Emerging Securi
and EU Governa.

MW01118826

This book examines the European governance of emerging security technologies.

The emergence of technologies such as drones, autonomous robotics, artificial intelligence, cyber and biotechnologies has stimulated worldwide debates on their use, risks and benefits in both the civilian and the security-related fields. This volume examines the concept of 'governance' as an analytical framework and tool to investigate how new and emerging security technologies are governed in practice within the European Union (EU), emphasising the relational configurations among different state and non-state actors. With reference to European governance, it addresses the complex interplay of power relations, interests and framings surrounding the development of policies and strategies for the use of new security technologies. The work examines varied conceptual tools to shed light on the way diverse technologies are embedded in EU policy frameworks. Each contribution identifies actors involved in the governance of a specific technology sector, their multilevel institutional and corporate configurations, and the conflicting forces, values, ethical and legal concerns, as well as security imperatives and economic interests.

This book will be of much interest to students of science and technology studies, security studies and EU policy.

Antonio Calcara is Adjunct Professor at the Vesalius College, Belgium, and Postdoctoral Researcher at LUISS Guido Carli, Italy.

Raluca Csernatoni is Guest Professor at the Institute for European Studies, Vrije Universiteit Brussel, Belgium, and Visiting Researcher at Carnegie Europe, Belgium.

Chantal Lavallée is Assistant Professor of International Studies at Royal Military College Saint-Jean, Canada.

Routledge Studies in Conflict, Security and Technology

Series Editors: Mark Lacy, *Lancaster University*,
Dan Prince, *Lancaster University*, and
Sean Lawson, *University of Utah*

The *Routledge Studies in Conflict, Technology and Security* series aims to publish challenging studies that map the terrain of technology and security from a range of disciplinary perspectives, offering critical perspectives on the issues that concern publics, business and policymakers in a time of rapid and disruptive technological change.

International Conflict and Cyberspace Superiority
Theory and practice
William D. Bryant

Conflict in Cyber Space
Theoretical, strategic and legal perspectives
Edited by Karsten Friis and Jens Ringsmose

US National Cybersecurity
International Politics, Concepts and Organization
Edited by Damien Van Puyvelde and Aaron F. Brantly

Cybersecurity Discourse in the United States
Cyber-Doom Rhetoric and Beyond
Sean T. Lawson

National Cyber Emergencies
The Return to Civil Defence
Edited by Greg Austin

Information Warfare in the Age of Cyber Conflict
Edited by Christopher Whyte, A. Trevor Thrall, and Brian M. Mazanec

Emerging Security Technologies and EU Governance
Actors, Practices and Processes
Edited by Antonio Calcara, Raluca Csernatoni and Chantal Lavallée

For more information about this series, please visit: www.routledge.com/ Routledge-Studies-in-Conflict-Security-and-Technology/book-series/CST

Emerging Security Technologies and EU Governance

Actors, Practices and Processes

**Edited by Antonio Calcara,
Raluca Csernatoni and
Chantal Lavallée**

Routledge
Taylor & Francis Group

LONDON AND NEW YORK

First published 2020
by Routledge
2 Park Square, Milton Park, Abingdon, Oxon OX14 4RN

and by Routledge
52 Vanderbilt Avenue, New York, NY 10017

Routledge is an imprint of the Taylor & Francis Group, an informa business

British Library Cataloguing-in-Publication Data
A catalogue record for this book is available from the British Library

Library of Congress Cataloging-in-Publication Data
Names: Calcara, Antonio, 1989- editor. | Csernatoni, Raluca, 1984- editor. | Lavallée, Chantal, 1978- editor.
Title: Emerging security technologies and EU governance : actors, practices and processes / edited by Antonio Calcara, Raluca Csernatoni and Chantal Lavallée.
Description: London ; New York, NY : Routledge/Taylor & Francis Group, 2020. |
Series: Routledge studies in conflict, security and technology |
Includes bibliographical references and index.
Identifiers: LCCN 2020009749 (print) | LCCN 2020009750 (ebook) |
ISBN 9780367368814 (hardback) | ISBN 9780429351846 (ebook)
Subjects: LCSH: European Union countries–Military policy. |
National security–European Union countries. | Military art and science–Technological innovations.
Classification: LCC UA646 .E445 2020 (print) | LCC UA646 (ebook) |
DDC 355/.03354–dc23
LC record available at https://lccn.loc.gov/2020009749
LC ebook record available at https://lccn.loc.gov/2020009750

ISBN: 978-0-367-36881-4 (hbk)
ISBN: 978-0-367-51098-5 (pbk)
ISBN: 978-0-429-35184-6 (ebk)

Typeset in Times New Roman
by Wearset Ltd, Boldon, Tyne and Wear

Contents

Contributors

Neven Ahmad is an MA student in Peace and Conflict at the University of Oslo and an intern at the Peace Research Institute Oslo. She has graduated in Social Sciences in Communications and Political Science at the University of Ottawa and has been an intern, *inter alia*, at the United Nations High Commissioner for Refugees, Protection Unit, Ottawa, as well as special assistant at the Office of the Hon. Bob Chiarelli, Ontario Minister of Infrastructure.

André Barrinha is Senior Lecturer in International Relations at the University of Bath and a Leverhulme Trust Fellow. He is currently working on cyber diplomacy as an emerging practice in international relations. In 2019, together with Thomas Renard (Egmont Institute), he was awarded the Best Article in Global Affairs Award for a co-authored piece on cyber diplomacy and the English School. He is one of the coordinators of the UACES RN INTERSECT: Technology-Security-Society interplays in Europe. He has published in high-profile journals such as *International Affairs*, *Mediterranean Politics*, *Third World Quarterly*, *Journal of Common Market Studies* and *Journal of European Integration*.

Clemens Binder is Researcher at the Austrian Institute for International Affairs and a PhD candidate at the University of Vienna. In his work, Clemens explores the intersections between the politics of border security and security technology development. He also has a broader interest in security theory, border security and migration and critical security studies.

Ciara Bracken-Roche is Assistant Professor of Criminology at the Department of Law, Maynooth University and Visiting Professor at the Department of Criminology of the University of Ottawa. Her current project explores the adoption and use of drone technologies in Canada and Ireland with a specific focus on their application by policing and public safety agencies. Her research interests are broadly: security, surveillance, technology-mediated policing practices, data and technocratic governance, privacy, civil liberties, media, and risk and governmentality studies.

Antonio Calcara is a Postdoctoral researcher at the LUISS Guido Carli University and Adjunct Professor at the Vesalius College in Brussels. He holds a PhD from LUISS Guido Carli in Rome. His dissertation on *The Decision-Making Dilemma of Arms Procurement Policy* won the Global Strategy PhD Prize 2019 awarded by Egmont – The Belgian Royal Institute of International Relations and the European Security and Defence College (ESDC). His research focuses on defence industry relations in France, Germany, Italy and the United Kingdom and their impact on the choice to cooperate or not in multinational defence procurement projects.

Raluca Csernatoni is Guest Professor at the Institute for European Studies (IES) of Vrije Universiteit Brussel (VUB), and Visiting Researcher at Carnegie Europe. Her research interests focus on international relations theory, security studies, and science and technology studies. She has published book and policy contributions on the European security and defence architecture and emerging technologies such as artificial intelligence and drones, as well as academic articles in peer-reviewed journals such as *European Security* and *Critical Military Studies*.

Delphine Deschaux-Dutard is Associate Professor in political science at the University Grenoble Alpes (France) and the vice-dean for International Relations of the Faculty of Law at this university. She holds a PhD from Sciences Po Grenoble (2008) dedicated to the role of French and German diplomatic and military actors in European Defence Policy and more precisely in CSDP since the 1990s. She teaches international relations and political science in Grenoble and Paris (ILERI, École de Guerre), and is supervisor of an online masters programme on International Security and Defence. Her latest publications deal with methods in defence studies, CSDP after Brexit, European cybersecurity and cyber defence, emerging powers and parliamentary scrutiny over military operations.

Benjamin Farrand is Reader in Law & Emerging Technologies at Newcastle University. His research focuses on the interaction between law and politics in areas of uncertainty, drawing insights from critical theory, political economy and conceptualisations of power. Areas he has worked on include the control of online disinformation, power relations in legislative change in the field of internet regulation and the security implications of Brexit for the UK and EU.

Daniel Fiott is a defence analyst at the EU Institute for Security Studies and Visiting Professor at the Institute for European Studies at the Vrije Universiteit Brussel (VUB) and the Brussels School of International Studies at the University of Kent. His research focuses on EU defence, defence industrial politics and emerging technologies.

Chantal Lavallée is Assistant Professor of International Studies at Royal Military College Saint-Jean. Prior to this, she was Marie Skłodowska-Curie Fellow (2017–2019) at the Institute for European Studies of the Vrije Universiteit Brussel (VUB) in Brussels working on 'The European Commission in the Drone Community: A New Cooperation Area in the Making'. She holds a PhD in Political Science from the Université du Québec à Montréal (UQAM). She conducted postdoctoral research at the European University Institute in Florence (EUI, 2010–2012) with a scholarship from the Fonds de recherche du Québec – Société et culture, and at the Institute for Strategic Research of the Paris-based École Militaire (IRSEM, 2015–2016) with a scholarship from the French Ministry of Defence. Her research and publications focus on the contribution of the European Commission to the security and defence as well as emerging technology (drones) sectors.

Samuel Longuet is a PhD Candidate at the Université libre de Bruxelles (ULB) and Research Fellow at the research centre REPI (*Recherche et Enseignement en Politique internationale*). He is currently finalising his doctoral thesis titled 'Military Drone Policies in Europe', funded by the Scientific Research Fund (FRS-FNRS) under the supervision of Christophe Wasinski.

Ilan Manor is Researcher at the Department of International Development of the University of Oxford. His research interests include digital diplomacy, public diplomacy, social media and framing theory. His monograph *Are We There Yet: Have MFAs Realized the Potential of Digital Diplomacy?* was published by Brill in 2016. He has also contributed to various scholarly journals such as the *Hague Journal of Diplomacy*, *Global Affairs*, *Place Branding and Public Diplomacy* and *International Affairs*.

Bruno Oliveira Martins is Senior Researcher at Peace Research Institute Oslo (PRIO), where he is coordinator of the Security Research Group and a member of the Migration and Law & Ethics Research groups. His main research interests lie at the intersection between technological developments, security practices and societal change. He is currently leading three projects at PRIO: Counter-Drone Systems, Transnational Academic Network for the Study of Armed Drones (TRANSAD) and INTERSECT: Technology – Security – Society Interplays in Europe.

Dagmar Rychnovská is Marie Skłodowska-Curie Fellow at the Techno-Science and Societal Transformation Group at the Institute for Advanced Studies in Vienna. She holds a PhD in International Relations (Charles University in Prague), an MA in Comparative and International Studies (ETH Zurich and University of Zurich) and an LLM in Law and Politics of International Security (VU University Amsterdam). Her research interests lie at the intersection of international relations, security studies, and science and technology studies. Her current research explores security controversies in research and innovation governance, with a focus on bioweapons, biotechnologies and biobanks.

Inga Ulnicane is Research Fellow at De Montfort University (Leicester, UK). Her interdisciplinary research focuses on governance and policies of science, technology and innovation, European integration in research and international scientific collaboration. Her recent work looks at governance of Artificial Intelligence, dual-use and research infrastructures.

Maximiliano Vila Seoane is a Postdoctoral researcher at the National Scientific and Technical Research Council (CONICET), Argentina. Besides this, he teaches courses on international relations, cyberpolitics and media at the School of Politics & Government of the National University of San Martín. Vila Seoane has an interest in science, technology and innovation, media and development studies. Currently, he investigates the expansion of the digital dimension of the Chinese Belt and Road Initiative to Latin America, vis-à-vis the power of US technology companies and the influence of EU norms.

Introduction

Emerging security technologies – an uncharted field for the EU

Antonio Calcara, Raluca Csernatoni
and Chantal Lavallée

Introduction

The past decade has been, without a doubt, one of dramatic transformations for technological innovation. Hence, scholars such as Klaus Schwab (2017), the World Economic Forum's founder and executive chairman, are labelling this new era as the 'Fourth Industrial Revolution', in line with the first Industrial Revolution of the eighteenth century. Are we indeed on the tipping point of the so-called the 'Industry 4.0'? Or, is this yet another trendy buzzword meant to hastily signify some of the more recent incremental technological developments of the twenty-first century? The term seems to be redolent of common framing tactics associated to other catchphrases such as the 'digital revolution' or the 'gig economy'. We are certainly witnessing something altogether quite unique in contrast to the three preceding Industrial Revolutions, that harnessed the powers of steam, electricity and computerisation. Compared to the digital revolution in the cyber domain from the 1990s, we are now seeing multiple, overlapping and converging technical revolutions in various domains.

This is due primarily to the unprecedented scale and speed of entirely new convergences between emerging technological breakthroughs in a number of spheres, as well as their yet-to-be-discovered impact. The constant increase in hardware performance and its decrease in price have empowered software solutions that scale up at unparalleled levels. Schwab has translated such advances in the usual cost-efficiency corporate-speak, issuing policy and economic recommendations to political leaders and young entrepreneurs to take advantage of this impending 'second machine age'. There are undeniably potential lucrative benefits to be drawn from the exponential and combinatorial effects of Artificial Intelligence (AI), autonomous robotics, digitisation and biotech on global economy, industry and society (Brynjolfsson and McAfee 2016). Both state and non-state actors have already taken note of the leadership potential provided by revolutionary tech-driven innovation and its conversion into economic and military power, fierce global competition bolstering big research and development (R&D) budgets and investments.

Nevertheless, several other issues take centre stage as regards emerging technologies, most importantly, the compliance of innovations with democratic and legal requirements, social norms and ethical values. From this perspective, there needs to be a greater mobilisation of theoretical and conceptual views as well as critical approaches to determine how these technologies are designed, implemented and meaningfully controlled, especially in sensitive areas such as security and defence. Most of the mainstream International Relations (IR) scholarship tends to theorise technology as either marginal, deterministic or instrumental by 'black boxing' it to be used in explanations or research designs, without ever having it explained (McCarthy 2018: 2–3 and 5). Besides, power struggles and contestation narratives are mostly absent from the IR literature, which largely focuses on strategic and market advantages without indeed opening the 'black box' of the politics governing emerging technologies. Notwithstanding their importance, there is undeniably a gap in the existing academic literature in Social Sciences in general and IR theory in particular, concerning the conceptualisation and operationalisation of these technologies. This ranges from definitional aspects, their application for both peaceful and military aims, different policy areas of interests or concerns, issues and challenges, to the hybridisation of civilian commercial interests, advanced multidisciplinary science and strategic military priorities.

Indeed, there are studies that focus on the increasing civilian use of dual-use technologies in Europe (Hoijtink 2014; Boucher 2015) or on emerging security technologies from an American perspective (Akhter 2017; Shaw 2017). Conversely, European Studies literature has been mostly focused on either functional and neoliberal institutional approaches explaining the European Union's (EU) construction and actorness as a civilian or normative power with some attempts to overcome the traditional distinction between intergovernmentalism and supranationalism in its external, security and defence policies. Less attention has been given to the technical, regulatory and normative controversies surrounding emerging security technologies, a key strategic sector where the EU is also progressively involved. Regarding this area, some studies have been conducted on the development of an EU security and defence research policy and market (Karampekios, Oikonomou and Carayannis 2018). However, there have been no significant analyses on how to problematise new security technologies and their governance in the European context.

In this respect, Science and Technology Studies (STS) offer a fertile ground for our understanding of them. STS has the potential to provide a more substantive analysis of such technologies as forms of power, as socially constructed processes which involve a complex interplay between actors, interests, norms, discourses and practices (Feenberg 2002; Latour 2005; Bijker 2010; Verbeek 2011; McCarthy 2018). Technology plays a key role in global politics, and yet in-depth reflection on its role has typically been sidelined to epiphenomenal or deterministic characteristics in IR theory in general and in Security Studies in particular. By contrast, work done in STS has a long-standing tradition of unpacking social and political dimensions within complex scientific and technological systems, thus shedding light on the governance practices and knowledge-production processes surrounding them. On the other hand, STS has rarely engaged in a sustained and systematic manner with IR scholarship, either by addressing the global and security dimensions of international politics or by engaging with the European Studies.

Therefore, this edited volume calls for a new research agenda, arguing that conceptual approaches at the intersection of the above-mentioned strands of literature can help to illuminate the various international, political, economic, security and normative mechanisms that encase technological artefacts. It refers to the concept of 'governance' as an analytical framework and tool to investigate how emerging security technologies are governed in practice, emphasising the relational configurations among different state and non-state actors, as well as regional and international organisations. By referring to European governance, it addresses the complex interplay of power relations, interests and framings surrounding the development of policies and strategies for the use of new security technologies. This shifts the attention from a descriptive to a substantive reflection on how emerging security technologies are framed by several state and non-state actors. In this regard, the strength of this collective work is to gather scholars using varied conceptual tools to shed light on the way diverse technologies are embedded in EU policy frameworks. Each contribution identifies actors involved in the governance of one of these technologies, their multilevel institutional and corporate configurations and conflicting forces, values, ethical and legal concerns, as well as security imperatives and economic interests.

The Introduction first clarifies this new wave of technological innovation to explore the implications for human–machine relations, especially in the security sector, emphasising the characteristics of these emerging technologies and the main ethical and legal concerns, as well as their definitional challenges. Then, it gives some indications about the broader governance mechanisms, especially regarding the role and position of state and non-state actors engaged at the national, regional and international levels in the management of the technical, industrial and political aspects of security technologies. Finally, it provides a comprehensive view of the distinctive EU policy-making process and its impact on the governance of emerging security technologies.

A new wave of technological innovation

The new wave of technological innovation that we are witnessing nowadays is marked by an unprecedented fusion of evolving technologies, increasingly blurring the lines between the digital, physical and biological. From a conventional human-centric environment, we are moving to a new age of ever-more sophisticated technologies. They are starting to exert an altogether different and increased impact in human–machine relations, mediating and dominating social interactions, as well as challenging our very ideas of what it means to be human. This new technological wave could be characterised by a blend of advances made in key fields such as AI, robotics, autonomous vehicles, unmanned aircrafts (drones), additive manufacturing or 3D printing, quantum computing, Big Data, biotechnology and so on. It also signals or obliges profound transformations in systems of governance. For instance, improvements in autonomous technologies are triggering an array of pressing and complex debates about their design characteristics, their legal and ethical dimensions, their dual-use applications, their military and security uses, as well as their broader impact on society and geopolitics. Autonomous and robotic systems, drones, self-driving cars, speech and image recognition systems, and chat bots are among the more known exemplifications of combining such technologies. This confluence has important dual-use applications for both civilian and military objectives and contributes to the blurring division as well as mutual transfers between the civilian and military sectors.

The challenge with these technologies is also related to difficulties in defining their revolutionary potential. In part, this is due to a proliferation of labels, ranging from the term of 'emerging' itself, to other descriptors such as 'dual-use', 'future', 'new', 'enabling', 'smart' and 'disruptive'. The definition of AI as 'dual-use', 'disruptive', or 'enabling' is particularly interesting. It sets the parameters for understanding the type of technology that an 'emerging' one encompasses. Although some of these technologies such drones, robotics and the Internet have been developed over the twentieth century, they are generally defined by the stakeholders as 'emerging technologies'. While now being hyped as *the* disruptive technology of the twenty-first century, AI has advanced out of a scientific field with deep historical roots dating back to the 1950s and the development of stored-programme electronic computers (Surber 2018: 3). Indeed, even once they have been created, their applications are still evolving and offering a variety of new potentialities. Though their potential is becoming clearer, their exact scope and impact on societies remain to be seen. AI has been generally framed as a disruptive weapon and likened to past revolutions, provoked by prior transformative technology cases such as nuclear, aerospace, bio or associated with issues of national security, balance of power and warfare (De Spiegeleire, Maas and Sweijs 2017; Cummings *et al.* 2018). Due to its broad civil–military applications across numerous types of technologies and domains, as well as its convergence potential with other security technologies such as drones or related to AI-enabled cybersecurity, the more likely comparison is with 'enabling technologies' such as electricity (Horowitz 2018). Nevertheless, seen as a strategic enabler (Fiott and Lindstrom 2018) for unmanned and robotic systems, the AI's comparison with electricity is not particularly helpful, since it has the potential to revolutionise decision-making in warfare, going as far as possibly creating a paradigmatic change in how conflicts are fought.

As regards the term 'disruptive', according to Christensen (2011), it involves a type of ground-breaking and radically novel technology. The main characteristic of such a technology is to have the capacity to completely dislocate established and recognised technologies, by creating an entirely new industry and market. An example is the email that displaced letter-writing and revolutionised the ways in which we communicate nowadays. By contrast, 'sustaining' technologies are relying on incremental advances in an already established technology. Illustrative examples are the improvements made in the case of existing drone technologies in terms of autonomy. Similarly, 'emerging' technologies

(Rotolo, Hicks and Benjamin 2015), while not necessarily completely new and equally including older and underdeveloped technology, could be construed as still having the capacity to transform the status quo; in part because of their comparatively emergent potential and fast development. Their management can generate new patterns of interaction among state and non-state, civilian and military actors, along the normative, knowledge-production and legitimation processes accompanying them. Such processes also have the potential to trigger and transform civilian–military relations, these implications further affecting strategic goals with regard to defence research and development. They could also be characterised by elements of ambiguity and controversy, as their progressive development, socio-economic impact and broader meaning remain indeterminate. From this point of view, 'emerging' technologies may have both disruptive and sustaining characteristics, combining the new and the old, but most importantly producing new technological convergences between different fields such as telecom and modes of transportation with the drones.

Technological advancements are also frequently accompanied by stark warnings from critics and technophobes alike, going as far as crediting them with science fiction and dystopic scenarios that will change the future of humanity. From the 'Terminator-style' and destructive rise of intelligent machines to fundamental changes in world politics and warfare, the spectrum is broad. Conversely, technophiles are hyping their positive effects, including their likely improvement of our standards of living, with clear benefits, for example, in healthcare applications: the EU funded project HOPE (Human Organ Printing Era), under the Future and Emerging Technologies (FET) Flagships of the Programme Horizon 2020 managed by the European Commission (2019), can help radically transform traditional surgical practices for donating human organs. By combining pioneering tech from robotic 3D bioprinting, tissue engineering, as well as Information and Communication Technologies (ICTs) for customisable implants, such innovative biofabrication applications have a huge potential for a positive impact on health care. They demonstrate once more the innovative and convergent potential of different cutting-edge technological domains, as well as their broader civil and societal applications. On the other hand, Benjamim Farrand's Chapter 12 in this book draws attention to the moral uncertainties, legal lacunae and debates concerning the safety of new medical equipment and biotechnologies, by exploring the gaps in their current governance structures. Related to this, Dagmar Rychnovská's Chapter 10 points towards new techniques of governance introduced in science and dual-use research, by integrating existing principles of scientific responsibility with security practices.

As in anything related to human activity, nothing is as black-and-white as either emerging tech opponents or enthusiasts would like to propose. Regarding the security applications of emerging technologies, there are countless possibilities of how they could fundamentally impact security-making in general and warfighting in particular. These technologies are increasingly deployed to enhance various functions related to war games, counter-terrorism, cybersecurity, cyber robots to protect communications and information platforms, cyber-surveillance, precision weaponry and data analytics – heralding a paradigmatic transformation in security technologies. The consequences for homeland security, armed conflicts and the future of warfare are still to be determined. However, broader trends could be identified concerning their uses in the security sphere, both in its internal and external dimensions. In this respect, Maximiliano Vila Seoane's Chapter 5 points out some of the risks associated with the increased digitalisation of our societies and the use of cyber-surveillance technologies, which bring about new threats such as human rights infringement acts. André Barrinha's Chapter 6 further engages with cyberspace as a central trope in European security agendas, as well as critically assessing how certain meanings associated to cybersecurity can create normative problems. Equally, in his Chapter 8, Ilan Manor shows us the civilian applications of cyber technologies in the case of social media, by exploring the potential and limitations of the EU's digital diplomacy as a tool for foreign policy.

Moreover, new security technologies could significantly impact military organisational and operational levels through the optimisation and automation of both institutional structures and technologies. For example, AI has the potential to alter the productivity and efficiency of human endeavours on almost all levels, being one of the most important and divisive inventions in human history. One technological trend is particularly challenging, namely, the AI's increasingly disruptive potential as regards the human monopoly on critical decisions that concern vital legal and ethical choices to be delegated to completely autonomous systems during conflicts. Presently, there are no fully autonomous weapon systems in operation and we cannot expect their wide implementation in the short term. Nevertheless, it is important to be aware of the possible consequences of the AI's deployment in automating security-making.

From this point of view, putting forward political, legal and ethical frameworks for the development and uses of emerging security technologies might be the key to mitigating a global potential arms race and power shifts that could be incurred by their implementation in critical fields such as security and defence. Equally, big investments, public–private partnerships, innovation, human capital and re-skilling and societal resilience will undoubtedly determine whether state and non-state actors will be well positioned to be at the forefront of their meaningful development and governance. In line with previous Industrial Revolutions, current new technologies are following similar patterns of development, clearly outpacing standards and regulation regimes to govern them. Even when a certain technology has clear harmful consequences, such as for example nuclear weapons and lethal autonomous weapon systems (LAWS) or so-called 'killer robots', global governance mechanisms are highly dependent on states' or more specifically great powers' political willingness to enforce them.

The challenge for traditional regulatory authorities in democracies is therefore to identify the best way to tackle related issues considering industrial, technological, economical, legal and societal perspectives. The difficult task is to find the right balance between the foreseen benefits and the risks. On the one hand, it means supporting the development of a strategic and dynamic sector for market growth, competitiveness and innovation. On the other hand, it means providing appropriate political and policy frameworks to address ethical and societal concerns towards their disruptive potential and mitigating the risks. The ultimate objective for the tech industries in general and the EU in particular is the public acceptance of such technologies, but this remains problematic due to closely associated problems of the risk perception (Clothier *et al.* 2015). The most appropriate way to include citizens is still not clear, for either regulatory authorities or for the stakeholders in the emerging tech communities. They are also challenged by the most suitable way to prepare societies and foster their awareness to upcoming technological changes, knowing that the more the public accepts normalising certain types of technologies, the more it is likely to buy it or buy into it.

For instance, the future huge-scale integration of civil drones into the airspace raises significant questions (Rao, Gopi and Maione 2016), notably regarding public safety if they are not properly used (Clarke and Moses 2014), privacy and data protection as drones can collect data (Volovelsky 2014), third-party liability for example in case of accidents, as well as environmental concerns, such as noise and visual pollution. It also poses some ethical apprehensions, for instance, related to the drone surveillance (West and Bowman 2016) as well as security issues with the risk of their misuse, which could also lead to largely damaging effects. The incidents of flying drones at the Gatwick Airport where thousands of passengers saw their flights cancelled shortly before Christmas 2018 and few weeks later at Heathrow Airport, where all departures were suspended for about an hour, are an illustrative reminder of the disruptive potential of drones and the risk of their misuse. Along the same lines, the trend towards more automation in our daily life opens many legal, ethical and political questions. Several key questions are of prime importance: How to regulate emerging technologies or to guarantee reliability of these systems? How to determine the human control and the level of autonomy, more precisely the human in/on/out of the loop issue? How to protect personal data and human rights abuses?

In this regard, technology is not by any means completely neutral and it should not be narrowly analysed as an object in itself, independent from specific socio-economic and political realities that engender its potential uses and meanings. On the contrary, more critical and constructivist STS interpretations posit that technology is neither socially nor politically neutral, but actually socially relative and constructed. From these perspectives, emerging technologies have clear-cut normative dimensions dependent upon specific historical contexts, economic or security interests and discursive framings, that in turn shape how subjects perceive, manage, implement and respond to technically mediated socio-political and security relations (Rao *et al.* 2015: 454). The concept of technology has a highly contested meaning and implies a general lack of consensus concerning its definitions. This could range from a narrower and materialist understanding of strictly speaking technological products to more nuanced conceptualisations of techniques that include, mediate and shape human existence, power relations, knowledge production, and the political and security implications of technological artefacts. Last but not the least, the politically laden concept of 'dual-use' as applied to emerging technologies brings about further complexities, namely, the legal and psychological barriers between civilian and military research as discussed by Daniel Fiott in Chapter 2 and Bruno Oliveira Martins with Neven Ahmad in Chapter 3, respectively. Dual-use technologies could be framed as such to justify either military or civil spending, duality being seen in terms of reconverting certain existing civilian or military technologies or representing different stages in the life cycle of technological production and applications.

The governance of emerging security technologies

The reference to the governance of emerging security technologies represents here an entry point to explore actors' rationale and relations between civilian and military, as well as public and private actors at the national, regional and international levels. Before introducing the plurality of actors, it is necessary to clarify what the term 'governance' means, as it has been widely used in the Political Science literature in so many different ways that its analytical precision has been blunted (Kohler-Koch and Rittberger 2006).

The concept of governance emerged in the late 1970s to describe the fragmentation of the political authority among public and private as well as subnational, national, regional and international actors (Rhodes 1996: 661). While government refers to an institutional system in which there is a centralised authority and vertical and hierarchical forms of regulation, governance indicates that states increasingly draw on experts outside governments, engaging interest groups, 'contracting out', 'outsourcing' and creating public–private partnerships (Bevir and Hall 2013: 24). Moreover, at the international level, governance has been a useful analytical device to describe the diffusion of authority towards subnational and transnational institutions, as well as to emphasise the role of multiple actors – institutions, states, international and non-governmental organisations – required to coordinate their efforts to regulate phenomena of global concern (Higgott 2005). Therefore, this book refers to governance for describing the 'coordinated management and regulation of issues by multiple and separate authorities, the interventions of both public and private actors, formal and informal arrangements, in turn structured by discourse, norms and practices, and purposefully directed towards particular policy outcomes' (Webber *et al.* 2004: 4). This broad conceptualisation takes into consideration a variety of public and private actors, as well as their formal and informal interactions. This definition also allows us to underline the role of discourse, norms and practices in structuring knowledge-production mechanisms, policy decisions and policy outcomes.

International organisations have often mentioned governance in their documents and strategies. For instance, since the 1980s, the International Monetary Fund (IMF) and the World Bank have been concerned with promoting 'good' governance in their lending policies. Similarly, the EU has been among the first organisations to write so-called 'good' governance into its agreements with external partners, especially regarding its neighbourhood policy (Schimmelfennig and Sedelmeier 2004). Therefore, the term governance, initially used as a descriptive tool, has progressively assumed a normative connotation. Other scholars have strongly criticised this concept, due to its neoliberal implications, and have used the Foucauldian term 'governmentality', as the organised practices, mentalities, rationalities and techniques, through which citizens and society are governed (Joseph 2010; Enroth 2014). Governance and governmentality denote two concepts rooted in different disciplinary and intellectual traditions, converging around a common core question: the problematics of steering, regulating and governing in modern society with regards to individuals, organisations, the state and society at large.

The concept of governance has been also widely used to shed light on international and regional security arrangements. Since the end of the Cold War, the concept of security, traditionally restricted to military threats, has been progressively expanded to cover a much more variegated set of phenomena and actors (Krahmann 2003). In particular, new security threats cross the established boundaries of internal security and external defence (Lutterbek 2005). Among these threats, we can include terrorism, the proliferation of weapons of mass destruction, organised crime and drug trafficking, as well as the manifold political, military and humanitarian challenges that arise from weak and failing states and the security vacuum they leave behind. In this regard, the Copenhagen and the Paris Schools of Security Studies, as well as the Critical Security studies at large, have also emphasised the importance of the subjective dimension of security and the importance of studying the social construction of security through discourses and practices (Buzan 1997; Bigo 2002).

Gradually, phenomena such as migration, human rights and the environment, among others, have been securitised. This widened security milieu involves both traditional state actors and non-traditional ones, such as international and transnational groups, individuals, national agencies, NGOs etc. The concept of security governance has been therefore employed to describe the multiple actors and levels of security engagement and assumes that norms, rules and ideas, besides interests, are also influential in the shaping of security policies (Webber *et al.* 2004). The literature, however, ranges quite a lot as far as the type of 'authorities' (states, non-states, private actors, international organisations), types of coordination (formal or informal arrangements) and the expansion of the policy areas to which they is applied according to the understanding of what security is (Sperling and Webber 2014). Policy frameworks of emerging security technologies are defined by various actors, shaped by multilevel institutional and corporate configurations, and they embody conflicting forces, values, ethical and legal concerns, security imperatives, as well as political and economic interests. Specifically, the governance of these technologies involves governments, private actors (defence and security as well as civil firms and high-tech companies), international and regional organisations, lobby and civil society groups.

Governments remain the main actors in the development of emerging technologies for political, legal and economic-related reasons. First, as emphasised in the previous section, security technologies have fundamental implications for international security. The American case is paradigmatic in this regard, given that Washington, through its 2014 'Third Offset Strategy', has committed to lead the process of innovation and research of emerging technologies and to include the development of these technologies within its military innovation strategy (Fiott 2016). Second, it is widely accepted that these technologies have a major impact on the economic, social and environmental welfare of a nation and they have triggered changes that are threatening existing markets. For instance, their management is challenging because traditional policy tools – regulations, taxes and subsidies – may not be as effective in new areas as in the more established sectors. Their use requires more information than is often available to governments as new technologies proliferate. Moreover, the development of new legal standards is necessarily slower compared to fast-evolving technologies.

Against this background, non-state actors such as the defence industry are also involved in technological developments. Given that, despite a large process of privatisation since the 1980s, they maintain constant relations with the governments, thus it is problematic to define these actors as completely detached from state control. This is principally due to the peculiarities of the defence market. Indeed, in weapons acquisition, free market principles are generally resisted because of many potential risks: specialisation could reduce the available military capabilities a state has at its disposal; it may become overly dependent on external suppliers; open procurement contracts could favour foreign firms and harm domestic industry and employment; competition could alter the shape of the defence supply chain to potentially disadvantage domestic firms. For all these reasons, the arms market is characterised by 'monopsony', namely, for the presence of a single buyer (the state) and a limited array of defence firms competing in a fragmented market landscape (Hartley 1991: 31). Since the end of the Second World War, R&D in defence was conducted in-house or commissioned to the industry (Mauro and Thoma 2016).

This picture has dramatically changed in the aftermath of the Cold War with the reduction of R&D budgets in almost all Western countries leading to a radical reconfiguration of the defence market. To give only a striking example, in 1960, 36 per cent of worldwide R&D was spent on American defence research, compared to 3 per cent in 2016 (Sargent 2018). Moreover, the dual-use nature of the emerging security technologies (see opening section of this chapter) has resulted in the tech industry being able to invest far more than the defence industry in relevant R&D. While large defence companies usually work closely with military officials to develop products that will be later purchased by the government, a number of large commercial corporations, such as Google, Facebook, Amazon and Toyota Motors, have been making huge investments in the development of technologies in recent years to access and secure the upcoming services market. Briefly, to give one concrete example: think about the computer processing technologies or the impact that the smartphones have had on the availability, performance, size and cost of computer chips, batteries and sensor technologies, from vision-based sensors (video cameras) to tactile sensors or touch screens (Boulanin and Verbruggen 2017: 105).

Although civil high-tech companies have clearly taken the lead with regard to the development and adoption of autonomy in robotic systems, the defence industry continues to play a key role, for the simple reason that commercial dual-use technologies can rarely be adopted by the military without modifications. While there are certainly civilian companies that might be prepared to fulfil a defence contract, commercial companies have little economic incentive to work with military customers, especially because contractual requirements in terms of proprietary rights are too stringent (Boulanin and Verbruggen 2017: 106). Defence companies are, therefore, bound to play a central role in delivering security technologies to the military. Furthermore, in today's interconnected and global world, it is difficult to attribute technological advances to specific actors. The tech industry gave us smartphones, but this would have been impossible without military advances in computing, battery and communication technologies.

Military and civil industries have also made efforts in recent years to form closer relationships with the academic institutions working on emerging security technologies, especially on AI and robotics. A relevant example is the multi-year collaboration agreement that Lockheed Martin signed with MIT's Department of Aeronautics and Astronautics (MIT 2016) in collaboration with the Computer Science and AI Laboratory to work on robotics and autonomous systems. In addition to governments, industries and academia, expert technical knowledge of international organisations is becoming progressively impactful on the development of security technologies (Martins and Küsters 2019). For instance, the OECD (2015) has constantly advised upon emerging policy issues related to the responsible development of security technologies, and assisted member countries in understanding and managing the changing nature of research, development and innovation.

Finally, civil society organisations are showing increasing attention to the advantages and risks that the development of new emerging security technologies entail and are pressuring governments to not underestimate these challenges. As for AI and its applications in the case of LAWS, the 'Campaign to Stop Killer Robots' in Europe has been stepping up its outreach at the national level to build support in key capitals for the call to ban development, production and transfer of fully autonomous weapons. Similarly, in spring 2018, some civil society organisations, as well as in-house resistance from Google developers, have put pressure on the company to interrupt its collaboration with the Pentagon. The concerns were related to Project Maven, which aimed at developing AI to analyse drone surveillance footage, the information generated then being used for military purposes with the potential to harm humans (Shane and Wakabayashi 2018).

Obviously, the nature of the industry (both civil and military) and the relations between public and private actors depend on the country or region in which they operate. For instance, in Israel, the tech sector and the military have strong ties due to the mandatory conscription and the resulting creation of extensive social networks among public and private actors (Swed and Butler 2015). In China, the civilian companies have members of the ruling party in their board of directors, creating an inextricable mix between public and private interests (Kania 2017). In the United States, some authors have noted the development of a hybrid partnership between state and non-state actors, in which the governments increasingly seek collaboration with civil entities to achieve its own security objectives (Weiss 2014).

The European Union: a distinctive approach to emerging security technologies

The concept of governance has been extensively used to shed light on EU policy formulation and implementation. In the late 1980s, the 'governance turn' in European Studies coincided with and was stimulated by a significant increase in European competencies in the wake of the Single European Act and the single market programme (Kohler-Koch and Rittberger 2006: 32). Studies focus on the simultaneous centralisation of authority in a continental polity and decentralisation to subnational regions. They have been shaped by the EU's hybrid features, which are hard to categorise with the standard toolkit of Political Science. Specifically, the EU appears to break the mould of state-like features, being not a state in itself. Overall, EU governance studies (Piattoni 2010) argue to move beyond European mainstream approaches that understood EU integration either as a natural spillover process (Haas 1958) or as driven by member states' national interests and actions (Moravcsik 1998), in order to analyse how the EU works as a decision-making system. In this regard, a plethora of analyses have come to see the EU as a multi-level governance (MLG) system, characterised by 'the simultaneous activation of governmental and non-governmental actors at various jurisdiction levels' (Piattoni 2010). MLG studies posit that decision-making authority is not monopolised by national governments but is diffused to different levels of decision-making – the sub-national, national and supranational levels (Hooghe and Marks 2001: 4). A lively debate has also emerged on new modes of governance, roughly defined as non-hierarchical means of political steering, a central characteristic of EU constrained authority vis-à-vis the member states (Sabel and Zeitlin 2010).

The literature on EU governance has predominantly dealt with former first-pillar issues (policy areas in which the EU has exclusive competence). However, with the adoption of the Treaty of Lisbon, which abolished the pillar structure, some scholars have explored the governance of the EU Common Foreign, Security and Defence policy (Webber *et al.* 2004; Kirchner 2006). The security governance research has been especially interested in the EU peculiar role as a security actor. In this regard, some scholars have argued that the EU can be defined as a civilian, normative, structural and global power (Manners 2002; Del Sarto 2016). Scholars have also analysed the social conditions of the EU's international identity as defined through practices, discourses, struggles of the actors enacting the EU external relations (Rogers 2009; Mérand and Rayroux 2016). Moreover, a strand of research has highlighted more complex governance structures in the EU security and defence field than that implied by the traditional intergovernmental cooperation among national governments. Some identified the governance in the European security and defence field as characterised by 'intensive transgovernmentalism' to indicate that the intensity of interactions and the density of structured and productive collaboration create transgovernmental relations that differ from the typical rational bargaining of intergovernmentalism (Howorth 2001; Wallace and Wallace 2007; Mérand 2008).

According to Cross (2011), transnational interactions in Europe have been conductive to the establishment of influential knowledge-based networks of state and non-state actors that, by sharing technical and specific professional behavioural rules, have the capacity to shape the mission of their organisations beyond the original formal mandate. Other scholars have examined the development of the EU's security architecture and capacity building, underlying the role of EU institutions (agencies and expert groups), bureaucracies at national and European levels, and non-state actors as part of 'epistemic communities' (Trondal 2008; Cross 2011; Gornitzka and Holst 2015). Nevertheless, emphasis has been given to expert knowledge production and its epistemic influence in policy-making. These 'epistemic communities' are often considered as homogenous and consensual sidelining technical, economic and political diverging interests in debates surrounding the governance of emerging technologies.

The academic literature on European security has not provided, so far, a systematic assessment of the main actors involved in the governance of emerging security technologies. First, European governments maintain a primary role in the development of these strategic technologies. To make only a striking example, the French government has developed its own AI strategy and has affirmed the strategic nature of these technologies for state security (Villani 2018). Second, European civil and military industries have an obvious economic interest especially as dual-use technologies are a simultaneously source of opportunity. However, if the equipment is unrestricted from military arms control or procurement policies it is subjected to EU dual-use control (see Vila Seoane, Chapter 5 in this book). Moreover, in contrast with other regional contexts, most European military companies have also a predominantly civilian component (Airbus is a case in point). The development of dual-use security technologies, therefore, questions the main features of both the European civil and military markets. This is actually a long-running debate in the European security field. Already in 1989, Walker and Gummett noted that:

> European defence industries are caught up in the powerful dynamics surrounding the Single European Act, not least because most defence contractors are substantial players in civil high-technology markets and because boundaries between civil and military technology are becoming harder to draw. Although different that regulatory structures of the two sectors cannot therefore be kept completely separate – which means that there is a potential serious clash of interests between the authorities concerned with civil and with military industrial activities.
>
> (Walker and Gummett 1989: 420)

The governance of emerging security technologies is further complicated by the distinctive policy-making at the European level. EU institutions have increasingly promoted the development and employment of 'new', 'dual-use', 'advanced', 'next generation' or 'emerging' technologies for countering their internal and external security threats. This is quite evident with regard to the policies and measures that have been adopted to foster the security domain of the EU Area of Freedom, Security and Justice. For instance, the pursuit of 'new technologies' for security purposes took on new dynamics following the adoption of 'The Hague Programme: Strengthening Freedom, Security and Justice in the European Union' (Council 2005). Moreover, security technologies, as indicated in the EU official documents, need to be developed through a close collaboration between the public and private sector, meaning EU public bodies and authorities, academia, research centres and industries (Bonfanti 2017: 39; Martins and Ahmad, Chapter 3 in this book). Significant budgetary resources have been allocated for the purpose of researching new security technologies. The EU has also promoted the involvement of representatives from the military sector in the definition of R&D, in particular the European Defence Agency (EDA). This involvement stemmed from the need to synchronise research initiatives carried out in the civil and military security domains with a view to avoiding duplications and to promote synergies.

The EU's institutions such as the European Commission and the European Parliament, as well as agencies like the EDA, and the member states have been actively involved in promoting the development of these technologies (drones and AI, for instance). Their common goals have been to bridge the technological-innovation gap, especially towards the United States and China, to transform the European technological and industrial base into a competitive advantage while also considering the need of the public acceptance. Hence, emerging security technologies are challenging the EU's representatives to find the balance between their promotion by creating markets and stimulating cutting-edge research and innovation, and the need to address their normative and ethical implications with legal controls regarding their use and the risks of misuse.

In this regard, the analysis of the European governance towards these technologies is also questioning the nature and scope of the European integration. Such technical advancements are transforming civil–military practices and might have unforeseen long-term effects on the EU imaginaries (what the EU is) and its global role. Concerning these changes, in the last few years, we have seen growing concerns in the critical literature and civil society about the militarisation of the EU. Some scholars engaged in the debate on armed drones within the EU (Csernatoni 2018; Paulussen and Dorsey 2016; Martins 2015), in line with the important academic debate on the legal, political and ethical issues regarding the extra-judicial 'drone killings' used by the American administration under the then President Obama as counter-terrorism measures in Afghanistan, Somalia, Yemen and Pakistan (Schulzke 2017; Barrinha and da Mota 2016; Hajjar, Levine and Naqvi 2014).

The apprehensions concerning the risks that the European contribution to the development of emerging technologies might transform the EU's scope and nature have further intensified with the 2016 'European Defence Action Plan' and the launch of the European Defence Fund by the European Commission. For instance, such fears have been openly expressed through demonstrations at the 2018 EDA's annual conference on 'From Unmanned to Autonomous Systems: Trends, Challenges and Opportunities'. In the international context where the 'Campaign to Stop Killer Robots' gains momentum, some critical voices expressed clear concerns about the possibility that European companies developing lethal autonomous weapons might have access to EU funds or criticised the military interest at national level to possess such weapons, raising the probability of a global arms race (Teffer 2018a, 2018b). With a new European discourse on civil drones, some scholars rather criticised the demilitarisation of dual-use technologies such as drones as a means to manage public acceptability by reducing the scope of debate in Europe (Boucher 2015).

Besides, almost all EU-level security strategies adopted in the last decade have also highlighted the crucial role of the private sector when it comes to countering a wide variety of contemporary security threats (Council 2015). For instance, Bures (2017) has noted that recent EU strategies have singled out the role of private sector actors in maritime security, including capability building, risk management, protection of critical maritime infrastructure and crisis response; crime prevention; private data protection and the fight against tax evasion and corruption. In its Security Industrial Policy, the European Commission stated that 'the security industry represents a sector with a significant potential for growth and employment' (2012: 2). In addition, the 2013 EU Cybersecurity Strategy mentions the term private sector more than 40 times (European Commission/HRVP 2013).

The EU has used extensively specialised expert groups for the development of emerging security technologies at the EU level. In this regard, in 2004, the European Commission (2004) established a 'Group of Personalities on Security Research', which comprised senior figures from European politics, industry and institutions. Afterwards, the Commission has set up expert groups driving the maturation phase of the European Security Research Programme (ESRP): the European Security Research Advisory Board (ESRAB) and the European Security Research and Innovation Forum (ESRIF), to devise strategic guidelines for the development of emerging security technologies in the scope of civil security, despite the fact that civil expertise has often been underrepresented (Lavallée 2016). Similarly, in 2016, Elzbieta Bienkowska, European Commissioner for Internal Market, Industry, Entrepreneurship and SMEs, has set up a 'Group of Personalities' composed by politicians, academics, think-tankers and defence company CEOs to advise on how the EU could support defence-related research (EUISS 2016). Besides this, while expert groups on AI and drones have been set up by the European Commission as legal obligation for the upcoming regulations, their input in the policy process remains to be seen. The European External Access Service (EEAS) has set up the Global Tech Panel. All these expert groups operate behind closed doors and by invitation. It shows how public–private partnerships are essential when it comes to the development of new emerging security technologies (see Martins and Ahmad, Chapter 3 in this book), characterised by a peculiar 'enmeshment between knowledge, technological development and security governance within the EU' (Martins and Küsters 2018: 4). The first section of the book is therefore devoted to investigating new patterns of authority and expertise in the EU governance of emerging security technologies, with a specific focus on the European Commission (Fiott, Chapter 2), the EDA and the European Parliament (Calcara, Chapter 1) and the role of public–private partnerships of experts in security research (Martins and Ahmad, Chapter 3).

Conclusion

Despite several ongoing debates on the fourth technological revolution, especially on the ethical, legal and political concerns about fast-evolving technologies, there are still no in-depth and systematic analyses on how emerging security technologies are conceptualised and integrated into new policies, practices and strategies in the EU. To date, not much attention has been given to the European governance of these technologies, nor on what their impact might be on the EU as such. Against this background, this book offers a comprehensive analysis of actors, policy dimensions, discourses and technological domains in the case of the European complex governance structures. It takes stock of recent EU policy initiatives such as for cyberspace, civil drones, AI and military research. In addition, by bringing together different theoretical perspectives and empirical case studies at the intersection of IR and STS literatures, the edited volume provides new and comprehensive insights on relevant aspects of the latest technological developments and innovations in Europe from their conceptualisation to their operationalisation. In the first section of this Introduction, we have therefore addressed why we need to integrate IR, STS and European Studies conceptual tools to shed light on the various international, political, economic, security and normative mechanisms that shape the development of emerging technologies. In this regard, we argue that the concept of 'governance' can be fruitfully used as an analytical and heuristic device to investigate how emerging security technologies are governed, by highlighting the diverse power configurations among different state and non-state actors, as well as regional and international organisations.

The book intends a timely and ground-breaking examination into the EU's approach to the research and development of new lines of technologies, out of which novel rationalities and dynamics of governance are emerging. The value added by research focusing on the European context is to advance knowledge into how a unique and complex institutional actor such as the EU adapts and puts forward the governance of innovative technologies. Moreover, it is also to conduct an in-depth analysis examining whether technological developments create new discursive rationalisations, patterns of authority, expertise and cooperation dynamics in key industrial domains, and transform the policy interface between national and EU levels and various stakeholders. As the development of new technologies is changing the way in which state and non-state actors deal with security challenges and thus identify public problems and policy issues, the book explores the governance responses and measures from EU institutions and member states in this respect.

In terms of chapters, each contribution follows the same structure, namely, it first provides the reader with the background information on EU initiatives (each chapter focusing on a specific case study) along with the presentation of the relevant theoretical approach and concepts which guide the analysis, then it identifies the actors involved in the chosen technological sector, their tools, relations and emerging practices. Finally, it assesses challenges and dynamics in this specific governance.

The first part of the book looks at the security and defence sector and initiatives that prioritise the interoperability of emerging and dual-use technologies in an effort to set the stage for a European vision of technological governance and innovation. In the wake of the latest transformations in the European security and defence architecture, following the 2016 European Defence Action Plan of the European Commission with the launch of the European Defence Fund, the focus is given to defence research and capacity building, as well as civil–military synergies. This part investigates how technological progress has been framed to be of strategic importance for the EU's future military capacity and strategic autonomy. Antonio Calcara assesses the new patterns of authority and expertise in the case of emerging technologies, emphasising the defence research field as prompted by the EDA and the European Parliament's Subcommittee on Security and Defence. Daniel Fiott analyses the European Commission's activity in framing and governing emerging security technologies in the context of its new crucial policy initiative, the European Defence Fund. In this regard, he highlights how the Commission has tried to balance civil, security and defence research when the EU is funding defence research projects. Bruno Oliveira Martins and Neven Ahmad examine the role of expertise in the EU's security research policy, underlining especially the configured hybrid nature of partnerships that are neither strictly public, nor strictly private, with the centrality of technological expertise. The book goes on to examine the impact of new surveillance technologies in the EU. Samuel Longuet focuses on surveillance drones underlining dual-use practices and analysing the implications in France and in the UK of the similar ways to conduct military and civil missions and operations. Maximiliano Vila Seoane assesses the role of 'market power' in the European governance of cyber-surveillance technologies. The book further addresses the EU's actorness through digital diplomacy activities and cyberspace initiatives. André Barrinha, inspired by Robert Cox, offers a critical reading of cybersecurity, questioning the meaning(s) of security embedded in the EU's approach to cyberspace and the normative problems that arise therein. Delphine Deschaux-Dutard examines the EU policy and capability initiatives regarding cyber defence. Ilan Manor evaluates the potential and limitations of the digital diplomacy of the EEAS. The book goes on to question the influence of 'technologisation' in European border management. Clemens Binder explores intersections between imaginations and understandings of border security as well as the R&D process of border security technologies, arguing that in this process, security understandings are reproduced. The last part of the book highlights the tensions between security and ethics. Dagmar Rychnovská and Benjamin Farrand's contributions are interested in the side effects, new dilemmas and societal concerns raised by biotechnologies and how that shapes the EU governance of dual-use research. Inga Ulnicane analyses the governance of dual-use research in the EU by focusing on the main EU-funded neuroscience project and one of the large-scale international brain initiatives – the Human Brain Project. Chantal Lavallée and Raluca Csernatoni are investigating the design and governance of interlinked technologies like drones and artificial intelligence (AI) in the EU, stressing the European Commission's leadership capacity in these sectors and the EU's 'smart governance' approach of the European emerging technologies field. Their approach is premised on the fact that technoscientific expert knowledge becomes particularly important in the case of cutting-edge technologies, by both establishing flexible, multi-stakeholder and marketable R&D initiatives, and by also putting in place ethically driven and regulatory governance mechanisms.

Finally, the book concludes with a critical assessment from Ciara Bracken-Roche, who not only reflects and comments on the book's contributions, but also opens the scope of the discussion to the rest of the world, notably comparing it with the North American context in order to identify potential convergences and divergences.

References

Akhter, M. (2017) The Proliferation of Peripheries: Militarized Drones and the Reconfiguration of Global Space. *Progress in Human Geography* 43(1): 64–80. https://doi.org/10.1177/0309132517735697.

Barrinha, A. and da Mota, S. (2016) Drones and the Uninsurable Security Subjects. *Third World Quarterly* 38(2): 253–269. DOI: 10.1080/01436597.2016.1205440.

Bevir, M. and Hall, I. (2013) The Rise of Security Governance. In Mark Bevir, Oliver Daddow and Ian Hall (eds), *Interpreting Global Security*. Abingdon: Routledge, 17–43.

Bigo, D. (2002) Security and Immigration: Toward a Critique of the Governmentality of Unease. *Alternatives* 27: 63–92.

Bijker, W. (2010) How is Technology Made? That is the Question! *Cambridge Journal of Economics* 34(1): 63–76.

Bonfanti, M.E. (2017) Let's Go for New or Emerging Security Technologies! … What About Their Impact on Individuals and the Society? *Democrazia e Sicurezza-Democracy and Security Review* 7(2): 37–85.

Boucher, P. (2015) Domesticating the Drone: The Demilitarisation of Unmanned Aircraft for Civil Markets. *Science and Engineering Ethics* 21(6): 1393–1412.

Boulanin, V. and Verbruggen, M. (2017) *Mapping the Development of Autonomy in Weapon Systems*. Stockholm: SIPRI.

Brynjolfsson, E. and McAfee, A. (2016) *The Second Machine Age: Work, Progress, and Prosperity in a Time of Brilliant Technologies*. New York: W.W. Norton & Company.

Bures, O. (2017) Contributions of Private Businesses to the Provision of Security in the EU: Beyond Public–Private Partnerships. *Crime, Law and Social Change* 67(3): 289–312.

Buzan, B. (1997) Rethinking Security after the Cold War. *Cooperation and Conflict* 32(1): 5–28.

Christensen, C.M. (2011) *The Innovator's Dilemma: The Revolutionary Book That Will Change the Way You Do Business*. New York: HarperBusiness.

Clarke, R. and Moses, L.B. (2014) The Regulation of Civilian Drones' Impacts on Public Safety. *Computer Law and Security Review* 30(3): 263–285.

Clothier, R.A., Greer, D.A., Greer, D.G. and Mehta, A.M. (2015) Risk Perception and the Public Acceptance of Drones. *Risk Analysis* 35(6): 1167–1183.

Council (2005) *The Hague Programme: Strengthening Freedom, Security and Justice in the European Union*. *Official Journal of the European Union* (2005/C 53/01). At: www. easo.europa.eu/sites/default/files/public/The-Hague-Programme.pdf.

Council (2015) Draft Council Conclusions on the Renewed European Union Internal Security Strategy 2015–2020, Brussels, 10 June.

Cross, M. (2011) *Security Integration in the European Union*. Ann Arbor, MI: University of Michigan Press.

Csernatoni, R. (2018) Constructing the EU's High-Tech Borders: FRONTEX and Dual-Use Drones for Border Management. *European Security* 27(2): 175–200.

Cummings, M.L., Roff, H.M., Cukier, K., Parakilas, J. and Bryce, H. (2018) Artificial Intelligence and International Affairs Disruption Anticipated. Chatham House Report. At: www.chathamhouse.org/sites/default/files/publications/research/2018-06-14-artificial-intelligence-international-affairs-cummings-roff-cukier-parakilas-bryce.pdf (accessed January 2019).

Del Sarto, R. (2016) Normative Empire Europe: The European Union, its Borderlands, and the 'Arab Spring'. *Journal of Common Market Studies* 54(2): 215–232.

De Spiegeleire, S., Maas, M. and Sweijs, T. (2017) Artificial Intelligence and the Future of Defence Strategic Implication for Small-and Medium-Sized Force Providers. The Hague Centre for Strategic Studies. At: https://hcss.nl/sites/default/files/files/reports/Artificial%20Intelligence%20and%20the%20Future%20of%20Defense.pdf (accessed January 2019).

Enroth, H. (2014) Governance: The Art of Governing after Governmentality. *European Journal of Social Theory* 17(1): 60–76.

EUISS (2016) Report of the Group of Personalities on the Preparatory Action for CSDP-Related Research. Paris: European Institute for Security Studies. At: www.iss.europa. eu/sites/default/files/EUISSFiles/GoP_report.pdf.

European Commission (2004) Security Research: The Next Steps, COM(2004) 590 final, Brussels, 7 September.

European Commission (2012) Communication Security Industrial Policy Action Plan for an Innovative and Competitive Security Industry, COM(2012) 417 final, Brussels, 26 July. At: http://eur-lex.europa.eu/LexUriServ/LexUriServ.do?uri=COM:2012:0417:FIN:EN:PDF.

European Commission/HRVP (2013) Joint Communication Cybersecurity Strategy of the EU: An Open, Safe and Secure Cyberspace, JOIN(2013) 1 final, Brussels, 2 July.

European Commission (2019) HOPE (Human Organ Printing Era). At: https://ec.europa. eu/futurium/en/content/hope-human-organ-printing-era-0 (accessed February 2019).

Feenberg, A. (2002) *Transforming Technology: A Critical Theory Revisited*. Oxford: Oxford University Press.

Fiott, D. (2016) Europe and the Pentagon's third offset strategy. *The RUSI Journal* 161(1): 26–31.

Fiott, D. and Lindstrom, G. (2018) Artificial Intelligence – What Implications for EU Security and Defence? European Union Institute for Security Studies (EUISS). At: www.iss. europa.eu/content/artificial-intelligence-%E2%80%93-what-implications-eu-security-and-defence (accessed February 2019).

Gornitzka, A. and Holst, C. (2015) The Expert–Executive Nexus in the EU: An Introduction. *Politics and Governance* 3(1): 1–12.

Haas, E. (1958) *The Uniting of Europe: Political, Economic and Social Forces, 1950–1957.* London: Stevens & Sons.

Hajjar, L., Levine, S.Z. and Naqvi, F.H. (2014) *Opposing Perspectives on the Drone Debate*. New York: Palgrave Macmillan.

Hartley, K. (1991) *The Economics of Defence Policy*. London: Brassey's.

Higgott, R. (2005) Theory and Practice of Global and Regional Governance: Accommodating American Exceptionalism and European Pluralism. *The European Foreign Affairs Review* 10(4): 575–594.

Hoijtink, M. (2014) Capitalizing on Emergence: The 'New' Civil Security Market in Europe. *Security Dialogue* 45(5): 458–475.

Hooghe, L. and Marks, G. (2001) *Multi-Level Governance and European Integration*. Lanham, MD: Rowman & Littlefield.

Horowitz, M.C. (2018) Artificial Intelligence, International Competition, and the Balance of Power. Texas National Security Review. At: https://tnsr.org/2018/05/artificial-intelligence-international-competition-and-the-balance-of-power/ (accessed January 2019).

Howorth, J. (2001) European Defence and Changing Politics of the European Union: Hanging Together or Hanging Separately? *Journal of Common Market Studies* 39(4): 765–789.

Joseph, J. (2010) The Limits of Governmentality: Social Theory and the International. *European Journal of International Relations* 16(2): 223–246.

Kania, E. (2017) 'Battlefield Singularity: Artificial Intelligence, Military Revolution, and China's Future Military Power'. *Center for a New American Security*. At: www.cnas.org/publications/reports/battlefield-singularity-artificial-intelligence-military-revolution-and-chinas-future-military-power.

Karampekios, N., Oikonomou, I. and Carayannis, E.G. (eds) (2018) *The Emergence of EU Defence Research Policy: From Innovation to Militarization*. Washington, DC: Springer International.

Kirchner, E.J. (2006) The Challenge of European Union Security Governance. *JCMS: Journal of Common Market Studies* 44(5): 947–968.

Kohler-Koch, B. and Rittberger, B. (2006) The 'Governance Turn' in EU Studies. *Journal of Common Market Studies* 44(9): 27–49.

Krahmann, E. (2003) Conceptualizing Security Governance. *Cooperation and Conflict* 38(1): 5–26.

Latour, B. (2005) *Reassembling the Social: An Introduction to Actor-Network-Theory*. Oxford: Oxford University Press.

Lavallée, C. (2016) La communautarisation de la recherche sur la sécurité: l'appropriation d'un nouveau domaine d'action au nom de l'approche globale. *Politique européenne* 51: 31–59.

Lutterbeck, D. (2005) Blurring the Dividing Line: The Convergence of Internal and External Security in Western Europe. *European Security* 14(2): 231–253.

McCarthy, D.R. (ed.) (2018) *Technology and World Politics: An Introduction*. London: Routledge.

Manners, I. (2002) Normative Power Europe: A Contradiction in Terms? *Journal of Common Market Studies* 40(2): 235–258.

Martins, B.O. (2015) The European Union and Armed Drones: Framing the Debate. *Global Affairs* 1(3): 247–250.

Martins, B.O. and Küsters, C. (2019) Hidden Security: EU Public Research Funds and the Development of European Drones. *JCMS: Journal of Common Market Studies* 57(2): 278–297.

Mauro, F. and Thoma, K. (2016) The Future of EU Defence Research. Brussels: European Parliament's Sub-Committee on Security and Defence. EP/EXPO/B/SEDE/2015–02 EN March 2016-PE535.003. At: www.europarl.europa.eu/RegData/etudes/STUD/2016/535003/EXPO_STU(2016)535003_EN.pdf.

Mérand, F. (2008) *European Defence Policy: Beyond the Nation State.* Oxford: Oxford University Press.

Mérand, F. and Rayroux, A. (2016) The Practice of Burden Sharing in European Crisis Management Operations. *European Security* 25(4): 442–460.

MIT (2016) Lockheed Martin Launch Long-Term Research Collaboration. 16 May. At: http://news.mit.edu/2016/mit-lockheed-martin-launch-research-collaboration-0516 (accessed January 2019).

Moravcsik, A. (1998) *The Choice for Europe.* New York: Cornell University Press.

OECD (2015) Digital Security Risk Management for Economic and Social Prosperity: OECD Recommendation and Companion Document, OECD Publishing, Paris. DOI: http://dx.doi.org/10.1787/9789264245471-en

Paulussen, C. and Dorsey, J. (2016) Towards an EU Position on Armed Drones and Targeted Killing? In C. Paulussen, T. Takacs, V. Lazic and E.V. Rompuy (eds), *Fundamental Rights in International and European Law. Public and Private Law Perspective.* Berlin: Springer, 9–44.

Piattoni, S. (2010) *The Theory of Multi-Level Governance: Conceptual, Empirical, and Normative Challenges.* Oxford: Oxford University Press.

Rao, B., Gopi, A.G. and Maione, R. (2016) The Societal Impact of Commercial Drones. *Technology in Society* 45(5): 83–90.

Rao, M.B., Jongerden, J., Lemmens, P. and Ruivenkamp, G. (2015) Technological Mediation and Power: Postphenomenology, Critical Theory, and Autonomist Marxism. *Philosophy & Technology* 28(3): 449–474.

Rhodes, R.A.W. (1996) The New Governance: Governing Without Government. *Political Studies* 44(4): 652–667.

Rogers, J. (2009) From 'Civilian Power' to 'Global Power': Explicating the European Union's 'Grand Strategy' Through the Articulation of Discourse Theory. *Journal of Common Market Studies* 47(4): 831–862.

Rotolo, D., Hicks, M. and Benjamin, R. (2015) What is an Emerging Technology? At: http://dx.doi.org/10.2139/ssrn.2743186 (accessed January 2019).

Sabel, C. and Zeitlin, J. (2010). *Experimentalist Governance in the European Union: Towards a New Architecture.* Oxford: Oxford University Press.

Sargent, J. (2018) Federal Research and Development Funding: Global Context and the FY2019 Request. Presented at ASTRA, 8 May. At: www.setcvd.org/wp-content/uploads/pdf_2018/Budget-Slides-5-08-18.pdf.

Schimmelfennig, F. and Sedelmeier, U. (2004) Governance by Conditionality: EU Rule Transfer to the Candidate Countries of Central and Eastern Europe. *Journal of European Public Policy* 11(4): 661–679.

Schulzke, M. (2017) *The Morality of Drone Warfare and the Politics of Regulation: New Security Challenges.* London: Palgrave Macmillan.

Schwab, K. (2017) *The Fourth Industrial Revolution.* Crown Publishing Group.

Shane, S. and Wakabayashi, D. (2018) 'The Business of War': Google Employees Protest Work for the Pentagon'. *The New York Times*, 5 April. At: www.nytimes.com/2018/04/04/technology/google-letter-ceo-pentagon-project.html.

Shaw, I.G.R. (2017) Robot Wars: US Empire and Geopolitics in the Robotic Age. *Security Dialogue* 48(5): 451–470.

Sperling, J. and Webber, M. (2014) Security Governance in Europe: A Return to System. *European Security* 23(2): 126–144.

Surber, R. (2018) Artificial Intelligence: Autonomous Technology (AT), Lethal Autonomous Weapons Systems (LAWS) and Peace Time Threats. ICT4Peace Foundation and the Zurich Hub for Ethics and Technology (Zhet). At: http://reachingcriticalwill.org/images/documents/Disarmament-fora/ccw/2018/gge/documents/ICT4Peace-and-ZHET (accessed January 2019).

Swed, O. and Butler, J. (2015) Military Capital in the Israeli Hi-Tech Industry. *Armed Forces & Society* 41(1): 123–141.

Teffer, P. (2018a) 'Killer Robot' Projects Eligible for EU Defence Fund. *EU Observer*, 23 May.

Teffer, P. (2018b) Rise of Killer Robots Seems Inevitable at EU Conference. *EU Observer*, 30 November.

Trondal, J. (2008) Images of Agency Governance in the European Union. *West European Politics* 31(3): 417–441.

Verbeek, P.-P. (2011) *Moralizing Technology Understanding and Designing the Morality of Things*. Chicago, IL: The University of Chicago Press.

Villani, C. (2018) For a Meaningful Artificial Intelligence: Towards a French and European Strategy. Mission assigned by the Prime Minister Édouard Philippe A Parliamentary Mission from 8th September 2017 to 8th March 2018. Paris. At: www.aiforhumanity.fr/pdfs/MissionVillani_Report_ENG-VF.pdf.

Volovelsky, U. (2014) Civilian Uses of Unmanned Aerial Vehicles and the Threat to the Right to Privacy – An Israeli Case Study. *Computer Law & Security Review* 30(3): 306–320.

Walker, W. and Gummett, P. (1989) Britain and the European Armaments Market. *International Affairs* 65(3): 419–442.

Wallace, H. and Wallace, W. (2007) Overview: The European Union, Politics and Policy-Making. In K. Jorgensen, M. Pollack and B. Rosamond (eds), *Handbook of European Union Politics*. London: SAGE, 339–358.

Webber, M., Croft, S., Howorth, J., Terriff, T. and Krahmann, E. (2004) The Governance of European Security. *Review of International Studies* 30(1): 3–26.

Weiss, L. (2014) *America Inc.? Innovation and Enterprise in the National Security State*. Ithaca, NY: Cornell University Press.

West, Jonathan P. and Bowman, James S. (2016) The Domestic Use of Drones: An Ethical Analysis of Surveillance Issues. *Public Administration Review* 76(4): 649–659.

1 The European Defence Agency and the Subcommittee on Security and Defence

A 'discursive coalition' for EU defence research

Antonio Calcara

Introduction

On 20 February 2019, the European Parliament (hereafter EP) and the Council approved the European Defence Fund (EDF). The Fund, proposed by the European Commission, will use the EU budget to finance cooperative defence research and to co-finance with member states the cooperative development of new military-related technologies and equipment (European Commission 2017a). From 2017 to 2020, the EDF has relied on the Preparatory Action on Defence Research (PADR) with a budget of €90 million and on the EU Defence Industrial Development Programme (EDIDP), with a budget of €500 million.

This activism in the defence–industrial field has been characterised by a strong intervention of the European Commission in a sector that was supposed to be the exclusive domain of the intergovernmental method (Lavallée 2016; see Fiott's Chapter 2). However, the Commission was not the only relevant actor in this context. The European Defence Agency (EDA)[1] and the EP's Subcommittee on Security and Defence (SEDE)[2] have been present in the process that led to EU defence research since its inception. The scope of the chapter is to assess the role of EDA and SEDE in the policy process that has led to the institutionalisation of defence research at the EU level. Specifically, this analysis suggests that EDA and SEDE, notwithstanding their respectively intergovernmental and supranational status, have formed a 'discursive coalition' to promote the contested institutionalisation of defence research and they have also developed important informal links to shape this policy process. Hence, the chapter aims to identify the main elements of this discourse and to test this argument on the recent developments in EU defence research.

The chapter makes three contributions. First, while there are several academic studies that have focused on the European Commission as a policy entrepreneur in EU defence (Edler and James 2015; Haroche 2019), very few studies have investigated the EDA and SEDE. Specifically, while the scholarly works on the EDA have highlighted either its institutional features (Karampekios and Oikonomou 2015; Calcara 2017) or its relations with the European Commission (Fiott 2015; Oiknomous 2018), there are few works on its discursive activity

(Barrinha 2015). In the case of the EP, there are recent insightful analyses on its role in security and defence (Rosén and Raube 2018), but – to my knowledge – there are no specific studies on the SEDE. Second, the chapter uses a conceptual framework that draws on discursive institutionalism to underline the importance of 'discursive coalitions' in the EU defence field, contributing to an innovative research strand on the importance of discourse within EU defence institutions (Rayroux 2014; Barrinha 2015; Heinikoski 2017). Third, it helps our under-standing of the policy process and the main actors involved in the EU governance of emerging security technologies (see the Introduction) and – through the explicit focus on the EDA and SEDE – naturally complements Fiott's Chapter 2 on the role of the European Commission in EU defence research. The chapter is structured as follows: first, it presents the theoretical framework and the methodological underpinning of the research. The second section highlights the EDA and SEDE discourse. The third section discusses the impact of this 'discursive coalition' on EU defence research. The conclusion identifies some limitations of the study and assesses some policy implications.

Discursive institutionalism in EU defence

The EU defence field is a policy domain in which there are day-by-day complex interactions among member states and EU institutions. Indeed, formally, EU defence policy decisions are taken at the level of the Council. However, these decisions are made on the base of policy provisions, scenarios, assumptions and ideas determined by lower-level Brussels-based actors in the framework of the Common Security and Defence Policy (CSDP; Tomic 2013: 224). Some studies have already highlighted how the intergovernmental nature of EU defence has been fading by a gradual socialisation among civil servants, bureaucrats and European and national officials with a similar educational background and iden-tity (Cross 2011; Howorth 2012; Calcara 2017). Moreover, as emphasised above, supranational institutions are also gradually assuming a major role in shaping EU defence initiatives (Haroche 2019). Members of EU institutions, committees, working groups and agencies, although receiving a set of instructions from member states, are the ones who write the texts that are dis-cussed by national decision makers. As noted by Tomic, these lower-level actors are the ones:

> that have the fact power of controlling the discourse of the whole EU. They do this by materializing policies in the form of texts [...]. While in the process the text and wording may change, the discourse is mostly preserved.
> (Tomic 2013: 224)

Given these considerations, a discursive perspective has a great potential to investigate the Brussels-based institutional context. In this regard, discourse can be defined as 'the space where intersubjective meaning is created, sus-tained, transformed and accordingly, becomes constitutive of social reality'

(Holzscheiter 2014: 145). Schmidt's (2008, 2010) discursive institutionalism is a useful conceptual framework to address how European institutions produce discourse in the defence domain. Briefly defined, discursive institutionalism deals with the substantive content of ideas and the interactive processes of discursive and policy argumentation in institutional contexts. Hence, this approach is able to connect the role of discourse to specific institutional settings, a crucial factor in the European security governance, in which there are multiple and overlapping institutions and centres of authority (see the Introduction).

Discursive institutionalism accounts for two types of discourse: coordinative and communicative. The coordinative discourse 'consists of the individuals and groups at the centre of policy construction who are involved in the creation, elaboration and justification of policy and programmatic ideas' (Schmidt 2008: 310). In contrast, the communicative discourse occurs in the political sphere, where individuals and groups inform and persuade the public with regard to these ideas. Since in EU defence there is little public input, I investigate the coordinative discourse in policy creation prior to decision-making. Investigating the coordinative discourse among EU defence institutions permits us also to shed light on the role played by individual agents within discursive practices (Rayroux 2014: 387). Indeed, the coordinative discourse concerns the policy actors (civil servants, bureaucrats, elected officials, experts), who elaborate a discourse on policy priorities. Moreover, these actors often join in discursive coalitions (Lehmbruch 2001), advocacy networks (Sabatier 1998) or epistemic communities (Haas 1992), to help them to connect and to circulate ideas in the policy field. Discursive coalition is the most general way of conceiving such discursive communities and of analysing the 'extra discursive practices from which social constructs emerge and in which the groups of policy actors who construct the new social idea or narrative' (Schmidt 2010: 14). Hence, the chapter aims to identify the coordinative discourse of the EDA and the SEDE in promoting defence research at the EU level, with particular attention to the role of individuals connected as the basis of a shared policy enterprise.

Discursive institutionalism has also specific methodological implications. In order to identify the discourse of EDA and SEDE, I examine official releases, research reports, strategy statements and political speeches produced by the two institutions. The analysis takes into consideration the period from 2004 (the year in which both EDA and SEDE were institutionalised) to 2018. In order to discover the internal logic of the discourse, I look for 'points of legitimation' in texts, meaning those claims that seem 'evident, natural and indisputable' and that serve to build a consistent discourse (Hansen and Sørensen 2005: 101). In addition, I collect media reports using the Factiva database for the period 2004–2017 and examined the proceedings of the European Parliament in the last three legislative mandates (2004–2009, 2009–2014, 2014–2018). I also conducted five semi-structured interviews with EDA and SEDE's members in Brussels.

The economic rationale

Market forces, globalisation and transatlantic competition

Arms market globalisation is presented as the main reason why it is impossible to sustain national defence–industrial policies. In this regard, the essential premise of the EDA's discourse is that the arms market is moving towards a progressive privatisation and liberalisation. In the European Defence Agency's 'An Initial Long-Term Vision for European Defence Capability and Capacity Needs' (LTV), armaments globalisation is depicted as 'an irreversible trend' (EDA 2006: 8), which will produce 'winners and losers, as between countries and regions' (EDA 2006: 11). This trend towards globalisation will force European producers towards intra-regional collaboration, if they want to maintain their competitiveness in the market. The Agency's officials stressed that: 'we recognise that a point has now be reached when we need fundamental change in how we manage the "business aspects" of defence in Europe – and that time is not on our side' (EDA 2007: 1). Moreover, the EDA points out that:

> We cannot continue routinely to determine our equipment requirements on separate national bases [...]. This approach is no longer economically sustainable – and in a world of multinational operations, it is operationally unacceptable, too.
>
> (EDA 2007: 1)

In other words, the Agency is developing a discourse that totally accepts the premises of the neoliberal narrative, for which defence firms will 'naturally' follow the laws of the market and will become more oriented to the global market (Oikonomou 2012). As highlighted by Barrinha (2010), the defence market has been subjected to a process of 'normalisation', similar to the neoliberal market dynamics that predominate in other areas of the international economy. As stated in the LTV:

> Government has a very special relationship with the defence industry [...]. But less and less does it remain owner; and, as defence companies move progressively from government to private ownership, and as shareholder funds become increasingly prominent in the control of companies, so one may expect the *normal*[3] laws of a globalised economy to apply; capital will migrate to optimise returns.
>
> (EDA 2006: 31)

This deterministic vision of the future of arms production is also shared by individual EDA's officials. Nick Witney, the EDA's first chief executive, recognised: 'it is no longer good enough to think just in terms of the national defence and industrial base'; but 'we [...] all start to think about the European industrial base as an entity in its own right' (quoted in Barrinha 2010: 15). Similarly, in an article for RUSI Defence Systems, the former EDA's Industry and Market director argues that 'more interdependence is less an issue of choice than of necessity [...] all recognise that self-sufficiency is no longer an option in defence. Competitive industries can no longer survive within national borders' (Hammarström 2008: 90). Moreover, the EDA's discourse has been also closely linked with the perceived increasing transatlantic competition in the defence–industrial sector. In this regard, the EDA's LTV highlighted that 'un-arrested, the trends point towards a steady contraction of the European defence industry into niche producers working increasingly for US primes' (EDA 2006: 31). This argument was also repeatedly pointed out by Domecq, the current EDA's chief executive: 'if we do not take action, the EU defence and technological industrial base will wane and we risk becoming a continent of subcontractors. This will cost us dearly' (2015: 2). Moreover, the EDA constantly warns of the lack of reciprocity between US and EU defence–industrial bases, especially for what concerns access to advanced technologies, arms exports and rules governing investments and property rights. According the EDA:

> We recognise that the problem of accessing the US defence market, and of establishing balancing technology exchange across the Atlantic, make it natural and necessary for Europeans to cooperate more closely to ensure the future of their own DTIB.
>
> (EDA 2007: 2)

A similar discourse is promoted by SEDE members. In 2011, the Lisek Report highlighted the fact that defence industry cannot be sustainable on a national basis and 'deplores the fact that, while a certain level of concentration has been achieved in the European aerospace industries, the land and naval equipment sectors are still overwhelming fragmented along national lines' (Lisek 2011: 11). SEDE has also been particularly active in showing the potential economic benefits of defence–industrial cooperation. Through a series of studies promoted by the Parliamentary Research Service on the 'Cost of Non-Europe in Defence' (Küchle 2006; Ballester 2013) and on 'The Impact of the Financial Crisis on European Defence' (Mölling and Brune 2011), SEDE has repeatedly pointed out the waste of financial resources on duplicative military capabilities. These studies have been important in shaping the SEDE parliamentary activity. As emphasised by Schlomach, the parliamentary assistant of Gahler (EPP), the study on 'The Impact of the Financial Crisis on European Defence', produced by the Stiftung Wissenshaft und Politik (SWP), served as the basis for the Lisek Report (Schlomach 2014: 57). At the same time, the series of studies on the 'Cost of Non-Europe' attracted considerable public attention and they are repeatedly quoted in the European Parliament's resolutions on defence.

As regards transatlantic competition, the lack of reciprocity between the USA and the EU and the need to protect the European market is also the basis of many of the SEDE's studies. In a recent report, this discourse takes a more dramatic tone:

> European defence research is coming close to an agonising point of no return. Its death is a silent one [...]. Should the trend not be reversed soon, in fifteen years, European will be no more than a mere customer of the US defence industry.
>
> (Mauro and Thoma 2016: 71)

These considerations are mostly shared by the MEPs of SEDE. The Lisek Report denounced 'a continuing disproportionate reliance on the US in defence matters' (2011: 4). Similarly, in their report on the topic, Mauro and Santopinto are very critical of the US defence–industrial policy mentioning that:

> In the face of the Buy American Act, which limits European companies' ability to export to the United States, it would be legitimate, against a backdrop of the US putting its own interests above all else, for Europe to do the same. [...] For which reasons should we have a level playing field with pure and perfect competition between European countries, but protectionist asymmetries in the transatlantic defence trade for the sole benefit of the US?
>
> (Mauro and Santopinto 2017: 35)

The proposal for an explicit 'buy-European preference' is exemplified in the Danjean Report:

> European national defence procurement agencies to take concrete steps, with the support of the EDA, towards making more European purchases, namely by sign up to a voluntary Code of Conduct that would introduce the principle of 'European preference' in some areas of defence equipment.
>
> (Danjean 2010: 15)

Therefore, we understand that the European competition with US defence industry has been one of the constant features of the EDA and SEDE discourse. Following this discourse, the only way to address the lack of reciprocity between the USA and EU is to consolidate an integrated European defence market and to introduce a buy European preference in defence procurement.

Defence budget cuts

Defence budget cuts have been used by EDA and SEDE as a powerful discursive tool to promote EU defence–industrial cooperation. SEDE has constantly warned about EU member states' shrinking defence budgets. The Lisek Report highlights:

> the culmination of a trend in recent years of cuts in the defence budgets of the majority of EU member states in the wake of the financial crisis, and the

potential negative impact of these measures on their military capabilities [… and] warns that uncoordinated defence cuts could result in the complete loss of certain military capabilities in Europe.

(Lisek Report 2011: 4)

Similarly, the Gomes Report emphasises the fact that the 'cutting of defence budgets is weakening the defence potential of EU member states and the EU, and leaves a question mark over the levels of preparedness to ensure national and European security' (2015: 4). According to the majority of the SEDE's members, the problem of shrinking defence budgets is also exacerbated by the duplication of European military equipment. As highlighted in the Lisek Report, the main problem resides in

> the way in which most of these funds are spent, based on uncoordinated national defence planning decisions, which results not only in persistent capability gaps, but often also in wasteful over-capacities and duplications, as well as fragmented industry and markets.
>
> (Lisek 2011: 5)

In this regard, SEDE's members have repeatedly quoted the EP's studies on 'The Cost of Non-Europe in Defence', as envisaged in the Paet Report (2016: 5) or in the Gahler and González Pons Report (2017: 5). According to the discourse promoted by the SEDE, the long-term effects of defence budget cuts could be even worse.

For instance, a SEDE's commissioned study emphasised the fact that the 'period of austerity may last for up to two decades until 2030. The exact time-frame depends i.a. on the fiscal discipline Member States show in consolidating public spending' (Mölling and Brune 2011: 11). Given these considerations, the only way to cope with a long period of austerity is to spend better at the EU level. In this regard, defence budget cuts from a negative element could turn into an opportunity. As emphasised in the Gomes Report 'the current budgetary constraints in EU member states should represent an opportunity for more and better cooperation in the field of defence equipment acquisitions' (2015: 7). Similarly, the Paet Report highlights 'the challenges which financial constraints represent to national budgets are at the same time accompanied by opportunities for progress arising from the evident need for closer cooperation between member states in defence matters' (Paet 2016: 8).

The EDA has developed a very similar discourse. Domecq, in his audition in front of the SEDE, argued that:

> let us be honest, in times of austerity it is politically difficult for member states to commit to an increase of defence spending […] if the increase in defence budgets is only devoted to solve short-term requirements and to fill urgent gaps […] we will harm out own future interests.
>
> (Domecq 2015: 6)

Member states' shrinking defence budgets, according to the Agency's discourse, can only be addressed through cooperation at the EU level. It is worth highlighting that in 2006, before the European financial crisis, the LTV emphasised already the

> need to increase the proportion of defence budgets going on investment – which implies the need to reduce operating costs. A significant part of these, of course, can be the costs of deployments – which, if met from defence budgets, are particularly damaging to coherent capability development.
>
> (EDA 2006: 29)

It is therefore interesting to note that the Agency's discourse was very consistent from the beginning, specifying how an apparently negative element, such as the reduction of defence budgets, could be also interpreted as a good opportunity for a better allocation of resources at the European level.

The security rationale

The economic rationale to promote EU defence–industrial cooperation has been accompanied by a parallel assessment of the risks and threats to the European security architecture. In this regard, EU defence–industrial cooperation is presented as a non-politicised issue, in order to ensure Europe's peace and stability (Barrinha 2015). In particular, as also noted by Heinikoski (2017: 40), a peculiar aspect in European debates is that the threats are not specified, but it is assumed that there is a mutual understanding of the existence of such threats. In this regard, the LTV strategically speaks about 'unknown threats', in which there are an increasing erosion of the 'distinction between what is regarded as the province of defence and what of security' (EDA 2006: 7).

The EDA's discourse argues that it is difficult to identify which threats the EU will have to face. Such unpredictability justifies the creation of common capabilities and trusting that the EDA knows how to tackle such threats. For instance, the former EDA's chief executive, Claude-France Arnould stated that 'I don't think it's possible to collectively define exactly what sorts of conflicts we will face, but I do think we can define the capabilities we will need' (Arnould 2012: 11). In the last few years, the terrorist threat has been crucial to promoting this discourse. As clearly expressed by the EDA's Chief Executive Domecq, one week after the November 2015 terrorist attacks in Brussels:

> Last week, Brussels has been in lockdown and under the highest possible security alert, meaning clear and present danger. This was also a first for Belgium. The point I would like to make: Do we really need events like Paris as a wake-up call? Do we really need to face imminent threats at home before we act and proceed in further European defence integration? I sincerely hope not.
>
> (Domecq 2015)

The SEDE has also developed a similar discourse. The Ehler Report pointed out that:

> internal and external security are increasingly intertwined [... and that] as present day crises and security threats can rarely be considered as being purely military or civilian [... so] effective responses need to be able to draw on both capabilities.
>
> (Ehler 2010: 4)

Similarly, the MEP Gualtieri, considers in his report:

> that it has become increasingly clear in modern times, and especially after 9/11, that many transnational threats such as terrorism, proliferation of weapons of mass destruction, organised crime, cybercrime, drugs and trafficking in human beings cannot be addressed without coordinated action.
>
> (Gualtieri 2012: 14)

Furthermore, the discourse promoted by SEDE also emphasises the difficulty in identifying the threats of the future. In the Klunhe Report in 2004, the MEP pointed out that the 'concept of security is continually changing and will change rapidly in the coming years. It is difficult to foresee the future evolution of threats' (Klunhe 2004: 13). The need to respond collectively to these unpredictable threats is well expressed by the Lisek Report, which emphasised that an 'increasingly complex and unpredictable security environment urges all EU member states to cooperate more closely and coordinate action against the common threats' (2011: 4). Similarly, the resolution on 'European Defence Union', drafted by the SEDE, emphasised that 'in recent years the security situation in and around Europe has worsened significantly, due to challenges like terrorism, hybrid threats or cyber and energy insecurity, that no country is able to tackle alone' (Lisek 2011: 4). However, this is not a homogeneous discourse within the SEDE. For instance, the discourse on 'unknown transnational threats' to be tackled collectively by the EU has been consistently criticised by the leftist forces of SEDE. The Confederal Group of the European United Left/Nordic Green Left (GUE/NGL) noted how SEDE's activities do 'not at least separate civil and military action instead pushed for greater and faster steps to be taken' (quoted in Klunhe 2004: 21).

Case study: EU defence research

Until now, I showed how the EDA and SEDE have developed a very similar discourse based on an economic and security rationale to spur defence–industrial cooperation. In this section, I investigate the impact of this discourse on the policy process that has led to the institutionalisation of EU defence research.

Dual-use civilian–military research

Funding instruments for the 2014–2020 EU budget (European Security Research Programme) provided support to companies involved in the development of dual-use technologies, namely, to those products, services and technologies that may have both a civilian and military application (see the Introduction).

The complementarity between civilian and military research has been important in the discourse promoted by the EDA. The starting point of this discourse has been recognition of the increasingly dual nature of technology and the significant potential that exists between the two fields. As highlighted by the former EDA's chief executive, Arnould:

> Europe still suffers from legal and psychological barriers between civilian and military research – barriers that our competitors do not have. [...] If we want the civilian and defence worlds to effectively cross-feed each other, then it is necessary to proceed with the de-segmentation of civil and military research. By allowing funding to flow from one side to the other, major spin-offs between defence and civil research could be achieved.
>
> (Arnould 2015: 1)

The EDA's support for dual-use technologies is not surprising. As previously noted by Barrinha,

> the close connection between civilian and military activities has important consequences in terms of the work the EDA is supposed to do in the defence field; in effect, not only EDA's activities go beyond the military sphere, as its aim, its *raison d'être*, seems to largely – and officially – surpass the field.
>
> (Barrinha 2015: 39)

In other words, the EU funding schemes allow the Agency to strengthen its position within the EU defence institutional landscape.

The SEDE has also been one of the main sponsors of this policy process at the EU level. The Ehler Report prepared the ground for establishing EU funded civilian–military research. This report emphasised the need to 'coordinate and stimulate investment in dual-use technologies and capabilities, so as to quickly close capability gaps whilst avoiding unnecessary duplication, creating synergies and supporting standardization' (Ehler 2010: 10). In the following Lisek Report, the call for EU investments on dual-use technologies was presented as crucial 'to stimulate European collaborative research and help bring together dispersed national fund' (2011: 10). Moreover, EU-funded dual-use technologies would benefit the broader European economy, given that 'just as the results of civilian research often have defence applications from defence research frequently benefit the whole of society; recalls in particular the examples of internet and GPS' (Lisek 2011: 10). Within SEDE, this position was supported by a majority of the three largest groups in the Parliament (EPP; S&D; ALDE). The strongest opposition to this idea came from the Greens, as they were not interested in using EU funds to finance tasks they deemed to fall under the remit of the member states (Schlomach 2014: 69).

The Pilot Project

In July 2013, the European Commission (2013: 5) expressed its intention to launch a Preparatory Action on CSDP-related research, aimed at financing defence-related projects with EU funds. At the end of the same year, the European Council (2013: 9) announced the future setting up of a Preparatory Action on CSDP as part of a broader effort to ensure long-term defence–industrial competitiveness. However, this process stalled at the institutional level, mainly due to the concern of some member states and the Barroso Commission's lack of appetite on this topic (James 2018: 29–30).

To overcome this stalemate, surprisingly, it was the EP, and specifically the SEDE, that drove this policy process. Indeed, after the successful motion of the MEP Gahler (2013), the SEDE proposed in autumn 2014 to fund a Pilot Project on CSDP research from the EU's 2015 budget. This agreement, worth a total of €1.4 million, was signed to develop three research projects on unmanned heterogeneous swarm of sensor platforms (Euroswarm), inside building awareness (Spider) and standardisation of a detector and avoid system for remotely piloted aircraft system (TRAWA) (EDA 2016a). The Pilot Project marked an important step in the EU defence panorama, because it was the first time that the EU, through its own budget, directly funded defence-related research.

The main promoter of the Pilot Project was the German MEP Gahler, chairman of the SEDE, who wrote the amendment and used the new EP budgetary powers to include funding for the Pilot Project into the EU budget (James 2018: 34). As Gahler emphasised

> In 2014, MEPs initiated an EU budget line for the first time with the pilot project on CSDP-related defence research [...]. The Pilot Project will be the litmus tests whether the Parliament and the Council will be ready to embark on further defence research activities.
>
> (EDA 2016a: 27)

Moreover, in an article published in 2016, Gahler clarified that 'I lead a group of MEPs [...] that turned words into deeds and launched a pilot project on CSDP related research [...] this Pilot Project was necessary because of delaying tactics within the Commission in early 2014' (2016: 53).

At this point, it is not surprising that EDA has actively supported the Pilot Project. Indeed, this was a chance for EDA to show that it could manage EU defence research funding successfully (Oikonomou 2018: 267). Furthermore, before the decisive initiative of SEDE, the EDA also helped to promote the discussion on EU defence research. In April 2010, Defence Ministries in the EDA's Steering Board discussed a 'Food for Thought' (FFT) paper prepared by EDA officials. The FFT recognised the need for a political decision on defence research and suggested a Preparatory Action, as part of the 7th Framework Programme for 2011–2013 in which the EDA envisaged it would have played a role in managing defence research programmes (James 2018: 28). The Pilot

Project promoted by the European Parliament paved the way for the 2017 Preparatory Action on defence research and for the following European Defence Research Programme (EDRP) in the next Multi-Annual Financial Framework. The EDA was the first beneficiary of this process, because it has been selected as the internal forum that has to coordinate all these research activities. In the context of the PADR Delegation agreement, the Agency agreed to manage and implement the Action on behalf of the Commission. The European Commission justified this choice for the EDA's

> knowledge and its recognised experience in the organisation and management of research projects and programmes in the area of defence, its unique role in the EU and its experience form the implementation of the Pilot Project in Defence Research in 2015 and 2016.
>
> (European Commission 2017b: 4)

The 'discursive coalition' in action

EDA and SEDE's members have been very active in promoting the institutionalisation of EU defence research. In 2004, the European Commission established a 'Group of Personalities on Security Research', which comprised senior figures from European politics, industry and EU institutions. In this group, the EP was represented by four members: McNally, an S&D member, Plooig-Van Gorsel, a Dutch member of the Liberals, Rovsing and von Wogau. The last two members have significantly shaped the institutionalisation of EU defence research, given also their strong links with the defence industry's lobbying in Brussels. Rovsing owns a company that delivers systems for complete satellite or satellite subsystems testing and, in its parliamentary experience, has promoted the idea of financing security and defence research activities with European funds. His company also benefited from the funds for the European satellite system, Galileo (Jensen 2007). Von Wogau has always been a staunch supporter of EU defence policy, especially as a political *trait d'union* and between the French and German political and industrial establishments (Edler and James 2015: 1261). Indeed, some studies have noted a decisive influence of the Kangaroo Group – Free Movement and Security, which brings together MEPs, business people and academics on EU defence research (Edler and James 2015; Oikonomou 2018). In early 2000s, the Kangaroo Group established a Working Group on European Security and Defence and Kangaroo Group's MEPs tabled a number of questions and resolution in the EP regarding the necessary EU funding for defence research. For instance, as highlighted by Edler and James (2015: 1258), the British MEP Titley was an active member of the Kangaroo Group's working group and he tabled questions in the EP on defence research. He also drafted the 'European Defence and Security Policy: The Challenges for Government and Industry', a paper for the Kangaroo Group, which emphasised the need for better European coordination in defence research and in the joint development of emerging security technologies. In 2002, the MEP Brok, also a member of the Kangaroo

Group, tabled a similar motion for a resolution on the need to finance research on new security and defence technologies (Brok 2002). Von Wogau was the first chairman of SEDE and in that period he was also a president of the Kangaroo Group. Oikonomou (2018: 273) has highlighted that the report on the basis of which the Parliament legitimised its pro-Pilot Project, pro-Preparatory Action and pro-EDRP stance was co-authored by Gahler and by another member of the Kangaroo Group (together with assistant – sherpa – of Fraunhofer – Gessellschaft). In this regard, it is also interesting to note that some of the most active members of SEDE on defence research are also part of the Kangaroo Group, such as Gahler (President), Mircea Pascu (Vice-Chairman) and Ana Gomes. Even Frédréric Mauro, lawyer and author of the EP's report on 'The Future of Defence Research' is a member of the Kangaroo Group, while von Wogau remains the Secretary-General of the group.[4]

Since its institutionalisation in the European framework in 2004, EDA officials have also been an integral part of the process leading to EU funding for defence research. In 2004, within the first 'Group of Personalities on Security Research', the Agency was represented by the Head of the EDA, Solana. EDA's members were also present in two key expert groups set up by the Commission driving the maturation phase of the European Security Research Programme (ESRP): the European Security Research Advisory Board (ESRAB) and the European Security Research and Innovation Forum (ESRIF). In the ESRAB, a group that had the goal to draw the strategic lines for EU defence research and to advise on the Seventh Framework Programme for Research and Technology development (FP7), the Agency was represented by Bertrand de Cordoue, former EDA's R&T director and now public affairs director of Airbus. In the ESRIF, a group aimed to developing a strategy for civil-security research, Ultimia Madaleno, EDA's Deputy R&T Director, chaired the Working Group 7 on Situation awareness and the role of Space.

It is particularly interesting to note that the contacts between EDA and SEDE members have intensified in recent years, in conjunction with the acceleration of the policy process on defence research and the launch of the Pilot Project and the Preparatory Action. In 2016, the Commissioner for Internal Market, Industry, Entrepreneurship and SMEs set up a new Group of Personalities (GoP) composed of politicians, academics, think-tankers and defence company CEOs. Both EDA and SEDE members were represented in the GoP. The EDA was represented by its chief executive Domecq and by its former chief executive Witney. SEDE was represented by the chairman of the subcommittee Gahler. During the signing of the Pilot Project, the EDA chief executive thanked:

> German MEP Michael Gahler and other members of the European Parliament's SEDE committee whose relentless efforts back in 2014 resulted in the EP funding for an EU Pilot Project in the field of defence research for the first time ever.
>
> (EDA 2016a)

Similarly, in a speech at the SEDE plenary session, Roger (2017: 3–4) – director of the EDA European and Synergies Innovations (ESI) department – declared: 'I must, first of all thank very warmly the SEDE subcommittee and its members at the origin of the Pilot Project. This Pilot Project was a great idea!' On 20 November 2016, a delegation from SEDE, led by the chair Fotyga, held discussion with EDA's chief executive. During a visit at the EDA's headquarters, Fotyga commented:

> I think I speak for all our members when I say that we are impressed with the work the EDA has done on the development of the EU member states security and defence capabilities. This is particularly important in a time of challenges for global security.
>
> (EDA 2016b)

In working to enhance the relationship between the EDA and the SEDE, Domecq said:

> I believe that regular EDA participation at the SEDE meetings, as well as visits of members of the SEDE Subcommittee to EDA, will improve transparency and information-exchange on EDA activities, at a time when European Parliament support in defence matters is key.
>
> (EDA 2016b)

Conclusions

This chapter has focused on the role of EDA, an intergovernmental agency and SEDE, a EP subcommittee, in the policy process that has led to the institutionalisation of EU defence research. The empirical analysis shows that both institutions have developed a converging discourse, based on clearly observable core features and on two points of legitimation: first, EU defence–industrial cooperation is needed for an economic rationale. The globalisation of the arms market, the competition with US military companies and member states' shrinking defence budgets are framed as 'challenges that need to be addressed collectively'. Second, the European cooperation is essential to face 'unknown' and 'unforeseen' threats and future transnational challenges. Hence, defence–industrial cooperation is not a political choice, but an indispensable necessity to ensure Europe's wealth and stability. Moreover, this chapter showed how some specific members of EDA and SEDE have been the promoters of this discourse and how they have strongly contributed to expert groups to push towards the institutionalisation of EU defence research. Contacts between EDA and SEDE members have also intensified over the past few years, coinciding with the launch of the Pilot Project and the Preparatory Action.

However, any attempt to draw on EDA and SEDE's discourse to make broader generalisations should be taken with a pinch of salt. First, the discourse analysis on EDA and SEDE member's involvement in this process should be integrated with a parallel study on the role of the European Commission in the defence–industrial sector (Fiott's Chapter 2). Second, the chapter has shown a substantial political convergence by the largest European parties (Christian-democrats, Socialists and Liberals) on the need to promote and fund EU defence research. However, the political conditions could also change in the short-term, for instance, through a greater role of the Greens, traditionally against EU defence itself, in the new European parliament's legislature (2019–2024).

Finally, this analysis opens up two further avenues for research. First, I show that there is a tension, in the discourse promoted by EDA and SEDE, between the desire to liberalise the defence market and the need to introduce protectionist arrangements to avoid excessive penetration of non-European companies in the EU market. More research is therefore needed to unpack the delicate balance between liberalisation and protectionism in the EU defence–industrial field. Second, it would be interesting to investigate the current institutional turf-battles in this sector. For instance, while the EDA has been at the centre of EU defence research from the beginning, recent analyses suggests that the European Commission is trying to marginalise its role in the management of EU defence–industrial projects (Haroche 2019: 11). Moreover, the recent decisions to create a DG on Defence and Space, closely connected with the wider EU industrial policy, may be seen as a further proof of the Commission political will to progressively marginalise the role of the intergovernmental EDA.

Notes

1 The EDA is an intergovernmental agency established in 2004.
2 The SEDE was created in 2004 to assist the Committee on Foreign Affairs (AFET) on security and defence issues.
3 Emphasis added.
4 This data is freely available at: www.kangaroogroup.de/who-we-are/.

References

Arnould, C.F. (2012) EDA's Key Mission is Delivering Capabilities. *European Defence Matters* 1: 9–11. At: www.eda.europa.eu/docs/default-source/eda-magazine/edmissue1.

Arnould, C.F. (2015) Three Ways to Reindustrialise Europe with Dual-Use Technologies. *Friends of Europe*. 9 January. At: www.friendsofeurope.org/security-europe/three-ways-reindustrialise-europe-dual-use-technologies/.

Ballester, B. (2013) The Cost of Non-Europe in Common Security and Defence Policy. European Parliamentary Research Service. At: www.europarl.europa.eu/RegData/etudes/etudes/join/2013/494466/IPOL-JOIN_ET(2013)494466_EN.pdf.

Barrinha, A. (2010) Moving Towards a European Defence Industry? The Political Discourse on a Changing Reality and its Implications for the Future of the European Union. *Global Society* 24(4): 467–485.

Barrinha, A. (2015) The EDA and the Discursive Construction of European Defence and Security. In Nikolaos Karampekios and Iraklis Oikonomou (eds), *The European Defence Agency: Arming Europe*. London: Routledge, 26–42.

Brok, E. (2002) Motion for a Resolution on European Defence Industries. European Parliament: Committee on Foreign Affairs, Human Rights, Common Security and Defence Policy on European Defence Industries.

Calcara, A. (2017) The Role of Experts in the European Defence Agency: An Emerging Transgovernmental Network. *European Foreign Affairs Review 22*(3): 377–392.

Cross, M. (2011) *Security Integration in the European Union*, Ann Arbor, MI: University of Michigan Press.

Danjean, A. (2010) Report on the implementation of the European Security Strategy and the Common Security and Defence Policy. European Parliament: Committee on Foreign Affairs. At: www.europarl.europa.eu/sides/getDoc.do?pubRef=-//EP//NONSGML+REPORT+A7-2010-0026+0+DOC+PDF+V0//EN.

Domecq, J. (2015) Intervention by EDA Chief Executive in the European Parliament's Subcommittee on Security and Defence, Brussels, 6 May.

EDA (2006) An Initial Long-Term Vision for European Defence Capability and Capacity Needs. European Defence Agency. 3 October. At: www.eda.europa.eu/docs/documents/EDA_-_Long_Term_Vision_Report_-_Paper_Version.pdf.

EDA (2007), A Strategy for the European Defence Technological and Industrial Base. Brussels. At: https://eda.europa.eu/docs/documents/strategy_for_the_european_defence_technological_and_industrial_base.pdf.

EDA (2016a) First EU Pilot Project in the Field of Defence Research Sees Grant Agreements Signed for €1.4 million. At: www.eda.europa.eu/info-hub/press-centre/latest-news/2016/10/28/first-eu-pilot-project-in-the-field-of-defence-research-sees-grant-agreements-signed-for-1.4-million.

EDA (2016b) Members of European Parliament Subcommittee on Security and Defence (SEDE) visit the EDA. At: www.eda.europa.eu/info-hub/press-centre/latest-news/2016/11/16/members-of-european-parliament-subcommittee-on-security-and-defence-(sede)-visit-the-eda.

Edler, J. and James, A.D. (2015) Understanding the Emergence of New Science and Technology Policies: Policy Entrepreneurship, Agenda Setting and the Development of the European Framework Programme. *Research Policy* 44(6): 1252–1265.

Ehler, C. (2010) Report on Civilian–Military Cooperation and the Development of Civilian–Military Capabilities. European Parliament: Committee on Foreign Affairs. At: www.europarl.europa.eu/sides/getDoc.do?pubRef=-//EP//NONSGML+REPORT+A7-2010-0308+0+DOC+PDF+V0//EN.

European Commission (2013) Communication from the Commission to the European Parliament, the Council, the European Economic and Social Committee and the Committee of the Regions: Towards a more competitive and efficient defence and security sector. Brussels.

European Commission (2017a) A Modern Budget for a Union that Protects, Empowers and Defends: The Multiannual Financial Framework 2021–2027. COM(2018) 321 final, 2 May, Brussels. At: https://ec.europa.eu/commission/publications/factsheets-long-term-budget-proposals_en.

European Commission (2017b) Annex 1 to the Commission Decision on the Financing of the 'Preparatory Action on Defence Research' and the USE of Unit Costs for the Year 2017. C(2017) 2262, 11 April.

European Council (2013) Conclusions of the European Council, 19–20 December. At: www.consilium.europa.eu/uedocs/cms_data/docs/pressdata/en/ec/140214.pdf.

Fiott, D. (2015) The European Commission and the European Defence Agency: A Case of Rivalry? *JCMS: Journal of Common Market Studies* 53(3): 542–557.

Gahler, M. (2013) Report on the European Defence Technological and Industrial Base. European Parliament: Committee on Foreign Affairs. 30 October. At: www.europarl. europa.eu/sides/getDoc.do?pubRef=-//EP//TEXT+REPORT+A7-2013-0358+0+DOC+ XML+V0//EN.

Gahler, M. (2016) The Added Value of EU Defence Research. *European View* 15(1): 47–56.

Gahler, M. and González Pons, E. (2017) Report on Constitutional, Legal and Institutional Implications of a Common Security and Defence Policy: Possibilities Offered by the Lisbon Treaty. European Parliament: Committee on Foreign Affairs and Committee on Constitutional Affairs. 17 February. At: www.europarl.europa.eu/doceo/ document/A-8-2017-0042_EN.pdf.

Gomes, A. (2015) Report on the Impact of Developments in European Defence Markets on the Security and Defence Capabilities in Europe. European Parliament: Committee on Foreign Affairs. 12 May. At: www.europarl.europa.eu/doceo/document/A-8-2015-0159_EN.pdf.

Gualtieri, R. (2012). Report on the Development of the Common Security and Defence Policy Following the Entry into Force of the Lisbon Treaty (2010/2299(INI)). European Parliament: Committee on Foreign Affairs.

Haas, P. (1992) Introduction: Epistemic Communities and International Policy Coordination. *International Organization* 46(1): 1–35.

Hammarström, U. (2008) A Strong European Defence Industry: What Needs to be Done. *RUSI Defence Systems* 11(1): 90–93.

Hansen, A.D. and Sørensen, E. (2005) Polity as Politics: Studying the Shaping and Effects of Discursive Polities. In D. Howarth and J. Torfing (eds), *Discourse Theory in European Politics: Identity, Policy and Governance*. Basingstoke: Palgrave Macmillan, 93–116.

Haroche, P. (2019) Supranationalism Strikes Back: A Neofunctionalist Account of the European Defence Fund. *Journal of European Public Policy* 1–20.

Heinikoski, S. (2017) 'Pool It or Lose It?' A Contrastive Analysis of Discourses Concerning EU Military Integration and Demilitarisation in the Baltic Sea. *Journal on Baltic Security* 3(1): 32–47.

Holzscheiter, A. (2014) Between Communicative Interaction and Structures of Signification: Discourse Theory and Analysis in International Relations. *International Studies Perspectives* 15(2): 142–162.

Howorth, J. (2012) Decision-Making in Security and Defense Policy: Towards Supranational Inter-Governmentalism? *Cooperation and Conflict* 47(4): 433–453.

James, A.D. (2018) Policy Entrepreneurship and Agenda Setting: Comparing and Contrasting the Origins of the European Research Programmes for Security and Defense. In Nikolaos Karampekios, Iraklis Oikonomou and Elias G. Carayannis (eds), *The Emergence of EU Defense Research Policy: From Innovation to Militarization*. Cham: Springer, 15–43.

Jensen, N.E. (2007) Interview with Christian F. Rovsing. *ESA Oral History of Europe in Space*. At: https://archives.eui.eu/en/oral_history/INT062.

Karampekios, N. and Oikonomou, I. (2015) *The European Defence Agency: Arming Europe*. London: Routledge.

Klunhe, H. (2004) Report on the European Security Strategy (2004/2167(INI)). European Parliament: Committee on Foreign Affairs.

Küchle, H. (2006) The Cost of Non-Europe in the Area of Security and Defense. Study for the European Parliament. Directorate-General for External Policies of the Union. At: www.bicc.de/uploads/tx_bicctools/bicc_study_for_ep.pdf.

Lavallée, C. (2016) La communautarisation de la recherche sur la sécurité: l'appropriation d'un nouveau domaine d'action au nom de l'approche globale. *Politique européenne* 51: 31–59.

Lehmbruch, G. (2001) Institutional Embedding of Market Economies: The German Model and its Impact on Japan. In W. Streeck and K. Yamamura (eds), *The Origins of Nonliberal Capitalism: Germany and Japan in Comparison.* Ithaca, NY: Cornell University Press.

Lisek, K. (2011) Report on the Impact of the Financial Crisis on the Defence Sector in the EU Member States. European Parliament: Committee on Foreign Affairs, 30 November. At: www.europarl.europa.eu/sides/getDoc.do?pubRef=-//EP//NONSGML+REPORT+A7-2011-0428+0+DOC+PDF+V0//EN.

Mauro, F. and Thoma, K. (2016) The Future of EU Defence Research. Brussels: European Parliament's Sub-Committee on Security and Defence. EP/EXPO/B/SEDE/2015–02 EN March 2016-PE535.003. At: www.europarl.europa.eu/RegData/etudes/STUD/2016/535003/EXPO_STU(2016)535003_EN.pdf.

Mauro, F. and Santopinto, F. (2017) Permanent Structured Cooperation: National Perspectives and State of Play European Parliament: Directorate-General for External Policies: Policy Department. 2 March. At: www.europarl.europa.eu/RegData/etudes/STUD/2017/603842/EXPO_STU(2017)603842_EN.pdf.

Mölling, C. and Brune, S.-C. (2011) The Impact of the Financial Crisis on European Defence. Directorate-General for External Policies of the Union. April. At: www.europarl.europa.eu/meetdocs/2009_2014/documents/sede/dv/sede190911studymoelling_/sede190911studymoelling_en.pdf.

Oikonomou, I. (2012) A Historical Materialist Approach to CSDP. In Xymena Kurowska and Fabien Breuer (eds), *Explaining the EU's Common Security and Defence Policy.* Basingstoke: Palgrave Macmillan, 162–187.

Oikonomou, I. (2018) The EDA-European Commission Connection in EU Military R&D: Not Seeing the Forest for the Trees. In Nikolaos Karampekios, Iraklis Oikonomou and Elias G. Carayannis (eds), *The Emergence of EU Defense Research Policy: From Innovation to Militarization.* Cham: Springer, 261–279.

Paet, U. (2016) Report on the European Defence Union. European Parliament: Committee on Foreign Affairs 31 October. At: www.europarl.europa.eu/doceo/document/A-8-2016-0316_EN.pdf.

Rayroux, A. (2014) Speaking EU Defence at Home: Contentious Discourses and Constructive Ambiguity. *Cooperation and Conflict* 49(3): 386–405.

Roger, D. (2017) Intervention SEDE – 25 January 2017 – Preparatory Action in the field of Defence Research. At: www.eda.europa.eu/docs/default-source/brochures/full-speech-of-roger-denis-at-sede-committee-(25-january2017)11309f3fa4d264cfa776ff000087ef0f.pdf.

Rosén, G. and Raube, K. (2018) Influence Beyond Formal Powers: The Parliamentarisation of European Union Security Policy. *The British Journal of Politics and International Relations* 20(1): 69–83.

Sabatier, P.A. (1998) The Advocacy Coalition Framework: Revisions and Relevance for Europe. *Journal of European Public Policy* 5(1): 98–130.

Schlomach, G. (2014) The European Parliament as the 'Driving Force' of the Common Security and Defence Policy, 6/2014 *KAS International Reports*, 51–72.

Schmidt, V.A. (2008) Discursive Institutionalism: The Explanatory Power of Ideas and Discourse. *Political Science* 11(1): 303.

Schmidt, V.A. (2010) Taking Ideas and Discourse Seriously: Explaining Change Through Discursive Institutionalism as the Fourth 'New Institutionalism'. *European Political Science Review* 2(01): 1–25.

Tomic, N. (2013) Coordinative Discourses in Brussels: An Agency-Oriented Model of EU Foreign Policy Analysis. *Perspectives on European Politics and Society* 14(2): 223–239.

2 Financing rhetoric?

The European Defence Fund and dual-use technologies

Daniel Fiott[1]

Introduction

In 2016, the European Commission announced that it would create a European Defence Fund (EDF) in order to support the European defence industry. After decades of capability fragmentation and duplication, plus the growing competition in European and international markets, the Commission stated that the Fund would be a way to boost the competitiveness of Europe's defence industry by investing a portion of the EU budget into defence research projects and capability development programmes. The Commission has asked for a total of €13 billion for such investments over a seven-year period from 2021–2027. The Fund was positively received by large parts of industry and the think-tank/academic community with many analysts calling it a 'game changer' for the way it breaks the taboo of EU funding for defence projects and the potential it has for reinvigorating defence cooperation between member states, research institutes and defence firms in Europe (Fiott and Bellais 2016; Ianakiev 2019; Haroche 2019).

However, after three years, the excitement surrounding its creation has subsided somewhat. It is therefore time to reflect on the practical implications that the Fund will have on the European defence market and for EU policy-making in defence. While there is still need for final agreement on the funding line for the Fund, it is worth thinking through how the EDF can make a difference in a rapidly shifting defence market and geopolitical landscape. In particular, the creation of this fund raises questions about the governance of EU security and defence as it takes the field from a largely intergovernmentally controlled policy domain to one with more supranational or communitarian involvement with the Commission. Furthermore, the EDF reveals an intriguing aspect of dual-use theory and practice, namely, that the European Commission insists on focusing the Fund purely on the 'defence' sector, even though the defence sector produces and integrates dual-use technologies and increasingly relies on civil sector innovation and technologies.

With reference to the development of disruptive technologies, this chapter asks how the European Commission intends to balance the defence, security and civil sectors under the EDF. In particular, the chapter enquires whether it is possible to maintain a strict division between civil, security and defence markets and how investments in defence research and capability programmes could incorporate dual-use technologies (see Chapter 3 by Bruno Oliveira Martins and Neven Ahmad and Chapter 10 by Dagmar Rychnovská). At the conceptual heart of the chapter is a focus on 'governance' and the way that various actors (state or otherwise) and interests intersect to inform ideas about what the EDF should focus on from a research and capability perspective. It is clear that while the EDF is largely seen as a communitarian tool, the range of policy actors involved is vast: industry, research institutes, civil society, experts (see Chapter 3 by Martins and Ahmad) and other EU institutions such as the EDA and/or the European Parliament's ITRE, AFET and SEDE committees (see Chapter 1 by Calcara).

More specifically on governance, this chapter is not interested in the typical policy process that begins with a policy problem, enacts a policy response and then leads to continuous evaluation or scrutiny (Knill and Tosun 2012). Instead, the chapter draws on the 'governance' literature to show how the European Commission has effectively branched into the defence domain with the EDF in addition to the competences it has claimed in security research. From this conceptual perspective, the chapter also highlights the theoretical limitations of existing work on European governance and remarks on a potential future research agenda. Before this conceptual debate, however, the chapter first looks at the ways in which the defence market is evolving based on an analysis of the defence economics literature. It then turns to how the European Commission understands 'disruptive technologies' before discussing how the EU has dealt with the management of dual-use technologies so far, and how future EU investments in defence may affect the overall governance of EU security and defence.

A shifting market for and approach to innovation

The global defence sector has been undergoing change for a number of decades and the ways in which governments manage the costs of defence have altered over time too. Back in 1984, the then US Army Under-Secretary Norman Augustine predicted that government budgets would not be able to keep pace with the rapid development of technology. Augustine predicted that defence budgets would be able to procure lower volumes of units of aircrafts because of the costs associated with sophisticated technologies such as on-board sensors, stealth technologies, precision-targeting systems, enhanced aerodynamics and more. As Augustine half-jokingly quipped,

> [i]n the year 2054, the entire defen[c]e budget will purchase just one aircraft. This aircraft will have to be shared by the Air Force and Navy 3½ days each per week except for a leap year, when it will be made available to the Marines for the extra day.
>
> (Augustine 1984: 48)

Readers can be the judge of how successful Augustine's prediction was: today, the US air force and navy are moving to a single aircraft (albeit with three variants) in the form of the F35 Lightening II fighter aircraft. This weapons programme is also likely to be the most expensive in history at $1 trillion over a 60-year period (US Government Accountability Office 2019).

Augustine's analysis of the increasing costs of defence in the USA has been empirically tested by defence economists. In particular, the work of Kirkpatrick (2004, 1995) has shown that – even when adjusted for inflation – the unit costs of weapon systems and equipment is on the rise because of their technological sophistication and because of the competitive development of defence systems between rivals and adversaries. What is more, it has been identified that even if generations of weapons systems share certain technologies, each generation nevertheless involves greater costs because of available technology, industrial production and the sophistication of military aims and equipment utility. Such a theory has been refined by other defence economists. For example, Bellais (2013) claims that the defence sector is heading towards a technology plateau where it will be extremely costly and counter-productive to rely solely on the defence sector for technological innovation. For such economists, relying on a technology-driven defence industry will ultimately lead to serious limitations in defence innovation.

Indeed, they argue that whereas the twentieth century was replete with new technological developments such as the tank, fighter aircraft and PGMs, today there is a limit or plateau to systems that can truly be classed as being 'disruptive' (see the Introduction). In fact, what is evident is that while there are certainly areas of continuity between defence systems in terms of design and technology, the room for real innovation appears to be plateauing – although this may change with the rise of Artificial Intelligence (AI) and bio/nano-technologies. For example, we tend to think of drones as an innovative or disruptive technology but most engineering and aerodynamic advances in this area have derived from past aeronautical R&D and development programmes. Accordingly, if defence firms are simply transferring and improving technological applications between generations of systems then increasing amounts of investment into defence R&D is unlikely to yield huge leaps forward in technology. It would be better, the argument goes, to harness the innovative power of civil R&D too (see the Introduction to this volume).

By way of an example, the US Department of Defence each year lists the Top 100 contractors it does business with. Out of the 100 firms listed for 2017, approximately 40 per cent can be classified as firms that make the bulk of their profits from defence-related business – the remaining 60 per cent focus on sectors such as health care, logistics and technology development in the commercial sector as well as defence markets (Federal Procurement Data System 2017). To give a more specific example, in 2017, the technology and communications firm Verizon ranked 64 out of the 100 contractors based on the overall value of DoD contracts – in the case of Verizon contracts stood at $427 million (compared to $48 billion to Lockheed Martin). Verizon is a commercial firm that principally sells telecommunications technologies worldwide, but it also sells its commercially developed products to the US military including digital streaming apps for personnel, switched line digital phone networks and data storage and networks. Other, more obvious, defence contractors such as SAIC (listed the 17th highest contractor) is also using augmented and virtual reality technologies and machine learning capabilities for its work to support the US national intelligence and military communities (SAIC 2019).

Of course, such an argument should not be read as a case against government investment into defence R&D. Instead, the point is for governments to stimulate a broader innovation environment that can develop defence-specific technologies. In the EU, meagre levels of government investment in defence R&D have contributed to the erosion of the EU's defence innovation potential, even if the EDF is designed to help reverse this trend. Although defence spending as a whole has been on the increase in the EU since 2013, this has not been reflected in the levels of investment in defence R&D spending. European Defence Agency (EDA) data for the period 2005 to 2017 shows us that while there was an overall increase in defence spending of €15 billion between 2013 and 2016, defence R&D investment remained static at around €8 billion during the same period (2018: 4, 10). Normally, in times of economic downturn, overall defence expenditure is decreased as a share of overall government spending, but within the defence budget innovation usually takes the biggest hit to investment and it can take a prolonged period of time to recover from periods of under-investment. For the EU, therefore, the challenge is not only unlocking the potential for civil-security-defence innovation but also ensuring healthy levels of investment across the board.

Unlocking this potential is not easy because many commercial firms are suspicious of defence contracts and they fear that Intellectual Property Rights (IPRs) may be lost (more on this later). Additionally, and as highlighted in many chapters in this book, the greater convergence between the civil and defence sectors also poses questions about the governance of research in the EU. The most basic question from an EU governance perspective is how to arbitrate between the 'civil' and 'defence' domains given the different intergovernmental and supranational governance methods. For the Commission, the growing importance of the civil and security sectors has already given rise to 'creeping competences'. For example, in the mid-1990s the Council of the EU insisted that all dual-use exports should fall under intergovernmental control, but, following the high-profile Leifer and Werner cases, the European Court of Justice ruled that dual-use items should be treated as goods that fall under the internal market and therefore legal purview of the Commission (Fiott 2019: 32). Since this time, the Commission has only increased its investment in and control over dual-use goods and technologies and this begs a question: does increasing communitarian involvement in defence also imply that the Commission will extend its competence over traditionally intergovernmental areas of defence policy (e.g. capability prioritisation and defence planning).

Scholars such as Citi have shown how the Commission can push for greater competences in a policy field under certain circumstances including: i) a collective action problem emerges that sits on the border of current treaty-based competences (e.g. fragmentation and duplication of defence capabilities and under investment collective European defence R&D); and ii) the progressive framing of the collective problem as an EU-level issue (i.e. intergovernmental action to reduce fragmentation and duplication has failed (Citi 2014: 149). For Citi, the Commission's increased competences in the defence field can be explained by a more ad hoc, 'incomplete contracting' perspective where the Commission and member states mutually agree to an indirect reformulation of the treaties based on collective action problems, rather than on functional spillover (as neofunctionalism prescribes) or 'opportunism' (as advanced by Blauberger and Weiss 2013). Although Citi helps us understand why European governance may evolve in a particular area of policy, the model does not precisely tell us how institutions such as the Commission rationalise technological developments, justify their role in an area such as defence or how they arbitrate between the civil, security and defence sectors.

Disruption: the EU way

The relationship between production and innovation in the defence sector bears some important challenges for the EU as it readies itself to invest in defence research and innovation. First, if scholars like Bellais are right, then the Union needs to pay much greater attention to civil research and innovation, or, at least, to ensure a greater symbiosis between civil, security and defence domains in Europe (Bellais 2013). In many respects, the fact that the European Commission is now prepared to invest a portion of the EU budget in defence removes the long-standing taboo that ensured that military innovation could not feature among the Union's broader efforts on research and innovation. It should indeed be pointed out that the EU has a far longer pedigree of managing and supporting civil research and innovation. For example, the EU is just winding up the term of its recent framework programme on research and innovation – Horizon 2020 – which from 2014 to 2020 has seen €80 billion invested in innovative projects such as enhanced medical imaging, rare disease research, Ebola vaccines, a 3D solution for the construction industry, a language learning app and more (European Commission 2017: 54). Compared to civil and security research, therefore, the Union has little experience in supporting defence innovation, although one could argue that the Commission's investments made under the European Security Research Programme (ESRP) and the European Structural and Investment Funds (ESIF) question the novelty of the EU's defence taboo. Indeed, under the ESRP, the Union deployed €1.7 billion from 2014–2020 for areas such as border management, police and internal security. More in line with defence-related investments, the EU's dual-use investments through the ESIF have also financed projects related to nano-technologies and maritime security.

Obviously, the calls to ensure that the research results from the Union's civil and security research programmes and those eventually supported by the EDF are to be expected – but more on the problems and challenges associated with this strategy later. One of the first largely rhetorical concepts that has captured the imagination of the European Commission, and been imported wholesale from discussions about innovation in civil and security research in the context of investments made under the ESRP, is 'disruptive technologies' (see also Chapter 13 by Csernatoni and Lavallée). In fact, in the proposed Regulation for a European Defence Fund, the Commission defines 'disruptive technologies' as 'a technology the application of which can radically change the concepts and conduct of defence affairs' (2018a: 21). Moving beyond rhetoric, however, the Commission has already pledged some €17.5 million on disruptive investments over the 2019–2020 period (i.e. €7.5 million in 2019 and €10 million in 2020) (European Commission 2019a: 14). This money has specifically been set aside for SMEs with a view to unlocking the innovation potential of the Union and to maintain a balanced approach to EU defence investments between larger, medium and small enterprises. The investment is also set aside for technology areas such as nano-modified composite materials, hyperspectral imaging, bio-based fuel production and innovative batteries.

However, the degree to which this strategy subscribes to more orthodox interpretations of 'disruptive technologies' can be questioned. First, it can be argued that truly disruptive technologies are very rarely identified prior to an investment call – that is, that by pre-conditioning or pre-defining what technologies should be financed by the EDF, there are less incentives for truly disruptive approaches. In this sense, devotees of Clayton Christensen's work would urge the Commission to use the term 'disruptive technologies' in its proper context. When the Commission speaks about investing 4–8 per cent of the Fund into 'disruptive innovation', it is mainly referring to technologies that could change the technology landscape. Yet, this understanding of the term is not exactly what Christensen had in mind: for him, disruptive technologies are less about the products or technologies developed and more about those innovations that emerge at the bottom of the market and have a wider consumer base than just a select few customers at the top of the market that are willing to pay more for technologies (see Introduction of this book). Examples include how cellular phones disrupted the fixed line telephone market or how discount retailers disrupted the department store market (Christensen 2019).

Obviously, in the defence sector, this 'democratisation' of innovation is not always beneficial because it would mean that a multitude of actors and governments could have access to once restricted defence technologies or systems. We therefore need to be careful about how we use the term 'disruptive innovation' in defence. While the Commission should be applauded for putting disruptive technologies on the agenda and making it a focus of the Fund, the point here is not just about the accuracy of language or calling for some sort of Christensen-ian orthodoxy. Rather, any strategy designed to fund defence innovation needs to focus less on the specific technologies being selected for financial support and more on the general effect the technology will have for the defence sector and for Europe's armed forces. Of course, financing technologies that do not yet exist will inevitably invite potential failures or experimentation that leads to a technology cul-de-sac. Beyond the mere act of financing such projects, however, there is a need for a 'disruptive culture' to take root in EU institutions such as the Commission and the EDA to ensure that the next big innovation drive is not overlooked if and when it comes along (e.g. Freeman *et al.* 2015).

Thinking about how the Commission may breed such a 'disruptive culture' gives way to important conceptual questions. Culture can be largely characterised as a body of practices, norms and understandings of a given society or network but the concepts developed by Citi and others (see Börzel 2005) focus on the causal explanation for increased supranational competences without necessarily acknowledging the role that social networks, experts and norms play in the formulation and legitimisation of policy and/or governance competences. As has been stated in multiple chapters in this volume, there is a certain difference between the 'governance' of a policy and the 'legitimacy' of a policy (see the Introduction and Chapter 10 by Rychnovská, Chapter 12 by Farrand and Chapter 9 by Binder; and Karlsson-Vinkhuyzen 2016). In this respect, any 'disruptive culture' must be understood not only as a method of identifying technologies but rather as a value system and sense-/meaning-making apparatus for how certain technologies (be they dual-use or otherwise) should be utilised by defence actors in the EU.

Dual-use technologies and EU defence

With the EU's new found focus on 'disruptive technologies' in defence, there is now even more reason to think about the ways that civil, dual-use and defence research can cross-pollinate to ensure a truly disruptive approach to defence innovation and capability development. Again, the European Commission has already stated in its proposal for a Regulation for an EDF that projects supported by the Fund 'may benefit from the results of civil or dual use research projects funded under Horizon Europe' (European Commission 2018a: 3). Behind this strategy sits a specific approach to how the Commission intends to proliferate the research findings of its investments under the EDF. In contrast to investments under Horizon 2020, which adopt open intellectual property rights (IPRs) so as to widely disseminate research findings, support under the Fund will see more restricted IPRs. Firms of all sizes will be able to safeguard IPRs for projects developed under the EDF, although the results of research projects could be shared among interested member states under certain conditions. Therefore, one challenge will be to effectively ensure cross-pollination between civil, security and defence research programmes (e.g. the ESRP, Horizon2020 and the ESIF) within the context of these different IPR regimes.

Of course, the EU's investments in dual-use technologies under its civil research programmes have already attracted the attention of a number of scholars. Molas-Gallart argues that a greater reliance on dual-use investments has occurred because defence became less important for R&D efforts after the Cold War period. In this regard, he shows how investments were focused on civil R&D in order to ensure *spin in* rather than *spin off*. Whereas in the past defence investments were justified on the overall societal benefits they could result in ('spin offs' such as touch screens, GPS, microwave ovens), investments after the 1990s switched to investments that could unlock technologies that could be spun into defence systems and equipment (Molas-Gallart 2002). Today, as evidenced by the discussion about disruptive technologies, it is clear that the commercial sector is out-performing defence when it comes to innovation. For example, if we look at the European Commission's 'R&D innovation scorecard' that ranks the world's top 2,500 companies according to how much they invest in R&D, one can see that the highest ranking aerospace and defence firm is Europe's Airbus at position 45. In fact, just over 2 per cent of firms listed in the top 2,500 innovators globally were aerospace and defence firms (i.e. 51 firms worldwide out of 2,500) (European Commission 2018b).

Despite the benefits of producing dual-use technologies that could be of use to the defence sector, however, one also needs to acknowledge the sensitive or more controversial aspects of dual-use investments. Indeed, Mawdsley has suggested that the blurring of lines between civil, security and defence research and product development has led to a greater securitisation of internal security matters, so much so that the 'rights of both EU citizens and non-citizens seem to play second fiddle to the overarching goal of security' (2011: 19). Furthermore, a greater reliance on technological solutions for security can be claimed to not only advance the idea that technology is a solution for every political or security issue, but that the use of technologies for security purposes can become 'normalised' without too much critical reflection (see Chapter 4 by Longuet and Chapter 9 by Binder). As Csernatoni (2018) states, the use of drones to monitor and police borders in the EU by agencies such as Frontex could introduce a military bias to policies and substitute longer-term solutions to border-related problems. With the introduction of the EDF, there will remain questions about what types of capabilities, technologies or weapons systems the EU should invest in (especially with regard to Artificial Intelligence). However, with the Fund, the EU has made its political intentions quite clear with regard to how it sees the necessity of investing in full spectrum technologies and capabilities.

In addition to the long-standing idea of and critique of 'securitisation', another aspect of dual-use technologies that has courted scholarly attention relates to exports. Although the EU's role in conventional arms exports is relatively curtailed, on dual-use exports, the European Commission has a significant role (see Vila Seoane, Chapter 5 in this book). The first attempt to establish an EU regime for dual-use goods was in 1994 and the aim under Council Regulation 3381/94 was to harmonise prohibitions and attain common agreement on authorised destinations. With Council Regulation 1334/2000 of 2000, however, the Commission's authority over dual-use exports was established by the European Court of Justice following the Leifer and Werner cases. The 'Dual-Use Regulation' was updated in 2009 and it further emphasised the Commission's role in harmonising and simplifying dual-use exports in line with the proper functioning of the internal market. In 2016, the Commission further refined the regime by adopting a proposal for a new regulation that included a 'human security' dimension to allow for export controls to prevent surveillance technologies getting into the hands of repressive regimes (Lavallée 2018). It is not entirely clear yet how the EDF could affect the Union's approach to exports of dual-use technologies. What is clear, however, is that the dual-use control regime will continuously need evaluating in light of new technologies that may or may not be financially supported by the EDF. Additionally, it seems more likely that a larger interplay between the Fund and conventional arms exports controls will occur, especially if EU member states cannot agree on a coherent export policy in advance of developing defence capabilities under the EDF.

Beyond export control, however, it will indeed be rather interesting to see how the European Commission cross-pollinates civil and dual-use research with projects it supports under the EDF. One element that bears reflection in this respect relates to the in-house capacity of the Commission to identify civil research results and to match them to the Union's defence needs. Given that the Commission has now created a dedicated Directorate-General for Defence Industry and Space (DG DEFIS), an important step will be recruiting staff with the know-how of managing capability programmes and identifying opportunities for defence innovation. Beyond simple staff numbers, however, the Commission will have to think rather more seriously about how it intends to establish and inculcate the aforementioned 'disruptive culture' in the new DG. Early results might be expected in the way that Commission officials work more closely together on defence and space issues. Not only is there a lot of research and pro-duction crossover (i.e. in the form of best practices and knowledge transfer) in the space and defence sectors, but the potential combined budgets of the EDF (€13 billion) and the space programme (€16 billion) gives the Commission the financial bandwidth to ensure coherence of the technological development it can support in defence and space, as well as provide an additional rationale for an increased role for the Commission in strategic sectors.

More critically, and beyond defence and space, there is also a need for Com-mission officials involved in the EDF to start cooperating with colleagues from various Commission services responsible for research and innovation. With the legal parameters set down by the proposed Regulation on the EDF, new working practices and groups could be established to ensure that officials working in the new DG are aware of the programmes being supported by the EU's framework programme on research and innovation. Regular staff-to-staff meetings and perhaps joint technology foresight studies could help with the cross-pollination of civil, security and defence research. Naturally, putting in place new bureau-cratic structures and working practices is the relatively easier aspect of greater civil–security–defence synergies. The really difficult part is in overcoming different mindsets and cultures – the truth is that those working in civil research and innovation do not always feel comfortable working on defence-related pro-grammes or initiatives. Thus, there is no guarantee that even if an intelligent official working at DG Defence Industry and Space identifies a promising civil research endeavour, that civil actors will feel comfortable with their efforts being fed into defence projects. Again, another important aspect to this debate is how the 'open' IPR regime for civil research can be taken up by the relatively closed regime under the Fund – some could argue that once open civil research findings could progressively become more closed the closer they get to defence and the need to classify certain research results.

Any such strategy of innovation in the Commission, will also rest upon the ability of policy makers to identify existing EU tools and mechanisms that apply to the development of dual-use technologies. For example, the Union has already mobilised the ESIF to support certain projects and in particular the ESIF's 'Strategies for Smart Specialisation' has helped regions utilise approximately €125 billion to support digitalisation and innovation. Furthermore, the European Regional and Development Fund (ERDF) is also being used to support dual-use projects in the EU (European Defence Agency 2014). When taken together with Horizon 2020 and future research and innovation framework programmes, it will be necessary for the Commission to stitch together the priorities and strengths of each of these tools to ensure that there is no unnecessary duplication of research projects. Here, it is also vital that the Commission continues to reach out to the main dual-use technology stakeholders through information sessions and conferences (European Commission 2018c).

Any discussion about stakeholder involvement or buy-in of the governance model underpinning the EDF needs a conceptual perspective. As Citi (2014) remarks, greater supranational involvement in hitherto intergovernmental domains occur because of a shift in the nature of collective action problems. Nevertheless, the increased power of a body such as the Commission in an area like defence forces one to think about the role of existing bodies and agencies. In EU security and defence, the rise of the Commission raises questions about the role of bodies like the European Defence Agency and the European External Action Service. Börzel (2005) has claimed that 'creeping competence' by institutions such as the Commission does not automatically translate into power for one set of bodies to the detriment of others – in this sense, the depth and scope of competences should be interrogated. With the EDF, what appears to be emerging is a re-organisation of the EU defence governance model away from outright intergovernmentalism to a more communitarian one that brings in member states, industry, research institutes and communities of interest under the overall guidance of the Commission. In this sense, not only is a collective action problem being configured at the EU level, but also financial incentives are being used to mould a new form of governance within the EU defence domain.

Yet, how the European Commission organises itself internally and manages the EDF is only part of the challenge of ensuring a crossover between the civil, security and defence domains. A bigger challenge can be found in the reluctance that some research institutes and commercial firms have with working with defence actors. While it is certainly true that many defence firms maintain civil wings to focus on value added sectors such as cyber, communications and security services, many civil firms do not wish to have their reputations tarnished by working with defence contractors or governments. As Verbruggen (2019) states, the main obstacles to greater collaboration between civil and defence actors are: 1) a lack of synchronicity in business cultures; 2) different cultures of innovation; and 3) a resistance by civil engineers to work in line with military standards. Another additional difficulty here is how IPRs are managed. Indeed, there is little incentive for researchers and engineers in the commercial sector to work on developing a technology if, as part of a process of integrating this technology into a defence system, commercial firms lose control over intellectual property. Should a technology take on a specific characteristic that makes it valuable from the perspective of national security, then governments and militaries may attempt to seize control of it.

Technology investments under the Fund: the story so far….

Despite all of the challenges highlighted above, it is interesting to note that the EU has already started to make defence investments that have implications for the development of dual-use technologies. For example, under the Preparatory Action on Defence (PADR), the Commission has set out a number of technology areas that can be exploited for dual-use purposes. In the PADR work programme for 2018, the Commission indeed specifies that €40 million shall be invested into three areas including: 1) the development of a system-on-a-chip package; 2) the elaboration of a high power directed energy system; and 3) strategic technology foresight. Whereas the third area is less about technology development per se, the first two areas have clear crossover potential with the civil sector. For instance, the system-on-a-chip call seeks to enhance the Union's high-resolution and high-speed data acquisition capacities with a view to improving communications, electronic warfare, encryption, radar, positioning and digital imaging (European Commission 2018c: 5). Yet, while general-purpose computer processors and chips can fulfil certain tasks, they are not usually compatible with the needs of defence. That is to say that while many high performance chips are already being used in the medical and automotive sectors, they need to be enhanced for the harsh environments in which military actors deploy them and they must ensure a much higher level of security.

Furthermore, under the European Defence Industrial Development Programme (EDIDP) of 2019, the Commission has also called for the development of specific defence capabilities including: disruptive technologies, future naval platforms, air combat capabilities, ground-based precision strike capabilities, command and control, satellite communications, cyber defence, air and space capabilities and remotely piloted air systems and a multipurpose unmanned ground system (European Commission 2019b). Of course, many of these areas include the possibility of integrating dual-use technologies (especially when it comes to cyber defence). What is clear from the Commission's initial EDIDP call is that the scope for 'off the shelf' commercial solutions is greatly reduced owing to the specific defence orientation of the investments. Of course, from both political and technical respects, this is important because otherwise the Commission could be accused of duplicating investments for certain technologies. In other words, the challenge will be maintaining a specific defence focus on investments. This will be easier for capability development programmes where specific technologies are integrated than perhaps it will be for defence research programmes. The lower one goes in the technological readiness levels, the more scope there is for sourcing commercially available technologies and solutions.

Yet, certain technology areas that could be integrated into defence capabilities still maintain a dual-use nature. Cyber is one obvious example. We know that cyber is an area that envelops all of society and multiple government agencies and commercial firms are attempting to ensure the cyber security of critical infrastructures. In a broader sense, strategies such as cyber hygiene and technologies that ensure data protection, the mitigation of distributed denial-of-service attacks, anti-phishing and fraud detection are commonplace. When applied to the defence sector, however, specific challenges arise such as the need to repel attacks on classified source material and communications networks, plus there is a need to safeguard against cyber espionage. As Lewis remarks, 'most cyber attacks will not produce destructive effects similar to kinetic weapons, but will instead seek to disrupt data and services, sow confusion, damage networks and computers (including software and computers embedded in weapons systems) machinery' (2015: 3–4). While technological solutions cannot be the only response to cyberattacks (e.g. cyber defence processes and doctrines are equally important, see Deschaux-Dutard, Chapter 7 in this book), military actors have specific needs. Ensuring, therefore, that the EDIDP call meets the needs of defence rather than broader security needs can be challenging.

Related to the importance of cyber defence is the development of artificial intelligence. While the PADR and the EDIDP do not specifically refer to AI for military purposes, it is clear that AI is not only a dual-use technology but also one that will have to respond to the specific needs of military actors. As a strategic enabler that could greatly enhance the military capabilities and defence industry of the EU, AI promises (or threatens, depending on one's perspective) to revolutionise the way armed forces communicate with each other, target adversaries and ensure the protection and durability of supply and logistics lines. For EU security and defence, the implications of AI are unclear but it should be recognised that AI systems are already used by the European Union to process and analyse data for crisis management purposes (e.g. the EU's Satellite Centre utilises basic AI to decipher data and images that are produced by European satellite systems; see Fiott and Lindstrom 2018). Much like cyber, however, AI is set to be a cross-sectoral factor that will not just lead to specific innovations in the defence field. In fact, the European Commission hopes to encourage investments of approximately €20 billion per year on AI (e.g. the digital economy, automotive sector and industrial production) (European Commission 2018d). Despite the wide application of AI, however, it will be critical from a defence perspective to tackle issues such as how AI stands up to the standards of International Humanitarian Law and the potential proliferation of such systems.

One strategy that can be deployed to ensure that technologies and capabilities developed under the Fund maintain a specific focus on defence is to develop standards. In fact, the Commission already makes clear in the proposed Regulation on the EDF that activities 'leading to common defence capability requirements and supporting studies as well as actions aiming at *supporting the creation of a common definition of technical specifications or standards* should also be eligible for support by the Fund' (emphasis added by the author) (European Commission 2018a: 14). Such action comes on top of the fact that member states, firms and research institutes will only be eligible for EDF support if they agree to harmonised technical requirements to begin with. Standardisation is a way not only to ensure higher degrees of interoperability between armed forces in Europe, but also to enhance the performance of pieces of equipment or technologies. In the defence sector, the issue of performance is critical because equipment is used in high-pressure environments and such equipment is also put to lethal ends. One of the expectations is that the Fund could help to stimulate standardisation and thereby reduce the costs associated with defence production processes and duplication. Finally, and perhaps most crucially, standardisation can also increase the security of supply of components and technologies (Fiott 2018).

Yet, as with the earlier point about ensuring relevant policy expertise in identifying civil–defence crossover opportunities, so too is it necessary to ensure that the Commission has the capacity to tap existing standards that have been certified by international and European standardisation organisations (SOs) and developed at NATO (i.e. the so-called STANAGs). Fortunately enough, the Commission already has a certain level of expertise in benefitting from existing 'hybrid' or 'dual-use' standards. Indeed, there have been interesting applications of these types of standards with respect to maritime information sharing and remotely piloted air systems (RPAS). For example, standardisation has already played a role in establishing and supporting the work of the EU's Safe SeaNet platform that helps share data on vessel traffic on the seas and oceans. With regard to RPAS, the Commission has already stated that it will look into how initiatives like the Single European Sky (SES) and the Single European Sky Air Traffic Management Research Joint Undertaking (SESAR JU) could inspire standards for the integration of RPAS into European airspace. On this basis, and with the support of the EDF and other instruments, there is scope for the Commission to explore how 'hybrid' standards could also be applied to initiatives such as military mobility, cyber defence and energy management for defence (Fiott 2018: 43–45).

Conclusion

This chapter began by asking how the European Commission intends to balance the defence and civil sectors under the EDF. In particular, it was necessary to establish whether it is possible or indeed necessary to maintain such a strict division between civil, security and defence markets and investments. To this end, the chapter has shown how defence markets continue to evolve in such a way that civil actors and firms are increasingly important for defence innovation. Long gone are the days where defence R&D drove forward innovation because today we observe a trend where commercial R&D is developing technologies in areas such as drones, cyber and AI at breakneck speeds (see Csernatoni and Lavallée, Chapter 13 in this book). The reality today is that defence firms, institutions and governments have to court the attention of commercial firms in ways not necessary in the past. The chapter has also highlighted how the rising cost of defence capabilities, which integrate high-tech and high-value technologies, is putting pressure on governments to save costs by avoiding duplication and to cooperate with partners. The European Defence Fund was singled out as a recent initiative developed by the EU to support member states with this challenge, and the chapter highlighted the challenges ahead for the Commission in terms of maintaining coherence between defence research and capability development.

After considering the implications of dual-use technologies and the civil sector, this chapter went on to show how there does not appear to be a contradiction in pushing for an EDF that supports defence research and capability development, despite the present nature of the defence market and its interlinkages with the civil domain. Indeed, without an express focus on and investment in the defence sector, there is a danger that Europe's defence industry will wither away in the coming years and decades. Clearly, the combination of a need for greater industrial competitiveness and a requirement to fill capability gaps means that the defence industry is and should be the key focus of EDF investments. This is not to imply that EDF support should serve as a subsidy for industry – far from it. Instead, the aim of the Fund is to ensure industrial competitiveness as a goal that simultaneously enhances cross-border cooperation in the EU and improves the Union's strategic autonomy in defence innovation and capabilities. It is therefore positive that the Commission directs a part of its investments directly to defence-relevant projects and work programmes.

Nevertheless, despite the focus on the defence sector the Commission also wants to stimulate a cross-pollination of civil, security and defence research. This chapter has shown how it can do so given its existing tools and instruments, but that there is still a need to refine its approach to IPRs and standardisation. If the Commission is able to successfully develop compatible IPR approaches in the civil, security and defence sectors, and if it is able to unlock the potential of hybrid standards, it will be able to better ensure a focus on defence while at the same time allowing for civil-initiated research and dual-use technologies to inform and possibly enhance EU defence innovation and capability programmes – if so required. Above all else, it is clear that the EU is not simply in the business of 'financing rhetoric'. Its preparatory programmes on defence research and capability development are underway, and there are high expectations that the fully-fledged Fund will enhance the competitiveness of Europe's defence industry and boost the European Union's strategic autonomy. Beyond the money that is now available, the real objective is to support a culture of innovation in the European Union that can lead to the identification and production of cutting-edge technologies, equipment and systems – capabilities that Europe's armed forces badly need.

Note

1 The views expressed in this chapter do not necessarily represent those of the European Union.

References

Augustine, N.R. (1984) *Augustine's Laws and Major System Development Programs*. Reston, VA: American Institute of Aeronautics and Astronautics.

Bellais, R. (2013) Technology and the Defense Industry: Real Threats, Bad Habits, or New (Market) Opportunities? *Journal of Innovation, Economics and Management* 12(2): 59–78.

Blauberger, M. and Weiss, M. (2013) If You Can't Beat Me, Join Me! How the Commission Pushed and Pulled Member States into Legislating Defence Procurement. *Journal of European Public Policy* 20(8): 1120–1138.

Börzel, T. (2005) Mind the Gap! European Integration Between Level and Scope. *Journal of European Public Policy* 12(2): 217–236.

Christensen, C. (2019) Disruptive Innovation. Clayton Christensen. At: http://clayton christensen.com/key-concepts/.

Citi, M. (2014) Revisiting Creeping Competences in the EU: The Case of Security R&D Policy. *Journal of European Integration* 36(2): 135–151.

Csernatoni, R. (2018) Constructing the EU's High-Tech Borders: Frontex and the Dual-Use Drones for Border Management. *European Security* 27(2): 175–200.

European Commission (2017) Horizon 2020 in Full Swing: Three Years On – Key Facts and Figures 2014–2016. https://ec.europa.eu/programmes/horizon2020/sites/horizon2020/files/h2020_threeyearson_a4_horizontal_2018_web.pdf.

European Commission (2018a) Proposal for a European Defence Fund. *COM(2018) 476 final*. Brussels.

European Commission (2018b) The 2018 EU Industrial R&D Investment Scorecard. https://iri.jrc.ec.europa.eu/publications/2018-eu-industrial-rd-investment-scoreboard.

European Commission (2018c) Decision on the Adoption of the Work Programme for 2018 of the Preparatory Action on Defence Research. *C(2018) 1383 final*, Brussels.

European Commission (2018d) Artificial Intelligence. Brussels, https://ec.europa.eu/commission/news/artificial-intelligence-2018-dec-07_en.

European Commission (2019a) Commission Implementing Decision on Financing the European Defence Industrial Development Programme. *C(2019) 2205 final*, Brussels.

European Commission (2019b) 2019 Calls for Proposals: European Defence Industrial Development Programme. https://ec.europa.eu/growth/content/2019-calls-proposals-european-defence-industrial-development-programme-edidp_en.

European Defence Agency (2014) Your Guide to European Structural Funds for Dual-Use Technology Projects. At: www.eda.europa.eu/docs/default-source/brochures/esf-brochure.

European Defence Agency (2018) Defence Data 2016–2017: Key Findings and Analysis. At: www.eda.europa.eu/docs/default-source/brochures/eda_defencedata_a4.

Federal Procurement Data System (2017) Top 100 Contractors Report. At: www.fpds.gov/fpdsng_cms/index.php/en/reports/62-top-100-contractors-report.

Fiott, D. (2018) European Armaments Standardisation. Study for the European Parliament's Directorate General for External Policies. At: www.iss.europa.eu/sites/default/files/EUISSFiles/Defence%20study.pdf.

Fiott, D. (2019) *Defence Industrial Cooperation in the European Union: The State, the Firm and Europe*. London: Routledge.

Fiott, D. and Bellais, R. (2016) A 'Game Changer'? The EU's Preparatory Action on Defence Research. *ARES Group Policy Paper* 1. Paris: French Institute for International and Strategic Affairs. At: www.iris-france.org/wp-content/uploads/2016/04/ARES-Group-Policy-Paper-Fiott-and-Bellais-04-16-OK.pdf.

Fiott, D. and Lindstrom, G. (2018) Artificial Intelligence: What Implications for EU Security and Defence? *EUISS Brief* 10. Paris: EU Institute for Security Studies. At: www.iss.europa. eu/content/artificial-intelligence---what-implications-eu-security-and-defence.

Freeman, J. *et al.* (2015) Innovation Models: Enabling New Defence Solutions and Enhanced Benefits from Science and Technology. *RAND Europe Report*. At: www. rand.org/content/dam/rand/pubs/research_reports/RR800/RR840/RAND_RR840.pdf.

Haroche, P. (2019) Supranationalism Strikes Back: A Neofunctionalist Account of the European Defence Fund. *Journal of European Public Policy*. At: doi: 10.1080/13501 763.2019.1609570.

Ianakiev, G. (2019) The European Defence Fund: A Game Changer for European Defence Industrial Collaboration. *ARES Group Policy Paper* 48. Paris: French Institute for International and Strategic Affairs. At: www.iris-france.org/wp-content/uploads/2019/11/ARES-48.pdf.

Karlsson-Vinkhuyzen, S.I. (2016) Legitimacy. In C. Ansell and J. Torfing (eds), *Handbook on Theories of Governance*. Cheltenham: Edward Elgar, 197–204.

Kirkpatrick, D.L.I. (1995) The Rising Unit Cost of Defence Equipment – The Reasons and Results. *Defence and Peace Economics* 6(4): 263–288.

Kirkpatrick, D.L.I. (2004) Trends in the Costs of Weapons Systems and the Consequences. *Defence and Peace Economics* 15(3): 259–273.

Knill, C. and Tosun, J. (2012) *Public Policy: A New Introduction*. Basingstoke: Palgrave Macmillan.

Lavallée, C. (2018) The EU's Dual-Use Exports: A Human Security Approach?. In Eva Pejsova (ed.), Guns, Engines and Turbines: The EU's Hard Power in Asia, *Chaillot Paper* 149. Paris: EU Institute for Security Studies: 43–50.

Lewis, J.A. (2015) The Role of Offensive Cyber Operations in NATO's Collective Defence. *Tallinn Paper* 8. Tallinn: NATO Cooperative Cyber Defence Centre of Excellence: 3–4.

Mawdsley, J. (2011) Towards a Merger of the European Defence and Security Markets?. In Alyson J.K. Bailes and Sara Depauw (eds), *The EU Defence Market: Balancing Effectiveness with Responsibility*. Brussels: Flemish Peace Institute, 11–20.

Molas-Gallart, J. (2002) Coping with Dual-Use: A Challenge for European Research Policy. *Journal of Common Market Studies* 40(1): 155–165.

SAIC (2019) Intelligence Community: Safeguarding our Future Relies on a Cohesive Picture of Threats. At: www.saic.com/who-we-serve/intelligence-community.

United States Government Accountability Office (2019) F-35 Aircraft Sustainment: DoD Needs to Address Substantial Supply Chain Challenges. *Report GAO-19–321*. At: www.gao.gov/assets/700/698693.pdf.

Verbruggen, M. (2019) The Role of Civilian Innovation in the Development of Lethal Autonomous Weapon Systems. *Global Policy* 10(3): 338–342.

3 The security politics of innovation

Dual-use technology in the EU's security research programme

Bruno Oliveira Martins and Neven Ahmad

Introduction

In 2007, the European Union (EU) initiated the Framework Programme 7 (FP7), the Union's Research and Innovation funding programme for the period 2007–2013. Totalling over €50 billion, FP7's budget marked a substantial increase compared with the previous Framework Programme FP6 (41 per cent at 2004 prices), a 'reflection of the high priority of research in Europe' (European Commission 2007). With a budget representing two-thirds of the overall budget, the core of FP7 was the Cooperation programme that was divided into ten themes, one of which was 'Security'.[1] This was the first time that security research had a dedicated theme in the EU's Framework Programme for research and innovation, and the following programme, Horizon 2020, continued along these lines, having 'Secure Societies' as a programmatic area. This security research funded through the EU's Framework Programmes constitutes the security research programme (SRP). Security-related research in FP7 was expected to generate new knowledge and promote the application of new technologies in the field of civil security' and would 'reinforce the competitiveness of the European security industry by stimulating the cooperation of providers and users for civil security solutions' (European Commission 2007).

Due to its civilian nature, the SRP prevented direct funding of defence and military technology. Yet, it enabled funding for dual-use technology, that is, technology that can have both civilian and military applications. Since then, the provision qualifying dual-use technology as eligible for receiving EU R&D funding has been instrumental for the development of new security technologies in Europe and for a number of different actors, including defence companies, to partake in EU-funded consortia that aim at developing 'security solutions' employing this type of technology (see Introduction in this book).

Like in other developed economies, the EU has equated increased security in the civilian realm with cutting-edge technology. As we will show in this chapter, the SRP pursued technology-based solutions for security problems. Yet the processes by which civilian technologies get military use (spin-in processes) are becoming increasingly common due to a combination of factors such as declining military expenditure, a highly innovative civilian industry and a more capability-oriented approach to military innovation (Verbruggen 2019: 338–339). For this reason, a strict distinction between civilian and military technology has become increasingly difficult to draw, and in this context, the concept of dual-use technology requires further scrutiny, particularly when it is promoted explicitly by political authorities.

While the SRP has received some attention from different theoretical perspectives, including critical security studies and sociology of knowledge production (Jeandesboz and Ragazzi 2010; Bigo *et al.* 2014; Edler and James 2015; Lavallée 2016; Carmel 2017; Leese, Lidén and Nikolova 2019; Martins and Küsters 2019), the centrality of the concept of dual-use technology in the broader picture of EU's security and defence research policies demands further inquiry and a multidisciplinary view that can illuminate both the sociological implications of dual-use technology and the security politics associated with it (see also Molas-Gallart 2002). The process by which the EU has promoted dual-use technology brings new elements for assessing civil–military relations within the EU, sheds light on how the politics of security meets the politics of innovation, and how the notion of dual-use technology has acted as a legitimising strategy that facilitates current spending on defence research (see Calcara, Chapter 1 and Fiott, Chapter 2 in this book).

The chapter offers a critical deconstruction of these developments through theoretical debates around the concept of dual-use technology in the disciplinary fields of innovation studies and Science and Technology Studies (STS). In its final section, the chapter promotes 'technology' as a conceptual arena where a dialogue between STS and critical approaches to security and militarism should take place.

Dual-use technology: controversies in the literature

At face value, the notion of dual-use technology as one that can have both civilian and military applications is very simple. Yet, any further consideration associated with this basic idea – how the technology is transferred from one field to the other, who defines what counts as a military application, what regulatory challenges do technology transfers imply, how to know whether something is potentially benign or malign, and so on – has been subject to much inquiry in different academic fields.

The concept of dual-use entered the discourse on weapons and technology exports following Second World War (Reppy 1999). This was unsurprising, considering that nuclear technology had the immense destructive power demonstrated in Hiroshima and Nagasaki in 1945, but also offered the promise of a new source of energy; in this case, not only uranium enrichment plants which may produce nuclear fuel for nuclear power plants, but also highly enriched uranium for a nuclear bomb. In the highly politicised and securitised Cold War environment, debates around dual-use technology were an important part of the strategic and geopolitical considerations of the time.

In the Cold War period, dual-use was framed mostly from an arms control perspective. The possibility of using a particular technology for both civilian and military purposes created a problem for the control and diffusion of cutting-edge weaponry (Brauch *et al.* 1992), particularly as advances in different scientific fields such as biotechnology, neurosciences and genetics created new possibilities for the conduct of war and the resort to political violence. In essence, this quarrel between the promise of scientific progress and the potential threat of a violent destruction constitutes what in the literature has been labelled the dual-use dilemma.

The public and political perception of dual-use technology has changed over time, following wider societal trends about the promise of scientific evolutions for the resolution of different problems. In many ways, then, dual-use technology became gradually perceived also as an industrial issue, in the way that it constitutes an opportunity to provide a wider exploitation of research and manufacturing beyond a given technology's initial objectives, whether they were military or civilian (Molas-Gallart 1997). Along with the perception of the technology, the dual-use dilemma in the security realm has also began to shift, from a narrative about the concern of the dual utility of research in military and civilian settings towards dual-use conversations which focus on how security enterprises should know when (and when not) to classify research, objects or even people as security threats (Vogel *et al.* 2017).

Te Kulve and Smit (2003) use the work of Gummett (1991) to show that the distinction between military and civilian technology can be understood as being institutional, rather than intrinsic. Te Kulve and Smit (2003) illustrate the fact that rather than an intrinsic feature of the technology itself, the civilian, military or dual-use character of a technology is often the result of its shaping within socio-technical networks, that is, not only the shaping of the technology but also the dual-use meaning attached to it depend on its institutional and cultural context. In the article, Te Kulve and Smit show how the bipolar lead-acid battery emerged in a military context in The Netherlands, where the Royal Netherlands Navy envisaged using the battery on future warships; at this initial stage, no civilian application was foreseen. Due a number of circumstances explored in the article, the research institute TNO, in particular its Environment, Energy and Process innovation laboratory (TNO-EEP), became involved in the project, and it was the fact that the TNO-EEP is a 'dual oriented institute' that allowed the battery to be understood as having potential civilian application (Te Kulve and Smit 2003: 961–962).

Therefore, dual-use is a dynamic and shifting concept, meaning that the civil, military or dual-use understandings attached to a technology may change, for example, during the development of the technology in interaction with changes in the number and nature of the actors involved in its socio-technical network (Te Kulve and Smit 2003).[2] The concept of dual-use technology, then, stands at the crossroads between two opposing views of technology: one that understands technology as artefacts and products versus one that understands technology as comprising a whole system of social relations (Molas-Gallart 1997).

A potentially dual-use technology may never be operationalised in all its capacities, and by the same logic, its duality can disappear, or it can appear late in its development and evolution based on the social network of the technology. Cowan and Foray (1995) explore the patterns of potential duality in order to establish the organisational and informational conditions that are required to realize the duality potential. They make a distinction between 'spillover' and duality based on the premise that duality is not intrinsic but rather dependent on the networks that the technology is designed and used in. 'Spillover' is defined as a situation in which the research is conducted within one domain and then adopted without change to another domain. Therefore, spillovers are not evidence of duality, but rather evidence of its absence, and so the promotion of spillover can be viewed as a policy designed to correct the 'duality failure' of an R&D programme (Cowan and Foray 1995). Molas-Gallart (1997) defines dual-use technology transfer as 'a special instance of technology transfer across applications that takes place when a dual-use technology developed for a military (or civilian) use, is transferred to a civilian (or military) application.' Therefore, dual-use technology is directly connected to dual-use technology transfers, which refer to the case when there is an intention to change the initial (military or civilian) application of a technology.

Alic *et al.* (1992) interpret military and commercial technological innovation as two systems that draw on a common technical knowledge but that involve two distinct institutions that operate differently. While the commercial industry depends on improving products through a feedback loop with clients, the military industry works with a different logic (see Introduction in this book; and Alic 1994). The differences extend to goals, technical requirements and managerial arrangements, and as a result, in most cases, military and commercial innovations have evolved in distinctive technical 'cultures' (Alic *et al.* 1992: 43).

The existence of a debate around everything that relates with the concept of dual-use technology has important consequences. In the formulation of Molas-Gallart,

> (g)iven its imprecision, it can easily fall prey to political orchestration. It can be used for instance, as a new, more palatable way of presenting measures of support to an industry that has lost some of its capacity to draw political backing.
>
> (Molas-Gallart 1997: 370)

In the next sections, we will show how this idea is fundamental for understanding the role played by the concept of dual-use technology in the development of the EU's security research programme.

Critical security and military studies approaches

The debates in the fields of innovation studies and STS, briefly introduced above, open relevant opportunities for intellectual cross-fertilisation with critical approaches to security and military studies. Even though the field for interdisciplinary exchange remains scarcely explored, some relevant incursions on this dialogue have been observed. These have focused on two main inter-related issues: circulation and ethicalisation.

Literature on critical security studies has pointed out how security concerns have converged with ethical dilemmas related to the governing of science. For critical security studies with a Foucaultian inspiration, dual-use emerges as a problem of organising circulations. For Foucault, circulation is 'the space of the operations of human beings and defines the principle of organization of modern biopolitics' (Ceyhan 2012). As explained by Aradau and Blanke (2010: 44), security to Foucault referred to biopolitical practices of 'organising circulation, eliminating its dangers, making a division between good and bad circulation, and maximizing the good circulation by eliminating the bad' (Foucault 2007: 18). From this perspective, policing scientific knowledge through the establishment of a 'culture of responsibility' can be understood as a part of broader shifts towards the subjectification of knowledge (Rychnovská 2016). For Foucault, then, circulation is in fact at the heart of modern security governance, constituting freedom and security as two complementary parts of the same system. Rychnovská argues that security concerns have converged with ethical dilemmas related to the governing of science causing an 'ethicalisation' of security. From this perspective, then, this 'ethicalisation' impacts the politicisation of security expertise (Berling and Bueger 2015), the prospects of resistance and the democratic accountability of science. Ethicalisation leads to moving an issue from the sphere of democratic deliberation not due to the immediate threat but rather to the need for upholding ethical norms (Rychnovská 2016).

The place of ethics in security research in a European context has been further explored by Leese, Lidén and Nikolova (2019). In their analysis of the place and function of ethics in the EU security research field – a field marked by the centrality of dual-use technology – they note how applied ethics faces challenges resulting from its 'location in the middle of numerous cross-pressures, such as political ambitions, economic interests, technological rationales and the demands of security professionals', which in turn 'risk turning what was intended to be the critical corrective of applied ethics into a legitimizing function of mere "ethics approval"' (Leese *et al.* 2019: 59). Indeed, these reflections bring new elements for a critique of the dual-use dilemma and expand the contours of its debate. In particular, they relate to a broader discussion on the regulation of scientific and technological developments (see also Burgess *et al.* 2018; Hurlbut 2015). To prevent the conversion of life sciences into 'death sciences' (Atlas and Dando 2006: 277), the United States established a new category of research that is subject to specific regulation. This 'dual-use research of concern' is defined as:

> life sciences research that, based on current understanding, can be reasonably anticipated to provide knowledge, information, products, or technologies that could be directly misapplied to pose a significant threat with broad

potential consequences to public health and safety, agricultural crops and other plants, animals, the environment, materiel, or national security.

(US Government 2014: 6–7)

As mentioned above, the regulation of emerging dual-use technologies and their control has been a classic theme in military studies. Yet, recent critical military studies approach open new opportunities for exploring the phenomenon. When addressing the question of what is critical military studies (CMS), Basham, Belkin and Gifkins address three main arenas of inquiry: the triangle practices/institutions, social practices and political contestation; CMS and the exploration of the 'in-between'; and interdisciplinarity and the place of technology in military discussions (Basham, Belkin and Gifkins 2015; for further discussions on how militarism and security dialogue, see also Stavrianakis and Stern 2018). These areas invite an interpretation of dual-use technology as an arena to re-question civil–military relations as well as a critical understanding of military socio-technical networks and the governance of weapons innovation. For CMS, then, STS, with its focus on the sociological elements of the process of technology production, can impact military studies by providing a crucial critical conceptual deconstruction and re-equation of military equipment and the political sociological elements that surround it.

An STS-inspired framework

The literature debates introduced above lay the ground for this chapter's theoretical framework, through which the EU's engagement with, and promotion of, dual-use technology will be introduced. Even though we do not have the space to provide a deep analysis of the topic, we propose this theoretical framework to conduct further studies of different, sectorial analysis of the governance of dual-use technologies in the EU. We draw insights from different bodies of literature that have had relevant contributions to academic debates on the topic, but we put an emphasis on the STS-based inquires. There are two main reasons driving our option. First, the aspects surrounding socio-political aspects of technology development and innovation are the ones that have made the most relevant contributions to the dual-use question (Molas-Gallart 1997; Vogel *et al.* 2017) and therefore they are the ones that can help us drive forward an informed discussion on the European governance of these technologies. Second, because many STS-based approaches share epistemological assumptions with critical approaches to security and military studies, this creates a favourable ground for theoretical innovation and contributes to a necessary cross-fertilisation between these areas of knowledge.

From these different bodies of literature, in particular inspired by Vogel *et al.* (2017), we build a framework of analysis around four ideas: developments in the dual-use dilemma; upstream and participatory governance of security concerns; the politics of security knowledge; and Responsible Research and Innovation.

Developments in the dual-use dilemma

The dual-use dilemma arises when a research finding or technology has the potential to be used for both civilian purposes and to be weaponised. This debate is by its nature an ethical dilemma (Selgelid 2009) and it is mobilised around all forms of dual-use technology, perhaps particularly in the field of biotechnology where for example the positive potential of genetic engineering can lead to a dangerous virus that could have the potential to kill millions (see also Pustovit and Williams 2008; Rath, Ischi and Perkins 2014). Discussions on this topic shed light on important concepts regarding responsibility, and question what is the responsibility of scientists in fully understanding the possible negative impact of their research findings.

Yet, the character of the dual-use dilemma has begun to shift. For Vogel *et al.*:

> Where once the primary concern was for the dual utility of research in military and civilian settings, today dual-use conversations focus instead on how security enterprises should know when (and when not) to classify research, objects, or even people as security threats.
>
> (Vogel *et al.* 2017: 977)

Today discussion around dual-use technology emphasises the potential industrial benefits of these technologies, and looks less into the security aspects that traditionally used to be mostly associated with it.

Upstream and participatory governance of security concerns

Related to the dual-use dilemma are the ideas of expertise and regulation. In other words, navigating the dilemma requires expertise to identify the full spectrum of possibilities emanating from the technology, in particular the full scope of potential threats associated with it. Due to this knowledge requirement, scientists and technology developers are often interested in contributing to the regulation of a particular scientific and technological field, with an understanding that governmental regulation stifles important research while possibly violating academic freedom and, in some cases, freedom of speech (Selgelid 2009). Associated with the dual-use dilemma, then, is the broader issue of the regulation of knowledge and scientific developments, as well as the relations between scientists and tech developers with the governance of the future. Upstreaming is the idea that 'broader public input involving a diverse array of expertise is needed on these contentious issues in order to have a more holistic understanding of the issues, problems, stakeholders, values, and agendas at play' (Vogel *et al.* 2017: 978; see also Resnik 2010; and Rychnovská 2016 on how the need for a 'bottom–up' approach with members of the specific fields is required for the creation of codes of conduct).

The politics of security knowledge

In the field of dual-use technology, the crucial issue at stake involving the politics of knowledge is how we know something is benign or malign as well as what it *is* in the first place (Vogel *et al.* 2017: 979; Hecht 2010). The politics of knowledge examines the interworking of who creates knowledge and for what purpose. In our case, it asks the question: who has the capacity to identify knowledge or a technology as a security issue? This question naturally opens up a larger set of questions that are at the core of critical security studies research agenda, namely, what counts as a security issue? Security for whom and security from what?

Responsible Research and Innovation

Responsible Research and Innovation (RRI) has gained a central position in the EU science and research policies. RRI emerges from the recognition of the power of science, and this recognition has forced reconsiderations of the responsibilities that should follow such power (Stilgoe and Guston 2017; Burgess *et al.* 2018). Owen, Macnaghton and Stilgoe (2012) argue that there are three main discourses associated with the idea of RRI: an emphasis on the democratic governance of the purposes of research; the idea of responsiveness (emphasising established approaches of anticipation in research and innovation); and the framing of responsibility itself in the context of research and innovation as collective activities with uncertain and unpredictable consequences (Owens *et al.* 2012). Yet, as will be explored here, recent research on the SRP (Martins and Küsters 2019; Leese *et al.* 2019) has showed that the logic of the RRI approach seems to be challenged in important ways by the prominence of the security consortia created through the SRP.

Dual-use technology in EU security and defence research

The Security Research Programme

From the outset, the security research funded under the FP7 had a very strong technological component. The areas to be covered by the SRP, illustrated in Table 3.1, included: technology solutions for civil protection, bio-security, protection against crime and terrorism; border security technologies; and technologies for communications, security systems integration, interconnectivity and interoperability. With a total budget of €1,400 million, the SRP had the expectation of generating both new knowledge and promoting the application of new technologies, while reinforcing the competitiveness of the European security industry. In this logic, we can observe the way in which the EU has seen improved security, advanced technology and industrial development as fully integrated.

The triangle security–technology–industry was further promoted in Horizon 2020, the Framework Programme that followed FP7. Its security programme was called *Secure Societies* and it comprised the areas displayed in Table 3.2.

Table 3.1 Areas for security research under FP7

Area	Description
Security of citizens	Technology solutions for civil protection, bio-security, protection against crime and terrorism
Security of infrastructures and utilities	Examining and securing infrastructures in areas such as ICT, transport, energy and services in the financial and administrative domain
Intelligent surveillance and border security	Technologies, equipment, tools and methods for protecting Europe's border controls such as land and coastal borders
Restoring security and safety in case of crisis	Technologies and communication, coordination in support for civil, humanitarian and rescue tasks
Security systems integration, interconnectivity and interoperability	Information gathering for civil security, protection of confidentiality and traceability of transactions
Security and society	Acceptance of security solutions, socio-economic, political and cultural aspects of security, ethics and values, social environment and perceptions of security
Security research coordination and structuring	Coordination between European and international security research efforts in the areas of civil, security and defence research

Source: European Commission 2014a.

Table 3.2 Areas for security research under Horizon 2020

Area	Description
Natural and man-made disasters	Enhance the resilience of our society against natural and man-made disasters, ranging from the development of new crisis management tools to communication interoperability, and to develop novel solutions for the protection of critical infrastructure
Crime and terrorism	Fight crime and terrorism ranging from new forensic tools to protection against explosives
Border security	Improve border security, ranging from improved maritime border protection to supply chain security and to support the European Union's external security policies including through conflict prevention and peace building
Cybersecurity	Provide enhanced cybersecurity, ranging from secure information sharing to new assurance models

Source: European Commission 2019.

Besides the SRP areas enunciated above, the EU has established numerous opportunities for the design and implementation of dual-use in the 2014–2020 programming period. Taken together, the European Structural and Investment Funds (ESIF), Horizon 2020, COSME and Erasmus+ programmes provide specific support for the various levels of development within the dual-use field. ESIF supports technology transfer, market intelligence, proof of concept and more, and these steps help businesses to diversify or to move from one sector to another. Horizon 2020 provides funding opportunities for the civil application of projects with dual-use nature, while the COSME programme presents opportunities to access certain funding for cooperation between clusters and for partnership-building. Finally, a strand of Erasmus+ contributes to the dual-use expansion by helping to create industry–university collaborations in this field. Through these programmes, all EU companies can benefit from the support of R&D through ESIF and Horizon 2020. Additionally, SMEs are able to benefit from COSME, Horizon 2020 and ESIF (European Commission 2014b).

From security to defence research

The EU views dual-use technology as a way forward for advancing innovation in Europe and the EU's strategic autonomy in the field of security and defence. Importantly, as explored in Martins and Küsters (2019), dual-use research within the SRP created practices, procedures and cultures that facilitated the opening up to EU-funded defence research operated since 2016 (on the differences between the SRP and the defence research programme, see also James 2018). Jean-Claude Juncker, former president of the European Commission, has made it clear that, while defence is a top priority for the EU (Mauro and Thoma 2016), the Commission views dual-use research as a solution for the lack of investment in research and innovation.

In 2014, the Commission proposed an industrial plan in the field of defence with the title *A New Deal for European Defence* expressing its intention to support CSDP-related research in three ways, one of which was dual-use research (European Commission 2014c). In order for this to happen, the EU recognises that it needs to invest in defence research and development and, for that reason, there has been a call to increase the 'dual-use' research share of the Horizon 2020 budget phase (2018–2020). Under Horizon 2020, a total of €164 million was allocated to 'dual-use' technologies including Critical Infrastructure Protection (2016 budget €20 million), Security (2016 budget €113.25 million) and Digital Security Focus Area (2016 budget €29 million; figures provided in Mauro and Thoma 2016). An additional push towards dual-use research came as the European Council invited member states to increase investment in cooperative research programmes and called on the Commission and the European Defence Agency (EDA) to develop proposals that would further stimulate dual-use research (European Parliament 2019).

Another important actor in the field of EU defence research is the EDA, who continuously work on defence-related SMEs with a focus on dual-use activities and cross-border cooperation across the European defence supply chain. The support for dual-use is clearly illustrated in the EDA's activities. Since

2013, the EDA has provided assistance for stakeholders in the defence sector to access ESIF co-funding for dual-use projects through various means such as raising awareness among defence stakeholders, providing coaching support for pilot projects and developing a methodology (European Parliament 2019). In concrete, the EDA's roadmap for dual-use technologies consists of the following elements:

- identifying and supporting dual-use Key Enabling Technologies (KETs);
- the development of nano-technologies through the public–private partnership Electronic Components and Systems for European Leadership Joint Understanding (JU ECSEL); and
- the research for dual-use technologies eligible for funding through Structural and Investment Funds

(EDA 2016)

An important means through which the EU promotes research on dual-use technology is through the publication of detailed, step-by-step brochures where it reaches out to different potential recipients of the EU funding. In some cases, it is the Commission that issues theses guides, for example, targeting SMEs and different regions (European Commission 2014b); at other times, it is the EDA (2015). Through its brochure 'Your Guide to European Structural Funds for Dual-Use Technology Projects', for example, the EDA (2015) provides a comprehensive document that breaks down the step-by-step process that a defence actor should follow in order to secure dual-use funding, therefore incentivising defence actors to access EU funding for the dual-use technologies.

The arms control dimension

An important aspect of the political debates around dual-use technology refers to its arms control dimension. Precisely because they can also be used for military purposes, dual-use goods are subject to expert controls mechanisms and, within the EU, the key document is the 2009 EU Dual-Use Regulation (Council Regulation 428/2009), that establishes a common legal basis for member states' controls of the trade of these goods. The Regulation has different annexes, that are updated on a regular basis, and that list the different dual-use technologies which are covered by the rules of said Regulation. These annexes follow closely the list of nine categories of dual-use goods covered by the Wassenaar Arrangement on Export Controls for Conventional Arms and Dual-Use Goods and Technologies.[3] In 2016, the European Commission published a proposal for recasting the regulation in order to provide it with a human security dimension and to cover certain types of cyber-surveillance (Lavallée 2018). At the time of writing, the three EU institutions involved in the recast process (Commission, Parliament and Council) have not agreed on the terms in which the Regulation should be amended.

Seeing EU dual-use technology through an STS perspective

In the EU, member states have the main responsibility for providing security to their citizens. This crucial principle of competence allocation opens a somewhat different trajectory of security politics at the EU level. This idea, coupled with an understanding of security as a derivative concept – that is, what 'security' is (or should be) is derived from one's political outlook and philosophical world-view (Booth 2007: 104–119) – implies that the definition of what counts/should count as a security issue for the EU is not provided by an external authority or a government, nor is it objectively defined. Rather, it results from a multi-layered process involving formal and informal decisions made by public and private actors, who create the knowledge base upon which policy decisions are made and priorities are defined.

In this context, the pursuit of technological knowledge in the security and defence realms becomes a political choice with relevant political consequences. Even if the European Commission frames much of the EU-funded dual-use research as being mostly an industrial policy – for example, by promoting it to SMEs and regions, as illustrated above – these options do not fall outside the domain of politics; rather, they bring elements to claim a new centrality of technology in IR and security studies, because security technologies are 'changing the way we conceive of foreign policy and security threats' (Martins 2019).

By promoting dual-use research as a way to reinforce EU defence R&D and advance industrial and innovation policies in the EU, the many EU actors involved in this process illustrate the above-mentioned shift in the understanding of the dual-use dilemma, that is, a growing focus on the synergies and possibilities opened up by these technologies, rather than on the risks they entail. This shift does not mean that risks are neglected. It means, instead, that the emphasis on the promise of dual-use technology reflects a strategy through which the peculiar character of these technologies is used to advance an agenda that is not only industrial but also political.

To recover the expression of Molas-Gallart mentioned earlier, these technologies 'can be used for instance, as a new, more palatable way of presenting measures of support to an industry that has lost some of its capacity to draw political backing' (Molas-Gallart 1997: 370). The provision qualifying 'dual-use' technology as eligible for receiving EU R&D funding through the SRP has been crucial for defence companies to receive EU funding, while direct defence R&D funding was prohibited and to foster consortia and projects that developed 'security solutions' employing this type of technology.

Additionally, the shift in the understanding of the dual-use dilemma impacts the participatory governance of security concerns, which are often not sufficiently addressed at the EU level. This, in turn, affects the RRI principle and threatens to render inefficient the efforts in making it a central premise of security and defence R&D in the EU.

The concept of dual-use technology in the security and defence realms adds value to the broader theoretical and empirical discussion on (the blurring of) the distinction between security and defence, and between the civilian and the military domains. A clear illustration of the growing enmeshment of all these concepts deals with issues of spin off and spin in, that can be cogently understood by using theoretical concepts such as circulation, vouching for the necessity of further dialogue between intellectual traditions emanating from STS and critical approaches to security and military studies.

Conclusions

In the context of this volume, a deeper incursion on the concept of dual-use technology plays a very important role for two main reasons. First, because the EU's engagement with security technologies happened mostly through fomenting, promoting and funding dual-use technology, as demonstrated in this chapter. Second, and most importantly, civilian and military technologies are becoming increasingly entangled and, therefore, a clear separation of both domains is increasingly impossible to draw. Technology transfers between both fields are happening on a constant basis and, most importantly, crucial technology used in military contexts emerged from civilian and commercial contexts. Throughout the Cold War, many technological breakthroughs happened in the military context and, only afterwards, were imported to the civilian sphere. Among these are nuclear energy, the Internet, jet engines, missile technology leading to space craft and the GPS navigation system, for example. Today, much of the technology used in military contexts is developed in the civilian and commercial sphere and further imported into the military sphere. Among examples of these technologies are face recognition tech, artificial intelligence and swarm drones.

These technologies, which will play an important role in the conduct of political violence in the near future, are dual-use per definition. Understanding the broader societal and scientific debates surrounding dual-use technologies is therefore pivotal for understanding the politics surrounding their use.

Notes

1 The other nine themes were Health; Food, agriculture and fisheries, and biotechnology; Information and communication technologies; Nanosciences, nanotechnologies, materials and new production technologies; Energy; Environment (including climate change); Transport (including aeronautics); Socio-economic sciences and the humanities; and Space.
2 Still, Haico te Kulve and Wim A. Smit (2003) argue that given a certain social-cultural setting, certain technologies will be more suitable for applications in both domains than others.
3 These are the nine categories: (1) Special Materials and Related Equipment; (2) Materials Processing; (3) Electronics; (4) Computers; (5 – Part 1) Telecommunications; (5 – Part 2) 'Information Security'; (6) Sensors and 'Lasers'; (7) Navigation and Avionics (8); Marine; and (9) Aerospace and Propulsion.

References

Alic, J.A. (1994) The Dual Use of Technology: Concepts and Policies. *Technology in Society* 16(2): 155–172.

Alic, J.A., Branscomb, L.M., Brooks, H., Carter, A.B. and Epstein, G.L. (1992) *Beyond Spinoff: Military and Commercial Technologies in a Changing World*. Boston, MA: Harvard Business School Press.

Aradau, C. and Blanke, T. (2010) Governing Circulation: A Critique of the Biopolitics of Security. In Miguel de Larrinaga and Marc G. Doucet (eds), *Security and Global Governmentality: Globalization, Governance and the State*. London: Routledge.

Atlas, R.M. and Dando, M. (2006) The Dual-Use Dilemma for the Life Sciences: Perspectives, Conundrums, and Global Solutions. *Biosecurity and Bioterrorism: Biodefense Strategy, Practice, and Science* 4(3): 276–286.

Basham, V.M., Belkin, A. and Gifkins, J. (2015) What is Critical Military Studies? *Critical Military Studies* 1(1): 1–2.

Berling, T.V. and Bueger, C. (2015) *Security Expertise: Practice, Power, Responsibility*. London: Routledge.

Bigo, D., Jeandesboz, J., Martin-Maze, M. and Ragazzi, F. (2014) *Review of Security Measures in the 7th Research Framework Programme*, Justice and Home Affairs (LIBE). Brussels: European Parliament.

Booth, K. (2007) *Theory of World Security*. Cambridge: Cambridge University Press.

Brauch, H.G., van der Graaf, H.J., Grin, J. and Smit, W.A. (1992) *Controlling the Development and Spread of Military Technology: Lessons from the Past and Challenges for the 1990s*. Amsterdam: VU University Press.

Burgess, J.P., Reniers, G., Ponnet, K., Hardyns, W. and Smit, W. (eds) (2018) *Socially Responsible Innovation in Security: Critical Reflections*. London: Routledge.

Carmel, E. (2017) Re-Interpreting Knowledge, Expertise and EU Governance: The Cases of Social Policy and Security Research Policy. *Comparative European Politics* 15(5): 771–793.

Ceyhan, A. (2012) Surveillance as Biopower. In Kirstie Ball, Kevin D. Haggerty and David Lyon (eds), *Routledge Handbook of Surveillance Studies*. London: Routledge.

Cowan, R. and Foray, D. (1995) Quandaries in the Economics of Dual Technologies and Spillovers from Military to Civilian Research and Development. *Research Policy* 24(6): 851–868.

Edler, J. and James, A.D. (2015) Understanding the Emergence of New Science and Technology Policies: Policy Entrepreneurship, Agenda Setting and the Development of the European Framework Programme. *Research Policy* 44(6): 1252–1265.

European Commission (2014a) FP7-SECURITY – Specific Programme "Cooperation": Security. At: https://cordis.europa.eu/programme/rcn/861_en.pdf.

European Commission (2014b) *EU Funding for Dual Use. Guide for Regions and SMEs*. REF Ares(2015)3866477, DG Enterprise and Industry, Brussels: European Commission. At: http://ec.europa.eu/DocsRoom/documents/12601/attachments/1/translations/en/renditions/native.

European Commission (2014c) A New Deal for European Defence, Brussels, 24 June COM(2014) 387 final. At: www.europarl.europa.eu/meetdocs/2014_2019/documents/sede/dv/sede110914dealeuropeandefence_/sede110914dealeuropeandefence_en.pdf.

European Commission (2007) What is FP7? The Basics. *FP7 in Brief*. At: https://ec.europa.eu/research/fp7/understanding/fp7inbrief/what-is_en.html.

European Commission (2019) Secure Societies: Protecting Freedom and Security of Europe and its Citizens. At: https://ec.europa.eu/programmes/horizon2020/en/h2020-section/secure-societies---protecting-freedom-and-security-europe-and-its-citizens.

European Defence Agency (2015) *Your Guide to European Structural Funds for Dual-use technology projects*. Brussels: European Defence Agency.

European Defence Agency (2016) *Dual-Use Research*. Brussels: European Defence Agency. At: www.eda.europa.eu/what-we-do/activities/activities-search/dual-use-research.

European Parliament (2019) *Fact Sheets on the European Union: Defence Industries*. At: www.europarl.europa.eu/factsheets/en/sheet/65/defence-industry.

Foucault, M. (2007) *Security, Territory, Population*. Basingstoke: Palgrave.

Gummett, P. (ed.) (1991) *Future Relations Between Defence and Civil Science and Technology*, Report for the UK Parliamentary Office for Science and Technology. London: Science Policy Support Group.

Hecht, G. (2010) The Power of Nuclear Things. *Technology and Culture* 51(1): 1–30.

Hurlbut, B. (2015) Remembering the Future: Science, Law, and the Legacy of Asilomar. In S. Jasanoff and S-H. Kim (eds), *Dreamscapes of Modernity: Sociotechnical Imaginaries and the Fabrication of Power*. Chicago, IL: University Of Chicago Press, 126–151.

James, A.D. (2018) Policy Entrepreneurship and Agenda Setting: Comparing and Contrasting the Origins of the European Research Programmes for Security and Defense. In Nikolaos Karampekios, Iraklis Oikonomou and Elias G. Carayannis (eds), *The Emergence of EU Defense Research Policy: From Innovation to Militarization*. Cham: Springer International Publishing AG, 15–43.

Jeandesboz, J. and Ragazzi, F. (2010) Review of Security Measures in the Research Framework Programme. Citizens' Rights and Constitutional Affairs, PE 432.740, Brussels: European Parliament.

Kulve, H. Te and Smit, W.A. (2003) Civilian–Military Co-Operation Strategies in Developing New Technologies. *Research Policy* 32(6): 955–970.

Lavallée, C. (2016) La communautarisation de la recherche sur la sécurité: l'appropriation d'un nouveau domaine d'action au nom de l'approche globale. *Politique européenne* 51: 31–59.

Lavallée, C. (2018) The EU's Dual-Use Exports: A Human Security Approach. In E. Pejsova (ed.), *Guns, Engines and Turbines*. Paris: EU Institute for Security Studies, 43–50.

Leese, M., Lidén, K. and Nikolova, B. (2019) Putting Critique to Work: Ethics in EU Security Research. *Security Dialogue* 50(1): 59–76.

Martins, B.O. (2019) Global Affairs and the Politics of Security Technologies. *Global Affairs* 5(2): 105–106.

Martins, B.O. and Küsters, C. (2019) Hidden Security: EU Public Research Funds and the Development of European Drones. *Journal of Common Market Studies* 57(2): 278–297.

Mauro, F. and Thoma, K. (2016) The Future of EU Defence Research. Brussels: European Parliament's Sub-Committee on Security and Defence. EP/EXPO/B/SEDE/2015–02 EN March 2016-PE535.003. At: www.europarl.europa.eu/RegData/etudes/STUD/2016/535003/EXPO_STU(2016)535003_EN.pdf.

Molas-Gallart, J. (1997) Which Way to Go? Defence Technology and the Diversity of 'Dual-Use' Technology Transfer. *Research Policy* 26(3): 367–385.

Molas-Gallart, J. (2002) Coping with Dual-Use: A Challenge for European Research Policy. *Journal of Common Market Studies* 40(1): 155–165.

Owen, R., Macnaghten, P. and Stilgoe, J. (2012) Responsible Research and Innovation: From Science in Society to Science for Society, with Society. *Science and Public Policy* 39(6): 751–760.

Pustovit, S.V. and Williams, E.D. (2008) Philosophical Aspects of Dual Use Technologies. *Science and Engineering Ethics* 16(1): 17–31.

Rath, J., Ischi, M. and Perkins, D. (2014) Evolution of Different Dual-use Concepts in International and National Law and Its Implications on Research Ethics and Governance. *Science and Engineering Ethics* 20(3): 769–790.

Reppy, J. (1999) Dual-Use Technology: Back to the Future? In A.R. Markusen and S.S. Costigan (eds), *Arming the Future: A Defense Industry for the 21st Century*. New York: Council on Foreign Relations Press, 269–284.

Resnik, D.B. (2010) Can Scientists Regulate the Publication of Dual Use Research? *Studies in Ethics, Law, and Technology* 4(1): 1–7.

Rychnovská, D. (2016) Governing Dual-Use Knowledge: From the Politics of Responsible Science to the Ethicalization of Security. *Security Dialogue* 47(4): 310–328.

Selgelid, M.J. (2009) Dual-Use Research Codes of Conduct: Lessons from the Life Sciences. *Nanoethics* 3(3): 175–183.

Stavrianakis, A. and Stern, M. (2018) Militarism and Security: Dialogue, Possibilities and Limits. *Security Dialogue* 49(1–2): 3–18.

Stilgoe, J. and Guston, D.H. (2017) Responsible Research and Innovation. In U. Felt, R. Fouché, C. Miller and L. Smith-Doerr (eds), *The Handbook of Science and Technology Studies*. Cambridge, MA: The MIT Press, 853–880.

US Government (2014) United States Government Policy for Institutional Oversight of Life Sciences Dual Use Research of Concern. 24 September. At: www.phe.gov/s3/dualuse/Documents/durc-policy.pdf.

Verbruggen, M. (2019) The Role of Civilian Innovation in the Development of Lethal Autonomous Weapon Systems. *Global Policy* 10(3): 338–342.

Vogel, K.M., Balmer, B., Evans, S.W., Kroener, I., Matsumoto, M. and Rappert, B. (2017) Knowledge and Security. In U. Felt, R. Fouché, C. Miller and L. Smith-Doerr (eds), *The Handbook of Science and Technology Studies*. Cambridge, MA: MIT Press, 973–1001.

4 Drone surveillance, a dual-use practice?

Samuel Longuet

Introduction

As stressed by the editors in the Introduction of this book, referring to governance 'also allows us to underline the role of discourse, norms and practices in structuring knowledge-production mechanisms' and this is precisely what I set out to do in this chapter about drones. The aim of this chapter is to deal with how discourse communities about drones developed within two European states, namely, France and the United Kingdom[1] and how such discourses coined a narrative that pushes for the use of MALE (Middle Altitude Long Endurance) drones for surveillance purposes in both war and peace contexts. Furthermore, those discourses participated in the blurring of the distinction between police action and war-fighting, making drone surveillance a dual-use practice, fit for both purposes. This, in turn, questions the actual difference (or lack thereof) between those two purposes that the term 'dual-use' presupposes.

Drones are often referred to as 'remotely piloted aircrafts' (RPA) or 'remotely piloted air systems' and are defined as airframes that do not transport their own crew. Although tele-piloted aircrafts have been flown throughout the twentieth century (Zubeldia 2012), the recent developments in this technology have resulted in it being referred to as 'emerging' today (see, for instance, Csernatoni 2019). Specifically, middle altitude, long endurance (MALE) drones are airframes capable of being flown for extended periods of time and piloted from half a world away through a satellite signal. They are often referred to as having completely transformed the way intelligence is gathered by armed forces (Ministry of Defence 2011: iii; Perrin and Roger 2017: 14). European states have used MALE drones for intelligence purposes in several theatres of war. For instance, the German Air Force has deployed Israeli-made *Heron-TP* drones in Afghanistan. The Italian Air Force deployed the American-made *Reaper* in Libya, during the 2011 military intervention. But the two states which have made the largest use of MALE drones in a situation of armed conflicts are the United Kingdom and France, largely due to the fact that they are the two European states that have taken the most active part in military operations over the past two decades. The Royal Air Force (RAF) has been operating *Reaper* drones since 2003 in Afghanistan and then over Iraq and Syria in the context of the ongoing operation against ISIS. The French Air Force has been using MALE drones since 2008, first with the *Harfang*, a version of the *Heron-TP* modified by EADS, in Afghanistan and then with *Reapers* in Mali and the Sahel–Saharan strip since 2013. Therefore, it is relevant to focus on France and the United Kingdom as cases to better understand how the practice of drone surveillance was coined in Europe.

An already extensive critical academic literature exists on the use of drones in a military context, however, most of this literature focuses on the United States' use of drones, with an emphasis on their participation in the targeted killing programme in Pakistan, Somalia and Yemen (Gregory 2011; Boyle 2013; Chamayou 2013; Coeckelbergh 2013; Holmqvist 2013; Gusterson 2016; Kindervater 2016). Very little work has been focused on the use of drones by European armed forces (Martins 2015). There is also some academic literature on the use of drones by police forces, mostly focusing on their use by police forces in the United States and emphasising their contribution to the 'militarisation of the police' (Salter 2014; Bergtora Sandvik 2016; Jensen 2016). Then again, little of this literature applies to this transformation in Europe; it focuses on the use of very small drones by police forces but not on the way military grade MALE drones are used or are planned to be used for security purposes outside of situations of armed conflicts (with the exception of Csernatoni 2018, 2019). It is also worth noting that some think-tanks and NGOs reports have focused on the development of long-endurance drones to monitor the external (and internal, in the case of the United Kingdom) borders of the European Union (Akkerman 2014; Hayes, Jones and Töpfer 2014; Jones 2014; Csernatoni 2016; Lavallée 2019a, 2019b).

The starting point of our discussion about drone surveillance as a dual-use practice is that institutionalised discourses (official strategic doctrines, publications in military para-scientific reviews, parliamentary reports and official discourses by high-ranking military and political personnel) about military drones in the United Kingdom and France form a discourse community. Those institutionalised discourses constitute the empirical material for this chapter. Their authors are the military officers, members of parliament and government officials who have written or spoken about the drone in their official capacity during the past decade. According to Hugh Gusterson and in line with Michel Foucault's earlier work,

> Members of discourse communities are bound together both by shared allegiance to explicitly formulated proposition about the world [...] and by common consumption of aspects of discourses that exist on the edge of awareness (figures of speech [...], for example).
>
> (Gusterson 1999: 326)

The discourses studied in that chapter share remarkable similarities in the arguments they deploy in favour of the acquisition and use of MALE drones by British and French armed forces, namely, their usefulness for intelligence gathering (which I will detail in this chapter) or the efficiency, legality and morality of their use as weapon systems. They also have a similar way of constructing their argument, basing it on feedback from experience and dismissing most discourses critical of drone strikes as those of insufficiently informed civilians.

Indeed, those discourses are part of what Michel Foucault named an apparatus ('*dispositif*'; Gordon 1980: 194–195): they provide the discursive framework for certain security practices to develop (that I refer to as 'drone surveillance') in order to respond to an urgent need to govern certain recalcitrant populations (whether they be abroad or on the state's territory). As such, the practices of drone surveillance and the discourses justifying them allow for a certain form of governance over the population subjected to them. The purpose of this chapter will be to demonstrate that the narratives produced by this discourse community participate in the militarisation of police action and the 'policisation' of military action. Therefore, to a large extent, drone surveillance, whether it be in war or peace contexts, is shaped in similar ways in those discourses and this allows for similar surveillance practices to appear both in war and peace contexts. To conduct that demonstration, I will notably draw on Mark Neocleous' analysis of colonial air control as a police power (Neocleous 2015) and see how his analysis of British air operations over Iraq in the 1920s echoes what had been written over the past decade about contemporary drone operations by France and the United Kingdom. I will also draw on Didier Bigo's concept of ban-opticon (Bigo 2006b) and see to which extent the practice of drone surveillance can be explained as a way of banning certain people from the rest of a given population.

In the first section of this chapter, I will detail how the inclusion of MALE drones in the British and French arsenals has been shaped as a revolutionary step in the gathering of military intelligence and that, hidden behind that revolution, is the heritage of the RAF's idea of airpower as police power in the 1920s. In the second section, I will emphasise how some European and French actors have advocated for these surveillance practices to be imported to the field of domestic security and what it says about the distinction between wartime and peacetime surveillance operations.

From the battlefield …

Since the beginning of their use by European air forces, MALE drones have been portrayed as bringing a revolution to the way military intelligence is gathered (Ministry of Defence 2011: iii; Perrin and Roger 2017: 14). By allowing air forces to switch from reconnaissance to surveillance missions, they have become an indispensable tool in counter-insurgency and counter-terrorism operations. However, this revolution is in fact very much in continuity with ancient considerations about airpower as a police power.

From reconnaissance to surveillance to air occupation

The ability of those drones to conduct surveillance missions has been emphasised as a revolution to military intelligence gathering in a very similar way, both in the British and French context. As acknowledged in the United Kingdom Joint Doctrine on drones, persistence 'is often quoted as the unique selling point of an unmanned aircraft' (Ministry of Defence 2011: para. 314). Indeed, MALE drones have the ability to stay in the air for more than a day. A French *Harfang* made a 26-hour flight during Operation *Serval* (La rédaction de DSI 2013) and a French *Reaper* made a 25-hour flight during Operation *Barkhane* (Lagneau 2015). Several *Reaper* drones can actually take turns hovering over the same area for even longer periods of time, sometimes up to 100 hours (Lagneau 2014). As a British officer points out, 'drones can survey an area of suspected militancy virtually indefinitely, often without the insurgents even realising it' (Roe 2012). This ability allows the air forces to perform not only reconnaissance but also surveillance missions. Often assembled under the acronym ISR (for 'Intelligence, Surveillance and Reconnaissance'), the distinction between those three terms is considered important by the officers discussing them. Intelligence is considered the end, and reconnaissance and surveillance the means towards that end (Boutherin 2014: 46). Reconnaissance refers to gathering information about the nature of terrain, the position of enemy forces or on the concentration of civilians but it is not supposed to do so over a long period of time. Surveillance, on the contrary, rather indicates observing continually an enemy or an area where he could be hiding for a long period of time. To use the picture metaphor, reconnaissance takes a photograph whereas surveillance takes a long video clip. The then commanding officer of the drone squadron of the French Air Force, Christophe Fontaine wrote:

> As true wardens-marauders, MALE drones allow to evolve from an intermittent reconnaissance to a multi-sensor (optical, radar, acoustic, electronic) surveillance of a target and its environment. This persistence is the real gain from the MALE drone system compared to other vectors or effectors.[2]
>
> (Fontaine 2012: 98–99)

Fontaine (2015a) also developed the concept of 'aerial occupation' to underline the ability of drones to persist in an airspace. Several other officers have emphasised the crucial importance of persistent drones in military operations (Boutherin 2014: 49; Thomas 2014: 101). The importance of persistence for a long-endurance drone is mentioned 12 times in a 2008 British parliamentary report and seven times in a 2014 report (Defence Committee 2008: 8, 10, 11, 14, 15, 17, 21, 28, 39 and 46, 2014: 18, 27, 30, 32 and 40). This feature is also emphasised at length in two French parliamentary reports (Vandewalle and Violet 2009: 18; Perrin and Roger 2017: 17–22). One of those reports shares the opinion of a British officer and go as far as to describe drones as a solution to the 'fog of war' problem (Vandewalle and Violet 2009: 18, Doyle 2013: 14).

Counter-insurgency, counter-terrorism and police

In the context of counter-insurgency and counter-terrorism operations in which MALE drones have been deployed, the surveillance often aims to identify an enemy hiding within the civilian population. This is the basic idea behind what is known as 'pattern of life analysis'. This approach to surveillance has been underlined by Fontaine (2015a: 60) notably in those words: 'in the framework of asymmetric conflicts, what is at stake is the mapping of patterns of life to detect anomalies.'[3] A British officer commenting on the second phase of the French Operation *Serval* mentioned that 'pattern-of-life surveillance was increased to locate hideouts, weapons and logistics caches and identify surviving militant leaders' (Byford 2013: 77). Another British officer, Andrew Roe, commenting on the United States drone campaign over Pakistan, summing it up in these terms:

> Round-the-clock surveillance and detailed imagery allow operators to build up a rich and detailed picture of the 'pattern of life' in a particular area of interest, allowing a distinction to be made between peaceful tribesmen and those facilitating hostilities before a target is engaged with laser-guided bombs or Hellfire air-to-ground missiles.
>
> (Roe 2012: 67)

In a nutshell, by doing long-term surveillance of a given area, drone systems can transmit tens of hours of video feed in which analysts can identify the habits of the local population. The individuals whose practice differs from the norm are then marked as suspected of being insurgents (Fontaine 2015b: 101). To this extent, the surveillance operated by MALE drones resembles civilian detective work.

Moreover, some drone surveillance missions resemble practices of hideout and tailing by civilian police forces. As the French Chief of Staff of the air force noted, drones were used during Operation *Barkhane* to follow groups of insurgents to their weapons cache in order to destroy them (Assemblée nationale 2015). The French armed forces' official doctrine on the use of drones also points out that those systems would be 'particularly efficient' in peacekeeping missions as they can permanently and silently observe if a truce or an embargo is respected. The resemblance with police practices is there again present in the subtext as drones are said to 'offer the ability to detect illegal actions and have a deterrent effect on the protagonists' (Centre interarmées de concepts, de doctrines et d'expérimentations 2012: 23).

Airpower as police power

The distinction between war-fighting and policing seems to be further eroded by the uses of long-endurance drones. Indeed, practices of surveillance in a counter-insurgency context increasingly resemble police detective work to identify and prosecute a suspect (although, in the military language, 'prosecuting' a target does mean something very different). Some work in Critical Security Studies has studied the erosion of this distinction between war and police (Bachman, Bell and Holmqvist 2015). Two of the most critical of such a distinction are Mark

Neocleous (2014: 138–190) and Thomas Hippler (2014: 75–91). Those authors go back to the very beginning of airpower doctrine, that is, the ability of air forces to play a central role in military operations. According to them, this conception dates back to the colonial wars of the 1920s, especially the actions of the newly created Royal Air Force to maintain colonial order in Iraq. Neocleous (2015) considers that drones are not just another step towards the militarisation of the police or the policisation of the military but that airpower has always been a form of police power and drone warfare is just the more modern avatar of that. From the beginning, the ambition of airpower has not been war-fighting in a traditional sense (that is, the defeating of an enemy) but the maintenance of a world order in which the colonies stay in submission to the colonising powers.

The discourses that emerge from the documents further reinforce the argument that airpower is still largely a police power today. For instance, the commander of the French drone squadron used the phrase 'air occupation' to describe the possibilities opened by the persistent ability of MALE drones (Fontaine 2015a). US Air Force officers had already used it in a 1996 research paper and described it as 'the ability to hold an adversary continuously at risk from lethal or nonlethal effects from the air' or 'the ability of *aerospacepower* to continuously control the environment of the area into which it is projected' (Carmichael *et al.* 1996: 1 and 11). However, it can be dated further back to the concepts of 'air substitution' or 'control without occupation' that were developed by the Royal Air Force in the 1920s, simultaneously with that of 'air police' (Neocleous 2015: 168). Furthermore, discourses emphasising the deterrent effect of the long-endurance drone to prevent some activities should be analysed in light of what the Royal Air Force wrote in a 1920 memorandum: 'from the ground every inhabitant of a village is under the impression that the occupant of an aeroplane is actually looking at *him* [...] establishing the impression that all their movements are being watched and reported' (Air Staff 1920).

Furthermore, several articles have been written in the Royal Air Force's *Air Power Review* about the lessons that could be learned from the operations over Iraq in the 1920s (Gray 2001, 2011; Pirie 2004; Horne 2010) and several more were written about other participations of the RAF in the policing of the Empire (in Palestine, Waziristan, Malaya, etc.; Parker 2010; Roe 2010, 2011).[4] While one retired general warned against drawing out of context conclusions from the air campaign over Iraq during the 1920s (Gray 2011), most of the other articles paint a positive picture of the doctrine of air control in the inter-war period and how it participated in successfully maintaining British rule over the Empire. For instance, regarding air policing over Iraq, one British Army officer notes that airpower allowed it to strike insurgent tribes with the element of surprise, virtually making the possibility of an air raid a constant concern to them (Horne 2010: 36). This kind of control, of maintaining a targeted population under the constant threat of bombing, could be read as a form of necropolitics (Mbembe 2003). According to Achille Mbembe, Michel Foucault's concept of biopower is not enough to account for modern forms of subjugation of human lives to the threat of death. Following that idea, necropower is, among other things, not only the capability of inflicting death upon someone, but also of maintaining them in a constant state of fear for their lives, making those people, to some extent, 'living dead'. This idea is very close to what drone advocates write that it is possible to do with persistence in the air. It is worth noting though, that in Mbembe's most advanced example of post-colonial necropower – the Israeli occupation of the West Bank – the ability to monitor and kill from the air is but one of the elements of this power and by no means not the only one.

All of this demonstrates how closely the French and British doctrines on the use of drones actually are to the origins of airpower as a police power. Therefore, it should come as no surprise that drones have been used in practices mimicking those of policing in counter-insurgency campaigns and that military officers claim them to be able to easily import those practices into domestic security.

… to domestic security

French and British police forces are using small drones and the European Union has funded several programmes of long-endurance drones for border control. Some European air forces have also used their long-endurance drones for various domestic security purposes and the case of France is particularly illustrative of the blurring of the borders between drone surveillance in external military intervention and in domestic security.

Police and border control with drones in Europe

Police forces are increasingly equipped with micro-drones both in France and the United Kingdom. In March 2017, '28 of the 43 police forces in England and Wales had either purchased at least one drone or had ready access to one' (HMICFRS Report 2017). In France, the police and gendarmerie forces are also acquiring a small number of those drones (Ministère de l'Intérieur 2016). Those drones, resembling private leisure drones, do not have the autonomy to be considered 'long endurance' as they often cannot fly for more than an hour, but drones much closer in capabilities to those used by the air forces either have been or are projected to be deployed for diverse tasks of domestic security in Europe.

At the regional level, the European Union has sponsored several projects to develop drone technologies for border control. One of the first was the Border Surveillance by Unmanned Aerial Vehicle (BSUAV) project, initiated in 2004 and led by the French aircraft manufacturer Dassault Aviation. The EU has financed a dozen projects since then, either to develop long-endurance drones for border control or ensure their integration into civilian airspace.[5] European institutions have tried to distinguish the civilian uses of drones as much as possible from their military uses. The European RPAS (Remotely Piloted Air Systems) Steering Group considered in 2013 that it was 'important to modify the vision of "killing machines" they have right now due to the actually military-specific utilisation and to some catastrophic movies' (European RPAS Steering

Group 2013: 30).[6] Before that, Catherine Ashton had acknowledged the link between the military uses of the drones and those the European Union was planning for, stating in February 2010 that: 'Unmanned Aerial Vehicles can monitor movement on the ground in deployed military operations or civilian missions abroad. The same UAVs, equipped with the same sensors, can be used to spot illegal immigrants at Europe's external borders' (Jones 2014: 32).

At the national level, a few European states have tasked the same MALE drones as those used by the military for domestic surveillance, following the example of the United States Customs and Border Protection, which was among the first civilian administrations worldwide to be equipped with *Predator* MALE drones (Vandewalle and Violet 2009: 71). The armed forces of Italy and Switzerland, for instance, have used MALE and tactical drones for surveillance of their borders, to fight both against drug trafficking and illegal immigration (Sécher 2013: 276).

The French example

Particularly interesting is the use of long-endurance drones in France, as they have been been more extensively used there than in other European state and also more reflexion has been produced about this. The French air force's *Harfang* MALE drones have been used for surveillance over special events such as the G8 summit in Evian in 2003, the visit of the Pope in Lourdes in 2008, the G8 summit in Deauville in 2011, the commemoration of the Normandy landing in 2015 and several editions of the French national holy days in Paris, Le Bourget air show and the *fête des lumières* in Lyon (Perrin and Roger 2017: 34). In many instances, it was underlined that synergies existed between the use of those drones in the context of armed conflicts and in the context of domestic security. A French officer, commenting on the use of drones over Lourdes in 2008, considered it a good opportunity to let the crews become familiar with flying their drones over mountainous terrain, a few months before being deployed in Afghanistan. In 2011, drone flying over the G8 in Deauville was used to monitor the anti-globalisation demonstrations to make sure they would not break the security bubble (Sécher 2013: 271–273). In a general way, those surveillance operations over special events have been used as both a laboratory during the first years and a showcase for military drones after that.

Some French officers are also pushing for the use of the air force's drones over the national territory for more than just surveillance over special events. In the French armed forces' 2012 official doctrine on the uses of drones, several potential civilian applications of drone technologies were already mentioned (Centre interarmées de concepts, de doctrines et d'expérimentations 2012: 26). Other administrations have also manifested an interest in using those drones. For instance, the French customs had identified a need for MALE drones for the surveillance of large areas (Vandewalle and Violet 2009: 73) – so do the national gendarmerie (Perrin and Roger 2017: 34). As an air force officer pointed out, the French Air Force has an expertise in the operation of MALE drones that could benefit other administrations. MALE drones could be used, for example, for the surveillance of places suspected of harbouring organised crime, the stalking of kidnappers or the surveillance of portions of railways where copper cables are often stolen (Mignot 2013: 280–283). The commanding officer of the French drone squadron, Fontaine (2015b: 102) emphasised the fact that drones could 'provide the same services' of persistent surveillance that they provide in counter-terrorism operations abroad for the fight against terrorism at home. In 2017, a French parliamentary report adopted those military arguments, stating:

> In addition to this surveillance of special events, the qualities of MALE drones could be taken advantage of in multiple domains of public security: surveillance of illicit trafficking on highways, itinerary reconnaissance for the protection of high-value convoys, fighting against clandestine gold panning in French Guyana, searching for missing persons.[7]
>
> (Perrin and Roger 2017: 34)

The French example also shows an important difference with the use of long-endurance drones for domestic surveillance in the United States: in France, those drones are still under the exclusive control of the armed forces and there is no plan, at this moment, to equip civilian administrations with them. An air force officer called for the organisation of an interdepartmental agency tasked with identifying and prioritising the needs for MALE drones from different administrations and making them correspond to the operational capacities of the air force (Mignot 2013: 285–287). The commanding officer of the French drone squadron, Christophe Fontaine (2014) went even further and proposed a three-step plan to share all surveillance resources in France: (1) organise an interdepartmental meeting on surveillance to map the needs of different administrations; (2) catalogue the surveillance capacities across all administrations; and (3) organise an interdepartmental command network for the repartition of those needs. In an organisational approach, such efforts can be analysed as translating the will of the French Air Force to remain a central actor in the operation of MALE drones, whether they be abroad or over the national territory, and not abandon that prerogative to a civilian agency.

Security and surveillance

Didier Bigo (2006a) analysed the 'de-differentiation between internal and external security' as the result of not only an insecure world after 9/11, but also the discourses and practices of actors having an interest in the blurring of this border. The discourses on drones in France that we have analysed tend to support this conclusion. Indeed, those discourses consider that internal security issues can be taken care of with the same technology and practices as for external security. Those who advocate for the use of MALE drones for domestic security purposes therefore participate in this 'de-differentiation'. They are air force officers and members of parliament from the defence committee, who have an interest in having the role of the military expanded to certain matters of internal security as long as the military stays in control of such an expansion.

Bigo has also participated in the development of a branch of critical security studies focusing on the question of surveillance, inspired by and trying to go beyond Michel Foucault's reflexion on the panopticon (Lyon 2006). Benjamin Noys characterises the drone as a 'mobile panopticon' (Noys 2015: 2) but the notion of ban-opticon, as developed by Bigo (2006b), seems closer to what drones actually do, both in war and peacetime. Jeremy Bentham's panopticon interpretation was there to heal and redress those who are being watched and there is no such redressing dimension in drone operation. Whether it is to find an insurgent or a terrorist in Afghanistan or Mali or to track an illegal migrant, the idea is to identify individuals that are in some manner considered as a threat and 'ban' them in some way. In the case of the surveillance of migrant ships or of anti-globalisation demonstrators, the ban is quite literal as the purpose of surveillance is to stop someone from entering somewhere, whether that be a state's territory or the premises of a G8 summit. In the case of the surveillance of an area of suspected militancy in Afghanistan, Iraq or Mali, a similar logic is at play as those identified as a threat also have to be separated from the rest of the population and 'banned' from the theatre of operation by either capture or killing. To that extent, there is a common logic behind drone surveillance in external military operations and in domestic security.

Conclusion

This chapter has demonstrated that drone surveillance has been shaped as a very similar practice whether it be in war or peacetime. It has first shown that most official discourses in the United Kingdom and France presented drone surveillance as a revolution in the gathering of military intelligence, thanks to its persistence and ability to detect and identify insurgents in an asymmetric conflict. Those discourses in fact showed that conceptions of airpower are still largely inspired from the colonial matrix, inherited from the RAF operations over Iraq in the 1920s. Indeed, this idea of control of a territory and its population from above is at the basis of the conception of airpower as a police power (Neocleous 2015) and can also be seen as an element of necropolitics (Mbembe 2003). It has then analysed how those surveillance practices have been imported back into domestic security, especially in France, under the argument that wartime and peacetime surveillance are similar enough to do so. This participates in the de-differentiation between internal and external security and drone surveillance seems to be animated by the same ban-optic (Bigo 2006b) logic in both war and peacetime contexts. This in turn questions the 'dual-use' label of drone surveillance technology since those uses seem to be extremely close to one another.

Notes

1 At the moment when those lines were written (November 2019), the United Kingdom was still *de jure* a member state of the European Union. All of the British discourses commented upon in the present chapter were written or spoken while the United Kingdom was a Member of the European Union over the past decade.
2 Author's translation.
3 Author's translation.
4 Comparatively, this does not appear to be the same in the French main military reviews (*Revue Défense Nationale*) or air force review (*Penser les Ailes Françaises*) about the uses of airpower to police the French colonies, such as over Morocco during the Rif War in the 1920s. More generally, the French military does not seem as eager to write about their past colonial operations as their British counterpart.
5 For a detailed enumeration and critical commentary of those research programmes, see the *Eurodrone, Inc.* report (Hayes *et al.* 2014: 26–38).
6 For a critique of this public relations strategy, see Boucher 2015.
7 Author's translation.

References

Air Staff (1920) *On the Power of the Air Force and the Application of this Power to Hold and Police Mesopotamia.* London: Air Staff, Air Staff Memorandum.
Akkerman, M. (2014) *Border Wars: The Arms Dealers Profiting from Europe's Refugee Tragedy.* Transnational Institute & Stop Wapenhandel.
Assemblée nationale (2015) Audition du général Denis Mercier, chef d'état-major de l'armée de l'air, devant la Commission de la défense et des forces armées, 15 April. At: www.assemblee-nationale.fr/14/cr-cdef/14-15/c1415055.asp.
Bachman, J., Bell, C. and Holmqvist, C. (eds) (2015) *War, Police and Assemblages of Intervention.* London: Routledge.
Bergtora Sandvik, K. (2016) The Political and Moral Economies of Dual Technology Transfers: Arming Police Drones. In Aleš Završnik (ed.), *Drones and Unmanned Aerial Systems: Legal and Social Implications for Security and Surveillance.* New York: Springer, 45–66.
Bigo, D. (2006a) Internal and External Aspects of Security. *European Security* 15(4): 385–404.
Bigo, D. (2006b) Security, Exception, Ban and Surveillance. In D. Lyon (ed.), *Theorizing Surveillance: The Panopticon and Beyond.* Cullompton: Willan Publishing, 46–68.
Boucher, P. (2015) Domesticating the Drone: The Demilitarisation of Unmanned Aircraft for Civil Markets. *Science and Engineering Ethics* 21(6): 1393–1412.
Boutherin, G. (2014) L'apport de la puissance aérospatiale à l'acquisition du renseigne-ment. *Revue Défense Nationale* (775): 45–50.
Boyle, M.J. (2013) The Costs and Consequences of Drone Warfare. *International Affairs* 89(1): 1–29.
Byford, A. (2013) Operation SERVAL: The Air Power Lessons of France's Intervention in Mali. *RAF Air Power Review* 16(3): 72–81.
Carmichael, B.W., DeVine, T.E., Kaufman, R.J., Pence, P.E. and Wilcox, R.S. (1996) *Strikestar 2025.* US Air Force, Research paper presented to Air Force 2025.
Centre interarmées de concepts, de doctrines et d'expérimentations (2012) *Emploi des systèmes de drones aériens.* Réflexion doctrinale No. 136 DEF/CICDE/NP.

Chamayou, G. (2013) *Théorie du drone*. Paris: La Fabrique.

Coeckelbergh, M. (2013) Drones, Information Technology, and Distance: Mapping the Moral Epistemology of Remote Fighting. *Ethics and Information Technology* 15(2): 87–98.

Csernatoni, R. (2016) *Defending Europe: Dual-Use Technologies and Drone Development in the European Union*. Brussels: IRSD.

Csernatoni, R. (2018) Constructing the EU's High-Tech Borders: FRONTEX and Dual-Use Drones for Border Management. *European Security* 27(2): 175–200.

Csernatoni, R. (2019) Between Rhetoric and Practice: Technological Efficiency and Defense Cooperation in the European Drone Sector. *Critical Military Studies*: 1–26.

Defence Committee (2008) *The Contribution of Unmanned Aerial Vehicles to ISTAR Capability*. House of Commons, No. 13/2007–08.

Defence Committee (2014) Remote Control: Remotely Piloted Air Systems – Current and Future UK Use. House of Commons, No. 10/2013–14.

Doyle, J. (2013) Rise of the Robots: Western Unmanned Air Operations in Iraq and Afghanistan, 2001 to 2010. *RAF Air Power Review* 16(2): 10–31.

European RPAS Steering Group (2013) Roadmap for the Integration of Civil Remotely-Piloted Aircraft Systems into the European Aviation System. Annex 3: A Study of the Societal Impact of the Integration of Civil RPAS into the European Aviation System.

Fontaine, C. (2012) La France a besoin d'orbites permanentes de surveillance de drones. *Défense et Sécurité Internationale* (81): 98–100.

Fontaine, C. (2014) Pour un Grenelle de la surveillance. *Revue Défense Nationale* (769): 103–104.

Fontaine, C. (2015a) L'occupation aérienne. Le chainon manquant à l'obtention de la maîtrise opérative dans les conflits de basse intensité. *Défense et Sécurité Internationale, Hors-Série* (42): 56–62.

Fontaine, C. (2015b) Les drones MALE : un atout maître contre les terroristes sur le territoire national. *Revue Défense Nationale* (781): 100–106.

Gordon, C. (1980) *Power/Knowledge: Selected Interviews and Other Writings by Michel Foucault 1972–1977*. New York: Pantheon Books.

Gray, P.W. (2001) The Myth of Air Control and the Realities of Imperial Policing. *RAF Air Power Review* 4(2): 37–52.

Gray, P.W. (2011) RAF Air Policing over Iraq – Uses and Abuses of History. *RAF Air Power Review* 14(1): 1–10.

Gregory, D. (2011) From a View to a Kill: Drones and Late Modern War. *Theory, Culture & Society* 28(7–8): 188–215.

Gusterson, H. (1999) Missing the End of the Cold War in International Security. In Jutta Weldes, Mark Laffey, Hugh Gusterson and Raymond Duvall (eds), *Cultures of Insecurity: States, Communities and the Production of Danger*. Minneapolis, MN: University of Minnesota Press, 319–345.

Gusterson, H. (2016) *Drones: Remote Control Warfare*. London: MIT Press.

Hayes, B., Jones, C. and Töpfer, E. (2014) *Eurodrones, Inc*. London: Statewatch & Transnational Institute.

Hippler, T. (2014) *Le gouvernement du ciel: histoire globale des bombardements aériens*. Paris: Les Prairies ordinaires.

HMICRFS (2017) Planes, Drones and Helicopters: An Independent Study of Police Air Support. Her Majesty's Inspectorate of Constabulary and Fire & Rescue Services, 30 November. At: www.justiceinspectorates.gov.uk/hmicfrs/publications/planes-drones-and-helicopters-an-independent-study-of-police-air-support/.

Holmqvist, C. (2013) Undoing War: War Ontologies and the Materiality of Drone Warfare. *Millennium: Journal of International Studies* 41(3): 535–552.

Horne, P. (2010) The RAF in Command: The Policing of Mesopotamia from the Air. *RAF Air Power Review* 13(2): 33–42.

Jensen, O.B. (2016) New 'Foucauldian Boomerangs': Drones and Urban Surveillance. *Surveillance & Society* 14(1): 20–33.

Jones, C. (2014) *Back from the Battlefield: Domestic Drones in the UK*. London: Statewatch & Drone Wars UK.

Kindervater, K.H. (2016) The Emergence of Lethal Surveillance: Watching and Killing in the History of Drone Technology. *Security Dialogue* 47(3): 223–238.

Lagneau, L. (2014) Les drones Reaper de l'armée de l'Air ont déjà dépassé les 2.000 heures de vol. *Zone Militaire*, 7 November. At: www.opex360.com/2014/11/07/les-drones-reaper-de-larmee-de-lair-ont-deja-depasse-les-2-000-heures-de-vol/.

Lagneau, L. (2015) Un drone Reaper français est resté en vol pendant plus d'un jour. *Zone Militaire*, 20 October. At: www.opex360.com/2015/10/30/drone-reaper-francais-reste-en-vol-pendant-plus-dun-jour/.

Lavallée, C. (2019a) The EU Policy for Civil Drones: The Challenge of Governing Emerging Technologies. *Institute for European Studies*, Policy brief No. 2019/01, 1–7.

Lavallée, C. (2019b) The New EU Policy on Civil Drones: A Paradigm Shift for European Airspace. PRIO Policy Brief No. 2019/5.

Lyon, D. (ed.) (2006) *Theorizing Surveillance: The Panopticon and Beyond*. Cullompton: Willan Publishing.

Martins, B.O. (2015) The European Union and Armed Drones: Framing the Debate. *Global Affairs* 1(3): 247–250.

Mbembe, A. (2003) Necropolitics. *Public Culture* 15(1): 11–40.

Mignot, B. (2013) Drones à longue endurance et sécurité publique, des perspectives intéressantes. In Centre d'études stratégiques aérospatiales, *Les drones aériens: passé, présent et avenir: approche globale*. Paris: La Documentation française, 279–288.

Ministère de l'Intérieur (2016) Les drones au service de la sécurité. At: www.interieur.gouv.fr/Archives/Archives-des-dossiers/2016-Dossiers/Les-drones-au-service-de-la-securite (accessed 7 November 2019).

Ministry of Defence (2011) *Joint Doctrine Note 2/11: The UK Approach to Unmanned Aircraft Systems*. The Development, Concepts and Doctrine Centre, Joint Doctrine Note No. 2/11.

Neocleous, M. (2014) *War Power, Police Power*. Edinburgh: Edinburgh University Press.

Neocleous, M. (2015) Air Power as Police Power. In Jan Bachmann, Colleen Bell and Caroline Holmqvist (eds), *War, Police and Assemblages of Intervention*. London: Routledge, 164–182.

Noys, B. (2015) Drone Metaphysics. *Culture Machine* 16: 1–22.

Parker, J. (2010) Air Power Lessons from the Counter Insurgency Operations in Malaya, Borneo and Aden. *RAF Air Power Review* 13(2): 33–42.

Perrin, C. and Roger, G. (2017) *Les drones dans les forces armées*. Commission des affaires étrangères, de la défense et des forces armées du Sénat, No. 559.

Pirie, G.C. (2004) Some Experiences of No 6 Squadron in the Iraq Insurrection, 1920. *RAF Air Power Review* 7(2): 1–12.

La rédaction de DSI (2013) 'Serval': succès foudroyant. *Défense et Sécurité Internationale* (90): 36–47.

Roe, A. (2010) 'Pink's War' – Applying the Principles of Air Control to Waziristan – 9 March to 1 May 1925. *RAF Air Power Review* 13(3): 97–118.

Roe, A. (2011) Aviation and Guerrilla War: Proposals for 'Air Control' of the North-West Frontier of India. *RAF Air Power Review* 14(1): 51–74.

Roe, A. (2012) 'Bugsplat' and Fallible Humans: the Hi-Tech U.S. Drone Campaign over North-West Pakistan. *RAF Air Power Review* 15(2): 65–82.

Salter, M. (2014) Toys for the Boys? Drones, Pleasure and Popular Culture in the Militarisation of Policing. *Critical Criminology* 22(2): 163–177.

Sécher, D. (2013) Les drones et les missions d'aide aux populations: cas particulier des DPSA. In Centre d'études stratégiques aérospatiales, *Les drones aériens: passé, présent et avenir: approche globale.* Paris: La Documentation française, 269–278.

Thomas, R. (2014) Le pilote, une alternative au drone? *Défense et Sécurité Internationale* (103): 100–103.

Vandewalle, Y. and Violet, J.-C. (2009) *Rapport d'information sur les drones.* Commission de la défense et des forces armées de l'Assemblée nationale, No. 2127.

Zubeldia, O. (2012) *Histoire des drones de 1914 à nos jours.* Paris: Perrin.

5 Normative market Europe?

The contested governance of cyber-surveillance technologies

Maximiliano Vila Seoane

Introduction

From 2011, the Arab Spring conveyed a beacon of hope for the potential democratisation of the region. However, journalists have unveiled that cyber-surveillance technologies, in many cases of European origin, played a key role in facilitating espionage on activists, which led to their interrogation and torture, such as in Bahrain (Arabian Business 2011). This and other examples have shed light on a shady aspect of the Fourth Industrial Revolution (see Introduction of this book), which opened the door to increased levels of surveillance. Although the contradiction between Western countries' allegiance to the defence of human rights, while exporting weapons to states that violate them is not new (Blanton 2000; Fuhrmann 2008; Yanik 2006), these incidents with digital technologies exposed a highly problematic double-speak by the European Union (EU), which claims to promote and protect human rights. Indeed, in the face of this inconsistency, the international dimension of the Cybersecurity Strategy of the European Union (2013) outlined the vision of promoting fundamental rights and freedoms in cyberspace, for instance, by monitoring the exports of cyber-surveillance technologies. In the same line, in 2014, the European Parliament (EP), European Commission (EC) and Council of the EU stated their intention of reviewing the Regulation No. 428/2009, which governs the control of exports of dual-use items. In 2016, the European Commission made public its proposal for updating the Union's regime for the 'control of exports, transfer, brokering, technical assistance and transit of dual-use items' in order to include the regulation of cyber-surveillance technologies. This proposal takes a normative stance on what type of trade is desirable and lawful. Yet, the policy process of this regulation has been very contested by companies as well as some member states, which have put into question whether the EU can actually govern cyber-surveillance technologies in line with its Charter of Fundamental Rights.

The challenge that the EU confronts is part of the broader problem of regulating dual-use technologies. During the Cold War, these were defined as those that could be employed both for military and civilian uses, but since then, its definition has become broader in scope (Rath, Ischi and Perkins 2014). Indeed, new non-state actors and new dual-use technologies have made the debate more complex, such as the rise of biotechnologies (see Rychnovská, Chapter 10 and

Farrand, Chapter 12 in this book) that led to the fear from bioterrorism and bioweapons, inspiring an academic literature investigating the challenges posed by the potential misuse of life sciences' knowledge by varied actors (Atlas and Dando 2006; Miller and Selgelid 2007; Rychnovská 2016). The rise of cyberweapons, a concept that includes cyber-surveillance technologies, adds a new chapter to these ongoing debates. Researchers believe that the governance of cyberweapons will be very difficult to implement in practice due to a number of specificities. First, cyberweapons are seen as important instruments in the arsenals of states, which would consequently be unwilling to limit their production (Stevens 2018). Second, authorities have far less choke-points to limit the proliferation of cyberweapons in comparison to nuclear or biological weapons (Lin 2016: 134). In effect, the skills and infrastructure to develop them are in general quite easy to access online and, thus, are hard to regulate (Lin 2016: 136). Third, in contrast to other dual-use items, cyber-surveillance technologies are easier to acquire, whether for commercial, personal or security reasons. For instance, firms selling spyware to snoop on loved ones or children, offer similar functionalities to those sold to states' security agencies (Brewster 2017). Therefore, the boundary between legitimate uses of cyber-surveillance technologies and malicious ones is far blurrier than with other dual-use items.

Despite the mistrust on the possibility of governing cyber-surveillance technologies, the EU's proposal assumes that it can overcome such challenges by updating the rules regulating the export of dual-use items. This EU's proposal has inspired a policy-oriented literature that explores its strengths and weaknesses (Alavi and Khamichonak 2016; Bohnenberger 2017; Kanetake 2019; Lavallée 2018). Yet, a more theoretical analysis of these processes has lagged behind. In particular, the dual-use items regulation proposal speaks directly to the debates on the EU's identity as a global power, since many members of the European Parliament advocating for the initiative assume that the adoption of stringent rules on such trade may shape global norms. In other words, they believe that the EU should be a normative power in cyberspace (Manners 2002, 2006), shaping global norms on what type of trade is considered 'good'.

By examining the contested process of governing cyber-surveillance technologies in light of the 'EU as a Power' debates (Damro 2012, 2015; Manners 2002, 2006; Young 2015), this chapter departs from the explanations that cyber-surveillance technologies are very difficult to regulate (Bohnenberger 2017; Lin 2016; Stevens 2018), or the counter view, that the EU will inevitably succeed given its allegiance to protecting human rights. Instead, this chapter adopts the Normative Market Europe (NME) approach to argue that, despite an initial approach by the European Commission and the European Parliament to uphold human rights in the export of cyber-surveillance technologies in the new regulation, the final outcome has been contested and the possible result will be far more limited due to the influence of the private sector in the Council of the EU's negotiating position.

The chapter proceeds as follows. First, it introduces the Normative Market Europe approach, which synthesises two important contending perspectives to understand the specific features of the EU as a global power: Normative Power Europe and Market Power Europe. Second, it characterises the specificities of cyber-surveillance technologies and then, analyses the EU proposal to update its regime for the export of dual-use items. Afterwards, it discusses the different policy preferences and interests shaping it, followed by the intergovernmental divisions at the Council of the EU. Finally, it concludes, stressing the challenges for the implementation of the EU's proposal to govern cyber-surveillance technologies.

Normative market Europe as a conceptual framework

The European Commission's proposal to update the dual-use items regulation is an example of the interface between security and trade (Gebhard and Norheim-Martinsen 2011), which cannot be understood as being separate from the ongoing debates on the *sui generis* character of the EU as an international actor. In particular, in order to examine the EU's governance of cyber-surveillance technologies, this chapter employs a Normative Market Europe (NME) approach, which is a synthesis of the Normative Power Europe (NPE) and the Market Power Europe (MPE) perspectives.

As regards the former, it was proposed by Manners (2002), who argued that after the Cold War, the EU's global influence derives from setting and disseminating norms to influence the international order, rather than by accumulating military or economic strength. Thus, NPE went beyond the previous (neo)realist understanding that mainly military power matters, or Duchêne's (1972) argument that the EU is a new type of civilian power in world politics. Instead, Manners identified five core norms that the EU aims to disseminate: peace, liberty, democracy, rule of law and respect for human rights and fundamental freedoms (Manners 2002: 242). According to Manners (2006), such normative power is precisely what is needed to overcome the destructive inter-state competition that characterised previous centuries. Despite its important contribution, NPE has not been exempt of criticism, for instance, for having a clear-cut division between norms and interests (Erickson 2013; Youngs 2004), or for neglecting the importance of non-state actors (Diez 2013). Thus, other approaches have been proposed to address such shortcomings.

The MPE is one such alternative conceptual framework (Damro and Friedman 2018; Damro 2012, 2015) that, in contrast to the NPE, suggests that the key feature of the EU as a global power is its capability to externalise its market-related policies beyond its borders, influencing other actors in the process. This derives from the fact that the European Single Market is one of the largest in the world, thus, its regulations have considerable external impact. In contrast to NPE, MPE does not accept an exceptional character for the EU's identity based on a specific set of norms written in its founding documents. Instead, it proposes a general framework, valid to empirically investigate any type of market power attempting to externalise its internal regulations, such as the USA or China. For this objective, it proposes to examine three dimensions (Damro 2012, 2015). First, the market size of the actor under analysis, assuming that the larger its size the greater its international influence is after setting a regulation. Second, the institutional features characterising the regulatory actor (Damro 2012), such as the varied types of stakeholders and networks that are part of the EU's processes of setting regulations, including EU member states and institutions, like the European Commission, the European Parliament, the Council of the EU, the decision-making rules and the EU's regulatory capacity. Third, interest contestation (Damro 2015: 1343), which considers the various types of pressures that different actors or coalitions (both internal and external to the market power) might put on its policy processes and its potential externalisation.

It is important to observe that MPE can include a normative aspect as well. Indeed, the outcomes of the interest contestation process might arrive to a particular normative consensus. Thus, MPE should not be seen as merely a reductionist economic approach. For this reason, instead of thinking of the NPE and MPE as mutually exclusive, Geeraert and Drieskens (2017) speak of Normative Market Europe, since, in their view, elements of both approaches can be identified in practice. For example, by analysing the case of international sports governance, they argue that the EU's external actions are always grounded on normative intentions. However, its success depends on the particular institutional features and interest contestation processes that arise in the specific norms under study, which define whether the EU acts or not in a normative way (Geeraert and Drieskens 2017: 89). In particular, they incorporate in their analysis the internal cohesiveness of member states as the key variable determining whether or not the externalisation of a market regulation might take place (Da Conceição-Heldt and Meunier 2014; Geeraert and Drieskens 2017).

The rest of the chapter shows how the NME approach helps to understand the challenges faced by the proposal to update the EU's dual-use items regulation to incorporate cyber-surveillance technologies.

Cyber-surveillance technologies and the EU's proposal for their regulation

Surveillance technologies are not new (Privacy International 2016: 16), but their scale and thoroughness in the contemporary digital era is far more intense than before (Ball, Haggerty and Lyon 2014). This justifies the use of the new concept of cyber-surveillance technologies, which, although it does not have an internationally agreed upon definition (Bromley *et al.* 2016: 143; SIPRI and ECORYS 2015: 40), conveys the idea that they facilitate new types of accessing and/or manipulating digital data in illegal and/or non-consented ways, violating different human rights, namely, freedom of expression and the right to privacy, which affects other rights, like freedom of assembly and association. Hence, the definition of cyber-surveillance technologies is usually list-based, for example, Bromley *et al.* (2016: 41) include the following technologies: mobile telecommunication interception equipment, intrusion software, IP network surveillance, monitoring centres, lawful interception systems, data retentions systems, digital forensics, probes and deep packet inspection. This approach can incorporate new technologies in the future, but it may also erroneously conflate very different types under a same category.

Cyber-surveillance technologies are developed by firms of different types, including large military contractors, big IT firms and also specialised SMEs (SIPRI and ECORYS 2015: 151), which sell to both military and civilian markets (see the Introduction of this book). These firms are located in countries that have a strong IT industry, such as the USA, UK, China, Germany, Israel, Italy and Russia. Privacy International (2016) identified 528 firms selling modern electronic surveillance technologies globally.[1] Although the USA has the largest amount of firms (122), as a whole, Privacy International (2016) reports that the EU has far more (279), distributed in 23 out of its 28 member states, that is, UK (104), France (45), Germany (41), Italy (18), Sweden (9) and Ireland (8). Thus, the EU represented more than 50 per cent of the market size of cyber-surveillance technologies acknowledged in the database. If the governance of biotechnologies puts a lot of focus on the community of scientists, their knowledge and facilities (Atlas and Dando 2006), these numbers also suggest that the proliferation of cyber-surveillance technologies could be curtailed significantly by regulating the firms specialising in their production. Notwithstanding, there is an illegal global market for zero-day vulnerabilities, which are errors in software unknown to its manufacturer and users (Stevens 2018). This is highly problematic because its suppliers are not always firms operating legally (Stockton and Golabek-Goldman 2013) and, thus, exist outside of any type of regulation.

In 2016, the EC made public its proposal for updating the Union's dual-use items regulation, which was based on different inputs from stakeholders and impact assessments, putting forward a number of key modifications, among which this chapter stresses two.

First, the proposal changed the definition of dual-use items in order to include a sub-item considering cyber-surveillance technologies that could be used to violate human rights, thus, incorporating a 'human security' perspective to the pre-existing military versus civilian definition of dual-use items. Second, the proposal adds new instruments to regulate cyber-surveillance technologies such as an EU autonomous control list of technologies not considered at the multilateral level (European Commission 2016) and an EU harmonised 'catch-all' clause that would allow the addition of new items to the control list if there is proof that they are being used for human rights violations (European Commission 2016). In this way, technologies will be regulated without depending on a long negotiation process to update the control list. In line with social constructivist strands of Science and Technology Studies (STS) (Bijker 1995; Kline and Pinch 1996), these regulations can be understood as an attempt to socially shape the trade and use of cyber-surveillance technologies. In effect, the introduction of such a 'human security' approach in the legislation understands that there may be 'legitimate' uses for such cyber-surveillance technologies, but also that there may be other aims which are quite reprehensible that they require considerable limits to its export.

Nonetheless, the ordinary legislative process at the EU requires that the passing of a new or updated regulation proposed by the EC must be approved both by the EP and the Council of the EU. This specific institutional feature of the EU permits interest contestation. Indeed, the next sections detail how during the initial phases of the policy process, the EC and the EP advocated for a 'value-based trade policy' in crafting the new EU's proposal, rooted in the market size of Europe in dual-use items. Although this initial policy preference has not been without disagreements and setbacks, the discussion at the Council of the EU shows far more contentious positions among governments, with many siding with the private sector, posing a serious challenge to the new normative positions that the EC and EP have agreed upon.

The main actors and their policy preferences

As we will quickly show, the EC, the EP and the Working Party on Dual-Use Goods of the Council of the EU, together with multiple stakeholders from the private sector and civil society have been the key actors shaping the outcome of the policy process to update the Dual-Use Regulation. It is relevant here to high-light their tools and relations as well as their emerging practices to better understand what is at stake. On the one hand, the EC and Members of the European Parliament (MEP), together with civil society organisations defending human rights in the digital space have been the main actors advocating stricter regulations for the export of cyber-surveillance technologies. Besides upholding their position in the ordinary legislative process, civil society organisations have released leaks to expose the double-speak of member states and the private sector. However, the policy process has also been moulded by the preferences of firms, which have been able to influence member states at the Council towards a negotiating position against new regulations for cyber-surveillance technologies.

With its proposal, the European Commission (2016) aims to protect human rights globally, while keeping a balance with the security and trade interests of the Union. Indeed, Cecilia Mälstrom, the EU trade commissioner, said that '... the introduction of a human security dimension that explicitly incorporates human rights into export controls reflects our commitment to a true value-based trade policy' (European Parliament 2018). This statement repeats the position of the "Trade for All" communication (European Commission 2015), which stresses the importance of trade policy for advancing the EU's interests and values, reinforcing development and foreign policies. Likewise, the EU's Cyber-security Strategy stresses the importance of protecting fundamental rights and freedoms in cyberspace (European Commission 2013). Therefore, the EC understands that regulating Europe's market of cyber-surveillance technologies can shape the global regulation of such dual-use items in line with the protection of human rights.

The MEPs largely shared the Commission's proposal. In effect, after introducing amendments to the EC proposal, in 2018, the majority of the MEPs voted in favour of starting the Trilogue negotiations – 571 in favour, out of 629 votes

(Stupp 2018). Two of the most vocal policy entrepreneurs in the review process have been: Klaus Buchner, the German rapporteur from the Green European Free Alliance, who was in charge of coordinating the proposal at the EP Committee on International Trade, and Marietje Schaake, Dutch shadow rapporteur from the Alliance of Liberals and Democrats for Europe Party, who has been very outspoken since the Arab Spring to update the EU's dual-use export control regime. Indeed, she has maintained that if European firms keep on facilitating human rights violations through their exports of cyber-surveillance technologies, they will damage the credibility of the EU's foreign policy to protect human rights (Schaake and Vermeulen 2016: 83). Likewise, updating the regulation is also important in terms of national security, since the export of cyber-surveillance technologies may pose a security risk to European firms and citizens abroad (Schaake and Vermeulen 2016: 82). The following fragments of Schaake's (2018) speech at the EP before voting for the proposal are illustrative of the consensus reached by MEPs:

> The billion-euro commercial market in ready-made surveillance systems remains largely unregulated. And that is astonishing in light of the capabilities that companies and surveillance, hacking and exfiltration technologies are further and further developing. While many politicians claim to be concerned with cybersecurity, anyone who can afford it can buy systems that collect massive amount of data, can break into people's devices without the consent of the user, and information can be removed unnoticed. This is unacceptable, and as I said, regulation lags behind. The digital surveillance market should worry us in Europe. But the consequences of exports to dictatorships, where the rule of law are absent, are even more grave and unacceptable. [...] It is taken long for EU action, but I am very glad we found broad consensus to update the dual use regulation that would tackle this toxic trade with targeted measures on the basis of human security. Surveillance systems will require licenses before exports, human rights will become clear criteria to assess before a license is granted, and definitions will be clear so that private sector will not suffer or be hindered unnecessarily, and we in turn count on their cooperation.
>
> (Schaake 2018)

This statement is in line with the idea of NPE, since it identifies a global problem caused by the unregulated market of cyber-surveillance technologies, where the EU could intervene by protecting human rights and fundamental freedoms, which is one of the norms identified in the NPE approach (Manners 2002: 243).

This main policy preference was influenced by the demands of a coalition of actors from civil society, the Coalition Against Unlawful Surveillance Exports (CAUSE),[2] that, in 2015, distributed a report that advanced many of the initiatives that would later appear in the first EC proposal. For instance, it requested a stricter evaluation of the potential end-user of cyber-surveillance technologies, together with an exempt of encryption technologies and other defensive legitimate uses

(CAUSE 2015: 16). Furthermore, CAUSE (2015) criticised regulating cyber-surveillance technologies through the Wassenaar Arrangement (WA), because it preserves the Cold War logic of considering dual-use items as either for military or civilian purposes, a division not well suited for cyber-surveillance technologies. Accordingly, CAUSE preferred a unilateral regulation by the EU, which, if successful, should then become the base for shaping global norms at the multilateral level through the WA, where it has 28 out of 41 members (CAUSE 2015: 15).

Corporate actors have been critical of the EC proposal even before it was made public. Due to its lobbying efforts (Stupp 2016), the proposal of the Commission released in 2016 excluded a number of technologies[3] from the autonomous list that firms considered to be too broad. Not surprisingly, even after this 'success', they still disputed many of the main amendments introduced in the EP's final proposal. Take the case of Digital Europe,[4] that still disapproved of the definition of cyber-surveillance technologies as being too ambiguous and broad, and opposed a unilateral European definition of dual-use items that would depart from the coordinated one with other multilateral arrangements (Digital Europe 2017: 2). Digital Europe also understands that a 'catch-all' control based on the potential misuse of cyber-surveillance technologies to harm human rights is a 'disproportionate measure' (Digital Europe 2017: 2), which exceeds the capabilities of the private sector to assess the end-user. Instead, they believe that states should make such judgements. These criticisms reveal the preference of the European digital industry for preserving the usual military versus civilian division of understanding dual-use items and rejecting the incorporation of extra human rights criteria in the regulation (Kanetake 2019). In their view, the new proposal would only harm the European digital industry, since buyers would still be able to obtain surveillance technologies from other less regulated markets (Digital Europe 2017: 4). Hence, they oppose the main changes introduced by the EC and the EP, undermining the intended update of the regulation to govern cyber-surveillance technologies. Although the corporate sector was unsuccessful in including all these claims during the discussion at the EP, the situation changed at the Council of the EU.

Intergovernmental divisions at the Council of the EU

Despite the fact that the contestation of interests at the EP sided with a normative approach, stark divisions have emerged among member states during the negotiations at the Council of the EU, which seriously put into question whether or not the new additions for the governance of cyber-surveillance technologies will remain.

Leaks of documents from the German delegation, which has taken the lead in regulating cyber-surveillance technologies, revealed strong opposition by other states to the introduction of a catch-all clause and a specific European autonomous list for cyber-surveillance technologies. Indeed, on 28 January 2018, Germany, France and other groups of countries, released a document to the

Working Party on Dual-Use Goods, to start negotiating a common position vis-à-vis the proposal voted at the EP. In contrast to the legislation received from the EP, this document says '... there is no need for additional catch-all controls' (Moßbrucker 2018), a neglect in line with the demands of the BDI (2017), the influential Federation of German Industries .The leaks suggest that excluding the catch-all clause was a concession to states opposing all new measures in order to reach a compromise that would have at least led to an EU autonomous list of cyber-surveillance technologies (Moßbrucker 2018).

However, even after this concession, unwavering opponents (Cyprus, Czechoslovakia, Estonia, Finland, Ireland, Italy, Poland, Sweden and the United Kingdom) to the new regulation gave additional reasons for rejecting an EU-autonomous list. Among the most relevant arguments, they expressed that:

> For EU companies, the EU-autonomous list would mean they were no longer operating on a level playing field in the global market, where sustained competitiveness is key for survival. Related to the issue of level playing field, it is important to point out that the effect of EU-only controls would be symbolic rather than preventative: those seeking cyber-surveillance technology have no shortage of non-EU vendors from which to choose. While EU industry has strengths in this area, it is far from having a global majority market share on high-end technology in the rapidly developing cyber-security sector. Controls on EU exports without parallel measures in the other major economies would serve only to push the development and production of relevant technologies outside of the EU.
>
> (Moßbrucker 2018)

This quote again echoes the position of the European cyber industry. Likewise, the countries opposing the EU autonomous list stressed the fact that the EU has always complied strictly with international regimes and should not do otherwise in this case. Therefore, they disapprove of taking a unilateral approach to govern cyber-technologies (Moßbrucker 2018).

Finally, in July, the Council of the European Union (2019) released its nego-tiating position, which deleted all the new proposals introduced by the EC and the EP to regulate cyber-surveillance technologies (Moßbrucker 2019). This document confirms that the member states – including Germany – finally sided with the policy preference of the private sector. Indeed, the BDI (2019) welcomed the rejection of the catch-all clause and specific treatment for cyber-surveillance technologies. Contrarily, Klaus Buchner criticised the fact that no effective tools were included to regulate cyber-surveillance technologies, exhibiting that 'Industry has done a great job' (Buchner 2019).

After initiating the move in 2015 to introduce stricter regulations for the export of cyber-surveillance technologies (Stupp 2015), it seems paradoxical that Germany also supported the Council's document. What explains such a reversal? The BDI has been an undeniable influence that criticised most of the additional measures to regulate cyber-surveillance technologies along the whole process. Yet, its success in shaping the policy preferences was contingent on the dynamics of German national politics. Actually, since 2013, Germany's government has been led by a grand coalition (*Große Koalition*) made up by the Christian Democratic Union (CDU), the Christian Social Union in Bavaria (CSU) and the Social Democratic Party (SPD). The pledge for a new regulation for cyber-surveillance technologies was initiated during the leadership of Sigmar Gabriel (SPD) at the Federal Ministry for Economic Affairs and Energy. However, after the 2017 German elections, a new Grand Coalition was formed, which in March 2018 assigned the Federal Minister for Economic Affairs and Energy to Peter Altmaier (CDU). This change coincides with the U-turn in the German negotiating position, suggesting the CDU's choice for defending the German industries' policy preferences. Indeed, Saskia Esken (SPD), member of the German Bundestag, asserted that 'The Federal Government has watered down the important initiative of our former Minister of the Economy Gabriel for the strict export control of digital dual-use goods and almost reversed it' (Meister 2018).

Overall, the Council of the EU has arrived to a negotiating position that expresses policy preferences in line with those of private industry. The exclusion of all the new additions proposed by the EC and the EP to advance with a human-rights-based approach to govern the trade of cyber-surveillance technologies presages a difficult Trilogue, which, in the worst case, may end up with no new measures to regulate such dual-use items (Moßbrucker 2019). Therefore, despite the initial normative inclination of the regulation, the final outcome will possibly be steered by the European business preferences.

Conclusions

This chapter has explored the proposal to review the EU's regulation regime for dual-use items, in particular its aim to govern the exports of cyber-surveillance technologies, an industry in which many European firms have an edge. Two opposing trends have been detected. On the one hand, during the first phase of the discussions within the EC and the EP, a normative approach prevailed, which has introduced new restrictions on the exports of cyber-surveillance technologies to prevent their likely misuse to harm human rights. Indeed, the institutional features of the EU allowed the advancement of these normative policy preferences, initially advocated by civil society actors and politicians defending human rights. On the other hand, the space for interest contestation in the EU's policy process has been stark at the Council of the EU, where, at first some states, but then all, have firmly opposed the most normative aspects of the proposal approved by the EP, mirroring the policy preferences of the European cyber industries. Accordingly, the new values-based proposals to govern cyber-surveillance technologies have been – so far – undermined.

In sum, this case sheds light on the EU's identity in governing new technologies, which seems to follow the NME approach. Indeed, in spite of a usual initial attempt to regulate new technologies in line with the Union's fundamental values, whether or not it succeeds, depends on the interest contestation that takes place during the policy process. Concomitantly, this depends on whether or not there is internal cohesiveness among member states to advance with such a normative position. Otherwise, as this case shows, the preferences of the private sector may influence the Council of the EU far from a stance that may threaten its interests. Despite the importance of the review to update the regulation to tackle new risks to human rights, these political challenges do not indicate an easy future for a human-rights-based approach to govern cyber-surveillance technologies at the EU. Nonetheless, they do show that its governance is possible, though highly dependent upon a new political consensus among member states.

Notes

1 It is worth pointing out that the NGO explains that the number of firms from China and Russia might be understated.
2 The critical report was composed by Amnesty International, Digitale Gesellschaft, FIDH, Human Rights Watch, Open Technology Institute, Privacy International, Reporters without Borders and Access.
3 The proposal of the Commission released in 2016 excluded a number of technologies, specifically: biometrics, location tracking devices, probes and deep packet inspection (DPI) systems were removed from the leaked draft version of the Commission's proposal.
4 Digital Europe represents the most important corporations and national associations of the European digital industry.

References

Alavi, H. and Khamichonak, T. (2016) A European Dilemma: The EU Export Control Regime on Dual-Use Goods and Technologies. *DANUBE: Law and Economics Review* 7(3): 161–172. DOI: 10.1515/danb-2016-0010.

Arabian Business (2011) Western Spy Tools Aid in Crackdown on Arab Dissent. At: www.arabianbusiness.com/western-spy-tools-aid-in-crackdown-on-arab-dissent-417 624.html (accessed 10 July 2018).

Atlas, R.M. and Dando, M. (2006) The Dual-Use Dilemma for the Life Sciences: Perspectives, Conundrums, and Global Solutions. *Biosecurity and Bioterrorism: Biodefense Strategy, Practice, and Science* 4(3): 276–286. DOI: 10.1089/bsp. 2006.4.276.

Ball, K., Haggerty, K.D. and Lyon, D. (eds) (2014) *Routledge Handbook of Surveillance Studies.* Paperback. London: Routledge.

BDI (2017) EU Dual-Use Reform: EC Proposed Regulation COM(2016). April. Berlin, Germany: Bundesverband der Deutschen Industrie e.V. At: https://english.bdi.eu/media/user_upload/20170401_BDI-Positioning_Dual_Use_Reform_Proposal.pdf.

BDI (2019) EU-Dual-Use Regulation: Council Mandate. At: https://e.issuu.com/embed.html?d=20190903_bdi_position_dual-use_en_final&hideIssuuLogo=true&u=bdi-berlin.

Bijker, W.E. (ed.) (1995) *Of Bicycles, Bakelites and Bulbs: Toward a Theory of Sociotechnical Change.* Cambridge, MA: The MIT Press.

Blanton, S.L. (2000) Promoting Human Rights and Democracy in the Developing World: U.S. Rhetoric versus U.S. Arms Exports. *American Journal of Political Science* 44(1): 123–131. DOI: 10.2307/2669298.

Bohnenberger, F. (2017) The Proliferation of Cyber-Surveillance Technologies: Challenges and Prospects for Strengthened Export Controls. *Strategic Trade Review* 3(4): 81–102.

Brewster, T. (2017) Meet the 'Cowboys of Creepware' – Selling Government-Grade Surveillance to Spy on Your Spouse. At: www.forbes.com/sites/thomasbrewster/2017/02/16/government-iphone-android-spyware-is-the-same-as-seedy-spouseware/#1d828bcf455c (accessed 18 August 2018).

Bromley, M., Steenhoek, K.J., Halink, S. *et al.* (2016) ICT Surveillance Systems: Trade Policy and the Application of Human Security Concerns. *Strategic Trade Review* 2(2): 37–52.

Buchner, K. (2019) Europäischer Rat veröffentlicht Position zu Handel mit Überwachungstechnolgie (Dual-Use). At: https://klaus-buchner.eu/europaeischer-rat-veroeffentlicht-position-zu-handel-mit-ueberwachungstechnolgie-dual-use/ (accessed 23 September 2019).

CAUSE (2015) *A Critical Opportunity: Bringing Surveillance Technologies within the EU Dual-Use Regulation.* June. Coalition Against Unlawful Surveillance Exports.

Da Conceição-Heldt, E. and Meunier, S. (2014) Speaking with a Single Voice: Internal Cohesiveness and External Effectiveness of the EU in Global Governance. *Journal of European Public Policy* 21(7): 961–979. DOI: 10.1080/13501763.2014.913219.

Council of the European Union (2019) Proposal for a Regulation of the European Parliament and of the Council Setting Up a Union Regime for the control of Exports, Brokering, Technical Assistance, Transit and Transfer of Dual-Use Items (recast) – Mandate for Negotiations with the European Parliament. At: www.consilium.europa.eu/media/39555/mandate-for-negociations.pdf.

Damro, C. (2012) Market Power Europe. *Journal of European Public Policy* 19(5): 682–699. DOI: 10.1080/13501763.2011.646779.

Damro, C. (2015) Market Power Europe: Exploring a Dynamic Conceptual Framework. *Journal of European Public Policy* 22(9): 1336–1354. DOI: 10.1080/13501763.2015.1046903.

Damro, C. and Friedman, Y. (2018) Market Power Europe and the Externalization of Higher Education: MPE and the Externalization of Higher Education. *JCMS: Journal of Common Market Studies* 56(6): 1394–1410. DOI: 10.1111/jcms.12749.

Diez, T. (2013) Normative Power as Hegemony. K. Nicolaïdis and R.G. Whitman (eds), *Cooperation and Conflict* 48(2): 194–210. DOI: 10.1177/0010836713485387.

Digital Europe (2017) Brussels, Belgium: Digital Europe. At: www.digitaleurope.org/wp/wp-content/uploads/2019/01/FINAL%20-%20DIGITALEUROPE%20paper%20on%20recast%20regs%20dual%20use[1].pdf.

Duchêne, F. (1972) Europe's Role in World Peace. In R. Mayne (ed.), *Europe Tomorrow: Sixteen Europeans Look Ahead.* London: Fontana, 32–47.

Erickson, J.L. (2013) Market Imperative Meets Normative Power: Human Rights and European Arms Transfer Policy. *European Journal of International Relations* 19(2): 209–234. DOI: 10.1177/1354066111415883.

European Commission (2013) European Commission and High Representative of the European Union for Foreign Affairs and Security Policy Cybersecurity Strategy of the European Union: an Open, Safe and Secure Cyberspace. At: https://eeas.europa.eu/archives/docs/policies/eu-cyber-security/cybsec_comm_en.pdf.

European Commission (2015) Trade for All: Towards a More Responsible Trade and Investment Policy. At: http://trade.ec.europa.eu/doclib/docs/2015/october/tradoc_153846.pdf.

European Commission (2016) Proposal for a Regulation of the European Parliament and of the Council. Setting up a Union regime for the control of exports, transfer, brokering, technical assistance and transit of dual-use items (recast). 28 September. Brussels, Belgium. At: https://eur-lex.europa.eu/legal-content/EN/TXT/?uri=CELEX%3A5201 6PC0616.

European Parliament (2018) Control of Exports, Transfer, Brokering, Technical Assistance and Transit of Dual-Use Items (Debate). At: www.europarl.europa.eu/doceo/document/CRE-8-2018-01-16-ITM-014_EN.html?redirect.

Fuhrmann, M. (2008) Exporting Mass Destruction? The Determinants of Dual-Use Trade. *Journal of Peace Research* 45(5): 633–652. DOI: 10.1177/0022343308094324.

Gebhard, C. and Norheim-Martinsen, P.M. (2011) Making Sense of EU Comprehensive Security Towards Conceptual and Analytical Clarity. *European Security* 20(2): 221–241. DOI: 10.1080/09662839.2011.564613.

Geeraert, A. and Drieskens, E. (2017) Normative Market Europe: The EU as a Force for Good in International Sports Governance? *Journal of European Integration* 39(1): 79–94. DOI: 10.1080/07036337.2016.1256395.

Kanetake, M. (2019) The EU's Export Control of Cyber Surveillance Technology: Human Rights Approaches. *Business and Human Rights Journal* 4(1): 155–162. DOI: 10.1017/bhj.2018.18.

Kline, R. and Pinch, T. (1996) Users as Agents of Technological Change: The Social Construction of the Automobile in the Rural United States. *Technology and Culture* 37(4): 763–795. DOI: 10.2307/3107097.

Lavallée, C. (2018) The EU's Dual-Use Exports: A Human Security Approach? In Eva Pejsova (ed.), *Guns, Engines and Turbines. The EU's Hard Power in Asia*, Chaillot Papers (EUISS), November, 43–50. www.iss.europa.eu/sites/default/files/EUISSFiles/CP_149_Asia.pdf.

Lin, H. (2016) Governance of Information Technology and Cyber Weapons. In E.D. Harris (ed.), *Governance of Dual-Use Technologies: Theory and Practice*. Cambridge, MA: American Academy of Arts & Sciences, 112–157.

Manners, I. (2002) Normative Power Europe: A Contradiction in Terms? *JCMS: Journal of Common Market Studies* 40(2): 235–258. DOI: 10.1111/1468-5965.00353.

Manners, I. (2006) Normative Power Europe Reconsidered: Beyond the Crossroads1. *Journal of European Public Policy* 13(2): 182–199. DOI: 10.1080/13501760500451600.

Meister, A. (2018) Reaktionen auf Dual-Use-Leaks: 'Offenbarungseid der Bundesregierung'. At: https://netzpolitik.org/2018/reaktionen-auf-dual-use-leaks-offenbarung-seid-der-bundesregierung/.

Miller, S. and Selgelid, M.J. (2007) Ethical and Philosophical Consideration of the Dual-use Dilemma in the Biological Sciences. *Science and Engineering Ethics* 13(4): 523–580. DOI: 10.1007/s11948-007-9043-4.

Moßbrucker, D. (2018) Überwachungsexporte: Bundesregierung stellt Industrie vor Menschen-rechte. *Netzpolitik.org*. At: https://netzpolitik.org/2018/ueberwachungsexporte-bundesregierung-stellt-industrie-vor-menschenrechte/.

Moßbrucker, D. (2019) EU States Unanimously Vote Against Stricter Export Controls for Surveillance Equipment. *Netzpolitik.org*. At: https://netzpolitik.org/2019/eu-states-unanimously-vote-against-stricter-export-controls-for-surveillence-equipment/.

Privacy International (2016) *The Global Surveillance Industry*. Privacy International. At: www.privacyinternational.org/sites/default/files/2017-12/global_surveillance_0.pdf.

Rath, J., Ischi, M. and Perkins, D. (2014) Evolution of Different Dual-Use Concepts in International and National Law and Its Implications on Research Ethics and

Governance. *Science and Engineering Ethics* 20(3): 769–790. DOI: 10.1007/s11948-014-9519-y.

Rychnovská, D. (2016) Governing Dual-Use Knowledge: From the Politics of Responsible Science to the Ethicalization of Security. *Security Dialogue* 47(4): 310–328. DOI: 10.1177/0967010616658848.

Schaake, M. (2018) Plenary Speech on Update of the Dual-Use Regulation. At: https://marietjeschaake.eu/en/plenary-speech-on-update-of-the-dual-use-regulation (accessed 25 July 2018).

Schaake, M. and Vermeulen, M. (2016) Towards a Values-Based European Foreign Policy to Cybersecurity. *Journal of Cyber Policy* 1(1): 75–84. DOI: 10.1080/237388 71.2016.1157617.

SIPRI and ECORYS (2015) Final Report for the European Commission. Data and Information Collection for EU Dual-Use Export Control Policy Review. At: http://trade.ec.europa.eu/doclib/docs/2016/september/tradoc_154962.PDF.

Stevens, T. (2018) Cyberweapons: Power and the Governance of the Invisible. *International Politics* 55(3–4): 482–502. DOI: 10.1057/s41311-017-0088-y.

Stockton, P.N. and Golabek-Goldman, M. (2013) Curbing the Market for Cyber Weapons. *Yale Law & Policy Review* 32(1): 239–266.

Stupp, C. (2015) Germany Leaves Brussels Behind on Surveillance Tech Export Controls, Euractiv. At: www.euractiv.com/section/digital/news/germany-leaves-brussels-behind-on-surveillance-tech-export-controls/.

Stupp, C. (2016) Juncker Postpones Controversial Export Control Bill on Surveillance Technology. At: www.euractiv.com/section/trade-society/news/juncker-postpones-controversial-export-control-bill-on-surveillance-technology/.

Stupp, C. (2018) MEPs Approve Export Controls Tailored to Stop Government Surveillance. At: www.euractiv.com/section/cybersecurity/news/meps-approve-export-controls-tailored-to-stop-government-surveillance/.

Yanik, L.K. (2006) Guns and Human Rights: Major Powers, Global Arms Transfers, and Human Rights Violations. *Human Rights Quarterly* 28(2): 357–388. DOI: 10.1353/hrq.2006.0026.

Young, A.R. (2015) The European Union as a Global Regulator? Context and Comparison. *Journal of European Public Policy* 22(9): 1233–1252. DOI: 10.1080/13501763.2015.1046902.

Youngs, R. (2004) Normative Dynamics and Strategic Interests in the EU's External Identity. *JCMS: Journal of Common Market Studies* 42(2): 415–435. DOI: 10.1111/j.1468-5965.2004.00494.x.

6 European security in cyberspace

A critical reading

André Barrinha

Introduction

The critical study of security became one of the most vibrant areas of activity in post-Cold War International Relations (see Buzan and Hansen 2009). Some approaches focused on unpacking the political nature of security, whereas others operated closer to the ethical ambitions of Critical Theory.[1] In common, they had 'the identification and denunciation of depoliticization [of security], both in the social realm and in the realm of academia' (CASE Collective 2006: 445). They also concurred in the subjective (or inter-subjective) meaning of the concept, highlighting its fundamental unsettled nature. But, whereas the emergence of Critical Security Studies[2] was very much focused on the debate between different schools and approaches, in recent years, those divisions have largely subdued and the debate seems to have moved beyond these imaginary silos towards a more empirical work (Dunn Cavelty and Wenger 2019: 9).

The problematisation/deconstruction/reconstructions of the concept of security itself is certainly the basis on which the remaining critical edifice is built. That constant search for transformative answers that contribute to the emancipation of individuals, groups and societies is an integral part of a robust critical analysis. In this chapter, we are particularly interested in exploring how these dynamics apply to cybersecurity in the European Union (EU) context.

Indeed, cybersecurity is fast becoming a key issue in European politics. Several high-profile attacks such as WannaCry and NotPetya, combined with foreign interference (or the fear of) in national and European elections have placed this topic on the top of the agenda. Surprisingly, the academic literature on European security, either critical[3] or 'traditional', remains relatively sparse (for exceptions, see Bendiek and Porter 2013; Christou 2016, 2018, 2019; Carrapico and Barrinha 2017, 2018; Dunn Cavelty 2018; Farrand 2018; Renard 2018; Sliwinski 2014).

This chapter intends to contribute to addressing this gap by applying some of the key ideas in the critical studies on security to the study of the EU's approach to cybersecurity. It has two main ambitions in that regard. First, it offers a basic framework through which to assess cybersecurity governance practices and policies from a critical standpoint. As will be suggested, only by dividing a security policy into its 'constitutive' and 'adjustment' phases can we unpack the normative principles that underpin it and offer alternative readings of what security 'should' be in a given area; only then can we move towards those 'more emancipatory ends'. This implies an initial identification of the embedded normative principles and a subsequent matching of those principles against the emancipatory potential of that policy. Second, it aims to problematise the EU's understanding of cybersecurity and question its emancipatory potential against alternative readings of what a human-focused cybersecurity approach *should* be. Finally, this chapter contributes to sheding light on how emerging security technologies (in this case, related to cybersecurity) are framed in the EU context.

In terms of structure, it starts by explaining the differences between the constitutive and the adjustment phases in security and the role of normative analysis within it. This will be followed by a brief discussion about the role of technology and cybersecurity from a critical perspective. The last part of the chapter looks specifically at the EU's approach to cybersecurity and the normative challenges it raises.

From constitution to adjustment: the sedimented nature of security policies

As mentioned in the Introduction to this volume, most critical approaches concur in that (in)security is a social construction, that can be manufactured, resulting from different expert views, representing specific cultural tendencies or dominant political forces. Security thus understood loses its deterministic mantle and opens the space for the contestation of specific security policies and practices; it opens the space for criticality. However, it also implies a political process of constant new beginnings. Whether it is through a speech act (Copenhagen School) or a set of practices (Paris School), it is clear something is created (Huysmans 2014: 3); security has a performative power in the lives of states, organisations and people.

This chapter proposes a slightly different reading, one in which security policies are not constantly redefined, but rather adjusted. That means that the logics of continuity are more sedimented than is often portrayed in the critical studies of security. It also means that security as a political process needs to be qualified: there is a distinction to be made between the politics of security that leads to the creation of something new and the politics of security that alters previously existing policies. Technology is often at the basis of the former, such as the discovery of nuclear fusion or the development of information systems. In the 1930s, there was no nuclear policy, in the same way that in the 1980s no European country had a cybersecurity policy. Technological development was fundamental for the constitution of these specific security fields, but that should not automatically endorse a deterministic understanding of technology, as a critical reading of Science and Technology Studies (STS) would tell us.

Andrew Feenberg, in his *Critical Theory of Technology* (1991), distinguishes between instrumental and substantive understandings of technology. Instrumental technology is 'the common sense idea that technologies are "tools" standing ready to serve the purposes of their users' (Feenberg 1991: 5), whereas the substantive understanding inverts the instrumental relationship, placing the human as a subordinate of technology. The aim of this distinction is not to highlight the deterministic character of technology. On the contrary, it raises the importance of shaping it. It is what Feenberg calls the 'ambivalence' of technology; or the idea that the design and implementation of technology is, as put by Columba Peoples, the result of a struggle whose outcome 'can be informed by and used towards more emancipatory ends' (2010: 28).

This struggle, that can assume the form of a 'democratic intervention'[4] (Feenberg 2017) is most effective in this constitutive moment of security. The constitutive moment of a security policy defines what the security issue is, who should be protected (referent object) and against what, how it should be approached and who should be responsible for dealing with it. The preliminary definition of the conditions of possibility therefore sets the constitutive ground from which the politics of security can operate. Security politics then becomes a boundary shifting exercise, akin to a parliament approving legislation within the framework of an *a priori* constitution. In that regard, separating the constitutive from the adjustment period enables us to chronologically understand the depth and importance of *a posteriori* change. Methodologically, this leads to a double move. First, the analyst extracts the normative claims embedded in both periods. To paraphrase Robert Cox (1981), it answers the question: security for whom and for what purpose? Second, it tests those normative claims against their emancipatory potential, answering questions such as: do those measures contribute to improving the lives[5] of the individuals under the jurisdiction of the political entity under analysis? If not, what alternative conceptions should be introduced in the political debate? The conclusion of that exercise can then be fed as a contribution to the boundary shifting exercise that is discussing and potentially changing the politics of security within a given field.

Applying this framework to cybersecurity implies removing the technological determinism of the concept and opening it to other emancipatory possibilities. Within such logic, security becomes a contrasting exercise between its constitutive elements and the political changes that are discussed or introduced. The security analyst becomes the jury of a higher court, constantly assessing the merits and shortcomings of policy proposals that are made against previously existing constitutional principles. This gives the analyst sufficient information to execute the above-mentioned two-step normative exercise: to identify the embedded normative principles enshrined in cybersecurity governance and to test their emancipatory potential against new policies in the field.

Defining cybersecurity: a political performance

What we 'do' when we say cybersecurity? First, it is important to understand that cybersecurity is a contested term, particularly by the IT community that has always preferred to use terms such as information security, network security or computer security. Its contemporary usage is therefore an attempt by policy makers to translate the complexity and importance that information networks have in our world.[6] That means that cybersecurity is, in itself, a policy construction (Nissenbaum 2005). But how to define it? Although definitions abound, we could say cyberspace is 'the realm of computer networks (and the users behind them) in which information is stored, shared, and communicated online' (Singer and Friedman 2014: 13). It is an 'information environment', that is 'made up of digitized data that is created, stored, and, most importantly, shared', but also 'comprises the computers that store data plus the systems and infrastructure that allow it to flow' (Singer and Friedman 2014: 13). In practice, cyberspace involves three distinctive levels: hardware, software and information (Segal 2016: 34), each of which needs to be protected. As for cybersecurity, one could follow the International Telecommunications Union definition, which considers it to be:

> the collection of tools, policies, security concepts, security safeguards, guidelines, risk management approaches, actions, training, best practices, assurance and technologies that can be used to protect the cyber environment and organization and user's assets. Organization and user's assets include connected computing devices, personnel, infrastructure, applications, services, telecommunications systems, and the totality of transmitted and/or stored information in the cyber environment. Cybersecurity strives to ensure the attainment and maintenance of the security properties of the organization and user's assets against relevant security risks in the cyber environment.[7]

From this perspective, cybersecurity is the policy area responsible for ensuring the normal functioning of cyberspace, in particular its availability, integrity and confidentiality. Issues such as privacy and surveillance are not commonly associated with cybersecurity. Even in documents that are not linked to national security that seems to be the case. The Report of the UN Secretary General's High-Level Panel on Digital Cooperation, published in 2019, whose ultimate purpose is to find 'ways we work together to address the social, ethical, legal and economic impact of digital technologies in order to maximise their benefits and minimise their harm' (2019: 7) clearly separates on Chapter 3 the right to privacy from security.

A more critical approach of the topic would, however, unpack cybersecurity beyond its technical components. As Myriam Dunn Cavelty highlights, also echoing previous definitions from Ronald Deibert, Rafal Rohozinski and Masashi Crete-Nishihata (2012) and Lene Hansen and Helen Nissenbaum (2009), cybersecurity can be seen as 'a heterogeneous set of discourses and practices with multiple, often contradictory effects' (Dunn Cavelty 2014: 703). This approach moves the core of the definition away from technological needs and places cybersecurity at the centre of the political debate. When doing so, alternative configurations of cybersecurity can be put forward. For instance, when referring to a human security-centred understanding of the term, Boulanin argues that we need a holistic understanding of cybersecurity 'that not only tackles risks related to cybercrime and sophisticated cyber-threats that jeopardize cyberspace, but also takes into account considerations for principles of the rule of law that can improve people's trust in ICT' (2016: 401). In her work, Madeline Carr also makes the connection between privacy and cybersecurity, arguing that the latter could be understood as 'the integrity of our personal privacy online, to the security of our critical infrastructure, to electronic commerce, to military threats and to the protection of intellectual property' (Carr 2016: 49–50).[8]

Currently, cybersecurity is perceived mostly in favour of 'a few and already powerful entities and has no or even negative effects for the rest' (Dunn Cavelty 2014: 707). Profit maximisation, sovereign oversight or higher strategic aims usually take priority over individuals' online (and offline) safety. If anything, the individual is from the state perspective often seen as a risk that needs to be managed via surveillance practices (see Seoane, Chapter 5 in this volume). Individuals are a threat, but they also serve a specific purpose as 'nodes in the network, needed to ensure the wealth and health of the networks, but not their own health' (Dunn Cavelty 2014: 706). Even issues that seem to benefit the individual, such as encryption or net-neutrality, are more often than not related to profit opportunities (see Horten 2016). Under the current circumstances, individuals are placed between a profit-driven private sector, sovereignty-obsessed states and the dependence on ultimately flawed technology (Eriksson and Giacomello 2007: 6). As expressed in a 2017 report by the London-based advocacy group Privacy International, 'cyber security should be considered a public good, in the same way as public health for example, which promotes collective responsibility for the benefit of everyone' (2017: 7). The protection of individuals, networks and devices is, in their view, interdependent, an understanding that is rarely taken into consideration by the major cybersecurity actors. Acknowledging the constitutive effects of cybersecurity policy in each given context, could, in that regard, be the first step towards offering specific normative suggestions on the issue. If we are able to unpack the meanings underlying each actor's constitutive cybersecurity policy, we can then match it against any future policy changes and suggest alternative meanings and approaches: in short, alternative forms of cybersecurity governance. This could also contribute to the formation of new publics, alert and willing to challenge the dominant perceptions of cybersecurity and its inherit tendency towards depoliticisation. It is that normative exercise which we will now do regarding the EU.

EU: Constituting cybersecurity

The EU's approach to cybersecurity started to gain momentum over a decade ago with the creation and development of a series of institutions, policies and initiatives, such as the 2005 Council Decision on Attacks against Information Systems, the creation of the European Union Agency for Cybersecurity (ENISA) in 2004 and the Communication from the Commission Towards a

General Policy on the Fight against Cyber Crime (COM(2007)267 final). But its major landmark came in 2013 with the approval of the EU Cybersecurity Strategy. The document proposed three action pillars – network and information security; law enforcement; and defence (European Commission 2013: 17) – attributing specific institutions and agencies to each of the pillars.

In parallel with its Cybersecurity Strategy, the European Commission proposed a Directive on the security of network and information systems (the so-called NIS Directive). Although significantly watered down when compared to the original proposal, the final text was eventually agreed by Commission, Parliament and Council in December 2015 and entered into force in August 2016.[9] Also, in 2013, the EU adopted the Directive on attacks against information systems that replaces the 2005 EU Framework Decision on attacks against information systems that built on the previous legislation but adds a more urgent requirement for communications and infringement for non-compliance.

All this activity could be defined as part of the constitutive period in which the edifice of EU's cybersecurity was built: a period that coincided with the progressive emergence of cyberspace as a priority issue in the international security agenda. The EU is now moving from a constitutive phase to an adjustment phase, embodied in a batch of policies and guidelines implemented or approved in the last three years. This second phase was heralded by the approval of the EU Global Strategy in June 2016, which placed cybersecurity among its top priorities (European Union 2016: 9). Cyber issues were, according to the strategy, to be 'weaved' across all policy areas, coordination with member states and cooperation with other actors, to which the strategy highlights the USA and NATO. The EU has indeed reached an agreement with NATO on the issue in November 2016 – the Cyber Defence Pledge (NATO 2016) – and the European Commission has included cyber defence as a top priority in its European Defence Action Plan (European Commission 2016b). A few months earlier, in July 2016, it had already adopted the Communication Strengthening Europe's Cyber Resilience Systems and Fostering a Competitive and Innovative Cybersecurity Industry (European Commission 2016a), two documents that place private initiative at the centre of cybersecurity development in Europe.

If 2013 was a crucial year for the EU by shifting a gear up in terms of its approach to cybersecurity, 2017 offered a renewed political mandate. In June, the Council (2017a) called for the development of a Cyber Diplomacy toolbox,[10] that will provide the EU with the necessary tools to engage with the rest of world both cooperatively and in response to cyberattacks, namely, through the imposition of economic sanctions (Moret and Pawlak 2017).

A few months later, in September, Jean-Claude Juncker, in his State of the Union address, placed the security of the Europe's critical information infrastructures at the centre of its future (European Commission 2017b). That came a week after the Council approved a comprehensive Cybersecurity Package that, among other elements, proposed the transformation of ENISA into a permanent Cybersecurity Centre, the creation of a new European Cybersecurity Research and Competence Centre and the development of an EU-based cybersecurity certification process. One new element in the EU's enhanced approach to cybersecurity is its ambition to offer concrete responses to cyberattacks: both through sanctions (Moret and Pawlak 2017) and through the development of an EU Cybersecurity Crisis Response Framework that would help operationalise a blueprint for joint action against large-scale cyberattacks (European Commission 2017a).

The year 2017 was also marked by the EU Council decision to approve the creation of a Permanent Structured Cooperation (PESCO) in defence, that together with the Commission-sponsored European Defence Fund will contribute to the significant development of defence within the EU framework (see Calcara, Chapter 1 and Fiott, Chapter 2 in this volume). Two of its initial 17 projects will be explicitly dedicated to the cybersecurity (Bendiek 2018: 4). That number has increased to three (out of 34) if one includes the project led by the Czech Republic on electronic warfare. What is most striking about these projects is the fact that none of the larger EU member states took the initiative to lead projects in this field,[11] which is not particularly surprising as the EU is only now starting to be seen as a credible actor in the field of cyber defence (see Deschaux-Dutard's Chapter 7 in this volume). This follows a wider trend as, until recently, the EU has acted more as a facilitator of member states' activities than as an enforcer of a specific worldview (Sliwinski 2014). Member states were, according to the EU's Cybersecurity Strategy, the main actors responsible for ensuring Europe's security in this sector. As we move away from the constitutive period to a consolidation phase (where adjustments become possible), there seems to be a progressive change of tone on the part of the EU in that regard. In the 2017 Joint Communication, a document that intends to offer concrete steps for the EU to advance in this field, it is recognised that:

> [w]hile member states remain responsible for national security, the scale and cross-border nature of the threat make a powerful case for EU action providing incentives and support for member states to develop and maintain more and better national cybersecurity capabilities, *while at the same time building EU-level capacity.*
>
> (European Commission, 2017a: 3, *our emphasis*)

In fact, some member states think the EU is already trying to overreach in this domain, with both France and Germany showing much scepticism regarding the EU's cybersecurity certification proposal (Stupp 2018). The next few months will tell if we are witnessing the start of an open turf war between the Commission and member states in this field and if that will have any implications in terms of how cybersecurity is perceived and done in Europe. The EU's recent efforts in cybersecurity seem to indicate a willingness to correct a certain lack of coherence (see Carrapico and Barrinha 2017) demonstrated in the constitutive phase of the policy, even if that means adopting a more pro-active stance that is not always cherished by all member states.

From consolidation to adjustment: analysing
EU's cybersecurity

The 2013 Cybersecurity Strategy of the European Union can be seen as the EU's foundational moment when it comes to cybersecurity as it was the first time the EU has adopted a structured, encompassing document that defined the limits of what cybersecurity should be and of how it should be approached. In the document, cybersecurity is defined as:

> the safeguards and actions that can be used to protect the cyber domain, both in the civilian and military fields, from those threats that are associated with or that may harm its interdependent networks and information infrastructure. Cyber-security strives to preserve the availability and integrity of the networks and infrastructure and the confidentiality of the information contained therein.
>
> (European Commission 2013: 3)

Its priorities are mostly centred on making information networks more 'resilient', reducing cyber crime, developing defence capabilities, developing the technological and industrial base and promoting the EU values abroad.

As indicated earlier, cybersecurity is, according to the strategy, translated into three main areas – cyber crime, CIIP and defence. From interviews conducted in Brussels with officials from the European Commission and European Parliament,[12] it is clear that issues associated with privacy and data protection are not seen as cybersecurity per se; they are taken to be about data protection and regulation. In one of the few rare occasions privacy is mentioned in the 2013 strategy, it appears as something that exists outside the cybersecurity sphere. Personal data and privacy are to be taken into full consideration as '[c]ybersecurity can only be sound and effective if it is based on fundamental rights and freedoms as enshrined in the Charter of Fundamental Rights of the European Union and EU core values' (European Commission 2013: 4). Also, '[a]ny information sharing for the purposes of cyber security, when personal data is at stake, should be compliant with EU data protection law and take full account of the individuals' rights in this field' (European Commission 2013: 4). However, as was also made clear in the same paragraph, '[r]eciprocally, individuals' rights cannot be secured without safe networks and systems' (European Commission 2013: 4). Ultimately, privacy and data protection matter as principles associated with the EU's fundamental rights that deserve to be respected in any EU cybersecurity policy, but they are *not* cybersecurity. This is visible in other recent documents. For instance, the term 'privacy' is entirely absent from the Cyber Diplomacy Toolbox (Council of the EU 2017a), the EU Cybersecurity Strategy Roadmap (Council of the EU 2017b) or even from the 2018 Conclusions on Malicious Cyber Activities (Council of the EU 2018). In the Resilience, Deterrence and Defence Joint Communication, it is mentioned once, but again, only in reference to the promotion of EU's core values internationally (European Commission 2017a: 18).

Although developments in the field of data protection and privacy are not seen as part of the cybersecurity remit, the EU has been rather active in this field, both inside and outside its borders. The European Parliament seems to be the institution most concerned with these issues, whereas the Commission and the Council often take a more pro-business position and are more susceptible to lobbying pressures, as was the case during the negotiations for new General Data Protection Regulation (GDPR), approved in April 2016 (see Horten 2016) and implemented in May 2018. In any case, and given the global context in this field, there is the perception that, as a whole, the EU is, internationally, at the forefront of data protection regulation (Segal 2016), a perception confirmed by the discussions around Cambridge Analytica and Facebook's use of its users' personal data (Hern and Pegg 2018). Internationally, relations with the USA have been particularly affected since the Snowden disclosures in 2013. The Safe Harbour agreement that regulated the transfer of information between the EU and the USA was declared void by the European Court of Justice in 2015, after an Austrian student filled in a complaint against Facebook, due to its participation in NSA's PRISM surveillance programme and subsequent lack of adequate protection for the transfer of data to the USA. A new agreement – Privacy Shield – was signed in June 2016 but its existence appears quite precarious, as the EU Court of Justice is currently assessing the legitimacy of its standard contractual clause (Walker 2019).

If the EU's cybersecurity was constituted as based on the cyber crime, CIIP, cyber defence triptych, there are not many signs of that changing in the near future. All the documents and policies published in the last couple of years indicate that the EU is more concerned in giving teeth to the current strategy than in radically changing its stance on the topic. This ultimately leaves the EU in a somewhat strange position: as a political entity, it does much to address issues of privacy and data protection – of the which GDPR certainly is its most recognisable feature – but as a cybersecurity actor its priorities lie elsewhere – in combating cyber crime, protecting critical infrastructures and defence. The move from its constitutive to its adjustment phase only seems to have consolidated such distinction.

Conclusion

This chapter conceptualises cybersecurity from a critical standpoint. It offers both an analytical tool – in the distinction between constitution and adjustment – and a backdoor within it for a normative discussion on what cybersecurity is or should be. As it argues, moving towards a more emancipatory understanding of cybersecurity implies redefining how we perceive the concept and how we define priorities; it also means extracting it from its technical dimension and accepting it as a political-normative construct. When looking at the EU's priorities in this field, it is clear it prioritises the consolidation of its 2013 Cybersecurity Strategy, which demands that its information networks are seen as reliable and secure. Issues such as privacy and personal data are contemplated, but mostly as part of its core values and as part of its internationally oriented value-promotion agenda. When it comes to its own member states, such issues are dealt in separate policy settings with different actors involved – such as in the case of the EU GDPR.

Should we be concerned with such division? Should cybersecurity at the EU level be redefined in order to include those issues that affect European citizens the most? Critics of the Welsh School have often highlighted that a problem with equating security with emancipation was that it could simply lead to the securitisation of the latter. By putting privacy issues at the centre of its cyber-security approach, we could end up securitising privacy as a principle. Another problem is the potential appropriation of an emancipatory discourse in order to achieve other goals. Nik Hynek and David Chandler (2013: 52) make that case, using the EU as an example of an institution that tends to appropriate itself of critical, emancipatory claims, in order to fulfil policy goals that are significantly different from the normative principles underpinning those claims, such as was the case with humanitarian interventionism.

There is an ethics of constant suspicion that comes with any solid critical analysis of security. As we enter the adjustment phase in the EU's cybersecurity policy, all these issues should be 'un-sedimented' and tested against emancipatory altern-atives of cyberspace. Only then can we contribute to a political discussion of what cybersecurity should be and of how the EU should engage with it.

Notes

1 As Robert Cox argues, 'Critical theory is a mode of thought that exposes the common current doctrines as inadequate in dealing with global problems, and that tries to find other elements that could be thought of, either separately or collectively, as an altern-ative' (2012: 20).

2 According to Michael Williams and Keith Krause's *Critical Security Studies*, 'the term critical to security studies [was] meant to imply more an orientation toward the discipline than a precise theoretical label, as we adopt a small-c definition of critical for both practical and intellectual reasons' (1997: x–xi).

3 For a broader approach to the topic, see Balzacq and Dunn Cavelty 2016; Choucri and Goldsmith 2012; Christou 2016; Saco 1999; Dunn Cavelty 2008, 2014, 2015; Hansen and Nissenbaum 2009; and Kello 2017. Also, for an overview of the field, see Dunn Cavelty and Wenger 2019. We find the literature in the field to remain sparse overall. From a brief analysis of two journals associated with Critical Security Studies, *Security Dialogue* and the more recent *Critical Studies on Security*, there were, until June 2018, a total of four articles with the prefix 'cyber' (Betz and Stevens 2013; Deibert, Rohozinski and Crete-Nishihata 2012; and Power 2007; Zajko 2015) in the title and only a handful seem to discuss issues associated with it (including Aradau 2010; Dunn Cavelty 2014 and Dunn Cavelty, Kaufmann and Kristensen 2015).

4 These are new forms of 'sociotechnical agency' that lead the public to intervene in order to alter its relation with a given technology or technology-based practice (Feenberg 2017: 4).

5 For a discussion about the principle of the good life in the interaction between humans and technology, see Verbeek (2013).

6 In their book *Cybersecurity* and *Cyberwar*, Peter W. Singer and Allan Friedman (2014: 5) offer a few curious examples of this, such as the FBI Director that did not have a computer in his office until 2001 or the fact that in 2013 eight out of nine US Supreme Court Justices did not use email.

7 Taken from the International Telecommunications Union, at: www.itu.int/en/ITU-T/studygroups/com17/Pages/cybersecurity.aspx.
8 I would like to thank the editors for pointing this out.
9 The Directive creates a Cooperation Group to coordinate the exchange of information between the different national Computer Security Incident Response Team (CSIRT) and it places significant responsibilities on member states and companies that are deemed to be operators of essential services (e.g. transport, banking and health) as well as those that are digital service providers (e.g. cloud computing and search engines). Member states had until May 2018 to transpose the directive to national legislation.
10 The April 2018 Council Conclusions on Malicious Cyber Activities gave a renewed (somewhat lost) impetus to the implementation of the Cyber Diplomacy toolbox, which eventually materialised in May 2019 when the EU set out a detailed sanctions regime and other restrictive measures against cyberattacks (Council of the European Union 2018, 2019a and 2019b).
11 That responsibility was given to Greece (Cyber Threats and Incident Response Information Sharing Platform), Lithuania (Cyber Rapid Response Teams) and the Czech Republic (Electronic Warfare). For more information, see Permanent Structured Cooperation (PESCO), at: https://pesco.europa.eu/.
12 Interviews conducted in May 2016.

References

Aradau, C. (2010) Security That Matters: Critical Infrastructure and Objects of Protection. *Security Dialogue* 41(5): 491–514.

Balzacq, T. and Dunn Cavelty, M. (2016) A Theory of Actor-Network for Cyber-Security. *European Journal of International Security* 1: 176–198.

Bendiek, A. (2018) The EU as a Force for Peace in International Cyber Diplomacy. *SWP Comments*, No. 19. April. Berlin: Stiftung Wissenschaft und Politik.

Bendiek, A. and Porter, A.L. (2013) European Cyber Security Policy within a Global Multistakeholder Structure. *European Foreign Affairs Review* 2: 155–180.

Betz, D.J. and Stevens, T. (2013) Analogical Reasoning and Cyber Security. *Security Dialogue* 44(2): 147–164. https://doi.org/10.1177/0967010613478323.

Boulanin, V. (2016) Information and Communication Technology, Cybersecurity and Human Development. *SIPRI Yearbook 2016*. Oxford: Oxford University Press, 389–411.

Buzan, B. and Hansen, L. (2009) *The Evolution of International Security Studies*. Cambridge: Cambridge University Press.

Carr, M. (2016) Public–Private Partnerships in National Cyber-Security Strategies. *International Affairs* 92(1) (January): 43–62. https://doi.org/10.1111/1468-2346.12504.

Carrapico, H. and Barrinha, A. (2017) The EU as a Coherent (Cyber)Security Actor? *Journal of Common Market Studies* 55(6): 1254–1272.

Carrapico, H. and Barrinha, A. (2018) European Union Cyber Security as an Emerging Research and Policy Field. *European Politics and Society* 19(3): 299–303.

CASE Collective (2006) Critical Approaches to Security in Europe: A Networked Manifesto. *Security Dialogue* 37(4): 443–487.

Choucri, N. and Goldsmith, D. (2012) Lost in Cyberspace: Harnessing the Internet, International Relations, and Global Security. *Bulletin of the Atomic Scientists* 68(2): 70–77.

Christou, G. (2016) *Cybersecurity in the European Union: Resilience and Adaptability in Governance Policy*. London: Palgrave.

Christou, G. (2018) The Challenges of Cybercrime Governance in the European Union. *European Politics and Society* 19(3): 355–375.

Christou, G. (2019) The Collective Securitisation of Cyberspace in the European Union. *West European Politics* 42(2): 278–301.

Council of the European Union (2017a) Draft Council Conclusions on a Framework for a Joint Diplomatic Response to Malicious Cyber Activities ("Cyber Diplomacy Toolbox"), 9916/17.

Council of the European Union (2017b) EU Cybersecurity Strategy Roadmap. 8901/17.

Council of the European Union (2018) Council Conclusions on Malicious Cyber Activities. 7925/18.

Council of the European Union (2019a) Council Decision Concerning Restrictive Measures Against Cyber-Attacks Threatening the Union or its Member States (EU). 2019/797.

Council of the European Union (2019b) Council Regulation Concerning Restrictive Measures Against Cyber-Attacks Threatening the Union or its Member States (EU). 2019/796.

Cox, R.W. (1981) Social Forces, States and World Orders: Beyond International Relations Theory. *Millennium: Journal of International Studies* 10(2): 126–155.

Cox, R.W. (2012) An interview with Robert Cox. In Shannon Brincat, Laura Lima and Joao Nunes (eds), *Critical Theory in International Relations and Security Studies. Interviews and Reflections*. London: Routledge, 15–34.

Deibert, R.J., Rohozinski, R. and Crete-Nishihata, M. (2012) Cyclones in Cyberspace: Information Shaping and Denial in the 2008 Russia-Georgia. *Security Dialogue* 43(1): 3–24.

Dunn Cavelty, M. (2008) *Cyber-Security and Threat Politics*. London: Routledge.

Dunn Cavelty, M. (2014) Breaking the Cyber-Security Dilemma: Aligning Security Needs and Removing Vulnerabilities. *Science and Engineering Ethics* 20(3): 701–715.

Dunn Cavelty, M. (2015) In(Visible) Ghosts in the Machine and the Powers that Bind: The Relational Securitization of Anonymous. *International Political Sociology* 9(2): 176–194.

Dunn Cavelty, M. (2018) Europe's Cyber-Power. *European Politics and Society* 19(3): 304–320.

Dunn Cavelty, M., Kaufmann M. and Kristensen, K.S. (2015) Resilience and (In)security: Practices, Subjects, Temporalities. *Security Dialogue* 46(1): 3–14.

Dunn Cavelty, M. and Wenger, A. (2019) Cyber Security Meets Security Politics: Complex Technology, Fragmented Politics, and Networked Science. *Contemporary Security Policy*, Online edition, October 2019.

Eriksson, J. and Giacomello, G. (2007) Introduction: Closing the Gap Between International Relations Theory and Studies of Digital-Age Security. In *International Relations and Security in the Digital Age*. London: Routledge, 1–28.

European Commission (2013) Cybersecurity Strategy of the European Union: An Open, Safe and Secure Cyberspace. European Commission and High Representative of the European Union for Foreign Affairs and Security Policy. Joint Communication to the European Parliament, The Council, The European Economic and Social Committee and the Committee of the Regions. JOIN(2013) 1 final, 7 February, Brussels.

European Commission (2016a) Communication from the Commission to the European Parliament, The Council, The European Economic and Social Committee and the Committee of the Regions, *Strengthening Europe's Cyber Resilience System and Fostering a Competitive and Innovative Cybersecurity Industry*, COM(2016) 410 final.

European Commission (2016b) *European Defence Action Plan: Towards a European Defence Fund*, Brussels, 30 November. Press release. At: https://europa.eu/rapid/press-release_IP-16-4088_en.htm.

European Commission (2017a) Joint Communication to the European Parliament and the Council. Resilience, Deterrence and Defence: Building Strong Cybersecurity for the EU, JOIN(2017) 450 final.

European Commission (2017b) Press Release. State of the Union 2017 – Cybersecurity: Commission Scales Up EU's Response to Cyber-Attacks. Brussels, 19 September.

European Union (2016) Shared Vision, Common Action: a Stronger Europe- A Global Strategy for the European Union's Foreign and Security Policy. June. At: www.eeas. europa.eu/archives/docs/top_stories/pdf/eugs_review_web.pdf.

Farrand, B. (2018) Combatting Physical Threats Posed via Digital Means: The European Commission's Developing Approach to the Sale of Counterfeit Goods on the Internet. *European Politics and Society* 19(3): 338–354.

Feenberg, A. (1991) *Critical Theory of Technology*. Oxford: Oxford University Press.

Feenberg, A. (2017) Critical Theory of Technology and STS. *Thesis Eleven* 138(1): 3–12.

Hansen, L. and Nissenbaum, H. (2009) Digital Disaster, Cyber Security, and the Copenhagen School. *International Studies Quarterly* 53(4): 1155–1175.

Hern, A. and Pegg, D. (2018) Facebook Fined for Data Breaches in Cambridge Analytica Scandal. *The Guardian*, 11 July. At: www.theguardian.com/technology/2018/jul/11/facebook-fined-for-data-breaches-in-cambridge-analytica-scandal.

Horten, M. (2016) *The Closing of the Net*. Cambridge: Polity.

Huysmans, J. (2014) *Security Unbound: Enacting Democratic Limits*. London: Routledge.

Hynek, N. and Chandler, D. (2013) No Emancipation Alternative, No Critical Security Studies. *Critical Studies on Security* 1(1): 46–63.

Kello, L. (2017) *The Virtual Weapon and International Order*. New Haven, CT: Yale University Press.

Moret, E. and Pawlak, P. (2017) "The EU Cyber Diplomacy Toolbox: Towards a Cyber Sanctions Regime?". Brief Issue 24, 27 July. At: www.iss.europa.eu/content/eu-cyber-diplomacy-toolbox-towards-cyber-sanctions-regime.

NATO (2016) *Cyber Defence Pledge*. Press Release (2016) 124.

Nissenbaum, H. (2005) Where Computer Security Meets National Security. *Ethics and Information Technology* 7(2): 61–73.

Peoples, C. (2010) *Justifying Ballistic Missile Defence: Technology, Security and Culture*. Cambridge: Cambridge University Press.

Power, M. (2007) Digitized Virtuosity: Video War Games and Post-9/11 Cyber-Deterrence. *Security Dialogue* 38(2): 271–288.

Privacy International (2017) *Cyber Security in the Global South: Giving the Tin Man a Heart*. May 2017. At: https://privacyinternational.org/sites/default/files/CyberSecurity_2017.pdf.

Renard, T. (2018) EU Cyber Partnerships: Assessing the EU Strategic Partnerships with Third Countries in the Cyber Domain. *European Politics and Society* 19(3): 321–337.

Saco, D. (1999) Colonizing Cyberspace: 'National Security' and the Internet. In Jutta Weldes, Mark Laffey, Hugh Gusterson and Raymond Duvall (eds), *Cultures of Insecurity: States, Communities, and the Production of Danger*. Minneapolis, MN: University of Minnesota Press.

Segal, A. (2016) *The Hacked World Order*. New York: Public Affairs.

Singer, P.W. and Friedman, A. (2014) *Cybersecurity and Cyberwar: What Everyone Needs to Know*. Oxford: Oxford University Press.

Sliwinski, K.F. (2014) Moving Beyond the European Union's Weakness as a Cyber-Security Agent. *Contemporary Security Policy* 35(3): 468–486.

Stupp, C. (2018) French Cybersecurity Chief Warns Against 'Step Back into the Past'. Euractiv.com. At: www.euractiv.com/section/cybersecurity/news/french-cybersecurity-chief-warns-against-step-back-into-the-past/ (accessed 11 May 2018).

UN Secretary-General (2019) UN Secretary-General's High-Level Panel on Digital Cooperation: The Age of Digital Interdependence, June. At: https://digitalcooperation.org/wp-content/uploads/2019/06/DigitalCooperation-report-web-FINAL-1.pdf.

Verbeek, P. (2013) Resistance is Futile: Toward a Non-Modern Democratization of Technology. *Techné: Research in Philosophie and Technology* 17(1): 72–92.

Walker, D. (2019) UK Firms May Soon Find it Impossible to Legally Receive Data from the EU. *ITPro*, 18 July. At: www.itpro.co.uk/general-data-protection-regulation-gdpr/33991/uk-firms-may-soon-find-it-impossible-to-legally.

Williams, M.C. and Krause, K. (1997) Preface: Toward Critical Security Studies. In M.C. Williams and K. Krause (eds), *Critical Security Studies: Concepts and Cases*. London: Routledge, vii–xxi.

Zajko, M. (2015) Canada's Cyber Security and the Changing Threat Landscape. *Critical Studies on Security* 3(2): 147–161. DOI: 10.1080/21624887.2015.1071165.

7 EU cyber defence governance

Facing the fragmentation challenge

Delphine Deschaux-Dutard

Introduction

Cyberspace has recently become the fifth battlefield (O'Connell 2012). As an international organisation, the European Union (EU) has become increasingly concerned with cybersecurity in the last decade. This topic is especially stimulating as the academic literature remains quite sparse (Dunn Cavelty 2013a, 2013b; Sliwinski 2014; Christou 2016; Barrinha and Carrapiço 2016, 2017, 2018). As Barrinha and Carrapiço (2018) underline, European cybersecurity constitutes an emerging field both for academic researchers and practitioners. In recent years, the EU has been summoned to be able to act as a security provider, which also entails the military aspects of the cyberspace. In this regard, cybersecurity encompasses the topic of this chapter, which lays emphasis on cyber defence. While cybersecurity designates both 'the insecurity created by and through [cyberspace] and [...] the practices or processes to make it more secure' (Dunn Cavelty 2013a: 363), cyber defence can be defined as the set of norms, organs, tools and procedures aimed at protecting critical infrastructures and networks dedicated to the military defence of a given country or group of countries from cyberattacks harming the national security of a country or collective security.[1] The paradox of cyberspace is that contrary to air, land or sea, in defence-related issues, it relies not only on the military but mostly on the civilian and private spheres. The specificity of cyberspace is its transnational nature relying on multiple stakeholders.

Faced with recurring cyberattacks and cyber threats against military infrastructure (emanating from Russia but not only, see Barrinha 2018), the EU started developing a discourse around cybersecurity and cyber defence (Christou 2016 and 2019; Barrinha and Carrapiço 2017). Yet, what is striking is that EU cyber defence is much less academically investigated than cybersecurity, even though the EU started developing a cyber defence architecture half a decade ago. Hence, this chapter focuses on EU cyber defence normative and institutional architecture to understand the governance of cyber defence at the European level as well as the challenges and limits it faces. This chapter aims at illustrating the global aim of this edited book seeking to open the black box of the politics governing new technologies in the EU. How does EU cyber defence emerge and work as a specific field? What are the characteristics and challenges of the governance of EU cyber defence? We rely on the concept of governance as defined in the Introduction of this book, which means as a tool enabling the exploration of how and by whom emerging security technologies are governed. Theoretically, the chapter borrows from the concept of strategic culture to explore these questions. Strategic culture designates a 'set of general beliefs, attitudes, and behaviour patterns' (Snyder 1977) affecting defence policy.[2] Norms, values, patterns of behaviour as well as historical experience shape the culture which the state (and at a regional level, the EU) tend to deploy in terms of military and strategic matters. We agree with Meyer's definition of strategic culture as 'a causal factor of relatively high permanence, which has practical implications for explaining decisions' about military matters (2013: 51). The concept of strategic culture is not predictive but helps us to understand why EU member states do not all share the same ideas about cyber defence, as the third part of the chapter demonstrates.

Thus, to show what impact strategic culture has on EU cyber defence initiatives, the chapter proceeds as follows. The first part analyses EU cyber defence normative architecture to show its still marginal position. The second part focuses on the governance of EU cyber defence by analysing its actors and tools. The final part uncovers the challenges of the EU cyber defence normative and institutional architecture by relying on the concept of strategic culture to explore the limits of the EU as an efficient cyber defence actor in the short term.

An emerging normative cyber defence architecture in Brussels

This part aims at understanding how the EU cyber defence is integrated into a global European normative framework.

A European framing of cybersecurity mostly based on economic and civilian aspects

The EU has shown a growing interest for cybersecurity matters since the late 1990s, seeing cyber technologies as a key sector as mentioned in this book's introduction. A first set of EU directives was issued by the European Commission between 1999 and 2002 with one main objective: protecting the EU citizens' fundamental rights and freedom, while securing economic and trade activities relying in the use of Internet. The economic logic underpinning these documents did not include the military dimension of cyber. Even in the European Security Strategy (Solana 2003), there is no mention of cyber threats. After the cyberattacks in Georgia in 2008, the EU included energy and transport as an important matter of cybersecurity. The EU also strongly focuses on the fight against cyber criminality with the involvement of the Commission, the Council and Europol (which developed a team dedicated to fighting cyber criminality: EC3; Christou 2016: 87–118).

The adoption of EU's Cybersecurity Strategy (EUCSS) released jointly by the Commission and the High Representative in February 2013 has become the nucleus of EU's cybersecurity normative architecture (European Commission/ HRVP 2013). The EU Cybersecurity Strategy emphasises cyber resilience by protecting critical information systems and fostering cooperation between the public and private sector, as well as civilian and defence authorities. Yet, the EUCSS does not provide a clear and common European definition of cyber-security (Sliwinski 2014). The document proposes a holistic approach necessi-tating cooperation among many public and private stakeholders, as in many other dual-technologic issues studied in this volume.[3] This cyberstrategy, updated in September 2017, comes together with the European Network and Information Security (NIS) directive adopted in 2016 and enforced in 2018, which is the first EU-wide legislation on cybersecurity and aims at creating common standards of cybersecurity within the member states. The driving concept under the strategy is resilience, which does not aim at the removal of the threat but rather at the capacity of the system to quickly recover in case of a cyberattack (Dunn Cavelty 2013a, 2013b). The last document adopted in May 2019 is the EU Cybersecurity Act, which mainly expands the mandate and resources of ENISA, the EU Agency for Cybersecurity located in Heraklion, and aims at producing a European certification framework. This rapid overview of EU cyber norms shows that defence has not been the priority in the framing of EU cybersecurity. However, in the last five years, the EU has started to look at the external dimension of cybersecurity, encompassing cyber defence. New technologies (drones, AI, big data, etc.) and their impact on warfare have prompted the need for a European reflexion on cyber defence, embedded in the quest for European strategic autonomy globally.

Cyber defence as a side issue in EU's framing of cybersecurity

The external dimension of cybersecurity encompasses both cyber diplomacy and cyber defence. In this regard, the EU launched a Framework for a Joint EU Diplomatic Response to Malicious Cyber Activities, also called the Cyber Diplomatic Toolbox, adopted by the Council in June 2017, looking at the best collective answer at the EU level regarding cyberattacks and creating a toolbox from sanctions until the ultimate level: the possibility to invoke the mutual defence clause (Article 42 §7) or the mutual assistance clause (Article 222 TFEU) in case of crossing of the threshold for a cyber conflict (or a cyberattack with lethal or conventional consequences; Moret and Pawlak 2017). Moreover, on 14 May 2019, the European Council agreed on the capa-bility to impose European sanctions to deter and respond to cyberattacks (Council Decision 7299/19). This shows a European will to exist as a diplo-matic actor in cyberspace, even though imposing sanctions raises the difficult issue of the attribution of cyberattacks to a state or a state-sponsored attacker (Bendiek 2018).

Cyber defence is the military side of EU's interest for the external dimension of cybersecurity. Even if cyber defence is not the main priority of the EU, the EUCSS remains the first norm introducing cyber defence at the European level. First, in this document, the EU recognises for the first time that it is now entitled to deal with cyber defence, which was not included in EU's defence activities (namely, in the Common Security and Defence Policy [CSDP]) before. Second, the cybersecurity strategy appeals to the solidarity clause (Article 222 for the Treaty on the Functioning of the European Union) as follows: 'A particularly serious cyber incident or attack could constitute sufficient ground for a member state to invoke the EU Solidarity Clause' (EEAS 2013: 19). This explains why cyber defence has been enriched with specific norms. The 2013 EU Cybersecurity Strategy underlines four main issues to be developed in cyber defence: the development of cyber defence capabilities with EU member states; the development of an EU Cyber Defence Policy framework; the promotion of the civil–military dialogue; and the dialogue with international partners like NATO. The need for a specific cyber defence document had already been expressed in the final report of the High Representative in October 2013 (eight months after the release of EU Cybersecurity Strategy). In November 2014, the Council issued an EU Cyber defence framework focusing on capability development, training, education and exercises (Council of the European Union 2018).

Since then, European cyber defence has been extended by several strategic documents. The EU Global Security Strategy published in June 2016 considers 'cyber' as one of the key components of EU's security and defence (see Barrinha and Renard 2018: 182). In September 2017, the European Commission and the High Representative issued a joint communication known as the '2017 Cybersecurity Package' emphasising the need for an EU cyber defence to better face hybrid threats (Pupillo *et al.* 2018). The European Commission and the European External Action Service (EEAS) also updated the EUCSS in September 2017 with a Joint Communication ('Resilience, Deterrence and Defence: Building Strong Cybersecurity for the EU'). Moreover, the European Parliament adopted a motion on Cyber defence in May 2018 stating: 'while cyber defence remains a core competence for member states, the EU has a vital role to play in providing a platform for European cooperation' (cited in Pupillo *et al.* 2018: 36). In June 2018, the European Commission, the European Parliament and the Council issued a joint communication titled 'Increasing Resilience and Bolstering Capabilities to Address Hybrid Threats' also putting emphasis on the need for cyber defence coordination at the European level.

To sum up, EU cyber defence norms take roots in a dense cybersecurity framework mostly based on civilian and economic principles at the European level. The main EU institutions (the Council, the Commission and the Parliament) have framed cybersecurity and cyber defence as a shared area of responsibility.[4] In reality, the securitisation process of cyber at the European level remains highly differentiated (Christou 2019), with cyber defence governance torn between the EU level and the national level as we analyse it in the next section. The EU's emerging cyber defence strategic architecture does not yet entail a consistent European cyberstrategic culture.[5]

The governance of EU cyber defence: an unstable balance between the national and European levels

This section explores the governance of EU cyber defence to show that as in many other dual-use technological issues, when it comes to the military dimensions of these technologies, the European level has to count with European governments maintaining a primary role, as stated in this volume's introduction. As EU cybersecurity architecture has already been well documented (Christou 2016; Barrinha and Carrapiço 2016, 2017), we only focus on the EU cyber defence governance. As cyber defence reports to EU's external action, the institutional structures involved are the ones working in the framework of CSDP, characterised by a governance torn between intergovernmentalism (the ruling principle of CSDP), and Europeanisation, represented by the nature of these structures incarnating the European interest within CSDP's institutional framework.

EU's actors operating European cyber defence torn between intergovernmentalism and Europeanisation

The architecture of EU cyber defence primarily relies on actors at the European level and at the member states level. At the European level, three main institutional actors and three tools can be identified. Regarding the institutions, the main actors dealing with cyber defence in Brussels are the European Defence Agency (EDA) and the EU Military Staff (EUMS) within the EEAS. Interestingly, these actors are included in European defence institutional framework (CSDP) but are not intergovernmental. Both the EDA and the EUMS are composed of detached national agents, which means these agents do not represent their own member states contrary to the agents working in the Political and Security Committee (PSC) or the EU Military Committee (EUMC).

The EDA is an important agency concerning EU cyber defence initiatives. The EDA's global role in CSDP is to support the member states in different areas of military capability development including cyber defence. It is also an actor participating in the creation of a military discourse at EU level (Barrinha 2015). Cyber defence has clearly become a priority of the EDA's capability development plan since 2010 and has been reaffirmed by the European Council of December 2013 as one of four key capabilities for EDA activity. The agency therefore set up a unique cross-national expert project team (coming from national MoDs and from the civilian sphere) in 2011 to promote the development of cyber defence capabilities both at the EU and national levels. As the success of military operations is increasingly dependent upon the access to cyberspace and the armed forces are reliant on cyberspace both as a user and as a battlefield, the EDA is active in the fields of cyber defence capabilities as well as in research and technology.[6] The EDA's action in cyber defence is more precisely developed within the Capability, Armament & Technology Directorate directed by Martin Konertz, working in close dialogue with the defence authorities of EU member states. Concretely, the EDA organises training and exercises and delivers cybersecurity and cyber defence courses for operational actors as well as decision makers, with the objective of creating a collaborative platform to exchange best practices and common standards.[7] Moreover, the EDA works at developing cyber defence situational awareness for CSDP operations with the objective of integrating cyber defence in the European military planning process. This issue is very accurate as, contrary to NATO, the EU does not possess its own planning assets and cyber threats raise the question of the protection of national critical infrastructures used in CSDP structures, missions and operations (Robinson 2014).[8] In this regard, the EDA works together with the EU Military Staff. The EDA also set up a Cyber Defence Research Agenda (CDRA) considered as a research and technology roadmap for the coming decade and appealing to coordination with other EU stakeholders, such as the Commission and the ENISA.

The other main EU institutional actor in cyber defence is the EUMS, located within the EEAS. Since the launch of EU's Cybersecurity Strategy, the EEAS has been actively involved in mainstream cyber issues related to the Common Foreign and Security Policy (CFSP): cyber dialogues have been established with key strategic partners, namely, the USA, Japan, South Korea, India and China. The EEAS works closely with the member states and the Commission so as to promote a coordinated EU cyber diplomacy in international relations, characterised by regular cyber consultations between the EU and other international organisations and also with third countries.[9] More precisely, the kingpin for cyber defence inside the EEAS is the EU Military Staff, which is the source of military expertise in the EU. Inside the EUMS, two directorates deal with cyber defence: the Concepts and Capabilities (CON/CAP) as well as the Communications and Information Systems (CIS). The former is responsible for developing concepts and doctrine in cooperation with the EDA, including cyber doctrinal aspects. For instance, the EUMS developed a European Concept for Cyber Defence for Military Operations and Missions in November 2016 (Rehrl 2018: 36). The latter provides communications and information systems planning expertise at both strategic and operational levels, including cyber-related issues. Last but not least, since 2018, the European Security and Defence College has been tasked with cyber defence education, training, evaluation and exercise to civilian as well as military staff.

However, member states remain the key players for the development of cyber defence capabilities, as with most other dual-use technologies. The motion on cyber defence adopted by the European Parliament in May 2018 is very clear on this: cyber defence remains a core competence for member states. As CSDP is an intergovernmental policy, this represents a strong limit to EU's potential as a cyber defence actor and to developing a consistent cyber strategic culture. At the member states level, the main actors are the national cyber commands when they exist, as in the cases of France or Germany, for instance. Should the EU experience a cyberattack with lethal consequences, the main principle to decide on what the response to oppose to such an attack (sanctions, hack back, etc.) should be, would rely on the intergovernmental principle of unanimity in the Council, as cyber defence remains a sovereign competence of the member states, where the EU can mainly act as a facilitator.

A governance completed by tools dedicated to cyber defence at the European level

Not only does EU cyber defence governance rely on the institutional actors presented above, but also on three specific tools included in the EU Treaties (TEU and TFEU). The first one is the solidarity and self-defence clause (Article 42 §7 TEU), which provides an institutional tool to address cyber incidents. Even though the clause does not state cyber defence as such, if the consequences of a large-scale cyberattack could legally qualify as an 'armed aggression', the clause could be invoked by the victim member state, as it has been by France after the terror attacks in November 2015. In such case, the EU member states should help the victim. But the use of this clause would raise the difficult question of the attribution of the cyberattack, in the same way as Article V of the NATO's treaty does. Such an attribution to a specific state or state-sponsored hacker would necessitate a consensus among the member states within the European Council, which would make it difficult as it tackles diplomatic strings and strategic priorities which keep diverging among the EU member states, as will be shown in our final part.

Thus, a second possibility would prove more effective in case of an unattributed cyberattack: the solidarity clause included in Article 222 of the TFEU. The 2017 Cybersecurity Package emphasises this clause as a well-suited institutional tool in case of a cyberattack not qualifying as an armed aggression. In such a case, this would qualify the cyberattack as a disaster and EU institutions and the member states would then have to respond with solidarity, relying on Article 222.

The last tool included in EU cyber defence architecture is the Permanent Structured Cooperation (PESCO), as four projects among the 43 projects developed in this framework explicitly deal with cyber defence. PESCO was officially launched by the European Council in December 2017 and 25 member states participate voluntarily in one or several projects. PESCO relies on the principle of unanimity among the participating member states. The projects including cyber defence aspects mainly concern training and coordination and bring together leading countries and observatory countries. For instance, a Lithuania-lead project titled 'Cyber Rapid Response Teams and Mutual Assistance in Cybersecurity' (CRRT) proposes to work on coordination in the area of cyber defence by developing penetration testing, joint capabilities and mutual operational support through Cyber Rapid Response Teams. This appeals to the case of EU battle groups for military conventional rapid response, as we show below.

This overview of EU cyber defence governance shows that EU cyber defence response is under construction and encounters the challenge of overlapping skills between CSDP cyber-related issues and global EU cybersecurity addressed by different agencies. Therefore, the EU as a cyber actor remains far from being coherent (Barrinha and Carrapiço 2017). EU cyber defence requires cooperation between the multiple stakeholders, which is not accomplished yet. Building a global EU cyber strategic culture not only requires a good level of inter-institutional cooperation (Christou 2016) but also a common understanding of cyber priorities in the military domain. The concept of strategic culture helps us understand the challenges and limits experienced by the EU in the construction of its cyber defence governance.

The fragmentation challenge of EU cyber defence: a puzzle between the EU, the member states and NATO's competing sets of priorities

EU cyber defence is embedded in a global environment, which encompasses the member states cyber defence architectures, as cyber defence mostly relies on states' sovereignty. The concept of strategic culture helps to grasp the difficulty of creating a European cyber defence governance in a context where many member states already have structured norms and preferences about cyber defence that differ from the EU level of ambition. As each national strategic culture is rooted in the countries' historical and political path, this constitutes a solid frame by which national decision makers establish their preferences and priorities in defence policy. Assuming that strategic cultures play an important role in framing the governance of cyber defence fulfils the argument that dual-use technologies are not neutral, as stated in this book's introduction, but relate to power as their governance and framing is based on a social construction rooted in each actors' culture. This helps to explain the conflicting forces at work. Therefore, after underlining the limits of EU cyber defence governance at the EU level, this part will focus on the challenges to the development of a European cyber defence self-standing culture in a strategic environment shaped by the member states and NATO's framing of cyber defence.[10]

The limits of the EU cyber defence governance

At the EU level, cybersecurity is still quite fragmented between its different components (cybersecurity, cybercriminality, cyber defence) (Barrinha and Carrapiço 2017). If the Commission plays a crucial role as a policy entrepreneur in cybersecurity, cyber defence remains in the intergovernmental area of the Council. Cyber defence reflects well the dilemma of European strategic autonomy, which it is supposed to fuel: the ambition may be wide, but the concrete realizations are always limited by the member states' concerns for their own strategic priorities.

The first striking element is that contrary to many states who frame cybersecurity primarily as a military threat giving a major role to the military institution in managing cybersecurity at the national level (like the US Cyber command set up in 2010 or the French or German cyber commands created since 2016–2017; O'Connell 2012), the EU has framed cybersecurity primarily as an economic and democratic challenge. This explains why cyber defence at the European level is still in its infancy and mainly focuses on prevention and resilience rather than on offensive capabilities as some member states do (Bendiek 2018). Therefore, in case of a massive cyberattack with lethal or conventional consequences, the burden of response would de facto fall on the member states and would be dependent on the unanimity principle.

A good example of this challenge is provided by PESCO. Even though it offers a way of building up EU cyber defence capabilities by committing the most willing states and having them work together within a constraining framework, the function of PESCO also limits the scope of such initiatives. The PESCO projects related to cyber defence aim at increasing the EU and member states' resilience to cyber threats by pooling resources and developing more coordination between the different actors (including private actors). But these projects are not EU-wide and are ruled by unanimity: all the states involved in the projects have to agree on the deployment of a Cyber Rapid Response Teams and Mutual Assistance in Cybersecurity (CRRT) on their networks, for instance. The same kind of dilemma as the one raised by EU's battle groups could lead to the project's inefficiency in reality.[11]

Another limitation to the EU's cyber defence governance is the scarcity of resources compared to the national resources dedicated by member states. The EEAS and the EDA combined currently disposed of a dozen staff working on cyber defence, whereas the French cyber command set up in 2017 aims at recruiting 4,000 staff over the next two years and NATO has disposed of several dozen staff. As Pupillo *et al.* underline, 'the resources allocated by the EU are neither commensurate [...] nor adequate' for EU cyber defence to be effective (2018: 44). These limits also come from the fact that the EU, unlike NATO, is not a military alliance but an organisation based on a wide political project of integration. Thus, the EU frames cyber issues as a way of exerting a soft power and promoting its core values in cyberspace (Bendiek 2018; Dunn Cavelty 2018). This is, of course, quite different from the member states and NATO's perspectives. Therefore, the EU mainly plays the role of a facilitator in cyber defence rather than the role of an actor per se. The member states remain responsible for the operational and strategic levels of cyber defence.

Diverging member states' priorities: a constraining environment for EU cyber defence

What is true about EU cooperation challenges in CSDP in general is also true when it comes to cyber defence. We share the idea developed by Biehl, Giegerich and Jonas that 'national strategic cultures are among the key factors that can explain why [...] progress on closer cooperation in security and defence remains slow and cumbersome' (2013: 7–8). The lack of consensus between EU member states about European defence in general reflects the range of different national strategic cultures, divergent military doctrines and strategic priorities within the EU and explains how difficult the achievement of European strategic autonomy, though claimed for few years, will remain. Cyber defence makes no exception. Many EU countries have started to include cyber into their defence strategies, even if disparity is high among the countries. Schematically, EU member states can be divided into three groups concerning cybersecurity and cyber defence (Christou 2016). The first group is composed of member states who invest in cyber defence and develop a cyber defence policy at the national level in order to dispose of the whole range of tools to face the cyber threats (France, UK, Germany, mainly). These states are also the ones that have been historically the most proactive in developing CSDP and EU military operations. To take the case of French cyber defence, the French government started to invest in cyber defence in 2010. The French government decided to invest over €1 billion and recruit about 4,000 persons for the development of French cyber defence in the coming years and a second cyber command was even launched in October 2019. The key document concerning the strategic culture shaping French cyber defence is the White Book on Defence and National Security of 2013. The White Book not only designates the cyberspace as falling within the state's sovereignty but even identifies 'offensive computer struggle' as a 'necessity'.[12] The underlying principle is proportionate response in case of cyberattack. This example clearly shows that French cyber defence policy relies on French strategic culture rooted in France's values of independence, autonomy and sovereignty in strategic matters and diverges from the EU's cyber defence framework mostly based on coordination and prevention.

The German cyber defence policy as well shows important financial investment in cyber but mainly relies on civilian means completed by measures taken by the *Bundeswehr* as a military cyber command was set up in 2018 in Bonn. German cyber strategy is more oriented towards defensive measures, whereas France also aims at developing offensive cyber capacities. A second group is composed of member states like Sweden, Finland and the Baltic states, who started to develop cyber responses but rely on NATO cyber defence assets. A third group consists mostly of the other EU member states that have not, until now, manifested a strong awareness about cyber defence. This shows how differentiated the involvement and investment of EU member states in cyber defence remains, as it relies upon different representations about cyber defence shaped by their own strategic cultures. Moreover, there is no consensus among the member states about an increased role for the EU in cyber defence.[13]

EU, NATO and cyber defence: complementary or contestant?

Another element constraining EU cyber defence governance is the existence of a consistent NATO cyber defence policy. EU cyber defence is driven by an important concern: to avoid as much as possible duplication with NATO cyber defence assets.[14] NATO and the EU have different normative perspectives regarding cyber defence. NATO frames cyber threats as a direct challenge for transatlantic and national security, as stated in the 2010 Strategic Concept, whereas the EU primarily focuses on the economic and social implications of cyber threats and on the diplomatic aspects of its external dimension more than on the military aspects (cyber defence). NATO may be the most advanced international organisation regarding cyber defence. NATO approved its first Policy on Cyber Defence in 2008 (revised in 2011 and 2014) and established a Cyber Defence Management Authority (CDMA) in 2008 and even a Cyberspace Operations Centre within NATO Command Structure in 2018 (Lété 2019). The Strategic Concept adopted in November 2010 fully acknowledges cyber defence capabilities as a necessity for the Alliance (NATO 2010). NATO also created tools to prevent cyberattacks and cyber offensive capabilities with a central objective: to defend the Alliance's own communications and information systems and to arouse its member states' awareness on the need to protect critical infrastructures implied in contemporary military operations. At the NATO Summit in Wales, in September 2014, the organisation recognised cyber defence as part of the Alliance's core task of collective defence and therefore included cyber threats as relevant Article V material.

If for both organisations cyber defence primarily lies in the hands of national authorities, NATO has taken an evident lead on this issue and the EU has to find a way of competing with NATO without decoupling it in cyber defence (Lété 2019). The EU does not aim to provide direct assistance to its member states in case of cyberattack but to act as a facilitator to help them share best practices, whereas NATO does. There is also a difference between NATO owning its information and the computer networks used in military operations and the EU depending on the member states' ICT infrastructures for CSDP missions. NATO started developing its own cyber defence culture, whereas the EU keeps looking for coherence and does not rely on a specific European cyber defence culture, therefore undermining EU's quest for strategic autonomy.

However, the EU and NATO have enhanced their cooperation in cyber defence since their joint declaration at the Alliance summit in Warsaw in 2016 (NATO 2016). They regularly organise common training and exercises and develop information sharing in order to raise mutual trust (Lété 2019). Cooperation is even more needed in a context of limited financial resources: some experts suggest using the Berlin Plus agreements in cyber defence (Robinson 2014). The EU and NATO have also concluded a technical agreement between their response teams for cyber incidents (NCIRC and CERT-EU) in February 2016 to intensify their cooperation on cyber defence. It has been used to commonly discuss cyber threats in the context of the 2019 European elections. Yet, the EU remains way behind NATO regarding cyber defence, even though strategic autonomy has become a leitmotiv as in European defence generally since the 2016 EU Global Security Strategy.

Conclusion

As part of its global effort on cybersecurity, the EU has started to invest normative and institutional efforts in cyber defence during the last decade. However, EU cyber defence remains beyond the scope of European ambition of strategic autonomy as its governance remains fragmented and its norms not really constraining. The member states keep framing cyber defence through their own strategic culture first, as it is a sovereign issue. This shows more generally that when it comes to strategic aspects of dual-use technologies, be it drones, cyber or AI, states remain the pivotal actor in their governance and can define the European level of governance to avoid risks for their sovereignty. This, therefore, limits the potentiality of a European strategic autonomy not only in cyberspace but also in international security in general. Thus, the EU develops initiatives in cyber defence, which remain to be fuelled with more substance. The EU has a cyber defence strategy still lacking in consistency and has designed a governance torn between the member states and European institutions. This can be explained by the weight of national strategic cultures framing cyber defence at the member states level and the still disputed existence of an emerging European strategic culture. Yet, EU cyber defence could be seen as a possibility for building a kind of cyber smart power at the European level, which would mean a kind of power that relates not only to persuasion and norm diffusion but also to a capacity for the use coercion if needed in cyberspace.

Notes

1 This definition is inspired by Ventre (2011: 102).
2 We will not discuss the debate surrounding the existence or lack of a common EU strategic culture which is much documented. See, for instance, Howorth (2002), Rynning (2003), Giegerich (2006), Norheim-Martinsen (2010, 2011), Biehl, Giegerich, Jonas (2013), Meyer (2013), Biava, Drent and Herd (2011) and Chappell and Petrov (2014).
3 The governance of cybersecurity varies depending on the concerned area, Network and Information Systems having a different governance than cyber defence, for instance; for a general perspective on EU's cybersecurity governance, see Christou (2016).
4 October is traditionally the European cybersecurity month and 2019 edition's motto was: 'Cybersecurity is a shared responsibility'.
5 We won't enter here into the debate surrounding EU's strategic culture, as it has been well documented in recent years: see, for instance, Howorth (2002), Rynning (2003), Meyer (2013), Giegerich (2006), Norheim-Martinsen (2010, 2011), Biava, Drent and Herd (2011) and Chappell and Petrov (2014).
6 See EDA Cyber Defence Activities, at: http://eda.europa.eu/what-we-do/activities/activities-search/cyber-defence (accessed 27 October 2019).
7 For instance, a pilot Decision-Making Exercise on Cyberspace Crisis Management took place in Lisbon in May 2014. The pilot exercise aimed at preparing strategic leaders for situations involving a major cyberattack.
8 However, a Military Planning and Conduct Capability has been established in Brussels in June 2017 but does not deal with cyber defence. This permanent operation headquarters is currently dedicated to non-executive military missions.
9 We come back to EU–NATO specific cooperation in the last section of this chapter.

10 As 22 EU states are also NATO members, it certainly plays an important role in the way that the EU is trying to define its own path in cyber defence.
11 EU battle groups have not yet been used, due to this unanimity principle.
12 Livre blanc sur la défense et la sécurité nationale (2013), 96. At: www.defense.gouv. fr/actualites/memoire-et-culture/livre-blanc-2013 (accessed 6 October 2019).
13 The lack of consensus also exists within NATO in this regard (see Joubert and Samaan 2014).
14 And yet, some experts estimate that 'finally, both NATO and the EU are pursuing similar activities in this area (albeit under different assumptions and limitations' (Robinson *et al.* 2013: 6).

References

Barrinha, A. (2015), The EDA and the Discursive Construction of European Defence and Security. In K. Nikolaos and O. Iraklis (eds), *The European Defence Agency: Arming Europe*. London: Routledge, 27–42.

Barrinha, A. (2018) Virtual Neighbors: Russia and the EU in Cyberspace. *Insight Turkey* 20(3): 29–42.

Barrinha, A. and Carrapiço, H. (2016) *The EU's Security Actorness in Cyber Space: Quo Vadis?* In L. Chappell, J. Mawdsley and P. Petrov (eds), *The EU, Strategy and Security Policy: Regional and Strategic Challenges*. London: Routledge.

Barrinha, A. and Carrapiço, H. (2017) The EU as a Coherent (Cyber) Security Actor? *JCMS: Journal of Common Market Studies* 55(6): 1254–1272. https://doi.org/10.1111/ jcms.12575.

Barrinha, A. and Carrapiço, H. (2018) European Union Cyber Security as an Emerging Research and Policy Field. *European Politics and Society* 19(3): 299–303. https://doi. org/10.1080/23745118.2018.1430712.

Barrinha, A. and Renard, T. (2018) The EU as a Partner in Cyber Diplomacy and Defence. In Jochen Rehrl (ed.), *Handbook on Cybersecurity: The Common Security and Defence Policy of the European Union – Volume V*. Vienna: EU Publications, 180–189.

Bendiek, A. (2018) The EU as a Force for Peace in International Cyber Diplomacy. *SWP Comments*, No. 19. April. Berlin: Stiftung Wissenschaft und Politik.

Biava, A., Drent, M. and Herd, G. (2011) Characterizing the European Union's Strategic Culture: An Analytical Framework. *Journal of Common Market Studies* 1–22. https:// doi.org/10.1111/j.1468-5965.2011.02195.x.

Biehl, H., Giegerich, B. and Jonas, A. (eds) (2013) *Strategic Cultures in Europe: Security and Defence Policies across the Continent*. Munich: VS Verlag.

Chappell, L. and Petrov, P. (2014) The European Union's Crisis Management Operations: Strategic Culture in Action? *European Integration online Papers* (EIoP), 18, Article 2, 1–24. http://eiop.or.at/eiop/texte/2014002a.htm.

Christou, G. (2016) *Cybersecurity in the European Union: Resilience and Adaptability in Governance Policy*. London: Palgrave.

Christou, G. (2019) The Collective Securitisation of Cyberspace in the European Union. *West European Politics* 42(2): 278–301. https://doi.org/10.1080/01402382.2018.1510195.

Council of the European Union (2018) EU Cyber Defence Policy Framework. http://data. consilium.europa.eu/doc/document/ST-14413-2018-INIT/en/pdf.

Dunn Cavelty, M. (2013a) Cyber-Security. In A. Collins (ed.), *Contemporary Security Studies*, 3rd edn. Oxford: Oxford University Press, 362–378.

Dunn Cavelty, M. (2013b) A Resilient Europe for an Open, Safe and Secure Cyberspace. UI Occasional Paper no. 23, Swedish Institute of International Affairs.

Dunn Cavelty, M. (2018) Europe's Cyber-Power. *European Politics and Society* 19(3): 304–320. https://doi.org/10.1080/23745118.2018.1430718.

EEAS (2013) Cyber Security Strategy – Open, Safe and Secure. European Union External Action Service (EEAS). At: http://eeas.europa.eu/top_stories/2013/070213_cybersecurity_ en.htm.

European Commission/HRVP (2013) Joint Communication Cybersecurity Strategy of the EU: An Open, Safe and Secure Cyberspace, JOIN(2013) 1 final, Brussels, 2 July.

European Parliament (2014) EU Cyber Defence Policy Framework, Brussels, 18 November, 14 pages. At: www.europarl.europa.eu/meetdocs/2014_2019/documents/sede/dv/sede160315eucyberdefencepolicyframework_/sede160315eucyberdefencepolicyframe work_en.pdf.

Giegerich, B. (2006) *European Security and Strategic Culture: National Responses to EU's Security and Defence Policy*. Baden-Baden: Nomos.

Howorth, J. (2002) The CESDP and the Forging of a European Security Culture. *Politique européenne* 4(8): 88–109.

Joubert, V. and Samaan, J.-L. (2014) L'intergouvernementalité dans le cyberespace: étude comparée des initiatives de l'Otan et de l'UE. *Hérodote* 152–153: 261–275. https://doi.org/10.3917/her.152.0261

Lété, B. (2019) Cooperation in Cyberspace. In G. Lindstrom and T. Tardy (eds), *The EU and NATO: The Essential Partners*, 28–36. European Union Institute for Security Studies (EUISS).

Meyer, C. (2013) European Strategic Culture: Tacking Stock and Looking Ahead. In S. Biscop and R. Whitman (eds), *The Routledge Handbook of European Security*. London: Routledge, 50–59.

Moret, E. and Pawlak, P. (2017) The EU Cyber Diplomacy Toolbox: Towards a Cyber Sanctions Regime? EUISS, Brief 24, July. European Union Institute for Security Studies. At: www.iss.europa.eu/sites/default/files/EUISSFiles/Brief%2024%20Cyber%20 sanctions.pdf.

NATO (2010) Strategic Concept for the Defence and Security of the Members of the North Atlantic Treaty Organization, 19–20 November. At: www.nato.int/nato_static_fl2014/assets/pdf/pdf_publications/20120214_strategic-concept-2010-eng.pdf (accessed 3 October 2019).

NATO (2016) Joint Declaration, North Atlantic Treaty Organization, Press Release, 8 July. At: www.nato.int/cps/en/natohq/official_texts_133163.htm (accessed 25 March 2019).

Norheim-Martinsen, P. (2010) EU Strategic Culture: When the Means Becomes the End. *Contemporary Security Policy* 32(3): 517–534. https://doi.org/10.1080/13523260.2011. 623055.

Norheim-Martinsen, P. (2011) Convergence Towards a European Strategic Culture? A Constructivist Framework for Explaining Changing Norms. *European Journal of International Relations* 11: 523–554. https://doi.org/10.1177/1354066105057899.

O'Connell, M.E. (2012) Cybersecurity Without Cyber War. *Journal of Conflict and Security Law* 17(2): 187–209. https://doi.org/10.1093/jcsl/krs017.

Pupillo, L., Griffith, M., Blockmans, S. and Renda, A. (2018) Strengthening the EU's Cyber Defence Capabilities. CEPS Task Force Report. Brussels: Centre for European Policy Studies. At: www.ceps.eu/ceps-publications/strengthening-eus-cyber-defence-capabilities/.

Rehrl, J. (ed.) (2018) *Handbook on Cybersecurity: The Common Security and Defence Policy of the European Union. Volume V*. Directorate for Security Policy of the Federal Ministry of Defence and Sports of the Republic of Austria.

Robinson, N. (2014) *EU Cyber-Defence: A Work in Progress*. EUISS, Brief No. 10, March.

Robinson, N., Walczak, A., Brune, S.-C., Esterle, A. and Rodriguez, P. (2013) Stocktaking Study of Military Cyber Defence Capabilities in the European Union (milCyberCAP): Unclassified Summary. Santa Monica, CA: RAND Corporation, Research Report no. RR-286-EDA.   At: www.rand.org/content/dam/rand/pubs/research_reports/RR200/ RR286/RAND_RR286.pdf.

Rynning, S. (2003) The European Union: Towards a Strategic Culture? *Security Dialogue* 34(4): 479–496. At: https://doi.org/10.1177/0967010603344007.

Sliwinski K. (2014) Moving Beyond the European Union's Weakness as a Cyber-Security Agent. *Contemporary Security Policy* 35(3) (December): 469–486. At: https://doi.org/ 10.1080/13523260.2014.959261.

Snyder, J.L. (1977) *The Soviet Strategic Culture: Implications for Limited Nuclear Options*. Santa Monica, CA: Rand Corporation.

Solana, J. (2003) European Security Strategy: A Secure Europe in a Better World. Brussels: European Council. At: www.consilium.europa.eu/uedocs/cmsUpload/78367.pdf.

Ventre, D. (2011) *Cyberattaque et cyberdéfense*. Paris: Lavoisier, Coll. Cyberconflits et Cybercriminalité.

8 Europe united

An analysis of the EU's public diplomacy on Twitter

Ilan Manor

Introduction: the digitalisation of public diplomacy

In my previous work, I have argued that one cannot understand the influence of digital technologies on the practice of public diplomacy without first characterising the digital society. This is because diplomats are social beings and ministries of foreign affairs (MFA) are social institutions (Manor 2019). Processes that affect society at large, such as digitalisation, influence diplomats and it through diplomats that such processes permeate into MFAs. Indeed, diplomats have already embraced the tools that have led to the digitalisation of society ranging from hardware, such as iPads and smartphones, to software, such as messaging applications. I have further asserted that diplomats' own use of digital technologies impacts their values and working procedures. For instance, when using social media diplomats have adopted the norm of maintaining close ties with distant friends and family. Overtime, this norm impacts the working procedures of MFA as diplomats employ digital platforms to strengthen ties with distant diasporas. Similarly, diplomats' personal use of Twitter to receive real-time information on breaking news, leads MFAs to regard Twitter as a tool for real-time crisis management. Like other members of the digital society, diplomats also search for a unique and authentic online voice influencing the type of content that embassies and MFAs share online. I, therefore, view the digitalisation of public diplomacy as a long-term process in which digital technologies influence the norms, values and working procedures of MFAs and their diplomats.

The digitalisation of public diplomacy has brought about two, new diplomatic practices. First, diplomats are now forced to practise a form of near real-time diplomacy as digital publics expect to learn about local and global events as they unfold on the ground. By practising near real-time diplomacy, diplomats can shape how digital publics interpret the world around them, while also becoming a credible source of information. Second, to attract large numbers of social media users, diplomats must author an online brand for their nation. Such a brand identifies the norms and values that a nation adheres to, while demonstrating how these values shape a nation's actions on the world stage. Values are central to national brands as they legitimise state action.

Despite the fact that the European Union's (EU) MFA, the European External Action Service (EEAS), has established a formidable digital presence, few studies to date have evaluated how it employs social media to practise online public diplomacy. Moreover, no study to date has examined how digitalisation has affected the public diplomacy activities of the EEAS, namely, its ability to practise near real-time diplomacy and create a distinct brand for the EU. This is a substantial gap as the EEAS may be able to use social media to create a brand of 'Europe United', one that depicts the EU as a unified political actor that speaks with one voice and promotes a single security and foreign policy. However, the EEAS may also be limited in its ability to practise near real-time diplomacy as policy statements must be approved by all member states. If this is the case, then the EEAS may fail to attract followers to its social media channels, thereby limiting its ability to shape how digital publics view the EU, its policies and its actions around the world. As such, digitalisation may be a double-edged sword for the EU.

This chapter seeks to address this important gap. Its research question asks: How has the emergence of the digital society impacted the digital activities of the EEAS? To answer this question, the chapter analyses 148 tweets published by the EEAS during December 2018 and January 2019, while identifying the issues that the EEAS addresses online, the values it promotes and its ability to comment on world events in near real time.

Structure of the chapter

This chapter begins by characterising the digital society and demonstrating how the norms and values of the digital society shape public diplomacy activities. The analytical prism of the digital society was adopted as it offers new insight into the EEAS's ability to leverage social media platforms. Indeed, EU diplomats may be using Twitter to bring the European dream to life as the EU is transformed online into a single political actor rather than assemblage of nation states, each attempting to obtain its own foreign policy goals. Yet, this prism also sheds light on the challenge of using social media in public diplomacy activities – that of interpreting the world for social media users. Failure to practise near real-time diplomacy may render diplomats' social media accounts redundant as digital publics search for other online channels that can help them to make sense of today's world, one which is perplexing as it is in a state of perpetual crisis. Beyond the EU case study, the prism of the digital society also highlights how technological advances shape society and, subsequently, the practice of public diplomacy. Next, the chapter identifies gaps in the existing literature pertaining to the EU's digital activities. Specifically, this chapter finds that few studies to date have examined the EEAS's use of social media, as scholars have tended to focus on the online activities of EU delegations. The third section of the chapter outlines the methodology used to analyse EEAS tweets, while the fourth section introduces the results of the analysis. This is followed by a discussion, which identifies the brand disseminated by the EEAS and reflects on its ability to attract social media users.

For the purposes of this chapter, public diplomacy is defined as foreign policy activities that are aimed at creating a positive climate among foreign publics in order to facilitate the acceptance of another country's foreign policy (Kampf, Manor and Segev 2015; Roberts 2007). The digital society is defined in the following section.

Characterising the digital society

Scholars have argued that the digital society is characterised by two important processes: the annihilation of time and space and the emergence of the iBrand; or social media users' need to create an authentic online brand through which they may attract large numbers of followers. Manuel Castells (2000; Castells and Cardoso 2006) maintains that the digital society constantly strives to annihilate time and space. Time is annihilated as digital technologies render it meaningless. This is evident in the global circulation of capital and information within second or the phenomenon of instant revolutions. As Phillip Seib (2012) writes, the almighty Hosni Mubarak was ousted from office in just three weeks, while the colour revolutions in Eastern Europe lasted less than two weeks. Space is annihilated as digital technologies enable two events to take place simultaneously, regardless of geographic proximity (Castells 2000; Castells and Cardoso 2006). Such is the case with a Parisian university student that attends an online course in New York, or drones in the Middle East that are operated from caravans outside Las Vegas (Bauman and Lyon 2013).

The annihilation of time and space has led to a form of real-time diplomacy (Seib 2012) as social media users expect to learn about world events while they are unfolding. They have become accustomed to this thanks to the work of citizen journalists and bloggers who use their smartphones to report in real-time on local events. For instance, Causey and Howard (2013) demonstrate how news channels and agencies were reliant on citizen journalists to report on the Arab Spring. Subsequently, diplomats and MFAs have taken to framing, or narrating, world events in near real time. Such was the case during the Turkish coup attempt in which MFAs commented on events in Istanbul and Ankara long before it was established that a coup was in fact underway. This was necessary as news agencies throughout the world used smartphone videos, shared by Turkish citizens, to report on the chaos that gripped Turkey (Sevin 2018).

Similarly, the Israeli MFA used Twitter to continuously narrate the 2014 Gaza War (Yarchi, Samuel-Azran and Bar-David 2017). Manor and Crilley found (2018, 2019) that the Israeli MFA used different narratives during different stages of the war. At first, the MFA argued that Israel *had* to invade the Gaza Strip as Hamas rockets had reached every major Israel city. Next, the MFA argued that Hamas was a consistent violator of the ceasefire agreements and was therefore responsible for prolonging the war. Finally, the MFA stated that a new government must be formed in Gaza as Hamas was using its citizens as 'human shields'. Other examples include Russia's real-time rebuke of NATO satellite images depicting Russian military troops in Crimea and the British

Foreign Office's use of Twitter to counter Russian conspiracy theories regarding the poisoning of Sergei Skripal (Bjola 2019). As this chapter will demonstrate, the EEAS has also taken to narrating world crises in near real time such as the contested elections in Venezuela and the domestic political paralysis that followed.

By practising near real-time public diplomacy, MFAs and diplomats may shape how digital publics make sense of local and global events. Moreover, by offering analyses of events as they unfold, MFAs and embassies become important sources of information for social media users. This can increase the number of followers that diplomats attract online thereby enhancing diplomats' ability to practise online public diplomacy. Indeed, one cannot practise public diplomacy without first attracting digital publics. Studies have shown that MFAs and diplomats who fail to narrate events in near real time become irrelevant to digital publics (Khatib, Dutton and Thelwall 2012). Lastly, near real-time diplomacy enables MFAs to explain geopolitical crises, thus, reducing feeling of uncertainty among social media users who are faced with a world that seems to be in a perpetual state of crisis.

The digital society is also the iBrand society. According to Storr (2017), social media has ushered in an era of social perfection as users promote a self-narrative of achievement and jubilation. Selfies, for example, are taken in trendy bars and champagne-infused parties, as opposed to the unemployment lines. Storr (2017) suggests that social media sites have become markets on which individuals are traded. The goal of social media users is to attract as many followers as possible. This logic is hammered into the minds of users as those who obtain the status of a Twitter celebrity are catapulted into a life of luxury. They ski down the slopes of Switzerland, or stroll along the beaches of the Bahamas, while promoting corporate sponsors (Manor and Soone 2018). To compete on the social media market, users must become an authentic brand, they must develop an online persona that has a distinct tone and appearance and that deals with one specific issue ranging from pop divas to Japanese manga. Succeeding on the social media market is also achieved by embracing the value of openness, or leading a transparent life, while sharing one's success and failures, marriages and divorces, awards and family drama. The norm of openness is enforced through the 'like' and 'retweet' buttons. It is these buttons that shape the activities of digital society members. The age of the iPhone and iPad is therefore also the age of the iBrand.

Social media sites enable diplomats to create an iBrand for their nation (Natarajan 2014). Diplomats can manage their nation's iBrand by identifying the norms and values their nation adheres to and demonstrating how these values shape its foreign policies. Diplomats can also use social media to demonstrate their nation's adherence with the norms and values celebrated by the international community. As Van Ham (2014) and Quelch and Jocz (2009) postulate, nations that adhere to international norms are more likely to succeed in implementing their foreign policies as morality breeds legitimacy on the international stage. Lastly, by turning to social media diplomats can manage their nation's reputation on both a global and a local scale.

One notable example is Poland's use of social media to create an iBrand of inclusivity and tolerance. In recent years, the Polish MFA has launched a global, digital campaign meant to distance Poland from the atrocities of the Second World War. The campaign, called 'Truth About the Camps', focuses on replacing the term 'Polish Death Camps' with that of 'Nazi Camps Operated on Occupied Polish Territory' (Polish embassy to Washington 2017).[1] To this end, the MFA has launched a dedicated Twitter page, which includes videos that depict Poland as the first victim of Nazi Germany.[2] Additionally, Polish embassies around the world have turned to Twitter to publically demand that newspapers retract articles that employ the term 'Polish Death Camps'.[3] Polish diplomats are thus attempting to refashion Poland's iBrand and to actively manage its global reputation. This social media campaign embraces the norm of authenticity as it deals with a specific issue while adopting a unique adversarial tone that lambasts publications for allegedly distorting history.

The digitalisation of the EU's public diplomacy

The European External Action Service (EEAS), the EU's MFA, was formally launched on 1 January 2011. Its stated goal is to help the EU carry out its common foreign and security policy. Based in Brussels, the EEAS oversees the EU's diplomatic ties with countries around the world by promoting human rights, facilitating trade with other countries, providing humanitarian and development aid and working with other multilateral organisations. The EEAS works in tandem with EU's High Representative for Foreign Affairs and Security policy, Federica Mogherini (EEAS website 2016).

As is the case with most MFAs around the world, the EEAS has also established a formidable social media presence that spans numerous platforms including Facebook, YouTube, Twitter, Instagram and Flickr. In total, the EEAS attracts more than half a million followers to its social media profiles. Despite the EEAS's migration online, few studies to date have investigated how the EEAS uses social media to practise public diplomacy. Most studies have focused on EU delegations rather than the EEAS itself. For instance, in a study from 2015, Bjola and Jiang investigated the digital activities of the EU's delegation to China, finding that social media was primarily used for disseminating information rather than interacting with digital publics. Similar findings were obtained in an analysis of the digital activities of European embassies in Kazakhstan (Collins and Bekenova 2017).

In one study from 2015, Vadura analysed the EEAS's use of social media to advance the cause of human rights in ASEAN countries. Vadura focused on this issue as the promotion of human rights has been recognised as a core EU value, in addition to democracy and the rule of law. Vadura's findings demonstrates that the EEAS lagged behind the United States (USA) and the United Kingdom (UK) in attracting social media followers, while also failing to interact with social media users.

In summary, studies examining the EU's use of social media have tended to focus on EU delegations rather than the EEAS itself. Moreover, studies focusing on the EEAS have examined its interaction with social media followers and its ability to attract online publics. As such, no study to date has examined how digitalisation and the emergence of the digital society has impacted the public diplomacy activities of the EU, namely, its ability to create a distinct iBrand and its practice of near real-time diplomacy. This chapter posits that this is a substantial gap for three reasons. First, the EEAS is a unique organisation as it promotes the foreign policy of a political union that does not entirely supersede its member states. Indeed, each member state of the EU has its own, independent foreign and security policy. This might limit the EEAS's ability to practise near real-time diplomacy as issues discussed online, and opinions expressed on social media, must be approved by all member states. Second, while the EU does not supersede its member states, it has moved towards greater integration, formulating a joint foreign and security policy and appointing an official foreign minister. The EEAS may thus employ social media to create an iBrand of the EU as a unified political actor that has a single foreign policy, a single security policy and a single foreign minister. Third, the EEAS may use social media to identify the values that the EU adheres to and exemplify how such values inform its actions on the world stage. This is important as values legitimise diplomatic action (Quelch and Jocz 2009; Van Ham 2014). This chapter seeks to address this important gap by analysing the EEAS's Twitter activity during December 2018 and January 2019. The research hypotheses that guided this analysis are presented in the following section.

Research questions, sample and methods

This chapter investigates how the norms and values of the digital society influence the online public diplomacy activities of the EEAS. Thus, it posed the following research question:

> RQ: How has the emergence of the digital society impacted the digital activities of the EEAS?

To answer this research question, three hypotheses were formulated. Previous studies suggest that diplomats now use social media to create a distinct iBrand for their nation. It is through this iBrand that diplomats may shape how digital publics view nations' actions on the world stage. It was hypothesised that the EEAS would use Twitter to create an iBrand that depicts the EU as a unified political actor, rather than assemblage of independent member states, each attempting to obtain its own policy goals. By so doing, the EEAS could influence how digital publics view the EU and its ability to shape global events through a shared vision. In other words, it is on the EEAS's Twitter channel that the European dream may come to life.

> H1: The EEAS would employ social media to depict the EU as a unified political actor.

The second research hypothesis stipulated that EEAS would use Twitter to identify the EU's core values and exemplify how such values shape its global policies. This assumption rests on the fact that morality breeds legitimacy in diplomacy. As noted earlier, diplomatic actors that promote desired norms and values are less likely to encounter resistance to their foreign policies. Moreover, morality can help manage the reputation of a diplomatic actor, as is the case with Poland.

H2: The EEAS would use social media to identify the EU's core values and exemplify how these values shape its foreign and security policies.

Lastly, it was assumed that the EEAS would fail to practise near real-time diplomacy, given the need for consensus between member states when formulating policy responses to local and global events. This could prove a major disadvantage for the EEAS as those MFAs that fail to comment on events as they unfold are at risk of losing their social media followers.

H3: The EEAS would not employ social media to comment on events as they unfold.

To answer this chapter's research question, all tweets published by the EEAS during December 2018 and January 2019 were analysed. This time period was selected as MFAs are especially active during these months, given the need to publicise diplomatic achievements gained over the past year. Twitter was selected as MFAs are most active on this social media platform (Kampf, Manor and Segev 2015). All Tweets were gathered using the TwimeMachine application that enables one to store up to 3,200 tweets published by any public Twitter account. In total, 148 tweets were analysed in the scope of this chapter.

All tweets were analysed using the methodology of thematic analysis. This analysis followed the roadmap offered by Braun and Clarke (2006), who define thematic analysis as a method for identifying, analysing and reporting on patterns, or themes, within a given data corpus. During the first phase of the analysis, half of all the tweets published by the EEAS were reviewed and grouped into issue-based categories. For instance, a large number of tweets depicted meetings between Frederica Mogherini and world leaders. Thus, a category of 'bilateral meetings' was created. Similarly, a large number of tweets focused on election monitoring in foreign countries, leading to the creation of the 'EU core values' category. Finally, several tweets dealing with nations slated to join the EU were grouped into the 'EU expansion' category. During the second phase of analysis, one-third of all EEAS tweets were reviewed yet again to ensure the relevance of the identified categories. This led to the creation of several new categories such as 'climate awareness' and 'fighting disinformation'. Finally, categories were grouped together into meta-categories such as 'A prosperous Europe' or 'A Globally Engaged Europe'. This process enabled the author to identify the issues addressed by the EEAS online and the themes that were prevalent in the EU's iBrand.

Results

Meta-category number 1: promoting European values

The most prevalent meta-category included tweets that identified the EU's core values and exemplified how these values shape EU policies. Tweets in this category dealt with three issues. The first was the need to combat climate change and protect the environment. These tweets depicted EU diplomats cleaning beaches around the world or dealt with EU initiatives during the COP24 Convention on Climate Change. In addition, tweets in category dealt with the promotion of human rights. Several EEAS tweets highlighted the EU's commitment to advancing the role of women in peace processes, specifically in Syria and Yemen. One such tweet argued that women spend less time looking for faults and more time looking for solutions. Thus, it is women who can help conflicted societies search for compromises.

Additional EEAS tweets dealt with the EU's commitment to fighting anti-Semitism and other manifestations of hate; celebrating human rights day; calling for the release of jailed journalists in Turkey; publishing EU authored reports on the state of human rights around the word and advancing migrant's protection and the safe passage of migrants around the world. Here, the EEAS emphasised its close cooperation with other multilateral organisations such as the International Maritime Organization (IOM). The issue of refugee security was quite visible on the EEAS Twitter channel, possibly due to the waves of migrants that have attempted to flee conflict zones by reaching the shores of European nations. Indeed, the EEAS highlighted the EU's commitment to protecting migrants around the world including in Europe, Asia and Africa. Lastly, the EEAS celebrated the release of human rights activists in Pakistan.

A substantial number of tweets also dealt with EU teams sent to observe elections in foreign states. These teams, which demonstrated the EU's commitment to promoting democracy, were sent to Nigeria, El Salvador and Senegal, while other EEAS tweets called for democratic reforms in Venezuela. Most of these tweets were accompanied by the hashtag #EU4Democracy.

Finally, EEAS tweets grouped into this category included links to Federica Mogherini's press conferences, press statements and questions and answers sessions from around the world. These tweets may have been published in order to depict the EU as an open and transparent political actor. Such tweets included remarks by Mogherini ahead of a NATO summit, remarks following a meeting of the EU's foreign affairs council, as well as press conferences following meetings with Serbian officials, Egyptian leaders and the African Union.

To summarise, tweets in this category identified the EU's core values including the protection of human rights, promoting democracy, combating climate change and a commitment to open and transparent governance. These tweets also exemplified how these values shape the EU's foreign policies and actions on the world stage ranging from the promotion of women as peacemakers to dispatching election-monitoring teams.

Meta-category number 2: a globally engaged actor

Tweets comprising this category framed the EU as a globally engaged actor. Such tweets depicted bilateral meetings between Mogherini and foreign leaders including the foreign ministers of Armenia, Bolivia, Ecuador and Ukraine. Tweets also summarised meetings between Mogherini and the president of Libya, the king of Jordan, the prime minister of Ethiopia, the president of Bosnia and Herzegovina and the king of Morocco.

Additionally, EEAS tweets dealt with the EU's commitment to protecting and strengthening the multilateral system. One tweet in this category stated that the EU was committed to working with the Organization for Security and Co-operation in Europe (OSCE) to reduce regional tensions. Another tweet stated that the EU was working to support the activities of the United Nations Human Rights Council (UNHCR) in Libya. In one public address, Mogherini argued that 'Today we need the United Nations (UN) more than ever' and that the EU would continue to support UN activities around the world. Lastly, EEAS tweets also addressed the EU's commitment to bringing a European perspective to the UN Security Council (UNSC), while strengthening the council's ability to resolve crises in a time of global turmoil.

Finally, tweets in this category dealt with EU diplomatic initiatives around the world including attempts to reforge the transatlantic relationship with the USA; the opening of an EU delegation in Kuwait; continuous dialogue with the authorities in Hong Kong on a range of issues; strategic meetings with the government of China; trade relations with Japan; establishing an international contact group to coordinate diplomatic efforts vis-à-vis Venezuela and a ministerial meeting between the EU and ASEAN countries. Tweets even dealt with the EU's space programme. All these tweets may have been used to exemplify the EU's desire to embrace its role as 'a global power', to quote a statement by Mogherini on Twitter.

Tweets comprising this category depicted the EU as a globally engaged actor whose diplomatic initiatives and relationships are in no way limited to the European continent. The EU was also depicted as taking part in shaping world events mostly through the multilateral system, which the EU would continue to protect and strengthen.

Meta-category number 3: EU security in the service of peace

The third, most prevalent category dealt with the EU's adoption of a single, unified security policy. However, EEAS tweets emphasised that the goal of this policy was not to militarise the EU. On the contrary, the EU's security policy was a tool for ensuring peace. In one of her speeches, Mogherini stated that there was a unique, European perspective to defence that prioritised peace over militarisation. Tweets comprising this category demonstrated how this security policy could maintain peace at home and abroad. Tweets, therefore, focused on the EU's attempt to reduce tensions between Ukraine and Russia; the EU's commitment to the Intermediate-Range Nuclear Forces (INF) Treaty that had helped secure peace for more than 30 years; stressing that cooperation and not confrontation was the key to peace in Eastern Europe; collaborating with partners in the Western Balkans to combat organised crime; collaborating with the government of Ethiopia to combat piracy; security collaborations with African governments; and collaborative actions with India to ensure maritime security.

A substantial number of tweets in this category also depicted the EU as a 'peacemaker'. Such tweets highlighted the EU's attempts to broker a peace agreement in Afghanistan; the EU's strides towards implementing an agreement between Greece and the Former Yugoslavian Republic of Macedonia regarding the latter's official name; the EU's ongoing negotiations with Iran and its attempts to rescue the Iran Nuclear Agreement; and EU negotiations with Colombia to uphold the peace agreement with the Revolutionary Armed Forces of Colombia (FARC-EP).

Finally, tweets in this category highlighted the EU's attempts to combat digital disinformation, which was labelled as a threat to peace as it undermined the health of many European societies. These tweets introduced: the EU's joint action plan to combat disinformation; joint EU efforts to minimise the impact of disinformation on European elections and elections in European states; the creation of a 'Red Alert' system that allowed European nations to jointly identify and combat disinformation campaigns and a future investment of €5 million in a rapid response programme that would tackle digital disinformation.

In summary, this meta-category included tweets that framed the EU's security policy as one that strives to promote and preserve peace while depicting the EU as a peacemaker working to mediate tensions and preserve peace processes around the world. Even the EU's efforts to combat disinformation were framed as peaceful measures used to promote the health of European societies.

Meta-category number 4: greater European integration

The least prevalent meta-category focused on the future integration of the European continent. Specifically, tweets in this category dealt with nations who are slated to join the EU. One such tweet reviewed the association agreement between the EU and Ukraine. Another tweet summarised meetings between the EU and Western Balkans leaders and the need for additional reforms before these nations could join the EU. Lastly, tweets included images from meetings with diplomats from Kosovo, which is also on the path to joining the EU. These tweets may have been used to depict the EU as a prosperous union, one still destined to grow. This is an important component of EEAS activities in light of Brexit and the UK's decision to exist the EU.

The results presented thus far demonstrate that the EEAS used Twitter to create a distinct iBrand for the EU, one of 'Europe United'. The tweets disseminated by the EEAS depicted the EU as a unified actor with a single foreign policy, a single security policy and a single, European foreign minister. Indeed, the majority of tweets evaluated in this chapter included a reference to Federica Mogherini. Some tweets contained statements made by Mogherini, while others included videos or images of the foreign minister. In this way, Mogherini became the face of a united Europe. However, the iBrand created by the EEAS also depicted the EU as a global actor that is committed to promoting its core values in all regions of the world. As was expected, the EEAS exemplified how the EU's core values shape its foreign and security policies including its efforts to promote human rights and democracy and to assist in the implementation of peace agreements. Lastly, despite the ongoing Brexit negotiations, the EEAS formulated an iBrand of a prosperous EU, one that was still viewed as attractive by nations throughout the continent. On social media, the EU was thus a united actor that strove to achieve a shared vision. The European dream therefore came to life on the Twitter profile of the EEAS.

True to the norms and values of the digital society, the EEAS's iBrand was both authentic and transparent. It was authentic in the sense that the EU spoke in a distinct tone, or in Mogherini's words, it promoted a 'distinct European perspective', one of ensuring peace through the multilateral system. The EU's various diplomatic actions were all framed through the logic of ensuring and sustaining peace, both in the continent and around the world. This was most evident when the EEAS, and Mogherini, framed the EU's security policy as a peaceful policy. The EU would also sustain peace through the multilateral system and international bodies such as the UNHCR, the UNSC and the IOM.

The EU's iBrand was transparent as dozens of tweets included press briefings, press conferences and question and answer sessions with Mogherini. Moreover, tweets focusing on disinformation, European integration and the EU's joint security policy included links to EU documents and EU websites where social media users could access additional information. Lastly, a video of Mogherini speaking to the press was published ahead of every important meeting including meetings with NATO members, nations destined to join the EU and EU ministerial meetings. As such, the EU's iBrand celebrated the digital society's norm of openness. These results validate H1 and H2. The following section evaluates the EEAS's ability to practise near real-time diplomacy.

Near real-time diplomacy in the EEAS

The months of December 2018 and January 2019 saw a rapid succession of important global events including terrorist attacks in Colombia, France, Iran, Kenya, Mali, Nigeria and the Philippines, as well as violent clashes between Israeli military forces and protestors in the Gaza Strip. In Spain, Catalan leaders went on a hunger strike following a constitutional crisis, while in France the Yellow Vest protests led to violent clashes with police forces. In the UK,

Theresa May was found in contempt of Parliament further deepening the Brexit crisis while the USA–China trade war intensified. In Syria, independent NGOs documented 223 massacres by forces loyal to the Assad regime, while the Civil War in Yemen worsened following a Houthi drone attack that killed several government officials and military personnel. Gabon experienced a failed coup attempt, while Italy's economy fell into an official recession.

None of these events were addressed by the EEAS on Twitter, even though these directly affected the EU or were in opposition to EU values. The massacres in Syria were not only a gross violation of human rights but would also motivate new refuges to set sail towards Europe. The Brexit debacle further increased tensions between the EU and the UK, while fuelling anti-EU sentiments in Europe and the USA. The USA–China trade war had a detrimental effect on European economies, while terrorist attacks in Europe and around the world increased feelings of uncertainty and insecurity. And yet, the EEAS ignored all of these events on its Twitter channel. It is possible that the EEAS could not address these events in near real time given the EU's need to act in consensus and formulate agreed upon policy responses to world events. This may have especially been the case with Brexit, a major policy shift by the UK, which threatened the very future of the EU.

These results demonstrate the tension that is at the heart of the EU. For, although the EU is a transnational political union that brings together numerous nation states, it does not entirely supersede its member states. Moreover, the foreign policy goals of different member states may be at odds with those of the EU as a whole. For instance, in the past, the EU has adamantly supported the two-state solution as a means of resolving the Israeli–Palestinian conflict. EU diplomats would often lament Israeli construction in the settlements and denounce violence between Israeli Defense Forces and Palestinian protestors in Gaza (Manor 2019). Yet, the emergence of right-wing governments in Eastern Europe has fractured this consensus as these governments frequently support Israeli security policies. As such, the EU's position on the Israeli–Palestinian conflict may be harder to define (Kalev 2019). This offline tension between the EU and its member states was manifest online as the EEAS was unable to interpret global events for its followers. This tension may also impact the EEAS's ability to create an iBrand of a unified, European actor as the EEAS can only deal with issues, events and actors that have been discussed by all member states. As such, these results demonstrate how the offline structures and working procedures of political actors shape their online activities and ability to fully leverage digital technologies. These results validated H3.

There was, however, one issue that was addressed in EEAS tweets and that was the crisis in Venezuela. The results of a contested election led to a political and financial crisis as millions of citizens attempted to cross the borders into neighbouring nations. During this crisis, several governments recognised opposition leader, Juan Guaidó, as the legitimate president of Venezuela, while MFAs commented daily on escalating tensions in the country. However, as noted in the analysis of tweets, when addressing the issue of Venezuela, the

EEAS merely stated that the EU had created an international contact group to coordinate diplomatic efforts opposite Venezuela and that the EU called for democratic reforms in the country. Unlike its peers around the world, the EEAS did not take to Twitter to narrate the rapidly escalating crisis or comment on the policies of the besieged Venezuelan government.

The practice of near real-time diplomacy (Seib 2012) demonstrates how the norms and values of the digital society permeate into MFAs giving rise to working procedures. Digital publics have become accustomed to learning about the world in near real time and they expect diplomats to offer up-to-date analyses of world events. Yet, the practice of near real-time diplomacy also enables MFAs to become important sources of information for publics looking to make sense of a chaotic world. Additionally, near real-time diplomacy helps MFAs, embassies and diplomats to increase their digital reach, thus facilitating the practice of online public diplomacy. Those MFAs that fail to practise real-time diplomacy risk being abandoned by the digital public. This not only limits MFAs' ability to practise online public diplomacy, but it also prevents MFAs from shaping how digital publics view an international actor, its policies and the values it subscribes to. As such, the EEAS's failure to practise near real-time diplomacy may soon lead to its abandonment by social media followers.

Discussion

Few studies to date have investigated the digital activities of the EEAS. This chapter argues that this is an important gap as the EEAS is a unique diplomatic organisation, one which represents a political union that does not entirely supersede its member states. Indeed, the EU comprises sovereign states that jointly pursue a foreign policy, while at the same time, each state also seeks to obtain its own policy objectives. Yet, it is exactly for this reason that digital technologies such as social media may prove an important public diplomacy resource for the EU.

Storr (2017) has postulated that social media sites are markets on which individuals are traded. To become an attractive commodity, individuals develop a distinct and authentic iBrand. Yet, for the nation state, an opposite process occurs. Diplomats now use social media to create an iBrand for their nation. In the process, the nation is individualised. It becomes a digital individual as it has a profile page, it can 'like' and 'retweet' content, it can comment on the activities of other social media users and it can interact with other users in real time. Indeed, social media users can now engage online with the State of Israel, or Egypt or even Colombia. The same is true of the EU. By creating an iBrand for the EU, the EEAS leads to the individualisation of the EU. It becomes a single, unified digital individual that speaks with one voice, promotes one foreign policy and has one official spokesperson. It is thus on social media sites, such as Twitter, that the European dream comes to life. The individualisation of the EU may have an immense impact on how digital publics view this union. It is no longer a semi-autonomous political actor forever destined to be limited by its member states; rather, it is a cohesive and coherent diplomatic actor that acts to promote a shared set of values. In this way, the EEAS's iBrand could increase the importance that digital publics ascribe to the EU and its actions on the world stage. Notably, online impressions shape the offline worldviews of millions of people around the world. To paraphrase Sandrin and Hoffmann (2018), EU digital activities do not only explain reality, but they also help to produce reality. As such, digital tools may be of special value to the EU.

It is worth noting that the EEAS is not the only diplomatic organ that may shape the EU's iBrand. The digital activities of EU diplomats and ambassadors, high-ranking officials (e.g. the President of the European Council; the President of the European Commission) and members of the European Parliament may all contribute to the EU's iBrand (Duke 2013). However, this is true of most diplomatic actors as national iBrands are also shaped by the digital activities of presidents, prime ministers, foreign ministers and high-ranking members of parliament. This plurality of digital channels poses a challenge to many nation states, as it is often hard to coordinate all the messages originating from multiple sources. However, some states such as Norway and Israel have established national communication forums in which all government ministries meet to coordinate their online messaging (Manor 2016). Future studies should examine whether the EU has been able to address the challenge of multiple digital channels.

The individualised, digital EU also has a clear set of values that determine its actions on the world stage. Indeed, the most prevalent meta-category identified in this chapter exemplified how the EU's values are manifest in its diplomatic initiatives. Scholars have argued that morality breeds legitimacy on the world stage (Quelch and Jocz 2009; Van Ham 2014). Yet, morality also breeds legitimacy in the digital society. States that are associated with negative values are lambasted online, while states associated with positive values are lauded by social media users. In this way, the EEAS's digital activities may enable the EU to obtain the support of digital publics for its policy initiatives, an important component of public diplomacy activities (Roberts 2007).

Notably, the EEAS placed an emphasis on the need to protect and strengthen the multilateral system. Moreover, the EEAS depicted the EU as a thriving and prosperous multilateral organisation, which is still destined to grow. This narrative may have been an effective one, given the ongoing paralysis of multilateral organisations and the crisis within the EU. In recent years, bodies such as the UNSC had failed to end the Syrian Civil War, broker a deal in Yemen's Civil War or protect the territorial integrity of Ukraine, while the EU's ability to reach consensus has been hampered by the rise of populist governments in Eastern Europe, anti-EU sentiments in the USA and the never-ending Brexit drama. The EU's narrative of a functional multilateral system may have thus reduced feelings of uncertainty among digital publics while reinstating confidence in the international system established in the wake of the Second World War.

However, the EU's iBrand may be nothing more than an impressive tree falling in a deserted forest. This is because the EEAS is limited in its ability to practise real-time diplomacy. MFAs that fail to narrate events, and help digital publics make sense of a chaotic world, are often abandoned by digital publics. It is the practice of near real-time diplomacy that enables an MFA to attract followers and, subsequently, shape publics' worldviews. Near real-time diplomacy is thus the Achilles heel of the EU and one that jeopardises its ability to reap the benefits of online public diplomacy. To face this challenge, the EU may need to adopt new working procedures and communications strategies that set free the EEAS and enable it to become an indispensable source of information for social media users.

Yet, here again, one must take note of how offline diplomacy impacts online diplomacy. Duke (2013) has argued that lack of coordination between the EEAS and EU member states may hinder EU public diplomacy activities as members ignore consensus and work pragmatically to obtain their own, narrow set of policy goals. Lack of coordination at the transnational and national levels may also prevent the EU from articulating a clear message or narrative of 'what exactly the EU stands for on the international stage' (Duke 2013: 33). Sandrin and Hoffmann (2018) assert that lack of coordination at the transnational and national levels also affects support for EU policies within member states. They further argue that the member states must clearly define the global role of the EU before addressing specific policies in specific regions. As such, effective offline public diplomacy rests on greater coordination of policy goals and agreements on the means to achieve these goals. This is also true of online public diplomacy for greater consensus between member states may increase the EEAS's ability to narrate world events and the EU's role in shaping these events and project an iBrand that clearly answers the question: what exactly does the EU stand for on the international stage?

Notes

1 The Facebook page of the Embassy of Poland, Washington, DC features a video under the heading 'Words Matter': stating 'Remember to use the correct terms when describing German Nazi Camps. It's not just a matter of semantics. It's a matter of historical integrity and accuracy.' See www.facebook.com/watch/?v=1291276330936637.
2 The Polish MFA's dedicated Twitter page is at: https://twitter.com/TruthAboutCamps.
3 This link to the Polish MFA's Twitter page provides an example of such activities: https://twitter.com/TruthAboutCamps/status/874280080389918721/photo/1.

References

Bauman, Z. and Lyon, D (2013) *Liquid Surveillance: A Conversation.* Cambridge: Polity Press.

Bjola, C. (2019) *The Dark Side of Digital Diplomacy: Countering Disinformation and Propaganda.* Madrid: Elcano Royal Institute.

Bjola, C. and Jiang, L. (2015) Social Media and Public Diplomacy: A Comparative Analysis of the Digital Diplomatic Strategies of the EU, US and Japan in China. In Corneliu Bjola and Marcus Holmes (eds), *Digital Diplomacy: Theory and Practice.* Abingdon: Routledge, 85–102.

Braun, V. and Clarke, V. (2006) Using Thematic Analysis in Psychology. *Qualitative Research in Psychology* 3(2): 77–101.

Castells, M. (2000) Materials for an Exploratory Theory of the Network Society. *The British Journal of Sociology* 51(1): 5–24.

Castells, M. and Cardoso, G. (eds) (2006) *The Network Society: From Knowledge to Policy*. Washington, DC: Johns Hopkins Center for Transatlantic Relations, 3–23.

Causey, C. and Howard, P.N. (2013) Delivering Digital Public Diplomacy: Information Technologies and the Changing Business of Diplomacy. In R.S. Zaharna, Amelia Arsenault and Ali Fisher (eds), *Relational, Networked and Collaborative Approaches to Public Diplomacy: The Connective Mindshift*. New York: Routledge, 144–156.

Collins, N. and Bekenova, K. (2017) European Cultural Diplomacy: Diaspora Relations with Kazakhstan. *International Journal of Cultural Policy* 23(6): 732–750.

Duke, S. (2013) The European External Action Service and Public Diplomacy. In Mai'a K. David Cross and Jan Melissen (eds), *European Public Diplomacy: Soft Power at Work*. New York: Palgrave Macmillan, 113–136.

Kalev, G. (2019) Theodor Herzl Was Willing to Tolerate Europe's Far-Right. Should Israel's Leaders Do the Same? *Foreign Policy*, 10 February.

Kampf, R., Manor, I. and Segev, E. (2015) Digital Diplomacy 2.0? A Cross-National Comparison of Public Engagement in Facebook and Twitter. *The Hague Journal of Diplomacy* 10(4): 331–362.

Khatib, L., Dutton, W. and Thelwall, M. (2012) Public Diplomacy 2.0: A Case Study of the US Digital Outreach Team. *The Middle East Journal* 66(3): 453–472.

Manor, I. (2016) *Are We There Yet? Have MFAs Realized the Potential of Digital Diplomacy*. Leiden: Brill.

Manor, I. (2019) *The Digitalization of Public Diplomacy*. Cham: Palgrave Macmillan.

Manor, I. and Crilley, R. (2018) Visually Framing the Gaza War of 2014: The Israel Ministry of Foreign Affairs on Twitter. *Media, War & Conflict* 11(4): 369–391.

Manor, I. and Crilley, R. (2019) The Mediatisation of MFAS: Diplomacy in the New Media Ecology. *The Hague Journal of Diplomacy* 1: 1–27.

Manor, I. and Soone, L. (2018) The Digital Industries: Transparency as Mass Deception. *Global Policy*, January.

Natarajan, K. (2014) Digital Public Diplomacy and A Strategic Narrative for India. *Strategic Analysis* 38(1): 91–106.

Quelch, J.A. and Jocz, K.E. (2009) Can Brand Obama Rescue Brand America? *The Brown Journal of World Affairs* 16(1): 163–178.

Roberts, W.R. 2(007) What is Public Diplomacy? Past Practices, Present Conduct, Possible Future. *Mediterranean Quarterly* 18(4): 36–52.

Sandrin, P.O. and Hoffmann, A.R. (2018) Silences and Hierarchies in European Union Public Diplomacy. *Revista Brasileira de Política Internacional* 61(1).

Seib, P. (2012) *Real-Time Diplomacy: Politics and Power in the Social Media Era*. New York: Palgrave Macmillan.

Sevin, E. (2018) Digital Diplomacy as Crisis Communication: Turkish Digital Outreach after July 15. *Revista Mexicana de Politicia Exterior* 118: 1–21.

Storr, W. (2017) *Selfie: How the West Became Self-Obsessed*. London: Pan Macmillan.

Vadura, K. (2015) The EU as 'Norm Entrepreneur' in the Asian Region: Exploring the Digital Diplomacy Aspect of the Human Rights Toolbox. *Asia Europe Journal* 13(3): 349–360.

Van Ham, P. (2014) Social Power in Public Diplomacy. In R.S. Zaharna, Amelia Arsenault and Ali Fisher (eds), *Relational, Networked and Collaborative Approaches to Public Diplomacy: The Connective Mindshift*. New York: Routledge, 31–42.

Yarchi, M., Samuel-Azran, T. and Bar-David, L. (2017) Facebook Users' Engagement with Israel's Public Diplomacy Messages during the 2012 and 2014 Military Operations in Gaza. *Place Branding and Public Diplomacy* 13(4): 360–375.

9 Developing future borders

The politics of security research and emerging technologies in border security

Clemens Binder

Introduction

AMASS, TALOS, OPARUS, SEABILLA, PERSEUS, ROBORDER, I2C, iBorderCtrl. These multiple abbreviations all describe research projects for developing security technologies in order to improve the EU's surveillance capabilities at the external borders and in consequence, to improve border security and control. These projects have all been funded under the calls for enhancing border security within the security research programmes of the EU's large-scale Research Framework Programmes, FP7 and Horizon 2020 (H2020). Annually, more than €40 million are specifically devoted to projects enhancing the EU's border surveillance capabilities solely within the FPs; other funds, such as the Internal Security Fund (ISF), receive even substantially more budgetary means. However, while the ISF supports also acquisition of material and training of border guards, within the FPs, Research and Development (R&D) of particular technologies is emphasised. In order to achieve this, calls explicitly addressing border security and control are issued in the security research themes of the FPs. As the FPs pursue a 'policy-driven' approach, these calls often seek to address specific political goals. In the case of border security, the two major policy initiatives are the European Border Surveillance System (EUROSUR, see Bellanova and Duez 2016; Jeandesboz 2017) and the European Travel Information and Authorisation System (ETIAS). This reflects in the kinds of devices that are developed – in the case of EUROSUR, automated border control technologies, such as drones (Csernatoni 2018; Martins and Küsters 2019) or so-called 'Smart Border technologies' such as biometrics and databases (Amoore and Hall 2009; Hall 2017; Jeandesboz 2016).

The importance of R&D of border security technologies represents a new reality in the field of border and migration control. This results from the increasing technologisation of the EU's border security (Andersson 2016; Bourne, Johnson and Lisle 2015; Dijstelbloem, Meijer and Hoijtink 2011) technologies have a central role in the EU's Integrated Border Management (IBM) approach, which also underlies the policies of EUROSUR and ETIAS. Securing the external border of the EU shall be achieved through 'making better use of the opportunities offered by IT systems and technologies' (European Commission 2015a: 11).

This is embedded within a larger set of demands for state-of-the-art security technologies, which is also outlined in the Agenda for Security as '[r]esearch and innovation is essential if the EU is to keep up-to-date with evolving security needs' (European Commission 2015b: 11). This has resulted in a steady and consequent expansion of security research efforts within the FPs.

However, the increasing role of technologies and R&D in border security has caused a crucial shift in the composition of the field of actors. As shown by Bigo *et al.* (2014: 19), the majority of funds in FP7's security research programme were distributed among private security and defence companies as well as applied research centres (e.g. Fraunhofer). Private companies are not only on the receiving end of funds, but through lobbying and consulting, for example, through the European Organization of Security or the Protection and Security Advisory Group, they are also capable of shaping the research programmes according to their interests. The EU has fostered this influence through the creation of Public–Private Partnerships (PPPs) in the field of security research. Scholars have problematised the involvement of private security companies (PSCs) and their effects on power structures and knowledge production in security politics (Abrahamsen and Williams 2009; Avant 2005; Berndtsson 2012; Leander 2005). For border security specifically, scholars such as Baird (2017, 2018) and Lemberg-Pedersen (2013, 2018) have investigated the multiple roles PSCs assume in controlling and protecting borders. However, the role of the private security industry in border security-related R&D and the effects of this involvement on practising border security have hitherto not been sufficiently addressed in academic debates.

While academics acknowledge and thematise possible negative consequences of PSC involvement in R&D, a systematic problematisation and criticism so far has been predominantly conducted by NGOs (Akkerman 2016; Hayes 2009; Jones 2017). Reports highlight precarious developments of how practices of PSCs exacerbate conditions for migrants and marginalised groups and might even result in violent practices (Akkerman 2016). At the same time, the private security industry profits massively in financial terms, hence, they are strongly involved in decisions of planning and designing security research programmes. The findings of these reports offer a strong rationale to investigate the different knowledges and practices introduced by the private security industry in border security-related R&D critically.

This chapter will assess the private security industry's modes and practices of involvement in border security through R&D. The focus will be explicitly on the EU's security industry and its role in the Research Framework Programmes, FP7 and Horizon 2020. In order to find out how conceptualisations and knowledges of security are articulated in the public–private dialogue within the FPs, I will proceed as follows. First, I will introduce the theoretical presumptions this chapter is based on, particularly, the concept of 'sociotechnical imaginaries' (Jasanoff and Kim 2009; Jasanoff 2015), which describes desired configurations of futures achieved through technological progress. I will then go on to outline the field of actors and introduce the various private actors and initiatives.

Drawing on the concept of sociotechnical imaginaries, I will then explore the imaginaries of border security that foster the border security-related R&D programmes and how they emerge from the interactions and negotiations of different actors, particularly of the private security industry. I argue that, through the creation of PPPs, private actors shape the sociotechnical imaginaries, which drive security research and therefore augment the importance of PSCs not only in the R&D process but also in the field of border security as a whole.

Theorising the field of R&D in border security

The field of R&D in border security comprises a multiplicity of actors; these are connected in various ways and interact through different intermediary means. Mapping the field, which consists of different practices (such as formulating programmes and calls or decisions of funding) of R&D is crucial in order to understand how imaginaries are formulated and translated into technology development. However, the field of security-related R&D is not to be understood as separated from security politics, rather, it is strongly embedded in the security assemblage (Abrahamsen and Williams 2009) of border protection in the EU. In this chapter, I aim to create an understanding of R&D not as a merely technical practice, but rather as a political practice in the wider field of the politics of border security in the EU.

Critical security studies have increasingly engaged with Science and Technology Studies (STS) in order to create a more political understanding of the role of technologies in security politics. As Amicelle, Aradau and Jeandesboz describe, '[security] devices are performative in that they (re)configure social spaces, (re)draw boundaries and (re)distribute meanings' (2015: 298). This notion of performativity states that security technologies are not operating in an empty space or reducible to mere tools of assistance, but they assume political agency. This role is fostered through what Davidshofer, Jeandesboz and Ragazzi refer to as 'technological imperative', which describes how:

> technology is referred to in terms of both necessity and novelty, it is a 'toolbox' to be managed and a matter where governmental authorities need to 'keep pace' with purported societal processes, including developments coined as new, unprecedented and unpredictable threats.
>
> (Davidshofer *et al.* 2016: 208)

As outlined in the introduction of this chapter, this holds true particularly in the field of border security and migration control, where technologies are regarded as a solution to quickly emerging threats and risks.

While the connections between the governing of border security and technologies have been widely debated (see Amoore 2006; Amoore and Hall 2009; Andersson 2016; Dijstelbloem *et al.* 2011; Hall 2017; Jeandesboz 2016, 2017), little attention has hitherto been devoted to the R&D process. Whereas Bourne *et al.* (2015) have investigated the process of security technology development in laboratories, Leese *et al.* (2019), Martins and Küsters (2019) and Möllers (2017) have analysed the larger structures of security R&D programmes, particularly the EU's FPs. I argue that, following the approach of 'border security as a practice' (Bigo 2014; Côté-Boucher, Infantino and Salter 2014), which explains the politics of border security and its prevalence for international security through the mundane everyday practices of border security professionals, R&D shall be regarded as a 'security practice' (Balzacq *et al.* 2010). Through this understanding, it is possible to analyse R&D as a set of security practices providing security professionals with tools specifically designed to tackle threats and mitigate risks at the EU's external border. Through making these specific devices available, the different practices that constitute the R&D process in its entirety perpetuate insecurities (see also Huysmans 2006), and as I will explain later in this chapter, sociotechnical imaginaries are a central tool in this perpetuation.

The role of technologies, particularly in border security, should be seen as a reciprocal process, where technologies that derive of political imaginations also shape the governance of the border. Border security and security technologies are therefore 'co-productive' (Jasanoff 2004). Emergent, even disruptive technologies, such as drones and biometrics (see Calcara, Chapter 1 in this volume) emerge from the specific socio-political environment that they are embedded within. When we speak, for instance, of the 'data border' (Hall 2017), technologies, that produce this data border, have resulted from political imaginations of border security that emphasise the gathering of data, for instance, biometrics or travel records. Similarly, aiming for border surveillance (as in the case of EUROSUR), leads to an emergence of devices such as drones or sensor technologies. R&D as a security practice has a central role in providing the technologies that produce modes of governing the border, but the central question is about the co-productive element: How do political conceptions of border security produce R&D as security practice?

In order to address this question, I draw on the concept of 'sociotechnical imaginaries'. I follow Jasanoff's definition of imaginaries as 'as collectively held, institutionally stabilized, and publicly performed visions of desirable futures, animated by shared understandings of forms of social life and social order attainable through, and supportive of, advances in science and technology' (2015: 4). In regard to security, however, I argue that desirable futures often centre on the reduction of insecurities, a large body of literature in critical security studies has delved into the precautionary security practices of rendering threats intelligible and counteracting these threats before they even occur (Adey and Anderson 2012; Anderson 2010; de Goede, Simon and Hoijtink 2014). Specifically, I draw on the definition of pre-emptive security of de Goede *et al.*, who define pre-emptive security as 'security practices that aim to act on threats that are unknown and recognized to be unknowable, yet deemed potentially catastrophic' (2014: 412). In this chapter, I aim to explore the pre-emptive imaginaries visible in the R&D process and how different actors introduce these precautionary imaginaries. By employing this pre-emptive logic, I analyse how power structures between those are redefined through imaginaries, following Vogel *et al.*, who state that '[h]ow security gets framed, therefore, and the kinds of knowledges that are brought to bear on it, matter enormously for what security means and the power and influence of security enterprises' (2017: 974). Imaginaries are not simply perspectives on how technology might improve security, they also represent an exertion of power.

In this regard, the central role of private actors is vital in analysing how imaginaries constitute and how actor-structures that produce these imaginaries are constructed. I focus on the specific role of private security companies and their specific knowledges (Abrahamsen and Williams 2009; Avant 2005; Leander 2005). Particularly, I will look into the civil security market, where Hoijtink (2014) has examined how the civil security industry attempts to create markets on the basis of often exaggerated threats. This connects to the notion of preemptive security that is often visible in imaginaries of border security. It is reflected in analyses on the private security industry in the realm of border security (Baird 2017, 2018; Lemberg-Pedersen 2013, 2018) showing the specific, often heavily securitised approaches employed by private companies. With this chapter, I aim to advance this scholarship in examining the specific paths of influence of the private security industry.

Analysing imaginaries in the context of security practices requires an understanding of security beyond practice. Practice-based approaches focus on (inter) actions of security professionals and devices, however, the move beyond practice extends this understanding to all instruments that comprise the field of border security. Moving beyond practice in this chapter means employing Mezzadra and Neilson's concept of the border as a method, which describes the border as 'finely tuned instruments for managing, calibrating and governing global passages of people, money and things' (Mezzadra and Neilson 2013: 3). Because R&D, as explained, in addition to its practices consists of what Huysmans (2011) describes as 'little security nothings', such as detailed research calls and tenders, it is rendered necessary to investigate these different instruments. These often provide insight into results of negotiation processes between public and private actors and therefore facilitate the analysis of different sociotechnical imaginaries prevalent in these interactions. Documents such as research calls and programmes as well as white papers by private security interest groups and official EU documents serve as the analytical base for this chapter.

Mapping the field of actors and their imaginaries in border security related R&D

Explaining the involved actors

The understanding of R&D as a set of security practices that co-produces the border requires a comprehensive analysis of the field within which the practices occur. The field of border security in the European Union is filled with complexities and complicated relations between states, the EU institutions and private actors. In this section, I will therefore outline the two major groups of actors involved in border security and R&D, public and private actors. I will also outline the modes of interaction, particularly through PPPs. In doing this, I aim to show how public–private interactions shape sociotechnical imaginaries that feed into border security related R&D.

The public side is largely constituted by EU actors, however, this should not be regarded as a monolithic, unified actor. Rather, it comprises a set of institutions that compete for power, resources and influence. With the Schengen system, the EU provides the major political framework for border security by putting the responsibility for external border protection on the states situated at the Schengen area's external border. In order to assist these states and strengthen border security, the EU established the European Border and Coast Guard Agency, better known as Frontex. Frontex has become a powerful actor in the EU's border security architecture that influences the practices of border security (Léonard 2010; Paul 2017), particularly since the expansion of its mandate in 2016. Other institutions concerned with border security tasks are, for instance, European Union Agency for the Operational Management of Large-Scale IT Systems in the Area of Freedom, Security and Justice (eu-LISA) and the European Maritime Safety Agency (EMSA). In this chapter, I will however focus on Frontex because it is the central institution in securing and controlling the EU's external borders.

Frontex is responsible for the implementation and execution of the EU's important border security policy initiatives, the surveillance system EUROSUR and the establishment of an automated Entry–Exit System with pre-arrival border checks through the European Travel Information and Authorisation System (ETIAS), which is planned to come into effect in 2021. While the scope of these instruments differs strongly – EUROSUR is mainly used to improve situational awareness and surveillance capabilities at the external border, whereas ETIAS's predominant application is to predetermine possibly dangerous individuals entering the EU, particularly at airports – the objectives of both systems are similar. Driven by the desire to detect illegal migrants constructed as dangers and threats, these policy initiatives should create infrastructures of border security comprising different emerging technologies (such as drones for EUROSUR or automated border controls for ETIAS). While the European Commission formulates the policy initiatives, it is the responsibility of Frontex to apply and maintain these systems correctly. Thus, the agency assumes a central role in multiple steps of the R&D process, particularly in planning.

Both EUROSUR and ETIAS underline the demand for state-of-the-art technologies to fulfil their objectives. For this reason, Frontex (and also other agencies such as eu-LISA) has set up divisions concerned with R&D efforts that seek to shape the security research programmes. This reflects in the larger EU's efforts, as the Agenda for Security states that:

> Horizon 2020 can play a central role in ensuring that the EU's research effort is well targeted, including factoring in the needs of law enforcement

authorities by further involving end-users at all stages of the process, from conception to market.

(European Commission 2015b: 11)

Frontex and other agencies are strongly involved in the R&D process and therefore also directly connect to the private security industry, particularly through a variety of events.

The FPs contribute to this extension of the field actors into the realm of PSCs. As noted in the introduction, private industrial actors such as Leonardo, Airbus, Thales and Indra are the major recipients of funding money.[1] These companies are members in various interest groups (such as the European Organisation of Security, EOS). Through these interest groups, private actors seek to shape border security and R&D policies in their favour, and in doing this, I will explain two organisations that are important vehicles for influence in the diverse field of industry actors (see also Baird 2017): EOS and the Protection and Security Advisory Group (PASAG).

EOS represents one of the central actors in the field, maintaining close ties to the relevant EU institutions such as Frontex and the Commission and is strongly involved in the politics of EU security research. Consisting of 40 members from the European private security industry, EOS provides knowledge and recommendations via reports but is also involved in lobbying efforts to benefit its members. As Lemberg-Pedersen states, 'EOS is, in other words, a comprehensive tool with which PSCs seek to influence the common European border politics so as to create a demand for their products' (2013: 162). In following this endeavour, EOS is actively involved in shaping Research Framework Programmes: the organisation was among the first to formulate its interests for the successor of H2020, FP9, also known as Horizon Europe. The knowledge and expertise held and articulated by EOS, therefore, are crucial in understanding the influence of the private security industry on imaginaries and the practising of R&D.

Another influential actor for the private industry is the Protection and Security Advisory Group (PASAG) of the European Commission. PASAG is an external advice group assembled by the Commission in order to set strategic and programmatic goals for security research within the Framework Programmes. The group consists of multiple members of the private security industry among others. PASAG strengthens the role of private security industry expertise in advising the EU and represents a direct channel for the private industry to shape imaginaries. Of great significance is the statement in the mandate of PASAG given by the EC that 'Advisory Group Members may even participate in consortia under Horizon 2020' (European Commission 2017a: 4). This adds to the role of the private security industry as companies, through increased investment in security research, directly profit from a possible securitisation. Enabling PASAG members to both influence decisions of the propositions of security research programmes and profit from them by receiving funds for R&D fits in Hoijtink's observation that '… the notion that threats could emerge from anywhere at any time has been joined with the desire to integrate security and economic profit in a seamless manner' (2014: 463).

The efforts to include the private security industry into security research through actors such as EOS and PASAG should be seen as embedded in the larger endeavours of the EU to strengthen the European security industry (European Commission 2012). This is also reflected in a major goal of the Horizon 2020 regulation, which is 'improv[ing] the competitiveness of the private security industry' (European Union 2013a). However, the influence and organisation of PSCs is not limited to EOS and PASAG. Numerous efforts have been made by the EU in order to create PPPs and involve private industry actors in security research. Fora such as the Group of Personalities for Security Research (GoP), the European Security Research Advisory Board (ESRAB), the European Security Research Industrial Forum (ESRIF) and the think-tank Security & Defence Agenda (SDA) have not only underlined the EU's efforts of developing a public–private security research programme, but have also produced substantial results in forms of reports and recommendations. Doing this has enabled the private security industry to introduce their specific knowledges and expertise, not to the same extent as through EOS and PASAG, but nevertheless these fora have had a transformative effect on the imaginaries upon which security research is planned and conducted.

Examining the imaginaries

The multiple negotiation and communication structures do not only result in a stronger inclusion of private security companies and interest organisations on the level of actors, it also hands them additional powers through the opportunity to express specific knowledges and conceptualisations of security. The sociotechnical imaginary of border security, which produces the specific practising of R&D, thus, is shaped by the specific political objectives of private and public actors alike. In this part, therefore, I will examine how, through the interactions of EOS, PASAG and EU actors, imaginaries are negotiated and rendered into one common position that is expressed in the H2020 Working Programmes. Imaginaries are not merely seen as definitive policy goals, but rather, following Jasanoff and Kim, I see them as 'less explicit, less issue-specific, less goal-directed, less politically accountable, and less instrumental' than policies (2009: 123). However, analysing policies and consulting reports are important to abstract the imaginaries from the definitive goals. I will therefore use a more interpretive approach (following Wagenaar 2011) to the analysis, through which I will describe the imaginaries as the socio-political condition 'that it is somehow constitutive of political actions, governing institutions, and public policies' (Wagenaar 2011: 4).

I will proceed by outlining the different standpoints of the private actors EOS and PASAG, the European Commission and Frontex and then proceed to show how these concepts and imaginations translate into the H2020 research calls for border security, in order to analyse the underlying sociotechnical imaginary of border security related R&D.

EUROSUR

EUROSUR has represented one of the major policy initiatives in the realm of border security. It depends strongly on technologies that improve 'the exchange of information and the operational cooperation between national authorities of Member States as well as with [Frontex]' (European Union 2013b). Frontex would therefore highly profit from interoperability and improved data exchange, which is also stated in the agency's strategy on IBM as 'the full implementation of the European Border Surveillance System (EUROSUR) and enhanced information and intelligence sharing through other appropriate channels will enable effective prediction and prevention of crises and events from occurring' (Frontex 2019: 30). The approach of EUROSUR is therefore highly pre-emptive; it is aiming to improve the capabilities to detect threats before they even occur. The policy also contains a humanitarian dimension through the objective of improving surveillance technologies in order to facilitate Search and Rescue, adding a humanitarian dimension (European Union 2013b), which in reality often is lacking (see Pallister-Wilkins 2015; Vaughan-Williams 2015).

In the context of EUROSUR, EOS outlines problems in terms of interoperability and harmonisation, 'innovative surveillance technologies [...] and networking of existing information systems so as to allow for a secure, timely and reliable exchange of data and information, whenever needed, should be implemented' (EOS 2009a: 11). For PASAG, in the context of surveillance, it is paramount to facilitate legal movement while detecting irregular migration. A focal area in this context is the detection of smugglers and traffickers, the group states in its 2015 recommendations for H2020 that 'developments of technologies and methods to follow and analyse the moving objects and detecting geographic interconnections for understanding the new way of migration (smuggling migrants) and the associated crime shall be envisaged' (PASAG 2015: 14). In terms of maritime surveillance, EOS sees a holistic, comprehensive approach as viable, underlining the quest for interoperability. EOS laments the lacking inclusion of the private security industry and lack of communication, which results in the deteriorating effectiveness of technological solutions provided by the security industry. One example would be the lack of knowledge on the EUROSUR regulation by members of the private security industry (EOS 2017: 10). The humanitarian dimension is completely absent in EOS's and PASAG's objectives.

ETIAS

The debate revolving around Automated Border Controls (ABCs) has had a prevalent role in the EU's border security architecture. In EOS's 2009 White paper 'A European Approach to Border Management' (EOS 2009b), the organisation calls for a harmonisation in approaches to biometric borders, with the objective to accelerate the flow of passengers and goods, while trying to 'understand "who is the person attempting to cross the border" and "what risks might they pose on entry to the country"' (EOS 2009b: 7). Similarly, PASAG states in its vision for

2030 that 'EU citizens of good standing should be able to cross all land, sea and air, internal and external EU borders, with no physical barriers' (PASAG 2016: 6). Priorities for the private security industry in this context is to provide devices that are able to sort travellers into categories of risky or safe, one example therefore would be the iBorderCtrl project.

The EU detected the same lack of interoperability and harmonisation in the different systems as were described by EOS and PASAG, however, it promised to address these issues via the creation of ETIAS (European Commission 2016). The ETIAS regulation developed these goals and reflected EOS and PASAG's vision of a system facilitating travel, while detecting possibly threatening individuals.

> ETIAS should provide a travel authorisation for third-country nationals exempt from the visa requirement enabling consideration of whether their presence on the territory of the Member States does not pose or will not pose a security, illegal immigration or a high epidemic risk.
>
> (European Union 2018)

In 2016, Frontex issued a report on the best-practices of ABCs (Frontex 2016), which outlined the importance of functional technological systems to improve passenger flows, reflecting both the need for interoperable devices and the desire for accelerating border crossing for people that are not seen as risks.

Objectives of border security R&D in the Horizon 2020 Working Programmes

Having now outlined the conceptualisations' central actors in the policy areas, I proceed to investigate how these are reflected in H2020's working programmes in the Secure Societies Programme. Three working programmes have been issued by the EU for different time-spans: for 2014–2015 (European Commission 2013); for 2016–2017 (European Commission 2015c); and for 2018–2020 (European Commission 2017b). All three programmes outline border security as one focal area and all three programmes reflect the EU's policy objectives through focusing on EUROSUR and Smart Borders. However, whereas the 2014–2015 programme contains aims to improve Search and Rescue capabilities in the context of EUROSUR, these endeavours disappear in the later programmes for the benefit of strengthening surveillance capabilities. The 2016–2017 Programme warns that 'without investments in technology and information systems, it is simply not feasible to manage borders and border crossing points' (European Commission 2015c: 37). This is particularly crucial, as it feeds into the 'technological imperative' by claiming that without innovation, political endeavours are not achievable. In the 2018–2020 programme, the main objective is:

> to develop technologies and capabilities which are required to enhance systems and their interoperability, equipment, tools, processes, and methods

for rapid identification to improve border security, whilst respecting fundamental rights including free movement of persons, protection of personal
data, and privacy.

(European Commission 2017b: 37)

Here, the vision of facilitating free movement while pre-emptively detecting
threats is reflected and outlined as an imperative goal. In terms of Smart Borders
and ETIAS, the 2014–2015 programme hints at a crucial vision.

The ever-growing number of travellers crossing the EU borders poses a
serious challenge to the border control authorities in terms of a reduced
amount of time for carrying out border checks. Consequently, efforts are
being undertaken to facilitate the travel of bona-fide and genuine passengers
and simultaneously to safeguard high level of security.

(European Commission 2013: 76)

Here, the notion of the *bona-fide traveller* comes into play, which describes the
unthreatening, law-abiding citizen for whom travelling should be facilitated.
While this is problematic in many ways, in terms of racialisation and exclusion
(see Aas and Bosworth 2013), it not only reflects the visions and recommendations of the private security industry, but it also reproduces those in a strong
fashion. This notion is even strengthened in the 2018–2020 working programme,
which states that border security 'should be facilitated by novel technologies and
sensing strategies characterized by risk-based protection and non-intrusive
security checks that can be implemented without disrupting business' (European
Commission 2017b: 40). The calls, therefore, contain three central elements that
reproduce both the EU's and the private actors' conceptualisations. First, pre-
emption and surveillance are important to tackle risks before they emerge.
Second, movement should be facilitated for some, while others need to be hindered in their movement. And third, technologies need to be interoperable and
harmonised to improve their specific usage, which is seen as an important aspect
for improving security as a whole.

Conclusion

The public and private conceptualisations of border security, both in terms of
ETIAS and EUROSUR, do not differ substantially. However, they reveal an
important facet of agenda-setting in Horizon 2020. Border security R&D shall
assist in achieving a pre-emptive mode of governance, detecting threats early
and emphasising the dichotomy between facilitating free movement and securing the borders of the EU. Technology and technological development are
described as paramount in achieving these goals of border security. This not
only shows the deep politicisation of the R&D process, but also the co-constitution
of technological devices and socio-political order. The sociotechnical imaginary
driving R&D and innovation in border security, therefore, can best be described

as a borderspace where citizens deemed unproblematic shall be granted accelerated movement, while those seen as risks and threats shall be excluded from entering pre-emptively, or as an area of 'free movement for some'. Surveillance and pre-emption are the central modes of this governance; technologies should perform these practices.

What has become visible in analysing working programmes and policy documents is that a large share of the interests common to the EU and the private security industry are reflected in the calls for H2020's border security research. This reveals that the private security industry indeed is a driving force in the EU's border security R&D politics. It also helps in understanding why decisions of planning, funding and developing technologies are made; and, particularly, why specific technologies, such as drones or Artificial Intelligence receive large shares of border security-related funding.

This chapter contributes to these debates by offering a mapping of the field of border security R&D and delving into the imaginaries different actors pursue in this field. Understanding R&D as a practice of border security allows us not only to understand the different actors in the field but also to examine the different entanglements between security and technology from the viewpoint of developing devices. My analysis has shown how security-related R&D contributes to a strong involvement of the private security industry in the EU and shifts power to the industry's advantage. It has also shown that we need to understand R&D as a political process that reproduces power relations and reifies understandings of security.

Note

1 However, not all of these companies are entirely private – for example, the Italian state holds 30 per cent of shares in Leonardo and France holds 25 per cent of shares in Thales. I refer to them to 'private' in the sense that their actions are not steered by state committees and are largely in private hands.

References

Aas, K.F. and Bosworth, M. (2013) (eds) *The Borders of Punishment: Migration, Citizenship, and Social Exclusion.* Oxford: Oxford University Press.

Abrahamsen, R. and Williams, M.C. (2009) Security Beyond the State: Global Security Assemblages in International Politics. *International Political Sociology* 3(1): 1–17. doi.org/10.1111/j.1749-5687.2008.00060.x.

Adey, P. and Anderson, B. (2012) Anticipating Emergencies: Technologies of Preparedness and the Matter of Security. *Security Dialogue* 43(2): 99–117. doi.org/10.1177/0967010612438432.

Akkerman, M. (2016) Border Wars: The Arms Dealers Profiting from Europe's Refugee Tragedy. Stop Wapenhandel and The Transnational Institute www.tni.org/files/publication-downloads/border-wars-report-web1207.pdf.

Amicelle, A., Aradau, C. and Jeandesboz, J. (2015) Questioning Security Devices: Performativity, Resistance, Politics. *Security Dialogue* 46(4): 293–306. doi.org/10.1177/0967010615586964.

Amoore, L. (2006) Biometric Borders: Governing Mobilities in the War on Terror. *Political Geography* 25(3): 336–351. doi.org/10.1016/j.polgeo.2006.02.001.

Amoore, L. and Hall, A. (2009) Taking People Apart: Digitized Dissection and the Body at the Border. *Environment and Planning D: Society and Space* 27: 444–464. https://doi.org/10.1068/d1208.

Anderson, B. (2010) Preemption, Precaution, Preparedness: Anticipatory Action and Future Geographies. *Progress in Human Geography* 34(6): 777–798. doi.org/10.1177/0309132510362600.

Andersson, R. (2016) Hardwiring the Frontier: The Politics of Security Technology in Europe's 'Fight Against Illegal Migration'. *Security Dialogue* 47(1): 22–39. doi.org/10.1177/0967010615606044.

Avant, D. (2005) *The Market for Force: The Consequences of Privatizing Security.* Cambridge: Cambridge University Press.

Baird, T. (2017) Who Speaks for the European Border Security Industry? A Network Analysis. *European Security* 26(1): 37–58. doi.org/10.1080/09662839.2016.1267146.

Baird, T. (2018) Interest Groups and Strategic Constructivism: Business Actors and Border Security Policies in the European Union. *Journal of Ethnic and Migration Studies* 44(1): 118–136. doi.org/10.1080/1369183X.2017.1316185.

Balzacq, T., Basaran, T., Bigo, D., Guittet, E.-P. and Olsson, C. (2010) Security Practices. In R.A. Denemark (ed.), *International Studies Encyclopedia Online.* Malden, MA: Wiley-Blackwell, 1–30. doi.org/ 10.1093/acrefore/9780190846626. 013.475.

Bellanova, R. and Duez, D. (2016) The Making (Sense) of EUROSUR: How to Control the Sea Borders. In R. Bossong and H. Carrapico (eds), *EU Borders and Shifting Internal Security.* Cham: Springer International, 23–44.

Berndtsson, J. (2012) Security Professionals for Hire: Exploring the Many Faces of Private Security Expertise. *Millenium: Journal of International Studies* 40(2): 303–320. doi.org/10.1177/0305829811425635.

Bigo, D. (2014) The (In)Securitization Practices of the Three Universes of EU Border Control: Military/Navy – Border Guards/Police. *Database Analysts, Security Dialogue* 45(3): 209–225. doi.org/10.1177/0967010614530459.

Bigo, D., Jeandesboz, J., Martin-Maze, M. and Ragazzi, F. (2014) *Review of Security Measures in the 7th Research Framework Programme FP7 2007–2013.* Study for the LIBE Committee.

Bourne, M., Johnson, H. and Lisle, D. (2015) Laboratizing the Border: The Production, Translation and Anticipation of Security Technologies. *Security Dialogue* 46(4): 307–325. doi.org/10.1177/0967010615578399.

Côté-Boucher, K., Infantino, F. and Salter, M.B. (2014) Border Security as Practice: An Agenda for Research. *Security Dialogue* 45(3): 195–208. doi.org/10.1177/0967010614533243.

Csernatoni, R. (2018) Constructing the EU's High-Tech Borders: FRONTEX and Dual-Use Drones for Border Management. *European Security* 27(2): 175–200. doi.org/10.1080/09662839.2018.1481396.

Davidshofer, S., Jeandesboz, J. and Ragazzi, F. (2016) Technology and Security Practices: Situating the Technological Imperative. In T. Basaran, D. Bigo, E. Guittet and R. Walker (eds), *International Political Sociology: Transversal Lines.* London: Routledge, 205–227.

De Goede, M., Simon, S. and Hoijtink, M. (2014) Performing Pre-Emption. *Security Dialogue* 45(5): 411–422. doi.org/10.1177/0967010614543585.

Dijstelbloem, H., Meijer, A. and Besters, M. (2011) The Migration Machine. In H. Dijstelbloem and A. Meijer (eds), *Migration and the New Technological Borders of Europe*. New York: Palgrave Macmillan: 1–21.

EOS (2009a) Priorities for a Future European Security Framework.

EOS (2009b) White Paper: A European Approach to Border Management.

EOS (2017) Towards Holistic European Security and a Competitive European Security Industry.

European Commission (2012) Communication from the Commission the European Parliament, the Council and the European Economic and Social Committee. Security Industrial Policy. Action Plan for an Innovative and Competitive Security Industry. COM 2012 (417).

European Commission (2013) Horizon 2020 Work Programme 2014–2015, 14: Secure Societies – Protecting Freedom and Security of Europe and its Citizens.

European Commission (2015a) Communication from the Commission the European Parliament, the Council and the European Economic and Social Committee. A European Agenda on Migration. COM 2015(240).

European Commission (2015b) Communication from the Commission the European Parliament, the Council and the European Economic and Social Committee. The European Agenda on Security. COM 2015(185).

European Commission (2015c) Horizon 2020 Work Programme 2016–2017, 14: Secure Societies – Protecting Freedom and Security of Europe and its Citizens.

European Commission (2016) Communication from the Commission the European Parliament, the Council and the European Economic and Social Committee. Stronger and Smarter Information Systems for Borders and Security. COM 2016(205).

European Commission (2017a) Mandate of the Horizon 2020 'Protection and Security Advisory Group' (PASAG).

European Commission (2017b) Horizon 2020 Work Programme 2018–2020, 14: Secure Societies – Protecting Freedom and Security of Europe and its Citizens.

European Union (2013a) Regulation (EU) No 1291/2013 of the European Parliament and of the Council of 11 December 2013 establishing Horizon 2020 – the Framework Programme for Research and Innovation (2014–2020) and repealing Decision No 1982/2006/EC.

European Union (2013b) Regulation (EU) No 1052/2013 of the European Parliament and of the Council of 22 October 2013 establishing the European Border Surveillance System (EUROSUR).

European Union (2018) Regulation (EU) 2018/1240 of the European Parliament and of the Council of 12 September 2018 establishing a European Travel Information and Authorisation System (ETIAS) and amending Regulations (EU) No 1077/2011, (EU) No 515/2014, (EU) 2016/399, (EU) 2016/1624 and (EU) 2017/2226.

Frontex (2016) Best Practice Operational Guidelines for Automated Border Control (ABC) Systems. At: https://op.europa.eu/en/publication-detail/-/publication/e81d082d-20a8-11e6-86d0-01aa75ed71a1/language-en.

Hall, A. (2017) Decisions at the Data Border: Discretion, Discernment and Security. *Security Dialogue* 48(6): 488–504. doi.org/10.1177/0967010617733668.

Hayes, B. (2009) NeoConOpticon: The EU Security-Industrial Complex. Statewatch and the Transnational Institute. At: www.statewatch.org/analyses/neoconopticon-report.pdf.

Hoijtink, M. (2014) Capitalizing on Emergence: The 'New' Civil Security Market in Europe. *Security Dialogue* 45(5): 458–475. doi.org/10.1177/0967010614544312.

Huysmans, J. (2006) *The Politics of Insecurity: Fear, Migration and Asylum in the EU.* London: Routledge.

Huysmans, J. (2011) What's in an Act? On Security Speech Acts And Little Security Nothings. *Security Dialogue* 42(4–5): 371–383. doi.org/10.1177/0967010611418713.

Jasanoff, S. (2004) The Idiom of Co-Production. In S. Jasanoff (ed.), *States of Knowledge: The Co-Production of Science and Social Order.* London: Routledge: 1–12. https://doi.org/10.4324/9780203413845.

Jasanoff, S. (2015) Future Imperfect: Science, Technology, and the Imaginations of Modernity. In S. Jasanoff and S. Kim (eds), *Dreamscapes of Modernity: Sociotechnical Imaginaries and the Fabrication of Power.* Chicago, IL: University of Chicago Press: 1–33.

Jasanoff, S. and Kim, S. (2009) Containing the Atom: Sociotechnical Imaginaries and Nuclear Power in the United States and South Korea. *Minerva* 47(2): 119–146. doi. org/10.1007/s11024-009-9124-4.

Jeandesboz, J. (2016) Smartening Border Security in the European Union: An Associational Inquiry. *Security Dialogue* 47(4): 292–309. doi.org/10.1177/0967010616650226.

Jeandesboz, J. (2017) European Border Policing: EUROSUR, Knowledge, Calculation. *Global Crime* 18(3): 256–285. doi.org/10.1080/17440572.2017.1347043.

Jones, C. (2017) *Market Forces: The Development of the EU Security-Industrial Complex.* Statewatch and the Transnational Institute. At: www.tni.org/files/publication-downloads/marketforces-report-tni-statewatch.pdf.

Leander, A. (2005) The Market for Force and Public Security; The Destabilizing Consequences of Private Military Companies. *Journal of Peace Research* 42(5): 605–622.

Léonard, S. (2010) EU Border Security and Migration into the European Union: FRONTEX and Securitisation through Practices, *European Security* 19(2): 231–254. doi.org/10.1080/09662839.2010.526937.

Leese, M., Liden, K. and Blagovesta, N. (2019) Putting Critique to Work: Ethics in EU Security Research. *Security Dialogue* 50(1): 59–76. doi.org/10.1177/0967010618809554.

Lemberg-Pedersen, M. (2013) Private Security Companies and the European Borderscapes. In T. Gammeltoft-Hansen and N. Nyberg Sørensen (eds), *The Migration Industry and the Commercialization of International Migration.* London: Routledge, 152–172.

Lemberg-Pedersen, M. (2018) Security, Industry and Migration in European Border Control. In A. Weinar, S. Bonjour and L. Zhyznomirska (eds), *The Routledge Handbook of the Politics of Migration in Europe.* London: Routledge.

Martins, B.O. and Küsters, C. (2019) Hidden Security: EU Public Research Funds and the Development of European Drones. *Journal of Common Market Studies* 57(2): 278–297. doi.org/10.1111/jcms.12787.

Mezzadra, S. and Neilson, B. (2013): *Border as Method or the Multiplication of Labor.* Durham, NC: Duke University Press.

Möllers, N. (2017) The Mundane Politics of 'Security Research'. Tailoring Research Problems. *Science & Technology Studies* 30(2): 14–33. doi.org/10.23987/sts.61021.

Pallister-Wilkins, P. (2015) The Humanitarian Politics of European Border: Frontex and the Border Police in Evros. *International Political Sociology* 9(1): 53–69. doi. org/10.1111/ips.12076.

PASAG (2015) Strategic Recommendations for Secure Societies Theme in Horizon 2020. At: https://ec.europa.eu/home-affairs/sites/homeaffairs/files/e-library/documents/policies/security/h2020_secure_societies_advisory_group_strategic_recommendations_for_secure_societies_theme_in_horizon_2020_en.pdf.

PASAG (2016) Secure Societies – Protecting Freedom and Security of Europe and its Citizens. At: https://ec.europa.eu/programmes/horizon2020/en/h2020-section/secure-societies-%E2%80%93-protecting-freedom-and-security-europe-and-its-citizens.

Paul, R. (2017) Harmonisation by Risk Analysis? Frontex and the Risk-Based Governance of European Border Control. *Journal of European Integration* 39(6): 689–706. doi.org/10.1080/07036337.2017.1320553.

Vaughan-Williams, N. (2015) *Europe's Border Crisis: Biopolitical Security and Beyond.* Oxford: Oxford University Press.

Vogel, K.M., Balmer, B., Evans, S.W., Kroener, I., Matsumoto, M. and Rappert, B. (2017) Knowledge and Security. In U. Felt, R. Fouché, C. Miller and L. Smith-Doerr (eds), *The Handbook of Science and Technology Studies*, 4th edn. Cambridge, MA: MIT Press, 973–1001.

Wagenaar, H. (2011) *Meaning in Action. Interpretation and Dialogue in Policy Analysis.* London: Routledge.

10 Security meets science governance

The EU politics of dual-use research

Dagmar Rychnovská

Introduction

In a guidance note to researchers working on H2020 projects, one can read that:

> *(e)xporting* certain goods/technologies can be a security threat, especially in terms of WMD (Weapons of Mass Destruction) proliferation. Transactions involving such *dual-use items* can be subject to certain *restrictions*, which may affect your research project.
>
> (European Commission 2018: 1, *emphasis in original*)

WMD are not the most typical theme in the guidelines for a research grant proposal. How did the topic get on the agenda of European researchers? What made it possible and what are the implications thereof? This chapter focuses on the European Union (EU) politics of dual-use research and specifically on how export control policy, as a traditional tool of security governance, intersects with the governance of research.

International trade in dual-use items, that is, those typically understood as having civilian as well as potential military applications (see Martins and Ahmad, Chapter 3 and Vila Seoane, Chapter 5 in this book) is an area under special scrutiny, because these goods and technologies can be used for the development of WMD on behalf of individuals or states. For instance, it is believed that the nuclear weapon programmes of North Korea, India and Pakistan have been made possible partly due to the ineffectiveness of international non-proliferation regimes (Wetter 2009: 1). Current export control regimes on dual-use items, thus, can be seen as a way to balance the promotion of commercial and research partnerships on the one hand and to limit the threat of proliferation of WMD on the other hand. In essence, export controls are a crucial complement to the international non-proliferation regimes (Vila Seoane, Chapter 5 in this book).

Any policy of export controls draws on an implicit or explicit threat scenario involving the products that are subject to this regulation. As such, export control regimes reflect the perception of the technological, political and economic realities and their mutual entanglements. Even though export controls have been of interest to scholars in International Relations, science and technology studies, law and so forth (Bromley, Cooper and Holtom 2012; Rath, Ischi and Perkins 2014; Reppy 2006; Micara 2012), the overlaps of the international control regimes with the workings of science and technology have been less explored (Evans and Valdivia 2012; Selgelid 2009). Given the increasing attention paid to the developments in science and technology in the governance of dual-use research (Atlas and Dando 2006; Danzig 2012; Revill and Jefferson 2013; Rychnovská 2016), the mutual relations between science and security in the politics of dual-use deserve more scholarly scrutiny and critical reflection.

This chapter looks at the governance of emerging security technologies in the EU as a product of developments both in the area of science and (international) security and their mutual interplays. In particular, it scrutinises the shifting meanings and practices of governing dual-use research in the EU and the implications thereof. It does so by situating the EU approach to dual-use research in three developments: the changing narrative about international security and the problem of WMD in particular; the emergence of security controversies related to biotechnology research; and the transformation of the EU institutional landscape. The chapter approaches the issue from the perspective of critical security studies, arguing that the EU politics of dual-use research may be read as a changing problematisation of security, which translates into the sphere of science governance and has implications for the constellation of power relations and the way authority, knowledge and subjectivity are constructed in security politics.

The chapter proceeds as follows. It first approaches the problem of dual-use research from critical security studies, arguing for reading it as a changing problematisation of security with socio-political effects on the performance of security expertise. Second, it briefly discusses the evolution of export control systems on dual-use items and the shifting narratives of international security within which this evolution needs to be contextualised. Third, recent security controversies in life sciences are discussed, which have affected the discourse on dual-use in the twenty-first century. After discussing the entanglements of security and science in the context of dual-use governance, the chapter provides a brief overview of the EU politics of dual-use and the contemporary practices of dealing with dual-use research. This part draws on the analysis of official EU documents relevant for the politics of dual-use from 2000 to 2019, which is the time-frame in which the EU formed a Community regime for the export control of dual-use items. Finally, the chapter concludes by discussing the implications of the novel approach to governing dual-use and misuse of research to the politics of security expertise, with some remarks on the politics of insecurity in the area of research and innovation governance.

Dual-use as a problematisation of security

How did dual-use research become a security concern for the EU and what are the implications of regulating it under the politics of export controls on dual-use items? Drawing on critical security studies, this chapter suggests that we need to look not only at what dual use *is*, but also at what it *does*. Critical security studies are a subfield of security studies that looks at security and threats as a result of social and political practices rather than as problems to be solved (Aradau *et al.* 2014). For critical security researchers, the emergence of specific problematisation of security (i.e. how security is made) is equally significant as a subject of study as are the wider implications of security practices (i.e. what security does). Critical security researchers typically look at the transformations of security governance and study how security threats are constructed in relation to valued referent objects, how these discourses of security change and what they legitimise (Buzan, Wæver and de Wilde 1998; Balzacq 2011).

The politics of dual-use in the EU can be understood as a result of similar processes of the changing problematisation of security, where new referent objects (scientific knowledge, technologies and the like) become seen as a source of insecurity if they get into the 'wrong hands' and become part of a newly imagined threat scenario. At the same time, the dual nature of certain items is an important aspect of this security discourse, which shall be understood in the context of broader thinking on security and innovation.

Drawing on critical theory and specifically on Michel Foucault, the problem of dual-use and the regulation of dual-use items may be embedded in the idea of *circulatory governance*, which has been on rise as a technology of governing the mobility of people, things and ideas (Aradau and Blanke 2010). According to Foucault, the circulation of ideas, goods, technologies, people and so forth are seen as crucial for neoliberal societies: 'organizing circulation, eliminating its dangerous elements, making a division between good and bad circulation, and maximizing the good circulation by diminishing the bad' is the core of modern security governance, which consequently constructs the duality of freedom and security in the same system (2007: 18).

In other words, the global movement of bodies, knowledges, materials and the like in current societies is cherished as a symbol of freedom, progress and eventually as the driving force of capitalism and profit-making. However, some types of mobility are not desired, for example, certain types of migration and travel. Dual-use governance then can be seen in the context of managing circulations, identifying wanted and unwanted mobilities and seeking to police the boundary between them. As pointed out by some critical security scholars, this type of governance can lead to exclusionary effects and shifting power relations (cf. Salter 2013; Vaughan-Williams 2009).

As such, dual-use can be seen as a powerful signifier which makes possible drawing a line between 'desired' and 'undesired' research and legitimising specific types of knowledge and expertise as being relevant for identifying and policing this boundary. Of particular interest are two areas in this regard: first, via what *practices* is this boundary policed; and second, what are the implications of this policing – that is, with the transformation of regimes of governance, what changes is also who becomes regarded as an appropriate speaker, and what kind of knowledge counts as relevant for threat assessment. This can be seen as an issue of *security expertise*. Both aspects are arguably relevant not only for understanding the changing nature of security politics, but also for understanding the effects of the changing nature of dual-use governance.

The politics of dual-use and export controls: from the Cold War to the war on terror

The notion of dual-use is a part of political discourse that brings together thinking on security threats and concerns about the non-desired use of technology in society. The very concept of dual-use has gone through much development in political and legal discourse and there are still many different meanings of the term used in diverse contexts – civilian versus military, benevolent versus malevolent, peaceful versus non-peaceful and so forth (Rath *et al.* 2014). The very concept of dual-use is, as noted by Reppy (2006), rooted in the Cold War and its geopolitical as well as technological dichotomies, when the commercial opportunities from technology exports started to be weighed against the potential military advantage to the enemy. It was in this context that modern export control regimes were established.

Export controls have a long history, yet the basic idea has remained the same over the centuries – to have a list of items whose export to other countries requires an official licence and an established process to gain this licence. A system of export control is established since certain items are seen as having the potential to contribute to an unwanted military advantage of an adversary. As Evans and Valdivia (2012: 171) point out, export controls have been mostly focused on balancing national security and economic interests and, therefore, can be seen as a tool of trade control. At the same time, as export controls also touch upon some scientific areas, such as the circulation of knowledge and information, they also become subject to national security concerns.

The current regimes of export control mostly draw on their predecessors from the Cold War, during which the control of exports was seen as a key tool of the politics of arms control and disarmament between the Western and Soviet blocs (Cupitt 2002). The template for modern export control regimes was provided by the Coordinating Committee on Multilateral Export Controls (CoCom), which was established after the Second World War by NATO countries, together with Japan and Australia, in order to put an embargo on sensitive materials and technologies exported to the Eastern Bloc countries. These included mostly hardware and electronics (such as machine tools or lasers), which could be used for the production of military technologies like tanks or fighter planes (Shaw 2016: 474).

The contemporary successor of CoCom is the Wassenaar Arrangement – a multilateral export control regime coordinating export policies on conventional arms and dual-use items among its 42 member states, including many from the former Warsaw Pact countries. Another export control regime is, for instance, the Australia group, formed in 1985 in response to the revelation of the chemical weapons programme in Iraq. The Australia group harmonises the export control policies of its members and seeks to prevent the export of dual-use materials and technologies that might contribute to the development of chemical or biological weapons (Shaw 2016).

The understanding of dual-use has shifted a lot with the changing interpretation of the international security environment after 9/11. The focus on non-state actors as a source of threat to state security shaped also the discourse on WMD – the new fear was the potential proliferation of WMD to terrorist groups and rogue states (Rath *et al.* 2014). This also affected the politics of export controls. Specifically, a major case for expanding and strengthening export control regimes globally came with the pronunciation of global terrorism as a security threat by the United Nations (2004), whose Security Council Resolution 1540 from 2004 urges member states to implement and improve export controls in order to prevent the acquisition of WMD by terrorist organisations. The effect of the UN call has been a new wave of export control laws and regulations at many levels, including in the EU.

Security controversies in life sciences

After 2001 and the rise of the global war on terror, much more attention among security professionals started to be paid to the possibility that non-state actors might get access to chemical, biological or nuclear technologies which could be weaponised and used in a terrorist attack. This fear has been partly triggered by the case of anthrax letters sent in the aftermath of 9/11 attack to several public figures in the United States, which caused the death of five people and fuelled the fear of bioterrorism and other novel types of terror and crime involving scientific material or technology (Vogel 2016: 212).

The case of anthrax mailings reminded national security professionals of the danger posed by biological weapons and reinforced some controversies in the scientific community about the potential security risks posed by rapidly evolving life scientific research, especially in the area of biotechnology – something that experts had already warned of earlier (Dando 1999; Henderson 1999). The narrative on controversial biotechnologies and the risks they pose was connected with that of global terrorism and the threat of malign non-state actors and the taxonomy of biological threats was widened to include bioterrorism, bio-crime, laboratory incidents and others (Koblentz 2010).

The threat of biotechnology misuse by malign non-state actors was described in detail in a report called *Biotechnology Research in an Age of Terrorism* (National Research Council 2004), prepared by the US National Academies. The report describes the dual-use dilemma posed by biotechnology and warns of the risk of the malevolent use of dangerous biological agents and the risk of creating a novel (and more dangerous) class of pathogens. As a response to these challenges, the report calls for a greater involvement of the scientific community, awareness-raising and its self-governance in conducting research in a responsible way. With the new framing of life sciences and biotechnology in particular as a potential source of threat providing tools for global terrorism, new policies started to be promoted and adopted in the United States and other states

(Rappert and Gould 2009) as well as by international organisations like the World Health Organization (WHO 2005).

A prime effect of this narrative about life sciences as a new source of threat and subject to security controversy has been the case of H5N1 research, in which the dual-use nature of scientific *knowledge* (understood as intangible technology) started to be discussed and was seen as a security concern (Evans 2016; Rychnovská 2016). The case started with the attempt by two separate scientific teams to publish their research on the H5N1 virus. The highly lethal virus appeared at the end of 1990s and the beginning of 2000s, causing several human deaths and stirring fear all over the globe about the potential pandemic it may cause in the highly interconnected world. The virus, though, did not prove to spread efficiently from human to human and the feared global pandemic did not arrive. This puzzling feature of the virus fuelled a question of whether the virus could be spread via airborne transmission, or if it were impossible, what the consequences thereof would be for the pandemic preparedness strategies. The question was raised by two scientific teams, working in the United States and in the Netherlands, who designed and conducted experiments on ferrets as a part of which the H5N1virus was genetically mutated. This so-called gain-of-function research showed that this enhanced and highly deadly H5N1 is in fact transmissible. The findings of the research were sent to the journals *Nature* and *Science*, where they triggered a wave of security concerns. The papers were read as containing a blueprint for a causing potentially catastrophic pandemic, which could be misused by malign actors or states as a biological weapon which could not be contained by existing medical drugs (Elbe and Buckland-Merrett 2019).

The approach to this controversy took very different form in the United States and in the Netherlands. The United States, unlike in Europe, established a special organisation with the purpose of deliberating and deciding on the governance of controversial life scientific research. The National Science Advisory Board for Biosecurity (NSABB) is a boundary organisation bringing together scientific and security expertise and was founded in 2004 to advise federal agencies on biosecurity issues. In the Unites States, therefore, the decision on the H5N1 research publication was put in the hands of the NSABB, which was supposed to assess the threat posed by the publications.

On the contrary, in Europe, the controversy was handled by the Dutch authorities and courts, who decided that the Dutch scientific team has to ask for an EU export control licence in order to publish the results. The reasoning behind the decision was that these research findings are a dual-use item and their publication comprises a transfer of intangible technologies, which falls under the EU export control regime on dual-use items (Charatsis 2015). This decision has had profound implications not only for the EU politics of export controls, under which the scope of controlled items became wider and brought with it new governance challenges, but also for research governance in the EU. As will be shown later, these areas gradually came closer together, with interesting implications for the scientific field and the status of scientific publications in the EU security governance.

The EU politics of dual-use

The EU politics on dual-use can be situated in the broader evolution of the European commercial and security policy (Micara 2012). During the Cold War, most European Community countries were members of CoCom, while European institutions did not participate in the multilateral export control regimes. With the advancement of EU internal market, the Council of the EU in 1994 set up a Community regime for the control of dual-use exports with Regulation 3381/94 and a Decision 94/942/CFSP in the realm of Common Foreign and Security Policy regulating the export of dual-use goods and setting up an authorisation of 'trusted' countries.

The EU first set up a Community regime for the export control of dual-use items and technology in 2000 with regulation 1334/2000, which integrates the existing system into one and gives a key decision-making role to the Commission (Vila Seoane, Chapter 5 in this book). The regulation defines dual-use items as:

> items, including software and technology, which can be used for both civil and military purposes, and shall include all goods which can be used for both non-explosive uses and assisting in any way in the manufacture of nuclear weapons or other nuclear explosive devices.
>
> (Council of the EU 2000: 3)

The export control regime relies mostly on the explicit list of items that are subject to oversight and it does not pay any special attention to the advances in science and technology.

In the early 2000s, in the aftermaths of the terrorist attacks in the United States and in the evolving global war on terror, the EU decided to strengthen its role in international politics and adopted its first security strategy, 'A Secure Europe in a Better World' (Council of the EU 2003a). The strategy acknowledges the complexity of contemporary security issues and argues for a common approach in dealing with them, with the aim to become a truly global security actor. One of the major themes of the strategy is the threat of WMD and the changing nature of the proliferation threat. The strategy argues that '[a]dvances in the biological sciences may increase the potency of biological weapons in the coming years; attacks with chemical and radiological materials are also a serious possibility' (Council of the EU 2003a: 4–5). The most frightening scenario in this regard becomes the acquisition of WMD by terrorist groups, which is seen as a threat comparable with the use of WMD by state actors (Council of the EU 2003a: 5). The direct answer to this call is the 'Fight Against the Proliferation of Weapons of Mass Destruction' (Council of the EU 2003b), in which the EU highlights that chemical and biological weapons in particular pose a special threat due to the dual-use nature of the relevant materials, equipment and know-how. It warns again that 'the potential for the misuse of the dual-use technology and knowledge is increasing as a result of rapid developments in the life sciences' (Council of the EU 2003b: 4) and argues for the development of export control policy that would effectively address also the transfer of intangible items.

In response to the changing approach to non-proliferation and the increasing attention paid to the specificities of biological and chemical weapons, the EU updated its export control regime. A complex framework for the export control on dual-use items is set by the EU regulation No. 428/2009 (European Commission 2009), which aims at better coordination with international regimes, greater harmonisation of the system of control and expands the scope of governance (Micara 2012: 588).

In its 2016 Global Strategy, the EU (2016) pledged to modernise its export control policy on dual-use goods as a part of its multidimensional approach to conflicts and crises and its contribution to the 'political economy of peace'. Three years later, the Council of the EU issued its position on a proposal by the European Commission, under which a new regime for the export control of dual-use items shall be set up. The modernisation of the dual-use policy shall, among other issues, better reflect the ongoing technological developments as well as the changing political and security environment and the threats to it. One of the aspects that the new regime of export control should take into account more is the role of researchers – as the proposal argues, 'academic and research institutions face distinct challenges in export control due to, inter alia, their organizational structures, technological developments and the international nature of their scientific exchanges' (Council of the EU 2019: 5). Even though exceptions from the regulation are considered for 'basic scientific research' and the spread of information 'in the public domain' (which is a provision that was set up already in the 2000 Council Regulation), the proposal calls for raising awareness of the risks and challenges associated with the handling of sensitive items among academics and researchers (Council of the EU 2019: 5).

The practices of governing dual-use research in the EU

Traditionally, there is a divide between military and civilian research, which is reflected in the institutional as well as the regulatory environment in which the research takes places. While military/defence research is still much in the hands of national governments, the EU has become a major player for funding and strategically shaping civilian research in Europe. With the new focus on dual-use as a security concern, the EU envisions the adaptation of novel regulatory practices in civilian research which shall help manage the risks of conducting dual-use research or research with potential risk of misuse.

How does the changing EU politics of dual-use effect research governance? Under the Horizon 2020 research programme, which is aimed at both basic and applied scientific research, researchers are supposed to apply only for funding that will be used for civil science. Concretely, as stated in Article 19(2) of the Horizon 2020 Framework Programme Regulation (EU) No. 1291/2013, '[r]esearch and innovation activities carried out under Horizon 2020 shall have an exclusive focus on civil applications' (European Commission 2013). This provision does not exclude the participation of military partners or the development of products that have both military and civil application (i.e. are of dual-use, as understood in the EU law), yet primarily the research shall focus on civil application (European Commission 2019).

Dual-use research is in this context understood as research involving dual-use items. According to the Article 2(1) of the EU Export Control Regulation No. 482/2009, 'dual-use items' shall mean items, including software and technology, which can be used for both civil and military purposes, and shall include all goods which can be used for both non-explosive uses and assisting in any way in the manufacture of nuclear weapons or other nuclear explosive devices (European Commission 2009: 5).

The definition of dual-use is adjusted to the scientific audience. As explained in the guidelines to the Horizon 2020 programme, 'dual-use items are normally used for civilian purposes but may have military applications, or may contribute to the proliferation of weapons of mass destruction' (European Commission 2019: 33). In this context, dual-use is presented to researchers as potentially a dangerous feature of their (otherwise benign) work, which they are supposed to detect and accordingly subject their work to a different regime of mobility.

Since the H5N1 controversy, the EU considers scientific publications as potential dual-use items and develops novel regulatory practices on how to identify and oversee such items. At the same time, more attention is now paid to the whole process of knowledge production so that security concerns are identified earlier than the publication stage. In order to raise awareness of the potential risks of dual-use research, the EU urges researchers to make sure that their research complies with relevant international treaties, especially regarding non-proliferation or humanitarian laws. The Biological and Toxin Weapons Convention and the Resolution 1540 of the UN Security Council on the non-proliferation of WMD are specifically mentioned in this context and worth further consideration (European Commission 2019: 33 and 34). For instance, in the guidelines to the Horizon 2020 programme, researchers are encouraged to appoint an independent ethics adviser/ethics board, with relevant ethics and security expertise, to carry out a risk-benefit analysis of the intended research and to suggest appropriate safeguards to cover security risks (during and beyond the lifetime of the project) and training for researchers (European Commission 2019: 33).

Besides *dual-use*, the European Commission also operates with the notion of *misuse*. Misuse of research is in this context understood as 'research involving or generating materials, methods, technologies or knowledge that could be misused for unethical purposes' (European Commission 2019: 37). This category is perhaps most directly targeted at disciplining researchers into critically scrutinising their own research and identifying its potential 'blind spots' that could be misused when appropriated in a different context. Researchers, thus, essentially become part of security governance and not only conduct research but, at some point, they also look at it as security experts and assess its potential dangerousness as neutral observers.

Interestingly, this category includes several quite diverse areas of concerns, even though they are brought together under a common theme of misuse. Specifically, researchers are supposed to conduct risk-assessment and as a guidance, ask themselves whether the materials, methods, technologies or knowledge that they work with could cause harm or whether they could serve unintended (and unethical) purposes and what the consequences would be if these were to end up in the 'wrong hands' (European Commission 2019: 37).

Risk mitigation measures are suggested for several areas of research that are more prone to misuse and these are, according to the European Commission (2019: 37–38), research on 'biological, chemical, radiological and nuclear security-sensitive materials and explosives' and 'research with a potential impact on human rights'. The strategies suggested include practices such as staff training, 'including security expertise', 'limiting the dissemination of research results' and so on.

To sum up, the EU over the past two decades has reformed and strengthened its policy of dual-use export controls. These changes can be accounted for by several factors: the changing narratives of international security and the threat scenarios that dual-use items are supposed to play part in; the developments in international export control regimes; the institutional changes that the EU has gone through; and the evolution of science and technology per se, as, for example, the H5N1 publication controversy demonstrates. As a result, the meaning of dual-use research has expanded to new areas, which have become seen as security concerns. Given the unpredictability of research and innovation development and the broadening threat scenarios, though, it becomes impossible to draw a clear line between secure and insecure research. For that reason, the EU resorts to novel security measures that are introduced in the governance of research. These practices are greatly based on enhancing the measures typically used in research ethics and the principle of responsibilisation – concretely, researchers are supposed to introduce practices that draw on self-assessment, shape community norms and eventually change the process of knowledge production and circulation.

Conclusions: security politics in research governance – what are the implications?

Since 2000, the EU has broadened the scope of goods and technologies, which it considers to have dual-use characters and which are subject to its export control regime on dual-use items. This development can be seen as a result of the EU's changing understanding of the international security environment and the way technology can be used in a harmful way on the society. Developments in science and technology have gradually become the subject of greater interest in the EU dual-use regime and the EU has adopted a more anticipatory approach to the governance of research and the circulation of its findings. In order to circulate materials, technologies and information that are of dual-use character, researchers may need to obtain an export licence, which is a rule that was introduced after the so-called H5N1 research controversy. What are the implications of these shifts in the governance of research seen as dual-use for the construction of authority and subjectivity and the politics of security knowledge?

First, this regime of governance promoted by the EU in the area of dual-use research and research misuse shifts the attention of regulatory oversight to the stage of science and technology development and makes researchers effectively co-responsible for the politics of security in the field of export controls. Researchers shall not only engage new actors as security experts in the process of research and development, but they are supposed to act as agents of security themselves. Drawing on their scientific knowledge and expertise, they shall assess the potential risks that their results – whether in the form of knowledge, software, technology or other – may pose in the future and as such, construct implicit or explicit threat scenarios which their research may become part of. This not only contributes to a blurring of the boundary between political and security decision-making and scientific knowledge and dispersing decision-making on security, but also, it transfers a great part of responsibility to individual actors and communities who are made responsible for 'doing' security.

Second, in addition to the *responsibilisation* of researchers for security governance, the mentioned developments may also be perceived as contributing to the *bureaucratisation* of security. This means that threat scenarios and deliberation on their relevance for the society are moved from the public sphere and political arenas to bureaucratic bodies – in this context, to ethics boards and other scientific bodies.

Finally, this also leads to making new connections between practices and institutions of research ethics with those of security policy-making – something that may be seen as *ethicalisation* of security (Rychnovská 2016). In the guidelines for researchers in the EU, very different types of research and different types of potential controversies are, for instance, labelled as being of potential misuse. The security framing and the suggested procedures of dealing with these controversies might not, however, be best suited to the diversity of problems that arise. Instead of looking at the structure of opportunities and the context in which such controversies may emerge, the uniform security framing (e.g. in the context of human rights) may supress broader discussion and the diversity of knowledges that should be taken into the account.

Emerging technologies build new synergies between actors and institutions, but the concerns about their use and misuse also create novel synergies, relations, power structures, policies and regulations in the realm of security governance. This chapter looked at these developments in the EU governance of dual-use research and pointed out different reconfigurations between security politics and research governance on the one hand and the relations between scientific knowledge, security assessment and political decisions on the other hand.

References

Aradau, C. and Tobias, B. (2010) Governing Circulation: A Critique of the Biopolitics of Security. In Miguel de Larrinaga and Marc G. Doucet (eds), *Security and Global Governmentality: Globalization, Governance and the State*. London: Routledge, 44–58.

Aradau, C., Huysmans, J. Neal, A. and Voelkner, N. (2014) Introducing Critical Security Methods. In Claudia Aradau, Jef Huysmans, Andrew Neal and Nadine Voelkner (eds), *Critical Security Methods: New Frameworks for Analysis*. London: Routledge, 1–22.

Atlas, R.M. and Dando, M. (2006) The Dual-Use Dilemma for the Life Sciences: Perspectives, Conundrums, and Global Solutions. *Biosecurity and Bioterrorism: Biodefense Strategy, Practice, and Science* 4(3): 276–286.

Balzacq, T. (ed.) (2011) *Securitization Theory: How Security Problems Emerge and Dissolve*. London: Routledge.

Bromley, M., Cooper, N. and Holtom, P. (2012) The UN Arms Trade Treaty: Arms Export Controls, the Human Security Agenda and the Lessons of History. *International Affairs* 88(5): 1029–1048.

Buzan, B., Wæver, O. and de Wilde, J. (1998) *Security: A New Framework for Analysis*. Boulder, CO: Lynne Rienner Publishers.

Charatsis, C. (2015) Setting the Publication of 'Dual-Use Research' Under the Export Authorisation Process: 'The H5N1 Case'. *Strategic Trade Review* 1(Autumn): 56–72.

Council of the European Union (2000) Council Regulation (EC) No. 1334/2000 of 22 June 2000 Setting Up a Community Regime for the Control of Exports of Dual-Use Items and Technology. At: https://publications.europa.eu/en/publication-detail/-/publication/adeadd68-9a0c-4c5b-acb2-6e2ae56dff11/language-en.

Council of the European Union (2003a) A Secure Europe in a Better World: European Security Strategy. At: http://data.consilium.europa.eu/doc/document/ST-15895-2003-INIT/en/pdf.

Council of the European Union (2003b) Fight Against the Proliferation of Weapons of Mass Destruction: EU Strategy Against Proliferation of Weapons of Mass Destruction. At: http://register.consilium.europa.eu/doc/srv?l=EN&f=ST%2015708%202003%20INIT.

Council of the European Union (2019) Proposal for a Regulation of the European Parliament and of the Council Setting Up a Union Regime for the Control of Exports, Brokering, Technical Assistance, Transit and Transfer of Dual-Use Items (Recast) – Mandate for Negotiations with the European Parliament. At: www.consilium.europa.eu/media/39555/mandate-for-negociations.pdf.

Cupitt, R.T. (2002) *Reluctant Champions: US Presidential Policy and Strategic Export Controls, Truman, Eisenhower, Bush and Clinton*. New York: Routledge.

Dando, M. (1999) The Impact of the Development of Modern Biology and Medicine on the Evolution of Offensive Biological Warfare Programs in the Twentieth Century. *Defense Analysis* 15(1): 43–62.

Danzig, R. (2012) *Innovation, Dual Use, and Security: Managing the risks of Emerging Biological and Chemical Technologies*. Cambridge, MA: MIT Press.

Elbe, S. and Buckland-Merrett, G. (2019) Entangled Security: Science, Co-Production, and Intra-Active Insecurity. *European Journal of International Security* 4(2): 123–141.

European Commission (2009) Council Regulation (EC) No. 428/2009 of 5 May 2009 Setting Up a Community Regime for the Control of Exports, Transfer, Brokering and Transit Of Dual-Use Items.

European Commission (2013) Regulation (EU) No. 1291/2013 of the European Parliament and of the Council of 11 December 2013 Establishing Horizon 2020 – the Framework Programme for Research and Innovation (2014–2020) and Repealing Decision No. 1982/2006/EC.

European Commission (2018) Guidance Note: Research Involving Dual-Use Items. At: https://ec.europa.eu/research/participants/data/ref/h2020/other/hi/guide_research-dual-use_en.pdf.

European Commission (2019) Horizon 2020 Programme: Guidance How to Complete your Ethics Self-Assessment. At: https://ec.europa.eu/research/participants/data/ref/h2020/grants_manual/hi/ethics/h2020_hi_ethics-self-assess_en.pdf.

European Union (2016) Shared Vision, Common Action: A Stronger Europe. A Global. Strategy for the European Union's Foreign and Security Policy. At: https://eeas.europa.eu/sites/eeas/files/eugs_review_web_0.pdf.

Evans, S.W. (2016) Biosecurity Governance for the Real World. *Issues in Science and Technology* 33(1): 84–88.

Evans, S.A. and Valdivia, W.D. (2012) Export Controls and the Tensions Between Academic Freedom and National Security. *Minerva* 50(2): 169–190.

Foucault, M. (2007) *Security, Territory, Population.* Basingstoke: Palgrave.

Henderson, D.A. (1999) The Looming Threat of Bioterrorism. *Science* 283(5406): 1279–1282.

Koblentz, G.D. (2010) Biosecurity Reconsidered: Calibrating Biological Threats and Responses. *International Security* 34(4): 96–132.

Micara, A.G. (2012) Current Features of the European Union Regime for Export Control of Dual-Use Goods. *JCMS: Journal of Common Market Studies* 50(4): 578–593.

National Research Council (2004) *Biotechnology Research in an Age of Terrorism: Confronting the Dual-Use Dilemma.* Washington, DC: The National Academy Press.

Rappert, B. and Gould, C. (eds) (2009) *Biosecurity: Origins, Transformations and Practices.* London: Springer.

Rath, J., Ischi, M. and Perkins, D. (2014) Evolution of Different Dual-Use Concepts in International and National Law and its Implications on Research Ethics and Governance. *Science and Engineering Ethics* 20(3): 769–790.

Reppy, J. (2006) Managing Dual-Use Technology in an Age of Uncertainty. *The Forum* 4(1).

Revill, J. and Jefferson, C. (2013) Tacit Knowledge and the Biological Weapons Regime. *Science and Public Policy* 41(5): 597–610.

Rychnovská, D. (2016) Governing Dual-Use Knowledge: From the Politics of Responsible Science to the Ethicalization of Security. *Security Dialogue* 47(4): 310–328.

Salter, M.B. (2013) To Make Move and Let Stop: Mobility and the Assemblage of Circulation. *Mobilities* 8(1): 7–19.

Selgelid, M.J. (2009) Governance of Dual-Use Research: An Ethical Dilemma. *Bulletin of the World Health Organization* 87: 720–723.

Shaw, R. (2016) Export Controls and the Life Sciences: Controversy or Opportunity? *EMBO Reports* 17(4): 474–480.

United Nations (2004) Security Council Resolution 1540 (2004) [Concerning Weapons of Massive Destruction], 28 April 2004, S/RES/1540 (2004).

Vaughan-Williams, N. (2009) *Border Politics: The Limits of Sovereign Power: The Limits of Sovereign Power.* Edinburgh: Edinburgh University Press.

Vogel, K.M. (2016) Aftershocks of the Anthrax Attacks. In F. Lentzos (ed.), *Biological Threats in the 21st Century.* London: Imperial College Press, 211–237.

Wetter, A. (2009) *Enforcing European Union Law on Exports of Dual-Use Goods.* Oxford: Oxford University Press.

WHO (2005) *Life Science Research: Opportunities and Risks for Public Health.* Geneva: World Health Organization.

11 The governance of dual-use research in the EU

The case of neuroscience

Inga Ulnicane

Introduction

An important element of the European governance of emerging technologies is the European Union (EU) Framework Programme (FP) rules on dual-use research. This chapter analyses the challenges that might arise in implementing them at the project level and the ways to tackle these challenges. To do that, it draws on the work of one of the largest projects ever funded by the FP, namely, the Human Brain Project (HBP), which is also one of the large-scale international neuroscience initiatives.

Neuroscience is seen as one of the most promising technologies of the twenty-first century that is expected to provide cures for mental disorders and contribute to the development of other technologies such as Information and Communication Technologies (ICT) and Artificial Intelligence (AI). At the same time, advances in neuroscience raise major concerns about potential misuse of sensitive research results. Neuroscience is seen as inherently a dual-use technology, which can be used for beneficial as well as harmful purposes (Ienca, Jotterand and Elger 2018).

Against this background, this chapter focuses on the governance of dual-use research in neuroscience in the EU. At a time when many countries are making unprecedented investments in the field of neuroscience, which sometimes are described as the 'gold rush' or 'golden age' of neuroscience, the European Commission has been supporting neuroscience – or brain research as it is sometimes called – via its research and innovation FP. In the FP7 that lasted from 2007–2013, the Commission invested €3.1 billion in neuroscience. In the first five years (until November 2018) of the following Horizon 2020 programme, a similar sum of €3.2 billion was invested (European Commission 2019a). This funding supports a number of neuroscience research projects included within the Future and Emerging Technologies (FET) programme.

The biggest EU project in this area is one of the FET Flagships projects – the HBP. The HBP is a ten-year, large-scale, multidisciplinary project (2013–2023), with an EU funding of approximately €400 million, bringing together more than 500 scientists and engineers at more than 100 universities and research institutes in some 20 countries (Human Brain Project 2020; Stahl *et al.* 2019). It is one of the large-scale neuroscience research projects in the world. Other major brain research initiatives have been launched or are about to be launched by the United States, Canada, Japan, South Korea, China and Australia (Savage 2019). These seven major neuroscience projects have established an International Brain Initiative, which is supported by the Kavli Foundation (International Brain Initiative 2020). While the International Brain Initiative aims to help these diverse projects to work together, it is also clear that they operate under very different governance, regulatory and ethical frameworks.

What is specific about the governance of neuroscience in the EU? At the moment, the EU has not adopted either a binding legislation or voluntary code of conduct or guidelines specifically dedicated to neuroscience, as has been the case in other technological areas (e.g. nano, AI; see Csernatoni and Lavallée, Chapter 13 in this book). However, all neuroscience research that is funded by the EU FPs is governed by specific regulations and rules, which notably specify that selected projects should have an exclusive focus on civil applications. This requirement distinguishes the EU's HBP from some of the other major brain initiatives around the world, in particular from the US Brain Initiative, which has been partly funded by the Defence Advanced Research Projects Agency (DARPA) with an explicit focus on developing neurotechnology for military use (DARPA 2020).

Thus, in the context when there is a clear military interest in the advancements of neuroscience that can be used for military purposes, it is necessary to better understand how the EU FP's commitment to fund only research that has an exclusive focus on civil applications can be implemented and what challenges might emerge in this process. Accordingly, the main research questions addressed in this chapter are – how is dual-use research in neuroscience governed in the EU and what challenges does it face?

To address these questions, this chapter first introduces the main EU initiative in neuroscience research – the HBP and the way dual-use research is tackled in the HBP, which goes beyond the compulsory EU framework and additionally applies the Responsible Research and Innovation (RRI) approach to deal with the dual-use issues. Second, the chapter reviews the main concepts of dual-use and RRI. Third, the chapter looks at the main actors involved in the governance of dual-use research in the HBP. Fourth, the chapter discusses challenges of governing dual-use research at the project level. Thus, this chapter aims to contribute to the studies of the European governance of emerging technologies by focusing on the governance of dual-use research in the fast-developing field of neuroscience at the project level by analysing one of the biggest research projects ever funded by the EU – the HBP.

The chapter draws on the review of academic literature and policy documents, as well as on the author's critical reflection on her two-year experience (December 2017–November 2019) of contributing to the development of the governance of dual-use research in the HBP, where she participated in the development of Opinion on Responsible Dual-Use and is co-chairing the HBP Dual Use Working Group.

The governance of dual-use research in neuroscience in the EU: the case of the Human Brain Project

The HBP was launched in 2013 as one of the two initial FET Flagship initiatives (with Graphene being the other one). Building on its well-regarded FET funding programme, the European Commission developed the FET Flagship model for large-scale multidisciplinary projects. This new funding model was established during a time of austerity with an aim to move the ICT research frontiers and establish the global EU leadership in FET research. According to the European Commission, the FET Flagships are 'visionary, science-driven, large-scale initiatives addressing grand scientific and technological (S&T) challenges' (2014). While the FET Flagships are often presented as 'one billion projects', in reality, the FPs fund only part of that amount (e.g. for the HBP, approximately 40 per cent) and the projects are expected to raise additional funding from other sources such as industry and national governments.

Thus, the HBP is supported by the EU funding for multidisciplinary ICT research and it aims to integrate research from neuroscience, computing and other research fields and scientific disciplines. According to the Commission, the HBP was launched with a promise that it:

> will create the world's largest experimental facility for developing the most detailed model of the brain, for studying how the human brain works and ultimately to develop personalised treatment of neurological and related diseases. This research lays the scientific and technical foundations for medical progress that has the potential to will dramatically improve the quality of life for millions of Europeans.
>
> (European Commission 2013)

While the original FP funding for this project is planned until 2023, it is envisaged to be turned into sustainable research infrastructure that helps to advance neuroscience, medicine and computing (Amunts *et al.* 2019). This research infrastructure aims to provide access to a wide range of brain data and computing services. The work in the HBP is organised according to a number of divisions such as Neuroinformatics, Brain Simulation, High Performance Analytics and Computing, Medical Informatics, Neuromorphic Computing and Neurorobotics. The HBP also has a dedicated Ethics and Society division that includes work on foresight, public engagement, compliance and researchers' awareness. Dual-use is one of the key ethical issues that the HBP has addressed.

As the project is funded by the FPs (initially by the FP7 and afterwards by the Horizon 2020), the HBP has to comply with the relevant regulations. Ethical principles set out in Article 19 of the Horizon 2020 regulation stipulate that 'research and innovation activities carried out under Horizon 2020 shall have an exclusive focus on civil applications' (European Parliament and the Council of the EU 2013). Issues of dual-use, exclusive focus on civil applications and potential misuse of research results is part of the Horizon 2020 ethics issues checklist and ethics self-assessment, which form part of the grant proposal, later becoming part of the grant agreement and can give rise to binding obligations that may be controlled through ethics checks, reviews and audits (European Commission 2019b).

The Commission's guidance document for completing the ethics self-assessment for Horizon 2020 draws on the EU Export Control Regulation in defining dual-use (European Commission 2019b; see Vila Seoane, Chapter 5 in this book). Accordingly, it focuses on research involving dual-use items that 'are normally used for civilian purposes but might have military applications, or may contribute to the proliferation of weapons of mass destruction' (European Commission 2019b: 33). Furthermore, this guidance document specifies that exclusive focus on civil applications:

> does not rule out the participation of military partners or the development of generic technologies, products or knowledge that may meet the needs of both civil and military end-users (known as 'dual-use' goods or technologies), provided that the research itself has a clear focus on civil applications.
>
> (European Commission 2019b: 35)

Additionally, the ethics issues checklist includes a question about a potential for misuse of research results that concerns 'research involving or generating materials, methods, technologies or knowledge that could be misused for unethical purposes' (European Commission 2019b: 37).

In practice, a number of challenges emerge in answering and dealing with these important questions. To address these challenges, the HBP Ethics and Society division has undertaken a broad research and practice agenda that focuses on applying the Responsible Research and Innovation (RRI) approach. The RRI will be introduced in the following section dedicated to explaining the key concepts, while the application of RRI in the HBP will be addressed in the later sections on actors and challenges.

What are dual-use research and Responsible Research and Innovation?

This section will review the literature on the key concepts used in this chapter: dual-use research and RRI.

Dual-use research

The concept of dual-use research and technology is rather imprecise and contested (see Martins and Ahmad, Chapter 3 in this book). Traditionally, research and technology have been considered to be dual-use when they have current or potential military and civilian applications, recognising that distinction between military and civilian technologies is not sharp and clear-cut (see, e.g., Molas-Gallart 1997).

It can include both turning civilian/benevolent technology into military/hostile uses as well as turning military technology into civilian (e.g. Vogel *et al.* 2017). The dual-use concept has been questioned analytically because it simplifies the link between scientific knowledge and technological innovation (Vogel *et al.* 2017: 977).

While historically, the meaning of dual-use had a military–civilian connotation, today it is used more generally to distinguish research that has the potential to have benevolent/beneficial as well as malevolent/harmful applications (Oltmann 2015). Tara Mahfoud and her colleagues (2018) highlight the problem that distinguishing between military and civilian applications of scientific research and technology has become increasingly difficult. They call for a more nuanced framework that would go beyond the binary world implied by the term 'dual-use'. According to them, policy makers and regulators need to identify and focus on undesirable uses in the political, security, intelligence and military domains (Mahfoud *et al.* 2018).

To clarify some of the questions involved, new terms such as 'intentional misuse' and 'dual-use research of concern' (DURC) have been introduced (Ienca *et al.* 2018: 269). The DURC label was introduced by the United States government to prevent the malicious application of life science research. While historically most attention to dual-use technology emerged in fields of molecular and cell biology, recently the focus has expanded to other fields such as neurotechnology (Ienca *et al.* 2018) and ICT (Langley and Parkinson 2017).

Attitudes towards dual-use research and technology have varied considerably across times, areas of activity and political beliefs. Haico Te Kulve and Wim Smit (2003) explained how the meaning of dual-use technology historically has shifted from a problematic to a desirable feature. According to Te Kulve and Smit, during the Cold War,

> dual-use was viewed as a negative feature that complicated export controls: countries might try to obtain military sensitive technology under the guise of buying civilian technology. The presumed dual nature of some products and technologies also created tensions between the economic and defence perspective on technology exports.
>
> (Te Kulve and Smit 2003: 955–956)

Te Kulve and Smit noticed a profound change in the discourse on dual-use products by the time the Cold War had ended, highlighting that then:

> rather than a negative feature, the dual-use aspect of technology was viewed as something that should be promoted and pursued, as it might solve the twin problem of maintaining a high tech defence technology base restrained by limited budgets, and improving a country's economic competitiveness by a more efficient allocation of R&D funds.
>
> (Te Kulve and Smit 2003: 956)

Similarly, Jordi Molas-Gallart (1997) demonstrates different understandings of dual-use technology from an arms control and industrial perspectives. According to him, 'from an arms control outlook, dual-use technology has been seen as a problem for the control of the international diffusion of advanced weaponry', while from industrial perspective, it is perceived 'as providing an opportunity for the wider exploitation of research and manufacturing efforts beyond their initial (military or civilian) use' (Molas-Gallart 1997: 370). Major differences in attitudes towards dual-use research and technology can also be seen when comparing the approach in research and innovation policy to promote dual-use research and technology (e.g. Molas-Gallart 1997) with the calls in bio- and neuro-ethics to regulate dual-use technology (e.g. Ienca *et al.* 2018).

Diverging attitudes become even more pronounced in the area of military research and technology that is related but not identical to dual-use research. Economists often emphasise many benefits for civilian technologies such as computers, electronics and commercial airspace technology that have originated from military research. A well-known example is the iPhone. Many technologies behind the iPhone have originated from defence research funded by DARPA, Department of Defence, US military and Army Research Office (Mazzucato 2013). However, the opposite argument emphasises the problem that military research leads to 'the diversion of funding from better understanding of root causes of insecurity' and therefore should be reduced (Langley and Parkinson 2017: 205).

Moreover, there are diverse views on the interaction and relationship between civilian, military and dual-use research and technology. In their case study of the development of an advanced battery in the Netherlands, Te Kulve and Smit investigate the cooperation between civilian and military actors and conclude that 'in view of the difficulties of realising civilian–military integrated joint development projects, the establishment of "dual capacity networks" is suggested as part of possible strategy towards an integrated civilian–military technology and industrial base' (2003: 955). In other contexts, interactions between civilian and military research are more restricted, either due to the secrecy of military research or because of funding rules such as the EU FP that require exclusive focus on civilian applications (but does not prohibit the participation of military partners).

The implementation of the EU FP rule about an exclusive focus on civil applications faces old and new challenges. Jakob Edler and Andrew James (2015) pointed out that already in the mid-1990s the European Commission itself recognised that, although the FP is civilian in focus, half of all FP-funded projects have had a strong dual-use dimension in particular in areas such as aeronautics, information technology and materials. Furthermore, since the FP7, a programme dedicated to security research has been introduced within the FPs (see Martins and Ahmad, Chapter 3 in this book). Recently, new defence-related EU research funding mechanisms have emerged outside the FPs (see Fiott, Chapter 2 in this book). These include explicit funding for dual-use research from the European Structural and Investment Funds as well as dedicated defence research funding from the European Defence Fund (EDF). The 2017 Communication from the European Commission on launching the EDF envisages that the planned funding for the EDF 'would make the EU one of the biggest defence R&T investors in Europe and the first investor in collaborative defence research' (European Commission 2017). It also stipulates that the EDF research proposals 'will be reviewed in relation to ethical, legal, or societal aspects by a group of experts on defence ethical and legal issues' and that the precise relationship between the EDF and the future FPs will be determined (European Commission 2017). These developments increase the complexity of dual-use research in EU countries and can raise new practical challenges, for example, if a research group receives funding from both – the FP with its exclusive focus on civil applications and the EDF – how does it practically separate in its lab its research with exclusive focus on civil applications from its defence research.

In the literature on dual-use research, a number of approaches have been suggested for addressing some of the challenges. These include regulation, self-regulation and education (Engel-Glatter and Ienca 2018) as well as participatory governance with a broader public input (Vogel *et al.* 2017). Putting these measures in place could intensify the tension between scientific freedom and public interest.

In recent years, many of these issues related to dual-use and the relationship between military and civilian research have been discussed in the context of neuroscience research (Ienca *et al.* 2018; Mahfoud *et al.* 2018; Royal Society 2012; Tennison and Moreno 2012). Concerns about dual-use and misuse of neuroscience are particularly relevant due to military funding for neurotechnologies in countries such as the USA and its applications including warfighter enhancement or neuroscientific deception detection and interrogation. For these reasons, Ienca and his colleagues (2018) suggest a 'neurosecurity framework' involving calibrated regulation, (neuro)ethical guidelines and awareness-raising activities within the scientific community.

Responsible Research and Innovation (RRI)

In the past ten years, the RRI approach has been promoted by researchers and funding agencies across Europe as a way to shape research and innovation towards social goods (De Saille 2015). According to a well-known definition by Jack Stilgoe, Richard Owen and Phil Macnaghton, 'responsible innovation means taking care of the future through collective stewardship of science and innovation in the present' (Stilgoe, Owen and Macnaghton 2013:1570). They operationalise responsible innovation along four dimensions of anticipation, reflexivity, inclusion and responsiveness.

The European Commission has been one of the major supporters of the RRI approach. The Horizon 2020 regulation recognises RRI as a cross-cutting issue that has to be promoted to improve societal engagement in research and innovation (European Parliament and the Council of the EU 2013). RRI is implemented in the Horizon 2020 via supporting thematic elements of RRI such as public engagement, open access, gender, ethics and science education as well as via integrated actions that foster uptake of the RRI approach by institutions and stakeholders (European Commission 2019c). One of the main political documents on RRI is the Rome Declaration on Responsible Research and Innovation in Europe, which defines RRI as an 'on-going process of aligning research and innovation to the values, needs and expectations of society' (Italian Presidency of the Council of the EU 2014). While the European Commission has extensively supported the implementation of RRI during the Horizon 2020, due to shifting political priorities (e.g. towards mission-oriented research), it is unlikely that RRI will receive the same amount of support in the following Horizon Europe programme.

Furthermore, a number of national research funding councils are also implementing the RRI approach. One of the first funders that started to implement this approach was the Engineering and Physical Sciences Research Council (EPSRC) in the UK. The EPSRC approach to responsible innovation highlights the need to continuously seek to anticipate, reflect, engage and act and is therefore known as the AREA framework (EPSRC 2019). According to this approach, anticipation implies describing and analysing intended and unintended economic, social, environmental and other possible impacts of innovation, while reflection focuses on purposes, motivations and potential implications of research and associated uncertainties. Engagement allows the opening up future visions to broader deliberation and dialogue, but action aims to influence the direction and trajectory of the research and innovation process itself.

While the RRI approach has an important aim of aligning research and innovation with societal values and needs, its practical implementation experiences a number of well-known research governance challenges, for example, how to deal with the diversity of societal values, what is the right balance between academic freedom and steering and how to address uncertainty inherent in research and innovation. The RRI approach still encounters the so-called 'Collingridge dilemma' according to which, during the early stages of research, too little is known to regulate emerging technology, while later when technology is more extensively developed and used, it is difficult to modify it via regulation (Stilgoe *et al.* 2013).

Actors involved in the governance of dual-use neuroscience research in the HBP

To address the complex issues described above, a wide range of actors, internal and external to the HBP, have been involved in developing and implementing the governance of dual-use research. Internal actors are the project's governing bodies, researchers and administrators from diverse disciplines and teams within the project. External actors are the European Commission as a funder as well as diverse stakeholders from citizens and patients to experts, other brain initiatives and international bodies such as the Organisation for Economic Co-operation and Development (OECD), which developed guidelines for governance of neuroscience and neurotechnology.

The HBP's Ethics and Society division has undertaken a leading role in the development of the governance of dual-use research in the HBP. The Ethics and Society division brings together research from social sciences and humanities, ethicists and public engagement practitioners from a number of universities and research entities across Europe. As a major EU initiative in a highly sensitive research area, the HBP implements a broad RRI agenda to identify and address major ethical and societal concerns (Stahl *et al.* 2019). In particular, the HBP implements the AREA framework of the EPSRC, which was one of the first frameworks available for a practical implementation of the HBP. According to the AREA framework, anticipation activities implemented by the HBP's Ethics and Society division include foresight analysis of future development of neuroscience and ICT developed by the HBP, while reflection activities focus on philosophical and neuroethical research. Engagement involves citizen workshops and online consultations to understand public views on neuroscience, while action focuses on developing and implementing processes, procedures and good practices to support RRI in the HBP. Thus, the HBP Ethics and Society division implements a wide-ranging research and practice agenda that goes well beyond complying with the FP regulatory requirements and includes anticipation, reflection, engagement and action on the conceptual and practical underpinnings of the regulatory require-ments, their limitations and the ways of overcoming them.

These principles of going beyond the legal FP requirements, critically reflect-ing on them and suggesting broader ethical and social agendas are also present in the HBP Ethics and Society team's work on dual-use. The key element of this work is the 'Opinion on "Responsible Dual-Use": Political, Security, Intelligence and Military Research of Concern in Neuroscience and Neurotechnology' (Ethics and Society 2018). This is the second opinion of the HBP Ethics and Society team, following the first one on Data Protection and Privacy published in the previous year. The Dual-Use Opinion starts with the recognition that 'current and newly emerging insights and technologies arising from research in brain sciences increase capabilities to access, assess and affect thought, emotion and behaviour' (Ethics and Society 2018). These capabilities can be used in socially beneficial as well as harmful ways. Examples mentioned in the Opinion include:

> brain inspired neuro- and ICT technologies that are already in use or in advanced stages of development, for example, in warfighter 'enhancement', intelligence gathering, image analysis, threat detection, manipulation of emotional states, incapacitation of adversaries, and the development of autonomous or semi-autonomous weapons, or weaponized robots using arti-ficial intelligence technologies and machine learning algorithms for target detection an elimination.
>
> (Ethics and Society 2018: 5–6)

Thus, the Opinion discusses important social and ethical questions these devel-opments raise and develops a set of recommendations for the HBP, the EU and social actors.

The preparation of the Dual-Use Opinion took several years and was done according to the RRI principles and the AREA framework of anticipation, reflection, engagement and action. The anticipation activities included a number of scoping reports to identify current and potential applications of brain research and brain-inspired technologies and their social and ethical implications. The reflection part focused on the conceptual clarification of dual-use terminology and identification of ambiguities in existing regulations and guidelines. The engagement part consisted of a broad range of activities involving experts on dual-use and neuroscience and research policy makers as well as citizens in webinars, workshops and online consultations. The results of the engagement activities have been made public to researchers and stakeholders within and beyond the HBP and some of these activities have been positively evaluated by neuroscience and dual-use experts as 'a first promising step in the direction of awareness-enhancing strategies' (Ienca *et al.* 2018: 273). The anticipation, reflection and engagement activities resulted in preparing recommendations for action.

One of the key insights from the preparatory work was the need to go beyond the binary civilian–military distinction of the dual-use definition used in the Horizon 2020 approach to ethics and to broaden it. To do that, the Dual-Use Opinion develops a broader set of terminology, building on terms such as dual-use research of concern, RRI and political, security, intelligence and military research of concern. The Opinion suggests that applying the principles of RRI to the concept of dual-use could increase the ability to identify which programmes and projects of research, development and innovation are 'of concern' and distinguish between 'responsible' and 'irresponsible' systems of research and technological development. Accordingly, the Opinion uses the term 'dual-use research of concern' to refer to:

> neuroscience research and technological innovations, and brain inspired developments in information and communication technologies, for use in the political, security, intelligence and military domains, which are either directly of concern because of their potential for use in ways that threaten the peace, health, safety, security and well-being of citizens, or are undertaken without responsible regard to such potential uses.
>
> (Ethics and Society 2018: 5)

Thus, the identification of research 'of concern' is not straightforward but rather is a matter of debate. The RRI principles should enable such a debate, capacity building to reflect and engagement of researchers and stakeholders. In the Opinion, responsibility does not simply refer to responsible conduct of individuals but also

> to processes and practices within research and development systems, and the extent to which they encourage or constrain the capacity of all those involved in the management and operations of research to reflect upon,

anticipate and consider the potential social and ethical implications of their research, to encourage open discussion of these, with a view to ensuring that their research and development does indeed contribute to the health and well-being of citizens, and to peace and security.

(Ethics and Society 2018: 9)

Thus, responsibility here means developing institutions and cultures that support socially beneficial research.

To implement these principles of responsibility, the Opinion recommends that the HBP evaluates the potential implications for dual-use research of concern, ensures a responsible use of its data and services, considers conditions for partnering with institutions that receive military funding and develops educational activities and materials on dual-use. Furthermore, the Opinion includes a number of recommendations for the EU. These include suggestions to extend its policies on dual-use research beyond the focus on aims, objectives and intentions of the researchers, to support research on dual-use research of concern and to establish an advisory body to have an oversight of all EU funded research with political, security, intelligence and military potentials. The recommendations to other social actors include a strong focus on the education of neuroscientists on social and ethical issues including questions of dual-use as well as on self-regulation of research institutions and industry.

The HBP governing bodies have approved the Opinion and established the HBP Dual-Use Working Group to implement its recommendations. This working group includes researchers, engineers and administrators from all HBP divisions.

Challenges for developing and implementing governance structures for dual-use research at the project level

Addressing issues related to dual-use research at the project level presents a number of challenges related to the complexity and sensitivity of the topic as well as uncertainties about potential uses and impacts of research results. On the basis of the ongoing work in the HBP discussed above, three challenges can be highlighted: first, limitations of the dual-use definition used in the EU FP; second, issues of education and awareness raising; and third, questions of global collaboration. These challenges can be relevant for research in other scientific disciplines and fields as well.

First, the FPs use a definition of dual-use from the EU export control regulation (see Vila Seoane, Chapter 5 in this book). According to that definition, the dual-use items are goods, software and technologies, which 'are normally used for civilian purposes but may have military applications, or may contribute to the proliferation of weapons of mass destruction' (European Commission 2019b: 13). Two limitations of this definition in particular can be highlighted. First, for basic research at the early stages of development, the definition's focus on goods, items and software often is not relevant. Second, this definition still defines dual-use in binary terms of military versus civilian, while practitioners and scholars in this field have recognised that a broader understanding of beneficial and harmful uses is needed (Ienca *et al.* 2018; Oltmann 2015). Thus, rather than inviting anticipation and reflection on the potential future uses of research that is at early stages, for many scientists doing basic research, this definition suggests that dual-use questions are not relevant for them. To address this challenge, the Ethics and Society division of the HBP suggested broadening the understanding of dual-use by bringing in concepts of dual-use research of concern, RRI and political, security, intelligence and military research of concern. In a similar manner, future EU research funding programmes could benefit by broadening their approach to dual-use and developing definitions that are dedicated to specificity of research by adjusting and going beyond dual-use definitions in export controls.

Second, building governance structures for dual-use research at the project level requires the involvement and support from the researchers. One limitation that such an approach faces is a lack of awareness about dual-use issues among researchers. Ethical and social issues of science and technology are not always included in science education nor are they required, supported or built into research career structures. The HBP has started to address these issues within the project's dedicated Education programme that includes workshops, online lectures and webinars on ethical and social issues including dual-use. To make such education and awareness-raising activities relevant, a particular challenge is to adjust them to the specificities of each scientific discipline and research field. That is not a straightforward task in a multidisciplinary project bringing together scientists and researchers with very diverse scientific backgrounds. At the institutional and policy levels, the importance of education and awareness of dual-use issues among scientists cannot be underestimated and novel ways to engage and support scientists in these endeavours need to be sought.

The third challenge focuses on global collaboration for addressing dual-use research issues. As research is global and scientific knowledge flows freely across national and regional borders, it is of paramount importance that dual-use issues are recognised at the global level. In the neuroscience field, the need to address issues of misuse has been recently recognised by the representatives of International Brain Initiative (Rommelfanger *et al.* 2018) that brings together the main large-scale neuroscience projects from the EU, USA, China, Japan, Australia, Canada and South Korea (see information in the Introduction) as well as by the OECD in its Recommendation of the Council on Responsible Innovation in Neurotechnology (OECD 2019). At the moment, the HBP is the only one among the main neuroscience projects that is developing and implementing dedicated governance structures to address issues of dual-use and potential misuse. To facilitate responsible neuroscience research globally, similar activities in other brain projects and global coordination efforts are needed.

Conclusions

This chapter demonstrates that the fast-developing field of neuroscience research not only promises major health, economic and technological benefits, but also raises important concerns about the potential misuse or harmful uses of research results. To address these concerns, appropriate governance structures should be built at the global, regional, national, institutional and project levels. The chapter shows that the research project level plays a key role in the governance of dual-use research. At the same time, the project-level governance is closely intertwined with governance at other levels.

The chapter reveals how one of the main neuroscience research projects worldwide – the EU-funded HBP – addresses a number of challenges such as the limitations of the EU FP's definition of dual-use based on the export control regulation and focusing on binary distinction between civilian and military applications by developing a novel approach that incorporates concepts of dual-use research of concern, RRI and political, security, intelligence and military research of concern. The development and implementation of such an approach benefits from engaging a broad range of researchers, stakeholders, experts and citizens. The lessons learned so far suggest the need for education and awareness-raising activities, global collaboration and reconsideration of policy definitions of dual-use and their suitability for research activities. The HBP, as a large-scale project, benefits from having dedicated Ethics and Society as well as Education teams for the development and implementation of its project-level governance of dual-use research. Nevertheless, lessons learned and practices developed in this project could be relevant for other brain initiatives as well as research projects in other disciplines.

Acknowledgement

This chapter has benefitted from feedback on earlier versions presented at the CPERI workshop in Lancaster (UK) in July 2018 and the INTERSECT workshop in Bath (UK) in November 2018. Conversations and interactions with researchers and stakeholders of the HBP are gratefully acknowledged. Research reported in this chapter has received funding from the European Union's Horizon 2020 Framework Programme for Research and Innovation under the Specific Grant Agreement No. 7202070 (HBP SGA1), No. 785907 (HBP SGA2) and No. 945539 (HBP SGA3).

References

Amunts K., Knoll, A.C., Lippert, T., Pennartz, C.M.A., Ryvlin, P., Destexhe, A., Jirsa, V.K., D'Angelo, E. and Bjaalie, J.G. (2019) The Human Brain Project – Synergy Between Neuroscience, Computing, Informatics, and Brain-Inspired Technologies. *PLoS Biology* 17(7): e3000344. https://doi.org/10.1371/journal.pbio.3000344.

DARPA (2020) DARPA and the Brain Initiative. At: www.darpa.mil/program/our-research/darpa-and-the-brain-initiative (accessed 13 January 2020).

De Saille, S. (2015) Innovating Innovation Policy: The Emergence of 'Responsible Research and Innovation'. *Journal of Responsible Innovation* 2(2): 152–168. https://doi.org/10.1080/23299460.2015.1045280.

Edler, J. and James, A. (2015) Understanding the Emergence of New Science and Technology Policies: Policy Entrepreneurship, Agenda Setting and the Development of the European Framework Programme. *Research Policy* 44(6): 1252–1265. https://doi.org/10.1016/j.respol.2014.12.008.

Engel-Glatter, S. and Ienca, M. (2018) Life Scientists' Views and Perspectives on the Regulation of Dual-Use Research of Concern. *Science and Public Policy* 45(1): 92–102.

EPSRC (2019) Anticipate, Reflect, Engage and Act (AREA). At: https://epsrc.ukri.org/research/framework/area/ (accessed 15 December 2019).

Ethics and Society (2018) Opinion on 'Responsible Dual-Use'. Political, Security, Intelligence and Military Research of Concern in Neuroscience and Neurotechnology. Human Brain Project, 21 December. At: www.humanbrainproject.eu/en/follow-hbp/news/opinion-on-responsible-dual-use-from-the-human-brain-project/.

European Commission (2013) Graphene and the Human Brain Project win Largest Research Excellence Award in History. At: https://ec.europa.eu/digital-single-market/en/news/graphene-and-human-brain-project-win-largest-research-excellence-award-history (accessed 6 December 2019).

European Commission (2014) FET Flagships: A Novel Partnering Approach To Address Grand Scientific Challenges and to Boost Innovation in Europe. Commission Staff Working Document SWD(2014) 283 final.

European Commission (2017) Launching the European Defence Fund. Communication COM(2017) 295.

European Commission (2019a) Brain Research. Commission activities in the area of Brain research. At: https://ec.europa.eu/info/research-and-innovation/research-area/health/brain-research_en (accessed 25 October 2019).

European Commission (2019b) Horizon 2020 Programme Guidance How to Complete your ethics self-assessment. Version 6.1. 4 February 2019.

European Commission (2019c) Responsible Research & Innovation. At: https://ec.europa.eu/programmes/horizon2020/en/h2020-section/responsible-research-innovation (accessed 15 December 2019).

European Parliament and the Council of the European Union (2013) Regulation (EU) No. 1291/2013 of 11 December 2013 establishing Horizon 2020 – the Framework Programme for Research and Innovation (2014–2020).

Human Brain Project (2020) Human Brain Project. At: www.humanbrainproject.eu/en/ (accessed 13 January 2020).

Ienca, M., Jotterand, F. and Elger, B.S. (2018) From Healthcare to Warfare and Reverse: How Should We Regulate Dual-Use Neurotechnology? *Neuron* 97: 269–274.

International Brain Initiative (2020) International Brain Initiative. At: www.international braininitiative.org/ (accessed 13 January 2020).

Italian Presidency of the Council of the European Union (2014) Rome Declaration on Responsible Research and Innovation in Europe. 21 November 2014.

Langley, C. and Parkinson, S. (2017) The Political Economy of Military Science. In D. Tyfield, R. Lave, S. Randalls and C. Thorpe (eds), *The Routledge Handbook of the Political Economy of Science*. London: Routledge: 194–209.

Mahfoud, T., Aicardi, C., Datta, S. and Rose, N. (2018) The Limits of Dual-Use. *Issues in Science and Technology* 34(4): 73–78.

Mazzucato, M. (2013) *The Entrepreneurial State: Debunking Public vs Private Sector Myths*. London: Anthem Press.

Molas-Gallart, J. (1997) Which Way to Go? Defence Technology and the Diversity of 'Dual-Use' Technology Transfer. *Research Policy* 26: 367–385.

OECD (2019) Recommendation of the Council on Responsible Innovation in Neurotechnology. OECD. At: www.oecd.org/science/recommendation-on-responsible-innovation-in-neurotechnology.htm.

Oltmann, S. (2015) Dual-Use Research: Investigation Across Multiple Science Disciplines. *Science and Engineering Ethics* 21: 327–341. https://doi.org/10.1007/s11948-014-9535-y

Rommelfanger, K.S., Jeong, A.J., Ema, A., Fukushi, T., Kasai, K., Ramos, K., Salles, A. and Singh, I. (2018) Neuroethics Questions to Guide Ethical Research in the International Brain Initiatives. *Neuron* 100(1): 19–36.

The Royal Society (2012) *Brain Waves Module 3. Neuroscience, Conflict and Security*. London: The Royal Society.

Savage, N. (2019) Brain Work: Large-Scale National Research Projects Hope to Reveal the Secrets of the Human Brain. *Nature* 574: 49–51.

Stahl, B.C., Akintoye, S., Fothergill, B.T., Guerrero, M., Knight, W. and Ulnicane, I. (2019) Beyond Research Ethics: Dialogues in Neuro-ICT Research. *Frontiers in Human Neuroscience* 13(105). https://doi.org/10.3389/fnhum.2019.00105.

Stilgoe, J., Owen, R. and Macnaghten, P. (2013) Developing a Framework for Responsible Innovation. *Research Policy* 42(9): 1568–1580. https://doi.org/10.1016/j.respol.2013.05.008

Te Kulve, H. and Smit, W.A. (2003) Civilian–Military Co-Operation Strategies in Developing New Technologies. *Research Policy* 32(6): 955–970. https://doi.org/10.1016/S0048-7333(02)00105-1.

Tennison, M.N. and Moreno, J.D. (2012) Neuroscience, Ethics, and National Security: The State of the Art. *PLoS Biology* 10(3): e1001289.

Vogel, K.M., Balmer, B., Weiss Evans, S., Kroener, I., Matsumoto, M. and Rappert, B. (2017) Knowledge and Security. In U. Felt, R. Fouché, C.A. Miller and L. Smith-Doerr (eds), *The Handbook of Science and Technology Studies*, 4th edn. Cambridge, MA: The MIT Press, 973–1001.

12 Managing security uncertainty with emerging technologies

The example of the governance of neuroprosthetic research

Benjamin Farrand

Introduction

This chapter seeks to analyse the challenges facing the management of security uncertainty in the European Union (EU) context, centring on the question 'how can policy makers govern an emerging technology from a security-related perspective, when their successful implementation, dissemination and use are largely speculative?' New and emerging technologies have the capacity to be highly disruptive. This is not intended in the sense of 'disruption' that is often used as a 'buzzword' in the context of Silicon Valley-based start-ups, grounded in an idea of Schumpeterian 'creative destruction' (Markides 2006; Gobble 2015), in which one business model is replaced by another. It is rather in the sense that these disruptive technologies can lead to unprecedented, unforeseen and even transformative changes to society and the economy. The McKinsey Global Institute has identified four characteristics that disruptive technologies possess: 'a high rate of technology change, broad potential scope of impact, large economic value that could be affected, and substantial potential for disruptive economic impact' (2013: 3; see also the Introduction to this book, by Calcara, Csernatoni and Lavallée). However, when 'disruptive' technologies are discussed, it is often in terms of the potential benefits and opportunities they present (and predominantly economic at that), with comparably less consideration given to the possible detriments. When considered, the focus is predominantly upon their impact on current forms and levels of employment (for an excellent consideration of the role of disruptive technologies on workers and the 'gigification' of the economy, see Prassl 2018). Even less discussed, when a technology is emergent, are the security risks (or opportunities) that they may present. This is not so surprising – an emerging technology is by its nature speculative, both in terms of its likelihood of success, as well as its conceivable social, economic and security impacts (Hoerr 2011).

Examples of this include nanotechnology, which became the centre of significant debate and controversies as the technologies developed and could be realized (Macnaghten 2010), or more recent discussions over blockchain technologies, the value of which is so far still unconfirmed, despite both media and academic speculation as to its future uses. In the early, formative stages of an emerging technology, research and discussion centre on its positive potential, rather than the negatives, as noted by Cordeiro, Hauptman and Sharan (2013). When a technology matures and emphasis is placed on the innovation and dissemination of a technology, then there is an increased attention on possible security threats and opportunities, which may also feature in EU funded research (Csernatoni 2019). Until such a time, however, these technologies exist in a legal, policy and knowledge lacuna, making the management of any security risks they may potentially create difficult to conceptualise and therefore implement. Hence, it will be demonstrated in this chapter through the use of a case study of a highly speculative and newly emergent technology, neuroprosthetics, that the inherent uncertainties when dealing with an untested invention make their security governance particularly complicated. Neuroprosthetics are artificial limbs or organs connected into nerve or muscle tissue that allow for the regaining of use and even sensation for individuals that have suffered limb damage as a result of injury or disease. However, they are at a very early stage of development, meaning that the focus of research is on the 'proof of concept' of the technology and its application in impaired individuals, rather than on a detailed consideration of their broader social, economic and security risks. Neuroprosthetics, and in fact biotechnological inventions more generally, are not generally framed in explicit security terms, but as technologies with the potential to present security concerns.

The first section of this chapter will provide further exploration of the purpose, use and science behind neuroprosthetics, as well as the inherent unforeseeability of the security implications of these technologies. The second section of the chapter will analyse the existing legal framework that may serve to govern their use and implementation, indicating the lacuna in which these devices exist and the difficulties in establishing a clear and effective legal regime for any security risks they may present. The third section of the chapter will then evaluate the dynamics of governance of emerging technologies more generally, and as applied to neuroprosthetics specifically, indicating how at these formative stages, knowledge gathering and reflective practice are key to understanding what potential risks and security threats may be posed by new disruptive technologies, and how the EU has attempted to provide for better understanding of the social, economic and security-related risks of new technologies through its Responsible Research and Innovation (RRI) approach. As the chapter will conclude, in areas of high uncertainty, low knowledge and in situations where a multitude of actors may be interested in the way in which a technology is governed, experimental governance is likely to emerge as a response to these uncertainties. Through networks of actors ranging from policy makers and legislators to academic researchers, industry and civil society organisations, a more careful, nuanced and potentially future-proof approach to the governance of security risks posed by neuroprosthetics could be made more likely.

Background on neuroprosthetics

According to the World Health Organization, as of 2006, more than one billion people worldwide suffer from neurological conditions impacting upon limb usage, ranging from injury or trauma, Parkinson's disease, Alzheimer's and multiple sclerosis (2006: 178). Furthermore, the increase in the incidence of diabetes mellitus type II-related neuropathy and subsequent amputations is leading to a reversal in the decreases of lower-limb amputations being carried out. According to the most recent available statistics, in the USA in 2008, it was determined that in 2005 there were 1.6 million individuals living with the loss of a limb, 38 per cent of which were the result of diabetes-related vascular disease, figures estimated to increase to 3.1 million by 2050 (Ziegler-Graham *et al.* 2008: 427). While comparable figures are not available for the entire European Union, approximately 58 million people have diabetes in Europe, of which 90 per cent are type II (European Commission 2017a). According to Behrendt *et al.*, diabetes is indicated in approximately half of amputations conducted in several countries in the EU, with incidence varying between 20 per cent in Finland, to up to 75 per cent in Slovakia (2018: 392). With these increases in diabetes and diseases such as Parkinson's and Alzheimer's, research in health care is becoming predominantly focused on the treatment of diabetes and these neurological conditions, along with the development of improved prosthetic devices for individuals rendered disabled by injury or disease. One promising avenue for this research and development is the creation of robotic limbs able to connect to nerve and muscle tissue, known as neuroprosthetics.

Neuroprosthetics have been defined as 'artificial devices designed to generate, restore or modulate a range of neutrally mediated diseases' (Glannon 2016: 1–2). Neuroprosthetic limbs are the result of a distinct field of neuroprosthetic research, facilitated by separate and distinct developments in neuroscience and robotics, making it possible to develop brain-controlled artificial limbs capable of restoring fine motor skills and a sense of touch to individuals affected by disease or serious injury (Berger 2019: 269). Operating through a brain-machine interface, signals coming from the brain's cortical neurons can be transformed into signals that can be interpreted by a computer system to move an external device. As the brain adapts to sending these signals, brain–machine interfacing improves, allowing for smoother, more nuanced manipulations of, for example, a robotic arm (Schweikard and Ernst 2015; Eapen, Murphy and Cifu 2017; Perlmutter 2017). Recent innovations have allowed for the insertion of electrodes in the form of an intracortical brain–machine interface at the point of cervical spinal cord injury and a functional electrical stimulation device in a paralysed arm, allowing for a tetraplegic individual to successfully drink coffee from a self-controlled mug after 463 days and to feed himself after 717 (Ajiboye *et al.* 2017). Neuroprosthetics have additional realized and emergent therapeutic benefits such as restoration of a sense of touch, as well as mitigating the effects of 'phantom limb syndrome', in which an individual experiences sensation of pain in a non-present limb (Blumberg and Dooley 2017; Bartolozzi 2018).

While it may be assumed that the majority of this research is conducted in the USA, there have been some significant breakthroughs in neuroprosthetic technology in the EU, with Horizon 2020 funded projects: SensAgain, which has focused on restoring sensory-motor functionality and the ability to 'feel' the artificial limb as part of their body, while striving to eliminate phantom limb syndrome (SensAgain Project 2016); and INPUT, specialising in upper-limb prostheses control systems intended to improve brain–machine interfaces allowing for increased dexterity and limb manipulation (INPUT 2018).

As stated above, neuroprosthetics, and in fact biotechnological inventions more generally, are not generally framed in explicit security terms, but as technologies with the potential to present security concerns. This is a reflection of two interlinked factors; the first is that due to their nature as therapeutic interventions, the predominant focus of research and writing pertains to health care and disability, including the treatment of disability in law (see, for example, Bockman 2009; Rosenfeld *et al.* 2008; Hanrahan 2015; Wright and Fins 2016). The second factor is the inherent uncertainty in determining the implications or consequences of many of these technologies, insofar as not only are the technologies themselves emergent, but so too are the social and economic impacts. Academic writers have focused on various different risks, social and ethical, that are potentiated by the use of advanced neuroprosthetics, should they reach that stage of development. In terms of security threats, there has been consideration of the potential dual-use of neuroprosthetics for enhancement as well as therapy in the military, by creating an enhanced form of solider (Girling, Thorpe and Auger 2017), the potential for 'brain-hacking' and a need for neurological security in the context of brain–machine interfaces (Denning, Matsuoka and Kohno 2009), or even the blurring of the lines between cyber crime and physical assault through attacks against human-embedded systems such as neuroprosthetics (Gasson and Koops 2013). Yet, one commonality that this scholarship possesses is the frequent use of the words 'could' and 'potential'. Due to the inherently speculative and emergent nature of these technologies, the security risks they are likely to pose are equally speculative, making formalised governance difficult. How can policy makers, therefore, effectively govern the security risks of a speculative technology?

The security governance of neuroprosthetics: the limitations of legislation in combating uncertainty

The management of these emerging and experimental technologies lies in an uneasy nexus between formal, legally binding rules, informal cooperation mechanisms and experimentalist governance (Sabel and Zeitlin 2012). Experimentalist governance can serve as a template for the governance of new areas (Sabel and Zeitlin 2012: 9) and the security dimension of emergent technologies is perfectly suited as a sector for this experimentation to arise (see, for example, Kuhlmann, Stegmaier and Konrad 2019), given its strategic uncertainty and the polyarchic power distributions, in which those with information and expertise (predominantly researchers) must engage with policy makers, industry and other stakeholders, with no one body having ultimate control or say (Sabel and Zeitlin 2012). In order to demonstrate the requirement for experimentalist governance in this field, it is first necessary to detail the somewhat ill-fitting nature of existing and applicable EU legislation. In terms of legally binding rules, the nature of prosthetics means that they are classified as 'medical devices' under the EU Medical Devices Regulation, which comes into effect in May 2020 (Regulation No 2017/754, 2017, European Parliament and Council of the European Union 2017a). According to Article 1, the European Regulation applies to the marketing, sale, distribution and putting into use of medical devices intended for human use, including clinical investigations concerning their use. For the purposes of neuroprosthetics, Article 2 defines a medical device as:

> any instrument, apparatus, appliance, software, implant, reagent, material or other article intended by the manufacturer to be used, alone or in combination, for human beings … [for the] diagnosis, monitoring, treatment, alleviation of, or compensation for, an injury or disability.

Neuroprosthetics are categorised as a Class III device under Annex VIII Rule 6, as they are 'intended specifically for use in direct contact with the heart or central circulatory system or the central nervous system'. In terms of security, while there are five references to security mentioned in the Regulation, they refer to information security for any software built into the implantable device (Annex I, Chapter I, Section 17) and the security of clinical data from breach (Annex I, Chapter II, Section 4). Furthermore, and as shall be discussed further, rather than prescriptive legal requirements, the security obligations that *do* exist are framed in terms of best practices and setting of minimum requirements. Similarly, in terms of the security dimension of the proprietary information upon which the neuroprosthetic is based, the EU provides for comprehensive legal protection under its intellectual property laws, ranging from the Information Society Directive (Directive 2001/29/EC 2001) for protection of any copyright in computer code serving to facilitate the brain–machine interface, the Trade Mark Regulation (Regulation No 2017/1001 2017, European Parliament and Council of the European Union 2017b) for any trade marks registered in association with the neuroprosthetic for names, logos and etc., as well as patents registered in the member states over the invention itself on the basis of national laws or the European Patent Convention. Similarly, confidential information regarding the neuroprosthetic and associated research may be protected by the Trade Secrets Directive (Directive 2016/943 2016), as confidential business information prior to the registration of a patent. This provides for comprehensive protection of the intellectual property rights inherent in the design, which can be framed as ensuring a form of economic security for the company or undertaking involved in a neuroprosthetic's commercial development.

Yet, such measures, under both the Medical Devices Regulation and the intellectual property framework, constitute a narrow perception of security based in the protection of information arising from neuroprosthetic research and development, as well as the ethics of the research involving human participants. The existing legal framework does not provide for a broader conceptualisation and understanding of security at a societal level arising from their use, indicative of the difficulties of formally regulating areas of emerging technological typified by uncertainty (see, for example, Weimer and Marin 2016). In particular, emerging technologies often result in a period of 'regulatory disconnection' (Brownsword 2012: 66), in which a technology may have outrun its regulatory framework. In such a scenario, the rules that may have ordinarily been applicable to such a technology (or type of technology) do not appear sufficient to regulate new uses of that technology or rapid advancements in its design or functionality. Indeed, new technologies suffer from what is referred to as the Collingridge dilemma (Collingridge 1981), in which, during the early stages of a new technology's development and application, regulation is difficult due to a lack of information regarding that technology's impact. However, once that technology becomes commonplace and entrenched in science, industry or business, any revision to that regulatory regime is both potentially expensive and resisted. For this reason, as Moses argues, those seeking to regulate an emerging technology need to act at an early stage, 'when the situation is more malleable' (Moses 2015: 8). Though, providing a robust regulatory framework is difficult when the impact of a particular technology is uncertain. This results in an 'uncertainty paradox' (Asselt and Vos 2006) in the regulatory sense, as it is deemed important to regulate before the technology becomes entrenched, yet determining the scope and function of that regulation is complicated by a lack of knowledge. For Easterbrook (1996), at this juncture, legislators must be careful to avoid a scenario in which they try to pull separate threads together in order to create a unified 'law of the horse'. A horse is a living thing and so may be protected by laws concerned with animal welfare. Its sale, in turn, may be regulated by contract law and its ownership by property law. Its use for sports such as horse-racing may in turn be regulated by specific legislation concerning competition and betting; and should the horse cause an accident through it being negligently ridden at speed through a crowded street, this action may be governed by tort, or even criminal law. Yet, these laws do not need to be brought together in a comprehensive law regulating horses. So, too, should it be ensured that legislation is not dependent on the technology in question, insofar as the utility of a 'law of the neuroprosthetic' is unlikely to be beneficial. Indeed, as discussed by Hildebrandt and Tielemans (2013), the law should strive to be technology neutral, considering the social or economic problem that the technology raises, rather than the technology itself. This is the view that was taken by the European Commission in the late 1990s, when it concluded that its audio-visual policy reforms proposed in light of the development of Internet streaming should be technology neutral (1999: 10). However, as Hildebrandt and Tielemans (2013) continue, this technology neutrality may require additional legislative interventions in order to ensure that the technology is specifically regulated in a neutral way that nevertheless addresses a perceived risk (in their argument regarding data protection, to human rights), safeguards innovation and achieves sustainability by 'future-proofing' law through the drafting of laws at appropriate levels of abstraction, guaranteeing that the law is not quickly rendered obsolete.

In the field of security, one such example is the implementation of the Network and Information Security Directive (2016), which requires member states to provide for high levels of protection for critical information infrastructures from cyberattacks, with the emphasis placed upon system resilience and the reporting of security breaches. The legislation does not specify the exact nature of cyberattacks and provides for a deliberately broad definition of network and information systems. Nevertheless, in order to ensure that the parties with obligations under the Directive are identified, it was necessary to provide for a definition of 'providers of essential service and digital service providers', which is covered by Annex II, including entities such as energy providers, financial services providers and a specific list of digital infrastructure providers. Should these change, by means of new energy technologies beyond oil, electricity and gas, or new types of digital infrastructure, then arguably, the legislation would not apply. Similarly, neuroprosthetics would not fall under the heading of providers of essential services and digital service providers; arguably it would only fall within the remit of the Directive should their use be targeted at initiating a cyberattack against these critical infrastructures. Would this be possible and are neuroprosthetics sufficiently regulated in terms of security in this field? It is very difficult at this time to say, but one would suggest not. Such endeavours still fall within the uncertainty paradox – when the technology is only just emerging and its potential unexplored, what are the risks and what level of abstraction should be afforded in any legislative regime? Furthermore, when considering security, which is predominantly concerned with the protection from threats and prevention of incidents rather than seeking legal redress should a negative event occur, these uncertainties become harder to legislate for. In this lacuna, between knowing and unknowing, or rather, certainty and uncertainty, alternative and indeed, less formal modes of governance are instead pursued.

Emerging informal security cooperation in neuroprosthetic research: the beginning of experimentation?

One potential reason that law alone is perhaps ill suited to resolving some of these tensions between innovation, security and uncertainty is that the law often perceives science as an objective field of binary answers – something is scientifically proven or unproven, risky or safe. This is not the view shared by scholars in Science and Technology Studies, however, which presents a more critical reflection of the role of science in society. As Jasanoff has stated, the questions regulators need to ask of science cannot in many instances be asked by science ... in the absence of sufficient hard evidence, decisions have to be made on the basis of available facts supplemented by a large measure of judgment.

(Jasanoff 1990: 7)

One such example is the use of assisted reproductive technologies, where in the absence of an absolute scientific certainty, a governable reality is constructed through the integration 'of the political, social, legal, ethical, bureaucratic, medical, technical and, quintessentially personal domains' (Sismondo 2009: 67). After all, as Sismondo (2009: 68) states, before scientific knowledge stabilises, disagreement is the rule, not the exception. Conflict *between* scientific experts can be based not only on empirical observations, but also on the different cultural, historical, political and social backgrounds of the scientists that impact upon how they perceive a particular technology and its social implications (McCarthy 2016; Rao, Gopi and Maione, 2016). For this reason, faith in an objective and relatively incontestable 'science' is misplaced.

Furthermore, this perception of objective science complements a self-critique that appears to permeate legal understandings of science and emerging technologies. This critique is that while science moves incredibly quickly, law is slow and reactive, and therefore cannot keep up with developments (see Braverman 2018). Instead, as Flear (2013) argues, the relationship is more nuanced – rather than playing catch-up with rapidly advancing technologies, law can play a leading role by orienting, shaping and directing the conditions of possibility for the development and market availability of emergent technologies. These twin misperceptions, namely, the objectivity of science and the law's inability to keep up with emerging technologies, serve to frame the processes by which these new technologies are governed and which actors engage in these processes. One purpose behind the governance of risk is to mitigate uncertainty as far as possible (see, for example, Rosa, McCright and Renn 2015; see also Renn and Klinke 2019: 204). Evaluating an uncertain risk requires consideration of trade-offs, both in terms of risk versus benefit, but also risk versus risk, requiring mediation between different actors concerning acceptable, tolerable and intolerable risk; in the field of technology, this can include consideration of occupational safety, routine emissions of waste into air, soil or water, or of accidents with the sudden emission of energy and/or material (Renn and Klinke 2019: 208–210). In the EU, this takes the form of reliance on expertise, and indeed networks of experts, in order to draw up guidelines for research, gather information and assess risks through technology and impact assessments. The framework for this to be done is the non-legally binding mechanism of the Commission's 'Responsible Research and Innovation' (RRI) approach under the Horizon 2020 funding system, which focuses on multi-stakeholderism, the accumulation of knowledge regarding the outcomes of scientific research and actions, the ability to evaluate outcomes and opportunities in terms of societal needs and moral values, and to subsequently use these as functional requirements for the design and development of new research, products and services (European Commission 2013: 5). These stakeholders range from policy makers, regulators and standardisation organisations to scientists, ethicists, civil society organisations and business/industry representatives (European Commission 2013: 20).

Under RRI, the Commission works through informal modes of governance (on this, generally, see Christiansen and Neuhold 2013; see also Kleine 2014) such as the coordination of member state activities such as identifying objectives, roadmaps and benchmarks, along with encouraging the adoption of voluntary codes of conduct and standardisation, based on the information gathered by the networks of actors involved in identifying the social, ethical and economic impacts of emerging science and technologies (European Commission 2013: 29–35). This, the Commission (2013: 49) reasons, would allow for the development of dynamic and flexible approaches to new technologies that a legislative initiative would lack. It must be stated, however, that security is not a topic that tends to be the exclusive focus of these networks of stakeholders; instead, it is one of many topics that may be discussed within the context of RRI, which also include issues such as justice, sustainability, democracy and efficiency (European Commission 2013: 56).

Furthermore, as an interim report on Horizon 2020 found, within the context of the societal challenges identified as subjects for funding, security gained only 2.3 per cent of the overall funding available, the smallest share recorded (European Commission 2017b: 126). While by 2019 this has changed somewhat with an additional €2 billion in funding being made available for the purposes of security research, the deadline for which closed in August 2019, these projects tend to be divided into discreet packages such as cyber security, the security of smart cities or protection against natural disasters.

In the context of disruptive technologies more generally, neuroprosthetic technologies can be considered a form of 'pioneering' research, with low ecosystem embeddedness, with the emphasis being on achieving 'breakthroughs' rather than systematic diffusion or incremental innovation (European Commission 2017b: 120). These are projects that have significant risks of failure, as well as uncertain futures. For this reason, less emphasis is placed upon considering their real-world application, including in the field of security. As the Interim Evaluation makes clear, many technology-related research projects are measured in terms of success based on traditional indicators, both by institutions and by researchers, such as prototypes, patents applied for, published outputs etc, rather than 'their impacts on e.g. decreasing CO_2 emissions, improving health of citizen, or their security, often on the longer term' (European Commission 2017b: 18). By way of example, the INPUT project mentioned earlier, does not mention security in any of its identified work packages. Similarly, SensAgain does not discuss security explicitly in its work, which is focused on getting an experimental and emerging technology to function. The Human Brain Project (HBP), a more advanced research project that is part-funded by the EU and began in 2013, has given some consideration to security in its discussion of brain–machine interfaces, but has made it clear that these security concerns are very much emergent and not particularly well understood at this stage; these emergent tech-nologies are discussed in terms of their *potential* to reinvigorate debates over ethics, privacy and computer security, and 'perhaps the major ethical challenges [will] arise in human–machine integration' (Rose, Aicardi and Reinsborough 2016: 26). However, due to the emergent and speculative nature regarding their application, use and feasibility, there is currently a lacuna in which their concep-tualisation as a security issue, either in terms of presenting security threats, or indeed, security opportunities is not prevalent in EU discourse.

This does, however, present an opportunity. Given the flexibilities built into RRI as a concept and the absence of legally binding commitments, RRI could serve as a basis for policy experimentation. According to a meta-analysis con-ducted by Burget, Bardone and Pedaste (2017: 14), the definition and dimen-sions of RRI are still being formulated, however, common themes appear to be inclusion, anticipation, responsiveness and reflexivity. This allows for a wide range of stakeholders representing different interests and concerns to be part of the discussion regarding how 'research and innovation can or may benefit society as well as prevent any negative consequences from happening' (Burget *et al.* 2017: 15). Florin (2019) argues that RRI can serve to complement risk governance, linking risk to responsibility and providing a normative framework for the governance of specific risk issues. Through the necessity of experimenta-tion and iterative governance design given the uncertainties of neuroprosthetic security risks, scientific research teams operating within the context of RRI can serve as informational nodes and help to make the unknown less uncertain, as well as providing ideas as to how a technology may be appropriately imple-mented, disseminated and used. This allows for the emergence of a range of possible solutions, any of which may result in the formation of a crystallised governance structure, including the possibility of binding legislation. As one example of this experimentation, the previously mentioned HBP recently published some specu-lative considerations on the regulation of dual-use technologies with security implications, concluding that the EU should consider extending its focus beyond the aims and objectives of the researchers involved in the project to the explicit consideration of the potential militarisation or securitisation of these technolo-gies and the subsequent risks for peace and stability where they are exploited in those capacities (Aicardi *et al.* 2018: 18). How to achieve this? Hasselbalch sug-gests a more nuanced approach to assessing new technologies going beyond impact assessments and technology assessments to consider innovation assess-ments as iterative processes of understanding a technology and its social impacts, allowing for policy makers to make 'effective and legitimate policy that manages to balance the viewpoints, interests and knowledge of attentive publics and experts' (2018: 1870). This, in turn, would allow for the development of governance networks that could then determine how the security risks posed by these new technologies could be addressed – formalised cooperation through agencies such as the European Union Agency for Cybersecurity (ENISA), Europol and the European Centre for Disease Prevention and Control, for example, with their networks of sector experts and national regulators, through expert committees, through binding regulatory mechanisms such as Directives or Regulations, or a combination of all three, with feed-in from relevant public stakeholders such as disability activist groups, charitable commissions and national medical regulators.

Conclusions

As this chapter has sought to demonstrate, emerging technologies can be highly disruptive due to their uncertain application and the security risks they present. In such scenarios, the effectiveness of hard, legally binding regimes is brought into question and the best way to govern a new technology such as neuroprosthetics is ultimately unknown. In this context, experimentalist governance, drawing in a range of actors from science, research, policy and the public can help to better identify risks and uncertainties, and through policy experimentation, find effective ways of managing the security risks presented by these new technologies. In such a situation, the uncertainty can act as an opportunity, in which different models of governance can be applied to that technology, through reflexive use of innovation assessments as iterative processes, rather than 'end-stage' proposals for regulation, allowing for the governance of security threats to be more reflective, nuanced and carefully thought out. The EU's RRI approach to funding for Horizon 2020 projects and the increased focus placed on the social implications of new technologies provides an opportunity for an approach to technology security governance that moves away from the binaries of 'objective' perceptions of science, incorporating the insights from Science and Technology Studies that allow for better understanding of the constructed nature of science, new technologies and the risks they present.

References

Aicardi, C., Bitsch, L., Badum, N.B. and Datta, S. (2018) *Opinion on 'Responsible Dual Use': Political, Security, Intelligence and Military Research of Concern in Neuroscience and Neurotechnology.* The Human Brain Project, 1–21.

Ajiboye, A.B., Willett, F.R., Young, D.R., Memberg, W.D., Murphy, B.A., Miller, J.P., Walter, B.L. *et al.* (2017) Restoration of Reaching and Grasping Movements Through Brain-Controlled Muscle Stimulation in a Person with Tetraplegia: A Proof-Of-Concept Demonstration. *The Lancet* 389(10081): 1821–1830.

Asselt, M.B.A. van and Vos, E. (2006) The Precautionary Principle and the Uncertainty Paradox. *Journal of Risk Research* 9(4): 313–336.

Bartolozzi, C. (2018) Neuromorphic Circuits Impart a Sense of Touch. *Science* 360(6392): 966–967.

Behrendt, C.-A., Sigvant, B., Szeberin, Z., Beiles, B., Eldrup, N., Thomson, I.A., Venermo, M. *et al.* (2018) International Variations in Amputation Practice: A VASCUNET Report. *European Journal of Vascular and Endovascular Surgery* 56(3): 391–399.

Berger, K.M. (2019) Emerging and Enabling Technologies in Biodefense. In S.K. Singh and J.H. Kuhn (eds), *Defense Against Biological Attacks: Volume I.* Cham: Springer International Publishing 253–281.

Blumberg, M.S. and Dooley, J.C. (2017) Phantom Limbs, Neuroprosthetics, and the Developmental Origins of Embodiment. *Trends in Neurosciences* 40(10): 603–612.

Bockman, C.R. (2009) Cybernetic-Enhancement Technology and the Future of Disability Law Note. *Iowa Law Review* 4: 1315–1340.

Braverman, I. (2018) Editing the Environment: Emerging Issues in Genetics and the Law. In I. Braverman, (ed.), *Gene Editing, Law, and the Environment: Life Beyond the Human.* Abingdon: Routledge, 1–27.

Brownsword, R. (2012) The Shaping of our On-Line Worlds: Getting the Regulatory Environment Right. *International Journal of Law and Information Technology* 20(4): 249–272.

Burget, M., Bardone, E. and Pedaste, M. (2017) Definitions and Conceptual Dimensions of Responsible Research and Innovation: A Literature Review. *Science and Engineering Ethics* 23(1): 1–19.

Christiansen, T. and Neuhold, C. (eds) (2013) *International Handbook on Informal Governance.* Cheltenham: Edward Elgar.

Collingridge, D. (1981) *Social Control of Technology.* Milton Keynes: Open University Press.

Cordeiro, J.L., Hauptman, A. and Sharan, Y. (2013) Foresight of Evolving Security Threats Posed by Emerging Technologies *Foresight.* At: https://doi.org/10.1108/FS-05-2012-0036.

Csernatoni, R. (2019) The EU's Technological Power: Harnessing Future and Emerging Technologies for European Security. In C.-A. Baciu and J. Doyle (eds), *Peace, Security and Defence Cooperation in Post-Brexit Europe: Risks and Opportunities.* Cham: Springer International Publishing, 119–140.

Denning, T., Matsuoka, Y. and Kohno, T. (2009) Neurosecurity: Security and Privacy for Neural Devices. *Neurosurgical Focus* 27(1); E7.

Directive 2001/29/EC (2001) Of the European Parliament and of the Council of 22 May 2001 on the Harmonisation of Certain Aspects of Copyright and Related Rights in the Information Society. European Parliament and the Council of the European Union.

Directive 2016/943 (2016) Of the European Parliament and of the Council of 8 June 2016 on the Protection of Undisclosed Know-How and Business Information (Trade Secrets) against Their Unlawful Acquisition, Use and Disclosure. European Parliament and the Council of the European Union.

Directive 2016/1148 (2016) Concerning Measures for a High Common Level of Security of Network and Information Systems across the Union. European Parliament and the Council of the European Union.

Eapen, B.C., Murphy, D.P. and Cifu, D.X. (2017) Neuroprosthetics in Amputee and Brain Injury Rehabilitation. *Experimental Neurology* 287: 479–485.

Easterbrook, F.H. (1996) Cyberspace and the Law of the Horse the Law of Cyberspace. *University of Chicago Legal Forum*, 207–216.

European Commission (1999) Communication: Principles and Guidelines for the Community's Audiovisual Policy in the Digital Age, No. COM(1999) 657, Brussels, 1–23.

European Commission (2013) Options for Strengthening Responsible Research and Innovation, Brussels, 1–78.

European Commission (2017a) Chronic Diabetes Affects Millions of People in the EU. *Eurostat*, 13 November. At: https://ec.europa.eu/eurostat/web/products-eurostat-news/-/EDN-20171113-1 (accessed 25 September 2019).

European Commission (2017b) Commission Staff Working Document: In-Depth Interim Evaluation of Horizon 2020, No. SWD(2017) 222 final, 1–146.

European Parliament and Council of the European Union (2017a) Regulation No 2017/754 (2017) Of the European Parliament and of the Council of 5 April 2017 on Medical Devices.

European Parliament and Council of the European Union (2017b) Regulation No 2017/1001 (2017) Of the European Parliament and of the Council of 14 June 2017 on the European Union Trade Mark.

Flear, M.L. (2013) Regulating New Technologies: EU Internal Market Law, Risk, and Socio-Technical Order. In M.L. Flear, A.-M. Farrell, T.K. Hervey and T. Murphy (eds), *European Law and New Health Technologies*. Oxford: Oxford University Press, 74–120.

Florin, M.-V. (2019) Risk Governance and 'Responsible Research and Innovation' can be Mutually Supportive. *Journal of Risk Research*, 1–15.

Gasson, M.N. and Koops, B.-J. (2013) Attacking Human Implants: A New Generation of Cybercrime. *Law, Innovation and Technology* 5(2): 248–277.

Girling, K., Thorpe, J. and Auger, A. (2017) *A Framework to Assess the Military Ethics of Human Enhancement Technologies*, No. DRDC-RDDC-2017-L167, Defence Research and Development Canada, 1–18.

Glannon, W. (2016) Ethical Issues in Neuroprosthetics. *Journal of Neural Engineering* 13(2): 1–22.

Gobble, M.M. (2015) The Case against Disruptive Innovation. *Research Technology Management* 58(1): 59–63.

Hanrahan, D. (2015) Neuroenhancement, Ethics & the Future of Disability Law. *Health Law Outlook* 8(1): 1–17.

Hasselbalch, J.A. (2018) Innovation Assessment: Governing Through Periods of Disruptive Technological Change. *Journal of European Public Policy* 25(12): 1855–1873.

Hildebrandt, M. and Tielemans, L. (2013) Data Protection by Design and Technology Neutral Law. *Computer Law & Security Review* 29(5): 509–521.

Hoerr, R.A. (2011) Regulatory Uncertainty and the Associated Business Risk for Emerging Technologies. *Journal of Nanoparticle Research* 13(4): 1513–1520.

INPUT (2018) Mission Statement. *INPUT Horizon 2020*. At: www.input-h2020.eu/the-mission/ (accessed 25 September 2019).

Jasanoff, S. (1990) *The Fifth Branch: Science Advisers as Policymakers*. Cambridge, MA: Harvard University Press.

Kleine, M. (2014) Informal Governance in the European Union. *Journal of European Public Policy* 21(2): 303–314.

Kuhlmann, S., Stegmaier, P. and Konrad, K. (2019) The Tentative Governance of Emerging Science and Technology – A Conceptual Introduction. *Research Policy* 48(5): 1091–1097.

McCarthy, D.R. (ed.) (2016) *Technology and World Politics: An Introduction*, Abingdon: Routledge.

McKinsey Global Institute (2013) *Disruptive Technologies: Advances That Will Transform Life, Business, and the Global Economy*, 1–176.

Macnaghten, P. (2010) Researching Technoscientific Concerns in the Making: Narrative Structures, Public Responses, and Emerging Nanotechnologies. *Environment and Planning A: Economy and Space* 42(1): 23–37.

Markides, C. (2006) Disruptive Innovation: In Need of Better Theory. *The Journal of Product Innovation Management* 23(1): 19–26.

Moses, L.B. (2015) How to Think about Law, Regulation and Technology: Problems with 'Technology' as a Regulatory Target. *Law, Innovation and Technology* 5(1): 1–20.

Perlmutter, S.I. (2017) Reaching Again: A Glimpse of the Future with Neuroprosthetics. *The Lancet* 389(10081): 1777–1778.

Prassl, J. (2018) *Humans as a Service: The Promise and Perils of Work in the Gig Economy.* Oxford: Oxford University Press.

Rao, B., Gopi, A.G. and Maione, R. (2016) The Societal Impact of Commercial Drones. *Technology in Society* 45: 83–90.

Renn, O. and Klinke, A. (2019) Risk Governance: Concept and Application to Technological Risk. In A. Burgess, A. Alemanno and J. Zinn (eds), *Routledge Handbook of Risk Studies.* Abingdon: Routledge, 204–215.

Rosa, E., McCright, A. and Renn, O. (2015) *The Risk Society Revisited: Social Theory and Risk Governance.* Philadelphia, PA: Temple University Press,

Rose, N., Aicardi, C. and Reinsborough, M. (2016) *Future Computing and Robotics: A Report from the HBP Foresight Lab.* The Human Brain Project, 1–46.

Rosenfeld, J., Bandopadhayay, P., Goldschlager, T. and Brown, D. (2008) The Ethics of the Treatment of Spinal Cord Injury: Stem Cell Transplants, Motor Neuroprosthetics, and Social Equity. *Topics in Spinal Cord Injury Rehabilitation* 14(1): 76–88.

Sabel, C.F. and Zeitlin, J. (2012) Learning from Difference: The New Architecture of Experimentalist Governance in the EU. In C.F. Sabel and J. Zeitlin (eds), *Experimentalist Governance in the European Union: Towards a New Architecture.* Oxford: Oxford University Press, 1–28.

Schweikard, A. and Ernst, F. (2015) Rehabilitation, Neuroprosthetics and Brain-Machine Interfaces. In A. Schweikard and F. Ernst (eds), *Medical Robotics.* Cham: Springer International Publishing, 349–361.

SensAgain Project (2016) About SensArs Neuroprosthetics. *SensArs.* At: www.sensars. com/about/ (accessed 25 September 2019).

Sismondo, S. (2009) *An Introduction to Science and Technology Studies*, 2nd edn, Chichester: Wiley-Blackwell.

Weimer, M. and Marin, L. (2016) The Role of Law in Managing the Tension between Risk and Innovation: Introduction to the Special Issue on Regulating New and Emerging Technologies. *European Journal of Risk Regulation* 7(3): 469–474.

World Health Organization (2006) *Neurological Disorders: Public Health Challenges.* Geneva: WHO, 1–232.

Wright, M.S. and Fins, J.J. (2016) Rehabilitation, Education, and the Integration of Individuals with Severe Brain Injury into Civil Society: Towards an Expanded Rights Agenda in Response to New Insights from Translational Neuroethics and Neuroscience. *Yale Journal of Health Policy, Law and Ethics* 2: 233–288.

Ziegler-Graham, K., MacKenzie, E.J., Ephraim, P.L., Travison, T.G. and Brookmeyer, R. (2008) Estimating the Prevalence of Limb Loss in the United States: 2005 to 2050. *Archives of Physical Medicine and Rehabilitation* 89(3): 422–429.

13 Drones and artificial intelligence

The EU's smart governance in emerging technologies

Raluca Csernatoni[1] and
Chantal Lavallée[2]

Introduction

In the past few years, the fast-paced and unprecedented development of new technologies has stimulated worldwide debates about their uses, risks and potential benefits. In addition, emerging and smart technologies are rapidly converging and are often interrelated, connected or fully integrated, such as Artificial Intelligence (AI) and machine learning, cyber networks, unmanned aircrafts (drones) and autonomous robotics (see the Introduction in this book). These technologies have been creating new synergies in key industrial domains at European and national levels, encompassing a host of implications for both civil and military objectives. Hence, their huge potential combined with their dual-use characteristics and interconnectedness have raised a series of questions about their unintended consequences and disruptive nature, leading to legal, ethical and societal concerns. In this context, intensive discussions about the best way to deal with and support their innovation and uptake have gained increasing traction in various national, regional and international fora (Lavallée 2019a; Hoijtink and Leese 2019; Boucher 2015). In this regard, the European Union (EU) has been (pro)active with several initiatives in emerging technology areas. EU member states, but also institutions and agencies such as the European Commission, European Parliament and European Defence Agency (EDA) have been actively involved in supporting research and development (R&D) to strengthen market growth, competitiveness and innovation (Calcara, Chapter 1 in this book). They have also pushed for the creation of legal frameworks in emerging sectors to mitigate potential risks and harness their benefits (Csernatoni 2019a; Lavallée 2019b). While recent academic literature has paid an increasing attention to emerging technologies in International Relations (IR) studies (Hoijtink and Leese 2019; Wilcox 2017; Shaw 2017; Aradau and Blanke 2015; Amicelle, Aradau and Jeandesboz 2015; Leander 2013), there is little research in European studies that substantively examines how the EU is tackling current technological challenges (Boucher 2015).

Against this background, this chapter examines how the EU has taken a position in the emerging technologies field. Especially, it analyses the leadership of the European Commission with the establishment of policy frameworks for drones and AI. This chapter focuses on these two key technological sectors, as the Commission has been particularly energetic in pushing their promotion and creating safeguards. In both domains, it has encouraged a 'smart' innovation and knowledge-based approach to policy-making, given their complexity, multi-disciplinary, interconnectedness and multi-stakeholder nature. Hence, this chapter analyses, from a comparative perspective, the EU processes behind the elaboration of policy frameworks for drones and AI, which have much in common, even if they have followed different paths towards different eco-systems. Both sectors offer rich material as case studies to assess whether there is a European distinctive approach and specificity when it comes to the govern-ance of emerging technologies. Informed by insights from field theory (Bigo 2014; Fligstein and McAdam 2011; Bourdieu 1986, 1985) and Science and Technology Studies (De Goede 2018; Amoore 2017, 2013), the chapter explores the techniques, expertise and power struggles that shape policy-making pro-cesses. It is interested in how discourses, interests, perceptions and practices cir-culate and are enacted by relevant actors to frame these new EU policy areas.

In this regard, this chapter argues that the European Commission's approach towards drones and AI policies, in stimulating intensive and strategic consulta-tions with and between key stakeholders, is engendering a 'smart governance'. The European Commission has taken a leadership role in elaborating European policy frameworks, shaping the EU's regulation as well as research and develop-ment priorities in line with a principled technological innovation model. The concept of 'smart governance' (Willke 2007) is used here as an analytical entry point to capture the complex dynamics in these fields and the nature of emerging technologies. It also refers to the idea that, in both cases, governance has been relying on expert and user know-how as well as specific strategic actions, struc-tured by relations with and among key stakeholders. In this regard, the European Commission has emerged as a policy entrepreneur in mobilising the European drone (Lavallée 2019a) and AI communities (Csernatoni 2019a) across civil–military, private–public, state–non-state nexuses in order to harness the innova-tion potential in the European emerging technologies field. It is (pro)actively pushing for and shaping a common European approach to the governance of emerging technologies by way of specific principled innovation frames of refer-ence for Europe itself and beyond the international community.

The chapter thus emphasises the EU's governance techniques in managing and evaluating the socio-political, ethical and legal challenges of a world increasingly dominated by new technologies in all aspects of activity. First, it clarifies how the EU became a proactive actor taking concrete actions in the field of emerging technologies regarding drones and AI, and how the concept of 'smart governance' provides us with a useful tool of analysis. Then, it examines the development of the EU drone and AI policies, by identifying who are the actors involved and how they interact, and what are their interests, narratives and tools. Finally, it analyses the commonalities, challenges and dynamics of a distinctive European governance of emerging technologies. It assesses how the European approach circulates new meanings, patterns, rationales and socio-material practices in the emerging technologies field. The chapter builds on data mostly collected through desk-based research, such as official discourses, key reports and policy documents, speeches and declarations, press releases, academic research and grey literature from think-tanks.

The EU: a newcomer in the European emerging technologies field?

IR and Science and Technology Studies (STS) bodies of literature are poised to tackle challenging global phenomena and major mutations of a so-called 'Fourth Industrial Revolution', an age of ever-more sophisticated systems with 'autonomous technologies', among which are drones, robotics, machine learning, deep learning and AI (Hoijtink and Leese 2019; see the Introduction in this book: xx). Such game-changing technical advancements have important dual-use applications in different sectors, by creating new markets, triggering new cooperation dynamics in key industrial domains and transforming civil–military relations. They galvanise a variety of actors and different levels of analysis, intertwining different socio-political, economic and security fields, that are made possible when STS, IR studies and multidisciplinary research approaches are taken into account. Therefore, the chapter builds on the very productive and notable developments of transversal research between IR and STS. By referring to the concept of 'smart governance' (Willke 2007) as an analytical lens, the research facilitates the encounter between insights from field theory (Bigo 2014; Fligstein and McAdam 2011; Bourdieu 1986, 1985) and engagements with critical work on technoscience (Ihde and Selinger 2003, Haraway 1997; Latour 1987). This chapter can thus better demonstrate the decisive role of the EU's position-taking in the field of emerging technologies and the dynamics between key actors, the structures of power and the struggles for competition in drone and AI domains.

From 2009 onwards, the European Commission (2012) has acknowledged the economic and transformative potential of drones, anticipating the proliferation of civil drones with their growing commercialisation. Although it did not yet have the capability to manage or regulate the sector, the Commission organised hearings and consultations with stakeholders to evaluate what could be its potential role to support the emergence of the sector. In these various fora, the European Commission (2012) has discussed on the one hand, the commercial questions acknowledging the competitiveness of the American and Israeli industries, the rising Chinese production and the so-called European 'technological-innovation gap' (Csernatoni 2019b). On the other hand, the Commission has considered societal concerns, namely, safety, security, privacy and data protection, third-party liability and environmental protection issues that needed to be addressed for the public acceptance of the increasingly important civil use of drones. While the EU has often been criticised for severely lagging behind in high-tech R&D, due to scarcities in human capital and the lack of commercial competitiveness (Lavallée and Zubeldia 2018), it has funded research projects related to drones from 1998 onwards. Indeed, through the fifth, sixth and seventh Framework Programmes (FPs), the European Commission managed R&D funds regarding drone-related projects mainly through its security research programme for civil purpose (Lavallée 2016), with a dual-use dimension potential (see Fiott, Chapter 2, as well as Martins and Ahmad, Chapter 3 in this book; Csernatoni 2018, 2019c). 'The Commission has spent [by the end of 2018] more than EUR 415 million via its research FPs on drone-related research' (Martins and Küsters 2019: 285). This drone-related research funding has indeed continued under the Horizon 2020 programme (H2020; 2014–2020) creating capacities and the emergence of patterns with individual projects (Martins and Küsters 2019), but also grants for the integration of the drones into the airspace through SES Air Traffic Management Research (SESAR) activities, namely, €9 million for exploratory research, €30 million for industrial R&D and €5 million for very large demonstrators (European Commission 2016).

Regarding the AI sector, the EU has only relatively recently started to elaborate a policy framework with a clear research and development strategy. Global players such as the USA and China have already been heavily investing in AI innovation over the past decades (Csernatoni 2019d). AI and autonomous robotics have become vital areas of international strategic competition, foreshadowing the impending possibility of becoming *the* revolutionary technologies of the current century. The acceleration of their uptake, the driving energy behind this new 'technological innovation race', at least in the narrative, has been justified by the AI's significant economic and social benefits and by the fact that early adopters are expected to become the next world leaders. The economic and innovation competition in this field is already playing itself out discursively, giving way to an ever-more urgent need to redouble efforts in mitigating the AI 'technological race' and to negotiate worldwide safety standards for AI research and usability. However, similarly, as for the drone sector, steps have been taken earlier than it seems to preserve Europe's claim to technological leadership. According to Juha Heikkilä, head of the Unit Robotics & Artificial Intelligence, the European Commission has allocated significant funding for cognitive systems, robotics and AI since 2004 (European Commission – Unit Robotics and Artificial Intelligence 2019b). A 'Short Overview of EU Activities and Policies in Robotics and Artificial Intelligence' lists a number of 15–20 new collaborative projects every year, with more than 80 projects currently in the Cognitive Systems and Robotics field between 2007 and 2013 (European Commission 2019b). As early as 2014, this overview confirmed that the Commission has invested significant amounts in AI-related areas, with around €1.1 billion under H2020 between 2014–2017, with more investments coming up until the end of 2020. According to this overview, between 2018–2020, further funding is dedicated to the research and development of AI, with €1.5 billion under H2020, topped by €20 billion of combined public and private investment. All this funding demonstrates a proactive commitment to take up a tailored approach to engendering a lucrative, innovative and competitive European AI environment.

Equally significant is the European Commission's agenda-setting capacity using its regulatory and market power to structure the field of emerging technologies in Europe and trigger innovation and legitimisation strategies around technoscientific issues in the drone sector and progressively as well as in the case of AI development. In particular, the European Commission's agenda-setter potential is a key driver in galvanising the drone and AI sectors, by building on expert technoscientific knowledges in order to chart their transformative impact on meanings, values, interests and practices. The Commission has used its tools to bridge the technological-innovation gap towards the international main players and to shape a European approach within comprehensive strategies in an era of rapid technological change and global insecurity.

Therefore, the chapter further contends that a defining feature of the EU's distinctive approach and specificity, when it comes to the governance of emerging technologies, is its capacity to strategically harness technoscientific knowledge. The EU, and the Commission in particular, leverage this form of knowledge 'capital' (Bourdieu 1986) to successfully compete on the emerging technologies 'battlefield'. Hence, the Commission can take a position in the field using its agenda-setting power and legitimating its role with the expertise it has gathered, as 'every field is the site of a more or less overt struggle over the definition of the legitimate principles of the division of the field' (Bourdieu 1985: 734). In this line of reasoning, technoscientific expert knowledge becomes crucial for the Commission to the European governance of emerging technologies on different levels, ranging from putting in place flexible decision-making processes, financial mechanisms to support innovative and lucrative R&D, to deciding on issues related to regulatory and ethical controls. Nevertheless, by paraphrasing Hellström (2000), the presence of technoscientific expert knowledge is one step in establishing the Commission's lead positioning in the field of emerging technologies. The second step is that of the actual *enactment* of such expertise by the Commission, which is carried out through culturally infused technocratic and procedural policy frameworks and management strategies typical to the EU (Vanhoonacker, Dijkstra and Maurer 2010; Trondal, Murdoch and Geys 2014).

In the case of the Commission, the 'smart governance' (Willke 2007) of emerging technologies builds on a specific policy culture that prioritises regulatory and market decisions, integrating both technoscientific and managerial expertise (Hellström 2000: 501). Furthermore, in order to occupy a strategic position in the field of emerging technologies, the Commission is ideally positioned as an essential node across various sociotechnical and expert networks and practices in Europe. Hence, by referring to 'smart governance' to explore and address these issues, the next section looks at the European emerging technologies sectors as a multilevel and multi-stakeholder playing field. The Commission's expertise and management strategies are shaping the EU's technological innovation model and R&D priorities in the case of drones and AI in line with built-in flexibility, accountability and ethical guidelines. However, as already mentioned, the possession of technoscientific knowledge does not necessarily translate into managerial knowledge in solving policy problem, here the Commission further potentially proving to possess technocratic and policy competencies in this regard.

EU drone and AI sectors: the emergence of new ecosystems

The EU Drone Policy

On 1 July 2019, the EU policy framework for civil drones entered into force. It 'provides requirements and obligations not only for the operators, but also for the manufacturers, importers, and distributors in the upcoming single drone market based on CE marking certification' (Lavallée 2019b: 2). At this stage, these detailed technical and operational rules, respectively, the 'Commission Delegated Regulation (EU) 2019/945 of 12 March 2019 on unmanned aircraft systems and on third-country operators of unmanned aircraft systems' and the 'Commission Implementing Regulation (EU) 2019/947 of 24 May 2019 on the rules and procedures for the operation of unmanned aircraft' should guide member states in the implementation process at the national level. The Commission has proposed in these new regulations a degree of flexibility to the member states, notably the identification of the drone zones. Most of the EU member states that have elaborated national rules already need to make sure that they will be in line with the European regulation by July 2020, but they still have room for manoeuvre. Some countries like France and, more recently, Belgium have developed exchange platforms such as the Belgian Civil Drone Council to coordinate actions between stakeholders and facilitate the implementation process. This new drone governance is the outcome of a long policy process involving different actors at different levels with diverse background in various fora.

As reported by the first 'Hearing on Light Unmanned Aircraft Systems' organised by the European Commission (2009: 1), drones are 'becoming a new paradigm for aviation, creating new potential usage, but requiring an adapted approach compared to the one applied to manned aircraft.' Drones have been considered earlier as unmanned aircrafts (also called Remotely Piloted Aircraft Systems, RPAS), which future integration into the airspace a main concern for civil aviation. Back then, the relevant European Regulation was on common rules in the field of civil aviation (known as the 'Basic Regulation' no 216/2008). It was stating that drones with a maximum take-off mass of less than 150 kg fall within the competence of the EU member states, while drones above 150 kg, excluding the military and state drones, fall into the competence of the EU under the responsibility of the European Aviation Safety Agency (EASA). Hence, if DG GROW was first involved for the economic potential with the opportunity for creating a new single-market dimension, DG MOVE took the leadership in the policy-making process leading to an EU-wide framework for drones, promoting aviation safety. It has coordinated its actions with DG GROW but also DG Research, which was managing drone-related research funding from FP5 and then DG HOME. As in this context, the EU member states were responsible for regulating their airspace, the European Commission (2014: 4) highlighted fragmented national standards requiring ad hoc individual authorisations and restricting market development for drones. In addition, the transnational dimension of the European drone industry and the cross-borders use of drones was justifying for the Commission the need for a European framework. Then, from the beginning, market and regulatory components were closely linked in the Commission narrative. This was a way for the Commission to use its regulatory and market power to take a position and structure the field of emerging technologies in Europe. The drone sector is indeed a rising aeronautical area, with new applications, a dual-use technology with many (but also as yet unidentified) potentialities. Hence Violeta Bulc, the EU Commissioner for Transport from 2014 to 2019 was insisting with high enthusiasm that:

> Drones mean innovation, new services for citizens, new business models and a huge potential for economic growth. We need the EU to be in the driving seat and have a safe drone services market up and running by 2019. The EU needs to take a leading role worldwide in developing the right framework for this market to flourish, by unleashing the benefits for key economic sectors.
>
> (European Commission 2017)

The key challenge about the regulation on the civilian use of drones for the Commission was earlier the balance between development of a market with high professional and economics opportunities and the protection of citizens' rights – the air users as well as the people on the ground.

Therefore, the Commission has played a leadership role working with all actors in the drone community to deal with multifaceted and interlinked aspects of drone-related issues. Besides the expert conferences and public consultations, the Commission (2012: 6) created the UAS Panel Process in 2011 to contribute with the organisation of a series of five workshops on key issues to the elaboration of a European strategy for the development of civil applications. It was open to key stakeholders such as Eurocontrol, the European Civil Aviation Conference (ECAC), European Civil Aviation Authorities, ICAO, Joint Authorities for Rulemaking on Unmanned Systems (JARUS), national representatives from the ministries of the interior and defence as well as EU agencies such as EDA and EASA (European Commission 2012: 7). The dual-use of the airspace as well as the interest in drones by civil and military users explain that, at an early stage, the discussions involved civil and military actors. The UAS Panel Process is an example of how the Commission stimulates and harnesses expertise to legitimate its action and strengthen its position in the field, especially with one of the conclusions saying that 'none of the European regulatory organisations is capable of carrying out the massive regulatory work for RPAS alone' (European Commission 2012: 17). Hence, the value-added and niche competence of the Commission is to provide the drone community with its regulatory power for an overarching regulatory framework. In its ambition to integrate civil drones into the European aviation system, the Commission pursues its smart governance establishing a European RPAS Steering Group in July 2012. This group, composed of the main civil and military stakeholders (EASA, EUROCONTROL, EUROCAE, SESAR JU, JARUS, ECAC, EDA, ESA, ASD, UVSI, EREA and ECA), submitted its report, including a roadmap for the Commission, in June 2013.

The Commission's strategy, based on this expert and user know-how, was finally presented in the 2014 Communication 'A new era for aviation. Opening the aviation market to the civil use of remotely piloted aircraft systems in a safe and sustainable manner.' The Commission mentioned the 'call of the European manufacturing and service industry to remove barriers to the introduction of RPAS in the European single market' as the key to stimulate the competitiveness of the European aeronautics industry (2014: 2). According to the Commission, 'while the exact nature and extent of potential RPAS operations are difficult to predict now, the service industry is expected to generate sufficient revenues to drive forward the manufacturing industry itself' (2014: 3). Therefore, the Commission's narrative framed the drone sector as an 'emerging market' with a huge potential to 'foster job creation and a source for innovation and economic growth' underlying the need for the creation 'a drone ecosystem', where 'citizens' fundamental rights' are protected (European Commission 2014). The official policy process for implementing its vision on drones started with the 2015 'Aviation Strategy for Europe', where the Commission did propose a new regulatory framework to update the Basic Regulation (European Commission 2015).

From 2015 to 2019, the Commission led intensive discussions across various committees and fora on the best way to frame the EU policy on drones. A series of annual, high-level conferences on drones with key stakeholders started in Riga (2015), then Warsaw (2016), Helsinki (2017) and Amsterdam (2018), which agreed on annual consensual non-binding declarations but provided the EU policy process with guidelines and input from the drone community. These declarations have offered the narrative, principles, definitions and expectations on which the EU could build its drone policy. Besides its dedicated working groups, the EASA also conducted extensive consultations with the stakeholders to develop guidelines for the 'Regulation (EU) 2018/1139' (called the 'new Basic Regulation'; EU 2018). This regulation has notably extended the competence of EASA under the authority of the Commission (DG MOVE) to deal with any drones irrespective of their weight. EASA could then submit its Opinion for more specific rules, norms and parameters to guide the safe use of civil drones, collaborating closely with the European Organisation for Civil Aviation Equipment (EUROCAE), which already develops standards in Europe, the ICAO to be in line with international standards and benefit from JARUS expertise. Despite this, the European Commission has only pushed for the regulation on the civil use of drones; as mentioned, the military have also been involved in an early stage, as they have been working for the integration of military RPAS in non-segregated airspace in the context of the Single European Sky (SES). In parallel, in 2017, DG MOVE created an Expert Group on Drones to assist the

Commission in the development of the Delegated Regulation (with various stakeholders) and Implementing Regulation (composed of national representatives). Through this intensive and comprehensive process, the Commission building its position on technoscientific expert knowledge has legitimised further its contribution and confirmed a smart governance for the EU drone policy.

At the time of the implementation of the new EU regulations on drones, the U-Space, the key initiative to facilitate the integration of drones into the airspace providing a platform for Unmanned Traffic Management, is now the centre of all discussions. In June 2017, SESAR JU (2017) presented the blueprint, based on several consultations, indicating that this framework will be:

> capable of ensuring the smooth operation of drones in all operating environments, and in all types of airspace (in particular but not limited to very low-level airspace). It addresses the needs to support all types of missions and may concern all drone users and categories of drones.
>
> (SESAR JU 2017)

Based on this document as well as on internal and external consultations, EASA is developing a draft regulation to be submitted to the Commission in 2020. In the perspective of urban mobility, cities are also invited to play an increasing role in this upcoming drone ecosystem at the local level through the European Innovation Partnership on Smart Cities and Communities (EIP-SCC) to then take part as well in this smart governance of emerging technologies.

The EU 'trustworthy' framework for AI

As the development of drones requested the EU's response, the unstoppable evolution of AI technologies has also questioned the role of the EU and its institutions. How can the EU, notwithstanding its gaps in both the areas of supercomputing and autonomous technologies, make a world with complex interconnected autonomous technologies and AI safe and secure for European citizens? Unprecedented improvements in AI and so-called 'autonomous' (digital) technologies have the potential to fundamentally transform human–machine relations and generate new and complex systems. AI offers potentially disruptive solutions for both civil and military uses and applications as an enabling and general-purpose technology. AI has been heralded by the High-Level Expert Group on Artificial Intelligence (AI HLEG) as 'one of the most transformative forces of our time and is bound to alter the fabric of society' (2018). Triggered by advances in quantum and cloud computing, hardware and Big Data intensive machine learning, the imminent new 'age' of AI signals far-reaching and profound transformations in all sectors of society, such as finance, health care, cybersecurity, education, social care and defence. Equally, such potential disruptions have ushered in an array of pressing and complex debates about the complementarity between humans and 'intelligent' machines, their governance, legal and moral dimensions, their various applications and uses, as well as their broader socio-economic and political impact.

The EU and particularly the European Commission appear here also as key drivers and agenda-setters in galvanising a comprehensive and more human-centred approach to the R&D of AI, to bridge the technological-innovation gap and to bring about an ethically informed and principled European strategy to AI (Csernatoni 2019a). Similarly, as with the strategies and processes in the drone sector, concrete and decisive actions have been taken at the EU-level, by promoting policy initiatives and projects, by creating specialised expert groups, by providing financing platforms for industry consortia and by fostering public–private partnerships in the AI technological area. Nevertheless, dilemmas still remain whether such initiatives are too little too late to consolidate the EU's position in the so-called AI global 'race' (Csernatoni 2019d).

In an effort to harness and consolidate its technoscientific expert knowledge in the case of AI, in 2018, the European Commission (2018b) created the High-Level Expert Group on Artificial Intelligence (AI HLEG), gathering 52 experts from academia, civil society and industry responsible for supporting the implementation of a European strategy on AI. The group acts as a steering body for the European AI Alliance, an interactive platform and multi-stakeholder forum set up by the Commission (2019c), engaging more than 3,000 European citizens and stakeholders in a dialogue on the future of AI in and across Europe. This expertise-building initiative is revealing as regards the Commissions efforts to proactively structure the European emerging technologies field, as well as in positioning itself via the group as an essential node across various sociotechnical and expert networks and practices. Furthermore, due to the fact that the High-Level Expert Group on AI provides recommendations concerning challenges and opportunities related to AI development, non-binding ethics guidelines as well as legal and policy frameworks, it equally plays a key role in shaping the EU's research and development priorities and technological innovation model in accordance with a specific normative stance.

By supporting the HLEG on AI's Communication on 'Artificial Intelligence for Europe' in April 2018 (European Commission 2018a) and the 'The Ethics Guidelines for Trustworthy Artificial Intelligence (AI)' in April 2019 (European Commission 2019a), the Commission has positioned itself as the key driver for a human-centric approach to AI. In addition, it has taken ownership of the AI's timely research and development: by directly dealing with technological, ethical, legal and socio-economic issues; and by boosting the EU's research and industrial capacity to put AI at the service of European citizens and economy. Consequently, initial steps have been taken towards capacity building in the case of AI to preserve Europe's claim to technological leadership, to bridge the technological-innovation gap in Europe and to bring about an ethically informed and principled European strategy to AI.

As mentioned above, the AI-related Communication and the Ethics Guidelines substantiated a 'European comprehensive approach' on three general pillars: being ahead of technological developments and boosting uptake in both public and private sectors; preparing for mid- and long-term socio-economic transformations engendered by AI; and last but not the least, providing appropriate ethical and legal frameworks for the design, production, use and governance of AI, robotics and autonomous systems. The HLEG on AI launched a pilot phase from 26 June until 1 December 2019 to ensure that the ethical guidelines for AI development and use could be implemented in practice. The Commission invited industry, research institutes and public authorities to test the detailed assessment list drafted by the High-Level Expert Group on AI, which complements the guidelines. On 26 June 2019, the HLEG on AI also presented a list of 33 recommendations on how to boost the European AI industry with the 'Policy and Investment Recommendations for Trustworthy AI' (European Commission 2019b), by drafting the most detailed plan and vision to date on setting the first steps towards defining the conditions under which AI should be developed and implemented in the EU's internal market.

There is a clear link between the overarching strategy and vision of the EU's intention to become a leader in responsible AI and the uptake of technologically robust and trustworthy European AI technologies that respect basic human rights engineered to mitigate potential harm. The EU's approach and narrative of 'Trustworthy AI', could indeed prepare the foundation for ethical guidelines as a reference for the creation and use of AI in Europe and potentially on the global stage. The underlying logic behind such a strategy is that the development of AI technologies adhering to high ethical and human rights standards will eventually provide European developers and manufacturers with a much-needed competitive edge, with consumers and users ultimately favouring such products over those sourced, for instance, in China or the USA. As in the case of the drone sector, the EU's strategic advantage as regards AI definitely resides in its market and regulatory power, as shown by the worldwide effect of the General Data Protection Regulation (GDPR), by setting industry standards, building trust, and ensuring legal clarity and public legitimacy in AI-based and autonomous robotics applications. The question remains whether the EU's ethical and human-centred approach runs the risk of stifling innovation in these fields, due to over-regulation, or lays the groundwork for a much-needed preventive and principled governance of technological development. This approach is certainly grounded in specific normative and cultural factors that go beyond policy and regulatory aspects and are embedded in a distinctive European-centric worldview.

According to the guidelines, 'trustworthy' AI should be: lawful and respecting all applicable laws and regulations; ethical and respecting ethical principles and values; and robust both from a technical perspective and while taking into account its social environment. Such an approach is substantiated on European AI technologies that respect basic human rights, human agency and data privacy. These are characterised by transparency, diversity and fairness, and are engineered to mitigate potential harm, allow accountability and oversight, ensuring social and environmental well-being. Nevertheless, such guidelines and any proposals put forward by the HLEG on AI are voluntary in nature and are not binding. Moreover, it is not yet certain how an ethics-first AI approach will establish global standards for development, implementation and regulation.

The European Commission has also emerged as a strategic managerial actor in mobilising the European AI community to optimise the technological and industrial potential in the field. It comes as no surprise that the composition of the AI HLEG brings together representatives from European AI politics, civil society, universities and above all industry, demonstrating the Commission's strategy to secure the industry's leaders in the field buy-in in the ethical development of AI. The AI HLEG Policy and Investment Recommendations (European Commission 2019b) with the 33 recommendations, provides a big picture and a non-exhaustive and holistic approach that should be taken together to achieve maximum uptake of AI in both private and private sectors. The recommendations focus on four main areas where Trustworthy AI development may help in attaining a beneficial impact: from humans and society at large, the private sector, the public sector, to Europe's research and academia. The European Commission has equally played an important role in stimulating a 'culture of cooperation' between industry and academia. Such efforts have been geared towards introducing a number of specialised instruments and to pushing innovation closer to market opportunities by stimulating cross-sectoral dialogue between producers, users and academia in emerging technologies. They also address the main enablers needed to facilitate such impacts, namely, the availability of data and infrastructure, upskilling and education, appropriate governance and regulation, and funding and investment.

Investments in AI development equally point towards increasing strides made in the last decade to foster a strong basis to innovate and create value added in cutting-edge technological domains. An overview of recent EU initiatives in AI and robotics (see Csernatoni 2019a) delineates clear steps taken to invest in front-line and interdisciplinary research, to carve value-based and human-centric guidelines and benchmarks, to ensure coordination at the European level by working with member states and to create a critical mass of cross-sectoral technoscientific expertise and cross-border collaborations in these domains. Although it is too early to judge the impact of such initiatives, the EU could have an agenda-setter potential in enacting its technoscientific expertise into policy frameworks. For instance, the European Commission has created a Unit Robotics & Artificial Intelligence within its DG for Communication Networks, Content & Technology. Its mission is 'the development of a competitive industry in robotics and Artificial Intelligence in Europe including industrial and service robots as well as the growing field of autonomous systems spanning from drones and driverless vehicles to cognitive vision and computing' (European Commission – Unit Robotics and Artificial Intelligence 2019a). This directorate manages the Commission's implementation and development of 'the relevant strategic industrial agenda', by managing the research and development and innovation priorities and projects in the field within the framework of Horizon 2020 (H2020). A 'Short overview of EU activities and policies in Robotics and Artificial Intelligence' presents the European Commission's (2019b) outlook on

AI as a 'significant component in robotics activities so far', as 'AI research and development' is key for related core technologies, and most pointedly 'AI as enabling technology' – for, for example, drones, autonomous vehicles and assistive systems.

According to Cécil Huet (2017), deputy head of the Unit Robotics & Artificial Intelligence, H2020 funding programmes have substantially supported AI-related European initiatives, with investments in Future and Emerging Technologies (FET), such as the AI-on-Demand Platform (AI4EU 2019) with €20 million to be continued in 2020. Launched in January 2019, the Commission and partners have started building the European AI on-demand platform (AI4EU 2019), the EU's landmark AI project, which seeks to develop a European AI ecosystem, bringing together an assemblage of knowledges, algorithms, tools and resources available and making it a compelling solution for users in order to unify Europe's AI community. Comprising 79 top research centres from 21 countries, the aim with this platform is to facilitate a wide uptake of AI in the business and public sectors across Europe and also provide courses for reskilling and upskilling. However, it is too early to assess whether such steps are enough to establish a solid basis for an AI culture of innovation and a pan-European collaboration ecosystem.

Towards a European approach to govern emerging technologies: challenges and dynamics

As the last section has showed, the advent of drones and AI has created new domains of action for the EU, interaction with and among various stakeholders, as well as new governance challenges due to their complexity, interconnectedness, circulations, applications and uses. This showed that the European Commission has put forward a unique and proactive normative entrepreneurship through a 'smart governance' approach, by harnessing its regulative and market power expertise to draw accepted standards for R&D and usability of AI and public acceptance for drones. While the EU has developed frameworks for civil use, the dual-use potential of drones and AI reveals deeper complexities in allocating controls in technological design and ethical standards of usability, without at the same time stifling innovation.

In the case of both drones and AI sectors, we noticed that the EU has followed a similar approach and rationale, namely, a knowledge-based approach (policy process) and an ethical and human-centred approach (policy outcome). There are some differences between both policy processes, given the specificities of each technological and policy domain, but there are enough commonalities to see comparable patterns. These are made apparent in how the European Commission has been (pro)actively pushing for and shaping a common European approach to the research and development as well as principled governance of emerging technologies by way of a specific innovation frames of reference not only for Europe itself, but also for the international community. This approach is consolidating a particular normative stand, thus positioning the EU as a legislative and ethical reference in a crucial moment where socio-material practices and the meanings surrounding these emerging technologies are not settled.

The second section demonstrated that the European Commission has emerged as a strategic actor in mobilising the European drone and AI expert communities to optimise their innovation potential and their development and applications according to a European normative approach. Therefore, special emphasis has been given to how expert technoscientific knowledges are being created and enacted as regards drones and AI, in order to chart their transformative impact on meanings, values, interests and practices. Some overlaps between, common grounds or same high-tech actors in both communities and emerging ecosystems are to be found in the consolidation of the European emerging technologies field. The European Commission has started regulation and implementation initiatives and proposing recommendations to establish ethical and legal frameworks with a human-centred use of drones and AI.

The involvement of the EU, thus, opens up new possibilities for regulating the innovation and specific use of drones and AI and for an ethically controlled technological design with a view to engendering a more encompassing and comprehensive process of reflection and dialogue in Europe and the world about the specific role such technologies should play in it. The EU has positioned itself as playing an essential role in ensuring that the benefits of advanced drone technologies and AI are broadly shared, while at the same time providing a platform for financing the research and development of such technologies in Europe. The rationale for a 'smart governance' of emerging technologies goes hand in hand with entrenching basic codes of conducts, liability regulations and legal and ethical principles, which need to be established and respected so that the technological development and the use of AI and drones is beneficial to society and at the same time economically lucrative. Finally, in both sectors, the European Commission has played an active role in promoting and legitimising through narratives, legal frameworks, market and research initiatives the design and governance of drones and AI in line with European values and interests.

Conclusions

The chapter has highlighted how the European Commission has emerged as a key policy-entrepreneur and manager. It has analysed its agenda-setter capacity in framing and translating principled innovation priorities into new EU policies in the case of frontier technology areas such as drone and AI sectors. The European Commission has indeed taken an important role in stimulating both sectors, especially in encouraging interdisciplinary cross-border research and a culture of cooperation between industry, users and academia, thus underscoring innovation as particularly important for a strong high-tech industrial base and to safeguard Europe's future competitiveness. The Commission's efforts have been geared towards introducing specialised instruments and mechanisms, pushing innovation closer to market opportunities and encouraging dialogue between producers, manufacturers, users, operators, regulators, service providers and academia.

This chapter has built on insights from field theory to demonstrate how the Commission has taken a distinctive position and legitimised its action based on its 'capital' (regulatory and market power as well as technoscientific expert knowledge) in the European emerging technologies field. From a critical STS perspective, this chapter stressed the technoscientific expertise required in the upcoming 'Drone and AI Age', especially as regards dual-use impact and dynamics between the norms (ethics and human-centric dimension) and the market. This chapter, by comparing two strategic sectors which the EU is now actively engaged in, has aimed to open up a new and comprehensive research agenda into the EU's 'smart governance' approach of the European emerging technologies field. In this respect, it has emphasised the fact that technoscientific expert knowledge becomes particularly important in the case of cutting-edge technologies, by both establishing flexible, multi-stakeholder and marketable R&D initiatives and also by putting in place ethically driven and principled regulatory governance mechanisms. Finally, the chapter has underlined the fact that while technoscientific expert knowledge is highly desirable and is needed to make sense of the brave new age of drones and AI, the enactment of such knowledge equally needs to be backed by technocratic managerial expertise and policy frameworks, for which the European Commission is particularly well placed as a nodal point to put forward comprehensive policy frameworks in both technological domains.

Notes

1 The research that led to this publication was conducted as part of the postdoctoral researcher fellowship (January 2017–January 2019) at the Department of International Relations, Institute of Political Studies (IPS), Faculty of Social Sciences, Charles University, Prague, Czechia.
2 The research that led to this publication was conducted in the framework of the project 'EU-Drones', which received funding from the EU's Horizon 2020 research and innovation programme under the Marie Skłodowska-Curie grant agreement No 747947.

References

AI-on-Demand Platform (AI4EU) (2019) About us. At: www.ai4eu.eu/.
Amicelle, A., Aradau, C. and Jeandesboz, J. (2015) Questioning Security Devices: Performativity, Resistance, Politics. *Security Dialogue* 46(4): 293–306.
Amoore, L. (2017) Securing with Algorithms: Knowledge, Decision, Sovereignty. *Security Dialogue* 48(1): 3–10.
Amoore, L. (2013) *The Politics of Possibility: Risk and Security Beyond Probability.* Durham, NC: Duke University Press.
Aradau, C. (2010) Security that Matters: Critical Infrastructure and Objects of Protection. *Security Dialogue* 41(5): 491–514.
Aradau, C. and Blanke, T. (2015) The (Big) Data-Security Assemblage: Knowledge and Critique. *Big Data & Society* 2(2). doi:10.1177/2053951715609066.
Bigo, D. (2014) The (In)Securitization Practices of the Three Universes of EU Border Control: Military/Navy – Border Guards/Police – Database Analysts. *Security Dialogue* 45(3): 2019–42.

Boucher, P. (2015) Domesticating the Drone: The Demilitarisation of Unmanned Aircraft for Civil Markets. *Science and Engineering Ethics* 21(6): 1393–1412.

Bourdieu, P. (1985) The Social Space and the Genesis of Groups. *Theory and Society* 14(6): 723–744.

Bourdieu, P. (1986) The Forms of Capital. In J. Richardson (ed.), *Handbook of Theory and Research for the Sociology of Education.* New York: Greenwood, 241–258.

Csernatoni, R. (2018) Constructing the EU's High-Tech Borders: FRONTEX and Dual-Use Drones for Border Management. *European Security* 27(2): 175–200.

Csernatoni, R. (2019a) An Ambitious Agenda or Big Words? Developing a European Approach to AI, *Egmont – Royal Institute for International Relations*, Security Policy Brief, No 118, November 2019. At: www.egmontinstitute.be/an-ambitious-agenda-or-big-words-developing-a-european-approach-to-ai/ (accessed November 2019).

Csernatoni, R. (2019b) The EU's Technological Power: Harnessing Future and Emerging Technologies for European Security. In C.A. Baciu and J. Doyle (eds), *Peace, Security and Defence Cooperation in Post-Brexit Europe.* Cham: Springer.

Csernatoni, R. (2019c) Between Rhetoric and Practice: Technological Efficiency and Defence Cooperation in the European Drone Sector. *Critical Military Studies.* https://doi.org/10.1080/23337486.2019.158562.

Csernatoni, R. (2019d) Beyond the Hype: The EU and the AI Global 'Arms Race'. European Leadership Network, www.europeanleadershipnetwork.org/commentary/beyond-the-hype-the-eu-and-the-ai-global-arms-race/.

De Goede, M. (2018) The Chain of Security. *Review of International Studies* 44(1): 24–42.

European Commission (2009) Report: Hearing on Light Unmanned Aircraft Systems, Brussels, 8 October.

European Commission (2012) Towards a European Strategy for the Development of Civil Applications of Remotely Piloted Aircraft Systems (RPAS), SWD (2012) 259 final, Brussels, 4 September 2012.

European Commission (2014) A New Era for Aviation: Opening the Aviation Market to the Civil Use of Remotely Piloted Aircraft Systems in a Safe and Sustainable Manner, COM (2014) 207 final, Brussels, 8 April.

European Commission (2015) An Aviation Strategy for Europe, COM(2015) 598 final, Brussels, 7 December.

European Commission (2016) The EU Drone Policy, Memo/16/4123, https://ec.europa.eu/commission/presscorner/detail/en/MEMO_16_4123.

European Commission (2017) Aviation: Commission is Taking the European Drone Sector to New Heights. Press release, 16 June.

European Commission (2018a) Communication artificial intelligence for Europe, https://ec.europa.eu/knowledge4policy/publication/communicationartificial-intelligence-europe_en.

European Commission (2018b) Call for High-Level Expert Group on Artificial Intelligence, https://ec.europa.eu/digital-single-market/en/news/call-high-level-expert-group-artificial-intelligence.

European Commission (2019a) Ethics Guidelines for Trustworthy AI, https://ec.europa.eu/digital-single-market/en/news/ethics-guidelines-trustworthy-ai.

European Commission (2019b) Policy and Investment Recommendations for Trustworthy AI, https://ec.europa.eu/digital-single-market/en/news/policy-and-investment-recommendations-trustworthy-artificial-intelligence.

European Commission (2019c) European AI Alliance, https://ec.europa.eu/knowledge-4policy/ai-watch/european-ai-alliance_en.

European Commission – Unit Robotics & Artificial Intelligence (2019a) https://ec. europa.eu/digital-single-market/en/content/robotics-and-artificial-intelligence-unit-a1.

European Commission – Unit Robotics & Artificial Intelligence (2019b) Short overview of EU activities and policies in Robotics and Artificial Intelligence, http://ec.europa.eu/ information_society/newsroom/image/document/2017-30/juha_heikkila_-_eu_policies_ and_activities_in_ai_and_robotics_620DBD48-E9E7-9583-0B3E7171B0B7E793_ 46144.pdf.

EU (2008) Regulation (EC) 216/2008 of 20 February 2008 on common rules in the field of civil aviation, *Official Journal of the EU*, 19 March.

EU (2018) Regulation (EU) 2018/1139 of the European Parliament and of the Council of 4 July 2018 on common rules in the field of civil aviation and establishing a European Union Aviation Safety Agency, *Official Journal of the EU*, 22 August.

EU (2019a) Commission Delegated Regulation (EU) 2019/945 of 12 March 2019 on unmanned aircraft systems and on third-country operators of unmanned aircraft systems, *Official Journal of the EU*, 11 June.

EU (2019b) Commission Implementing Regulation (EU) 2019/947 of 24 May 2019 on the rules and procedures for the operation of unmanned aircraft, *Official Journal of the EU*, 11 June.

Fligstein, N. and McAdam, D. (2011) Toward a General Theory of Strategic Action Fields. *Sociological Theory* 29(1): 1–26.

Haraway, D. (1997) *Modest_Witness@Second_Millennium.FemaleMan©Meets_OncoMouse™: Feminism and Technoscience*. New York: Routledge.

Hellström, T. (2000) Technoscientific Expertise and the Significance of Policy Cultures. *Technology and Society* 22: 499–512.

High-Level Expert Group on Artificial Intelligence (2018) First Draft Ethics Guidelines for Trustworthy AI. At: https://ec.europa.eu/digital-single-market/en/news/draft-ethics-guidelines-trustworthy-ai.

Hoijtink, M. and Leese, M. (eds) (2019) *Technology and Agency in International Relations*. Abingdon: Routledge.

Huet, C. (2017) European Commission's Initiatives in Artificial Intelligence. At: www. oecd.org/going-digital/ai-intelligent-machines-smart-policies/conference-agenda/ai-intelligent-machines-smart-policies-huet.pdf.

Idhe, D. and Selinger, E. (eds) (2003) *Chasing Technoscience: Matrix for Materiality –A State-of-the-Art View of Technoscience Studies, Featuring the Work of Donna Haraway, Don Idhe, Bruno Latour, Andrew Pickering*. Bloomington, IN: Indiana University Press.

Latour, B. (1987) *Science in Action*. Milton Keynes: Open University Press.

Lavallée, C. (2016) La communautarisation de la recherche sur la sécurité: l'appropriation d'un nouveau domaine d'action au nom de l'approche globale. *Politique européenne* 51: 31–59.

Lavallée, C. (2019a) The EU Policy for Civil Drones: the Challenge of Governing Emerging Technologies. *IES Policy Brief*, 2019/01.

Lavallée, C. (2019b) The New EU Policy on Civil Drones. A Paradigm Shift for European Airspace. *PRIO Policy Brief*, 05/2019.

Lavallée, C. and Zubeldia, O. (2018) A European Drone Space. *IRSEM Research Paper*, No. 52.

Leander, A. (2013) Technological Agency in the Co-Constitution of Legal Expertise and the US Drone Program. *Leiden Journal of International Law* 26(4): 811–831.

Martins, B.O. and Küsters, C. (2019) Hidden Security: EU Public Research Funds and the Development of European Drones. *Journal of Common Market Studies* 57(2): 278–297.

SESAR JU (2017) 'U-Space Blueprint', June. www.sesarju.eu/sites/default/files/documents/reports/U-space%20Blueprint.pdf.

Shaw, I.G.R. (2017) Robot Wars: US Empire and Geopolitics in the Robotic Age. *Security Dialogue* 48(5): 451–470.

Trondal, J., Murdoch, Z. and Geys, B. (2014) Representative Bureaucracy and the Role of Expertise in Politics. *Politics and Governance* 3(1): 26–36.

Vanhoonacker, S., Dijkstra, H. and Maurer, H. (eds) (2010) Understanding the Role of Bureaucracy in the European Security and Defence Policy. *European Integration online Papers* (EIoP), Special Issue 14(1). http://eiop.or.at/eiop/texte/2010-004a_htm.

Wilcox, L. (2017) Embodying Algorithmic War: Gender, Race, and the Posthuman in Drone Warfare. *Security Dialogue* 48(1): 11–28.

Willke, H. (2007) *Smart Governance: Governing the Global Knowledge Society*. New York: Campus Verlag.

Conclusion

The governance of emerging security technologies – towards a critical assessment

Ciara Bracken-Roche

Introduction

Throughout this volume, each chapter aims to open the 'black-box' (McCarthy 2018) around dual-use technologies in the EU by focusing on a specific technology and the corresponding policies and politics that accompany it. Many of the contributions lend themselves well to the material turn in International Relations (IR) and critical security studies more broadly by engaging with Science and Technology Studies (STS) and attempting to approximate a more holistic understanding of technologies through an analysis of the actors, conditions, policies and politics shaping their development and deployment. Technology is understood as being socially relative and constructed. And as the editors outline in the Introduction,

> emerging technologies have clear cut normative dimensions dependent upon specific historical contexts, economic or security interests, and discursive framings, that in turn shape how subjects perceive, manage, implement, and responds to technically mediated socio political and security relations.
>
> (Rao *et al.* 2015: 454)

This collection makes a unique theoretical contribution by building its assessment on a framework substantiated on conceptual approaches across critical security studies, international relations, science and technology studies and sociology in order to better assess the unique way that emerging technologies are governed by actor-networks in the European Union (EU). More so, it offers a unique empirical contribution in that each chapter focuses on a distinct technology in the EU context and offers a snapshot in time of the EU actors, networks and policies that relate to it. Much work on emerging technologies or dual-use technologies speaks specifically to the military context or to cases related to America and, so here, this contribution fills a gap. My own work on the Canadian drone market is drawn upon as it has limited use of drones in the military realm, but a dual-use has been found in the domestic market. I contrast the findings from this research against the EU case to show how – regardless of the size of the economies, the specific context of a technology or geographical region – similarities in the 'various international, political, economic, security and normative mechanisms that encase technological artefacts' (see Calcara, Csernatoni and Lavallée, Introduction in this volume) are striking.

This collection builds on previous work, which examines the adoption of dual-use technologies for civil applications within the EU (Boucher 2015; Hoijtink 2014) and the adoption of security technologies in the domestic context in the United States and Canada (such as Akhter 2017; Shaw 2017; Bracken-Roche 2016; Topak *et al.* 2015; Wall and Monahan 2011). Through an in-depth study of specific technologies within the EU context, each chapter engages with the technical, social, political and normative controversies that emerge around the technologies and their governance within the EU. The agential role of technologies and the extent to which they shape and are shaped by the actors and the spaces within which they engage is essential in understanding technologies as socially constructed and the ways in which they contribute to existing power structures (Behrent 2013; Walters 2012; Aas, Gundhus, and Lomell 2009). However, a key consideration is how these technologies are governed. Some broad questions that are addressed throughout the collection are broken down as follows: To what extent are these emerging technologies governed by traditional state-led institutions versus non-state actors? How do regional and international organisations impact the governing of these technologies within the EU? Does the role of the EU in governing emerging technologies pose problems for state sovereignty? Why should an assessment of governing dual-use technologies in the EU include a mapping of the actors and controversies that surround it?

What's in a name?

The Introduction to this collection includes a list of possible labels or names that stakeholders employ for new, emerging, dual-use technologies and the need for this to be an accurate descriptor of their revolutionary potential. The authors further speak to the need, on the part of stakeholders, for specificity in the label of these technologies as 'it sets the parameters for understanding the type of technology that an "emerging" one encompasses' (see Calcara, Csernatoni and Lavallée, Introduction in this volume). While this book is dedicated to the European dynamics, similar debates relating to appropriate terminology have occurred worldwide, for instance, around the emergence of civil drone technologies in the Canadian context. I encountered this debate directly during research interviews, with one industry stakeholder stating:

> There's a very good discussion going on about the word drone because 'drone' had a generally negative connotation to it so industry doesn't like it. On the other hand, it's easy and accessible. It's in the vernacular, and that's the way it is.
>
> (Bracken-Roche, Interview 12, 2018)

The use of the word 'drone' itself was the topic of much debate within the drone industry, internationally, during the early years of their adoption into domestic applications (approximately, 2010–2016), but the word drone has a much longer history.

The history of the drone as a military technology long resulted in perceived public caution on the part of industry that, for many years, resisted using this term in protest against the military stigma and a particular representation of the technology (Bracken-Roche, field notes, March 2015 and November 2013). The belief was that the public thought of military, weaponised UAS any time they heard the word drone (Bracken-Roche, field notes, March 2015 and November 2013). While many industry representatives claimed there was a need to use other terms that were more accurate in their approximation of the technology (Whittle 2013), I would argue that the push away from the word drone was primarily driven by the need to distance the technologies from the military context, in order to increase their commercial viability. While feeble attempts have been made at international industry conferences to dissuade the media from using the term, including in the case of AUVSI in 2013 where the media room Wi-Fi password was 'DONTSAYDRONE' (Mehta 2013), many credited the announcement of Amazon's drone delivery tests with removing the old stigma (Bracken-Roche, field notes, March 2015).

Why is this vignette on the word drone significant to the overall story of drones in Canada? Or, indeed, why is it significant for the discussion and labelling of new, dual-use technologies in the EU? Following from Foucault (1988) and the approach taken by the editors in the Introduction to this collection, it holds that knowledge is tied up in relations of power; therefore, knowledge is never neutral or impartial. Power relations further shape the rules that determine what can be said and written, what language can be used, and what is accepted as knowledge and truth, thus, discourse shapes reality (Fairclough 2001; Foucault 1995). Since language is tied up in power relations, the etymological debate linked to these technologies, while seemingly innocent and lacking depth, is in fact a key component of the knowledge-production, legitimation and normative processes that accompany their adoption within various fora. The role of various publics in accepting the development and use of new technologies is often shaped by the language tied to them and, therefore, plays a key role in their acceptance or rejection at every step. The ability to govern technologies and the controversies and politics that accompany them can be significantly helped or hindered by perceptions of the technologies. Many of the contributions throughout this volume, and my own research on the emergence of drone technologies in Canada, point to the role of actors and discourses in creating and shaping, as well as in governing new, dual-use technologies.

In this concluding chapter, I introduce my research on drone technologies in the Canadian context, with specific focus on the controversies and discourses that emerge alongside them. I will then highlight the key themes that emerged from the research in this collection and in the Canadian drone context. I will conclude with a discussion of the key contributions from this collection, and the takeaway from the research findings regarding both academic pathways, as well as policy pathways as they relate to dual-use, or emerging, technologies.

Finding commonalities across contexts

Each chapter generally addresses a particular technology and corresponding EU initiatives around said technology, whether in terms of research and development or governance more broadly. This is then followed by a theoretical framing of the author's analysis. The actors, tools, relationships and emerging practices that result in relation to the technology are mapped and the dynamics of the governance structures around the technology are assessed. Despite variability in theoretical framing and research methods, overlapping themes are manifest from the study of these varying emerging technologies that frame the question of their governance within the EU. In my assessment, the key themes that can be seen across the cases of the technologies in this collection and in the case of drones in Canada are: speed, competing interests, and pre-emption and risk. All of these themes are linked to questions of governance throughout. Speed is linked to the rapid development of new technologies and how these conflict with lagging regulations. Competing interests are seen in the clash between states, non-state actors and publics in relation to a new technology, as well as the possible clashes in the goals of a single actor. Lastly, is the final theme of pre-emption and risk; many of the technologies are being presented as ways to eliminate or mitigate risks and so they are being developed with the view of pre-empting various negative futures. All three of these themes, in their assessment by the authors, are highly contingent on economic interests across various actors.

In the Canadian context, I undertook an in-depth examination of the stakeholder networks and narratives that were driving and shaping drone technologies and corresponding policy. A key line of investigation for this research programme was to examine how and why some stakeholder groups were excluded from various regulatory processes for drones, and how the inclusion and exclusion of certain groups in regulatory processes impacts the deployment of these technologies, and their broader social impacts. Thus, how do various groups of actors shape drone development, deployment and the social, economic and political consequences of their use in a civilian context? Drones, here, are conceptualised as dynamic sociotechnical systems that are part of a larger material assemblage of technologies, politics and social life. As socially constructed technologies, drones cannot be separated from their contexts of design or use. Thus, instead of simply accepting the technology as a tool that can be discretely applied to security or social problems, the technologies must be understood in the ways they are thoroughly embedded in social practices, institutions and materialities (Pfaffenberger 1992; Bowker and Star 1999; Monahan 2005).

Bourdieu's (1984) field theory argues that fields of power are spaces of contestation in which agents struggle to gain access to the statist capital granting power. This, thus, intersects further with questions of economic capital and governance. Drawing on Bourdieu's field theory to frame and map the space that emerged around drones, I argue that particular actor groups disproportionately shape this sociotechnical space. The logics of dominant actors shape this space in a way that pushes for innovation and collaboration across public and private agencies but does not leave the real time of space to engage with ethical or humanitarian questions that accompany the adoption of the technologies. The exclusion of publics from the regulatory and development processes around new technologies in the Canadian case created misperceptions on the part of government, industry and military actors about how the 'public' felt about the technologies. This lacuna between public opinion and perceived public opinion is not productive for any group and leads to the further marginalisation of key issues that arise in relation to the adoption of the technologies.

The seemingly benign, informal relationships that develop across actors and organisations are not, in fact, benign. This is exemplified across the chapters in this volume for dual-use and emerging technologies in the EU context, and in the case of drones in Canada. The relationships that emerge within and between certain groups of actors (primarily government, industry and military) show how other groups (such as civil liberties advocates, lawyers and privacy experts) have long been excluded from the governance of new technologies. The field of power within which actors operate contributes to them: a) only associating with specific actor groups; b) upholding particular logics and predispositions about the technologies; and c) perpetuating particular discourses and narratives about the technologies that fulfil particular agendas. Drawing on semi-structured interviews with stakeholders as well as extensive analyses of primary documents obtained through Access to Information and Privacy requests, these data were parsed through thematically to demonstrate the contrasting positions of various actor groups engaged in the regulatory process, in assessing risk and the market and in media portrayals of drone technologies.

Many of the chapters throughout this collection draw on similar data collection methods to those of my research project and all of the chapters, including this one, accept technology as socially contingent. Although there is some variance in terms of theoretical underpinnings, it is clear that the challenges of governing new technologies are not limited to a particular geographical region, or indeed a particular security community, but are located in the engagement between the social and the technical in any space.

Thematicising a sociotechnical understanding of new technologies

In order to better define the concept of governance as it relates to dual-use technologies within the EU, the Introductory chapter draws on Webber *et al.*'s understanding of governance as the 'coordinated management and regulation of issues by multiple and separate authorities, the interventions of both public and private actors, formal and informal arrangements, in turn structured by discourse, norms and practices, and purposefully directed towards particular policy outcomes' (2004: 4). This definition was introduced by Webber *et al.* (2004) in the context of the European security community but could be more broadly applied to other regional contexts, especially as it does not require 'a pre-existing and specific constellation of state behaviours that permit the practice of governance; it only requires that there be alternative forms of security practices beyond the state' (Sperling and Webber 2014: 138).

This understanding of governance is complemented by related concepts in Science and Technology Studies (STS), thus aligning with the goals of this collection in terms of bridging a gap between IR and STS. Jasanoff and Kim's concept of sociotechnical imaginaries is defined as the 'collectively imagined forms of social life and social order reflected in the design and fulfilment of nation-specific scientific and/or technological projects' (Jasanoff and Kim 2009: 120). Together, what these definitions do for our understanding of governance in the context of new technologies, more than anything else, is to highlight the role of coordination (across state and non-state actors) in order to achieve a common goal or outcome (the development or adoption of particular technologies). However, the themes that emerge from the various technologies in the EU context and from researching the Canadian drone context demonstrate that the coordination of various actors to achieve a common goal is not very straightforward (see Molas-Gallart 1997, as well as the contributions throughout this book). Achieving a cohesive governance structure, let alone cohesive and all-satisfying policies, around diverse, emergent technologies is fraught with controversies, big and small.

Speed

The theme of speed speaks not only to the need to develop efficient and fast technologies on the part of state and non-state actors but also to the desire for rapid economic growth. Paul Virilio (1977) highlights the desire, at least in the Western world, for faster and more mobile technologies but warns that an ever-increasing speed would overwhelm humanity. As is pointed to throughout the collection, the rapid development of new technologies and the desire for economic growth by state and non-state actors alike might result in the sidelining of appropriate safeguards to ensure public good as regulatory development is delayed by traditional bureaucracy. Virilio's work is applied in the context of economic growth by Armitage and Graham (2001), who propose that a political economy of speed is constituted by two contradictory extremes: trade and war. This links to Foucault's notions on governance, which postulate dual-use technologies as part of circulatory governance as discussed by Rychnovská (Chapter 10 in this volume), which govern mobilities of people, things and ideas (Aradau and Blanke 2010). Other authors, such as Lee and LiPuma (2002), highlight the speed of economic growth as being reliant on future uncertainties and risks, therefore, the development of technologies to help mitigate these future possibilities of risk help to tame uncertainty, with regard to economic well-being and security.

Echoing the contradiction introduced by Armitage and Graham (2001), Rychnovská highlights how the duality of 'the global movement of bodies, knowledges, materials and the like in current societies is cherished as a symbol of freedom, progress and eventually as the driving force of capitalism and profit making' (Chapter 10 in this volume). Hoijtink (2014) discusses how the question of uncertainty around technologies, or emergence, has spurned both danger and new enterprises, with others pointing to the intersection of emergence and profit and the ways in which risk and uncertainty create new areas for economic growth and development (Aradau and van Munster 2011; Martin 2007; Ericson and Doyle 2004). Manor's Chapter 8 certainly points to the challenges that result from the need for rapid adaption to new technologies, as well as the need for actors to engage in near real-time diplomacy through social media to keep various publics informed. This need for information clashes with the goals of maintaining a coherent brand, at times.

Speed is also seen in the divergences between the development of new technologies and the corresponding regulatory processes that accompany traditional modes of governance. Typically, technology is seen to be developing too rapidly to be adequately addressed by existing regulations. Canadian drone regulations were heralded internationally for being forward-looking and open to the inclusion of industry expertise in terms of engineering and innovation (Bracken-Roche *et al.* 2014; Gersher 2014). However, there were concerns by various state and non-state actors regarding the differing speeds at which government regulation and technological innovation occur. In interviews and public presentations, government representatives consistently stated that their primary concern was safety, thus, they would only allow for the deployment of drones with a particular payload capacity or application when and if the technology is reliable and safe (Bracken-Roche 2018). As such, a repeated comment throughout industry interviews and in conversations at industry conferences was that the market was limited by the speed at which regulations were being developed; and further, that it was only as a new set of regulations opened up and allowed for new applications and uses that a whole new opportunity arises for industry.

Hence, the regulations, on the one hand, aimed to play catch-up with the innovation that was happening within the drone industry and, on the other hand, the regulations control and limit what technologies can be deployed and used across applications and spaces. As one industry stakeholder recounted in an interview:

> I would say every time a new set of regulations is released, the related operations are booming like crazy, it's shaping it from the bottom. Because regulations are starting with the small UAVs, small drones, it's creating this industry capability before the industry for large ones.
>
> (Bracken-Roche, Interview 7, 2018)

This comment picks up on the idea that areas of innovation are emerging in order to respond to new opportunities that arise as a result of regulatory changes.

Farrand's Chapter 12 counters the traditional perception of varying speeds between technologies and regulations by drawing on Flear (2013). Farrand asserts that, contrary to lagging behind, the 'law can play a leading role by orienting, shaping and directing the conditions of possibility for the development and market availability of emergent technologies' (Chapter 12 in this volume: [243]). Moreover, the alleged objectivity of science and the slow pace of the law in appropriately regulating new technologies might, in fact, frame the governance of these technologies and new actors entering the space according to Farrand. So, this discourse becomes self-serving and causes pause for the efficacy of traditional governance structures.

Conflicting interests

The governance of new technologies is not straightforward due to the large number of organisations and groups of actors, and states, involved in their development and the numerous, conflicting interests that each brings to the table. The inclusion and exclusion of other actors from the discourses around new technologies demonstrates how sociotechnical spaces, or imaginaries,

> cannot be understood as something like a set of spaces in which rational discussion simply takes place in an unmediated fashion. [...] Rather they are arrangements of persons and technical devices formed in particular settings, within which it is possible to articulate a range of rhetorical forms.
>
> (Barry 2001: 10)

This quotation proposes that the spaces for discussion and deliberation around new technologies in the public sphere are not open forums where anyone can engage in debate but rather key actors and technologies shape the spaces of debate in very particular ways. Indeed, Martins and Ahmad's Chapter 3 in this volume points to the blurring of lines between actors involved in governing new technologies, which is often further impacted by questions surrounding public input and acceptance. Fiott highlights further the ways in which a seemingly unified actor might struggle to reconcile various policies and initiatives through their assessment of the EU's governing of new technologies in the context of balancing civil research against new research for the European Defence Fund (Chapter 2 in this volume).

Transport Canada (the government regulatory agency) has controlled and operated the regulatory working groups for drones in Canada in very particular ways, where industry and military stakeholders tend to represent the majority of these working groups due to their expertise on drone technologies. In this sense, there is a privilege of expertise in engaging in regulatory rhetoric around drones in Canada. On the one hand, this seems completely reasonable as those with expertise, those who understand the technological make-up and capacities of drones, are best placed to examine and address the implications and concerns of the technologies. However, theorists such as Feenberg (2002) and Winner (1980) assert that 'rationality and expertise' are not 'valid reasons for excluding publics and secondary actors' (Bracken-Roche 2020) from the conversation around the acceptance and adoption of new technologies. Calcara highlights the tensions that arise between agencies within the EU as they emerge from new patterns of authority and different types of expertise in relation to new dual-use technologies (Chapter 1 in this volume). Drawing on the concept on strategic cultures, Deschaux-Dutard engages with the challenges faced within and across EU cybersecurity policy and how conflicting interests at the EU versus state level result in negative outcomes for cybersecurity (Chapter 7 in this volume).

Competing interests across groups of actors, and well as conflicts and tensions within groups are seen across new technologies in the EU and in the case of drones in Canada. Winner argues:

> if our moral and political language for evaluating technology includes only categories having to do with tools and uses, if it does not include attention to the meaning of the designs and arrangements of our artifacts, then we will be blinded to much that is intellectually and practically crucial.
>
> (Winner 1980: 125)

This naivety of a technologies' history is further assessed in Longuet's Chapter 4. They look at the adoption of drone technologies that come from colonial, militaristic contexts and parse the controversies that emerge around their use in civil and military spaces. Vila Seoane's Chapter 5 demonstrates the process of merging potentially conflicting interests when they discuss the impact of lobbying efforts around new technologies on EC proposals.

In the context of civil drones in Canada, Transport Canada is home to the primary regulatory working group, which develops and implements the regulations that govern drone technologies within the Canadian domestic context. Based on data obtained through Access to Information and Privacy requests, over 60 per cent of this working group's membership over a number of years (2012 and 2016) was made up of industry actors, with the remaining being state actors (with representatives from government agencies and the military) (Bracken-Roche 2018; Gersher 2014). Despite requests for greater involvement on the part of the Officer of the Privacy Commissioner of Canada and national civil liberties organisations (Bracken-Roche, Interviews, 2018), these groups have never been invited to the working group and must instead give feedback on the regulations with the rest of the general public when they are posted for public consultation and feedback. As argued elsewhere (Bracken-Roche 2020), the revolving door of stakeholders around new, emerging technologies, who migrate between roles in government, military and industry represent a serious concern for the inclusion of other voices. Industry actors have an economic interest in the successful introduction of drone technologies into the domestic space and this might compromise their ability to help shape regulations in their capacity as working group members in unbiased ways. Here, Csernatoni and Lavallée's Chapter.13 offers a good counterpoint by speaking to the positive role of the EU in bringing together a cohesive, holistic form of governance that involves various actors in response to new technologies. As a supranational organisation, the EU might be able to balance conflicting interests in a more considered way than that of a state government. Ulnicane's Chapter 11 also speaks to the role of the EU in creating positive governance structures that would help mitigate ethical concerns that arise with new technologies.

Pre-emption and risk

For the purposes of this analysis, and as a reflection of the way risk has been framed in theorisations around sociotechnical imaginaries, risk is understood in the sociological sense as a result of subjective perceptions and social constructions of risk, which often emphasises controversies on risk (Zinn 2015). And so risk is understood in the context of a risk society in Beck's (1992) conception, where harm (objective harm) as well as concerns about the future (expected harm) shape various political and social negotiations. However, the way in which these various negotiations play out depends on the socio-structural positioning of particular groups of actors, either at the centre or at the boundary of a society (Zinn 2015). Theorisations around risk and security have been discussed in critical security by Aradau and van Munster (2011), who link the risk of future, possible catastrophes to current practices and policies around security and governance. Hoijtink (2014) touches upon questions of pre-emption and risk in relation to the emergence of new security technologies in the EU context. They demonstrate that the growth of the security market transcends the American context on the one hand. While, on the other hand, demonstrating that the EU market capitalises on 'potential emergencies and broader discussions about threat pre-emption and anticipation', that can be traced to 'military discourses, strategies and technologies that can themselves be traced back to the emergence of new information-based technologies in the second half of the 20th century' (Hoijtink 2014: 471).

In this context of pre-emption and risk mitigation in response to future threats and security challenges that can be solved with new technologies, Barrinha's Chapter 6 argues that the policies that emerge, in his case regarding cybersecurity governance in the EU, are indeed more of the same. Instead of abrupt changes in policy in response to a perceived risk, Barrinha argues that the policy and security responses are calculated and adjusted slowly over time. Complementing this assessment by Barrinha, Binder's Chapter 9 engages with R&D of border security technologies in the EU as they reproduce a particular conceptualisation of security by different actors. Indeed, Binder's work reveals the power of the private security industry in shaping security research programmes based on potential, future sociotechnical imaginaries.

Conclusion

A key argument throughout this collection has been that technologies cannot be understood as impartial, objective tools but as embedded in particular dis-courses, logics and networks of actors that shape and are shaped by them. More so, the involvement of various actors with different interests engaging in the development of new technologies means that new elements are being introduced that could fundamentally alter relationships of power and security, with the potential to intensify pre-existing tensions that exist in society as well as bring technology and policy to the point of pre-emption entirely. Could it be said that many of these new technologies are simply solutions looking for a problem or are they genuinely beneficial to human flourishing?

My research with drones in Canada and the study of the new technologies introduced throughout this collection demonstrate the regulatory privilege given to particular groups of actors around emerging technologies. The result seems overwhelmingly that these technologies emerge from power structures, in dynamics controlled by government, industry and military and policing actors. The exclusion of other groups such as civil liberties advocates and privacy experts, let alone the public writ-large, from the conversation about the risks and implications around new technologies is often reasoned as an exclusion due to lack of expertise but it is really a bureaucratic politics of exclusion. However, could these dynamics be shifted if an organisation as influential as the EU took a stand against this technocratic governance?

The research presented throughout this collection has demonstrated that the competing discourses, logics and narratives that have been perpetuated by various groups are often ill founded and inaccurate. Instead, these narratives reflect the dispositions or interests of particular groups, shaped by their privileged position within the field of power. Technocratic governance is dominating the field of power around new, emerging technologies in the EU and in Canada as seen in this chapter and throughout this collection. By drawing on a number of interdisciplinary conceptualisations of governance, technology and the role of actors, economics and politics, this collection better illuminates our understanding our dual-use technologies and the ways they are governed in this contemporary period. It acts as a stepping stone for future pathways for interdisciplinarity in this area of research, for deepening our understanding of these spaces using these interdisciplinary approaches and helps us to understand contemporary governance of technologies in ways that might lead to positive policy interventions of the part of academics.

These findings reveal the need for increased regulatory oversight and for the inclusion of other groups of actors and the public in the regulatory process around new technologies. This is even more important for new technologies with security and surveillance capabilities. As a society, we should question whether we want to live in a world of pre-emption and risk that spurns capitalist enterprise at the expense of increasingly marginalised populations. Moreover, the concerns are ethics and humans that civil liberties and privacy advocates bring to the table are forward-thinking ones that consider worst-case futures. Thus, the early inclusion of broader groups of actors in the policy process would be beneficial in the long term. The inclusion of these experts alongside technical experts might also go a long way to developing public trust in these regulatory processes.

References

Aas, K.F., Gundhus, H.O. and Lomell, H.M. (2009) Technologies of (In)Security. In K.F. Aas, H.O. Gundhus and H.M. Lomell (eds), *Technologies of InSecurity: The Surveillance of Everyday Life*. New York: Routledge, 1–18.

Akhter, M. (2017) The Proliferation of Peripheries: Militarized Drones and the Reconfiguration of Global Space. *Progress in Human Geography.* https://doi.org/10.1177/030 9132517735697.

Aradau, C. and Blanke, T. (2010) Governing Circulation: A Critique of the Biopolitics of Security. In M. de Larringa and M.G. Doucet (eds), *Security and Global Governmentality: Globalization, Governance and the State.* London: Routledge.

Aradau, C. and van Munster, R. (2011) *Politics of Catastrophe.* London: Routledge.

Armitage, J. and P. Graham. (2001). Dromoeconomics: Towards a Political Economy of Speed, *Parallax* 7(1): 111–123.

Barry, A. (2001) *Political Machines: Governing a Technological Society.* London: Athlone Press.

Beck, U. (1992) *Risk Society: Towards a New Modernity.* London: Sage.

Behrent, M.C. (2013) Foucault and Technology. *History and Technology* 29(1): 54–104.

Boucher, P. (2015) Domesticating the Drone: The Demilitarisation of Unmanned Aircraft for Civil Markets. *Science and Engineering Ethics* 21(6): 1393–1412.

Bourdieu, P. (1984) *Distinction: A Social Critique of the Judgement of Taste.* Cambridge, MA: Harvard University Press.

Bowker, G.C. and Star, S.L. (1999) *Sorting Things Out: Classification and its Consequences.* Cambridge, MA: MIT Press.

Bracken-Roche, C. (2016) Domestic Drones: The Politics of Verticality and the Surveillance Industrial Complex. *Geographica Helvetica* 70: 285–293.

Bracken-Roche, C. (2018) Navigating Canadian Drone Space: A Sociological Analysis of the Stakeholders, Narratives, and Policy Shaping Canadian Unmanned Systems (Unpublished doctoral dissertation). Queen's University, Kingston Canada.

Bracken-Roche, C. (2020 forthcoming) Drones as Political Machines: Technocratic Governance in Canadian Drone Space. In N. Klimburg-Witjes, N. Pöchhacker and G.C. Bowker (eds), *Sensing Security: Sensors and the Making of Transnational Security Infrastructures.* Manchester: Mattering Press.

Bracken-Roche, C. *et al.* (2014) 'Privacy Implications of the Spread of Unmanned Aerial Vehicles (UAVs) in Canada'. Surveillance Studies Centre. Research Project for the 2013–2014 Contributions Program of the Privacy Commissioner of Canada, Ottawa, 30 April.

Ericson, R. and Doyle, A. (2004) Catastrophe Risk, Insurance and Terrorism. *Economy and Society* 33(2): 135–173.

Fairclough, N. (2001) *Language and Power.* Ann Arbor, MI: The University of Michigan.

Feenberg, A. (2002) *Transforming Technology: A Critical Theory Revisited.* Oxford: Oxford University Press.

Flear, M.L. (2013) Regulating New Technologies: EU Internal Market Law, Risk, and Socio Technical Order. In M.L. Flear, A.M. Farrell, T.K. Hervey and T. Murphy (eds), *European Law and New Health Technologies.* Oxford: Oxford University Press, 74–120.

Foucault, M. (1988) *Madness and Civilization: A History of Insanity in the Age of Reason.* New York: Vintage Books.

Foucault, M. (1995) *Discipline and Punish: The Birth of the Prison.* New York: Vintage Books.

Gersher, S. (2014) Drone Surveillance is Increasing in Canada. Ottawa Citizen, 10 April. At: http://ottawacitizen.com/news/drone-surveillance-is-increasing-in-canada.

Hoijtink, M. (2014) Capitalizing on Emergence: The 'New' Civil Security Market in Europe. *Security Dialogue* 45(5): 458–475.

Jasanoff, S. and Kim, S. (2009) Containing the Sociotechnical Imaginaries and Nuclear Power in the United States and South Korea. *Minerva* 47(2): 119–146.

Lee, B. and LiPuma, E. (2002) Cultures of Circulation: The Imaginations of Modernity. *Public Culture* 14(1): 191–213.

McCarthy, D.R. (ed.) (2018) *Technology and World Politics: An Introduction*. London: Routledge.

Martin, R. (2007) *An Empire of Indifference: American War and the Financial Logic of Risk Management*. Durham, NC: Duke University Press.

Mehta, A. (2013) AUVSI: Don't Say 'Drone!' No, Really, Don't Say Drone. Intercepts Defense News, 15 August. At: http://intercepts.defensenews.com/2013/08/auvsi-dont-say-drone-no-really-dont-say-drone/.

Molas-Gallart, J. (1997) Which Way to Go? Defence Technology and the Diversity of 'Dual Use' Technology Transfer. *Research Policy* 26: 367–385.

Monahan, T. (2005) The School System as a Post-Fordist Organization: Fragmented Centralization and the Emergence of IT Specialists. *Critical Sociology* 31(4): 583–615.

Pfaffenberger, B. (1992) Social Anthropology of Technology. *Annual Review of Anthropology* 21(1): 491–516.

Rao, M.B., Jongerden, J., Lemmens, P. and Ruivenkamp, G. (2015) Technological Mediation and Power: Postphenomenology, Critical Theory, and Autonomist Marxism. *Philosophy & Technology* 28(3): 449–474.

Shaw, I.G.R. (2017) Robot Wars: US Empire and Geopolitics in the Robotic Age. *Security Dialogue* 48(5): 451–470.

Sperling, J. and Webber, M. (2014) Security Governance in Europe: A Return to System. *European Security* 23(2): 126–144.

Topak, Ö.E., Bracken-Roche, C., Saulnier, A. and Lyon, D. (2015). From Smart Borders to Perimeter Security: The Expansion of Digital Surveillance at the Canadian Borders. *Geopolitics* 20(4): 880–899.

Virilio, P. (1977) *Speed and Politics, an Essay on Dromology*. New York: Semiotext(e).

Virilio, P. (1994) *The Vision Machine*. Indianapolis: Indiana University Press.

Wall, T. and Monahan, T. (2011) Surveillance and Violence from Afar: The Politics of Drones and Liminal Security-Scapes. *Theoretical Criminology* 15(3): 239–254.

Walters, W. (2012) *Governmentality: Critical Encounters*. New York: Routledge.

Webber, M., Croft, S., Howorth, J., Terriff, T. and Krahmann, E. (2004) The Governance of European Security. *Review of International Studies* 30(1): 3–26.

Whittle, R. (2013). Don't Say 'DRONES', Beg Drone Makers. *Breaking Defense*, 14 August. At: http://breakingdefense.com/2013/08/dont-say-drones-beg-drone-makers/2/.

Winner, L. (1980) Do Artefacts Have Politics? *Daedalus* 109(1): 121–136.

Zinn, J. O. (2015) Towards a Better Understanding of Risk-Taking: Key Concepts, Dimensions and Perspectives. *Health, Risk & Society* 17(2): 99–114.

Index